# The Retail Environment

Designed specifically for student use and based on the authors' extensive teaching and consultancy experience, this textbook takes a fresh look at the American retailing system. It describes and explains retailing, with a particular emphasis on the problem of store location, and combines a spatial approach to consumer demand with a corporate and institutional view of supply. Linking the theoretical and applied traditions of location analysis, it uses a wealth of real-life examples to illustrate its theoretical points.

The authors cover the subject broadly, dealing with the basic principles and components of the retail system and introducing students to consumer behavior, the spatial structure of markets, and the social concerns that affect retailing. They describe the spatial structure of retail activity, and how it is affected by such factors as changes in the distribution system and in the retail structure. Retail structure is examined from the viewpoint of business, many of the most widely used procedures in store locations studies are described, and students are encouraged to evaluate those techniques. Finally, the authors look at the policy implications of retail activities and the possible directions for change in the retail system of tomorrow.

Rooted in the world of retail chains, *The Retail Environment* shows clearly how market power and risk rather than economic theories affect the decisions of people developing real life business strategies. Essential reading for all students of geography, the book will also be of great value to business, retailing, and marketing students.

## The authors

Ken Jones is Professor of Applied Geography at Ryerson Polytechnical Institute, Toronto; Jim Simmons is Professor of Geography at the University of Toronto. They both also act as consultants to the private and public sectors, and are the authors of numerous articles and books on urban and marketing geography.

# The Retail Environment

## Ken Jones and Jim Simmons

**London and New York**

First published 1990
by Routledge
11 New Fetter Lane, London EC4P 4EE

Simultaneously published in the USA
by Routledge
a division of Routledge, Chapman and Hall, Inc.
29 West 35th Street, New York, NY 10001

© 1990 Ken Jones and Jim Simmons

Typeset by Leaper & Gard Ltd, Bristol
Printed and bound in Great Britain by
Mackays of Chatham PLC, Chatham, Kent

*British Library Cataloguing in Publication Data*

Jones, Ken, *1945–*
    The retail environment.
    1. United States. Retailing
    I. Title    II. Simmons, Jim, *1936–*
    658.8'7' 00973

ISBN 0-415-04984-9
        0-415-04985-7 (pbk)

*Library of Congress Cataloging in Publication Data*

Jones, Kenneth George, 1945–
    The retail environment / Ken Jones and Jim Simmons.
        p.        cm.
    Includes bibliographical references.
    ISBN 0-415-04984-9. — ISBN 0-415-04985-7 (pbk.)
    1. Retail trade—United States.    2. Store location—United States.
    I. Simmons, James W., 1936–    .    II. Title.
    HF5429.3.J595    1990
    658.8'7—dc20
                                                                    89-49763
                                                                    CIP

# Contents

Contents

# List of figures

# List of Tables

# List of Exhibits

# Preface

This text evolved from undergraduate courses taught within the geography departments of the University of Toronto and Ryerson Polytechnical Institute. These courses serve many students from outside the field of geography, especially business and other professional programs. At the University of Toronto there are 400 students, of whom 25 per cent are geography majors. At Ryerson two separate courses introduce 450 business students and fifty applied geography majors to the retail sector. The business students are attracted to the empirical and applied approach: they like to study real firms and real cities. Many of the location issues are new to them. Perhaps most important, the material gives these students a different perspective and a broader context for decision making by introducing consumer behavior, the spatial structure of markets, and the social concerns that affect retailing. Geography students, on the other hand, benefit from seeing spatial problems from the viewpoint of the various actors in the retail system, particularly the retail chains and shopping center developers. They are surprised by the degree of concentration and the level of uncertainty in the retail sector, and we try to suggest how market power and risk rather than economic theories affect the decisions of people developing real-life business strategies. Some students benefit from exposure to potential career opportunities in the retail sector.

The book combines a spatial approach to consumer demand with a corporate and institutional view of the supply side. We also take the view that retailing and commercial services are a significant and visible part of our social system. They both reflect and shape our preferences, lifestyles, and mores. We are what we consume, and our consumption priorities describe our society. These preferences are mediated through the actions of institutions and organizations such as retail chains, shopping plaza developers, and urban planners, acting either jointly or in competition.

Each of the four parts of the text has a slightly different flavor. In Part one we introduce the student to the basic principles and components of the retail system. The spatial pattern of demand is emphasized, but income and demographics are discussed as well. The chapter on the supply side looks at the corporate composition of retailing in some detail, stressing the degree of concentration in the industry. A final chapter introduces the study of consumer behavior.

Part two may be most familiar to geographers. Here we describe the spatial structure of retail activity, at both the settlement and intra-urban scale, but always with an eye on the location decisions of retail chains and developers. The complementary chapters on the directions and processes of change in retail structure introduce new topics and themes and lay the framework for later applied studies.

In Part three we look at retail structure from the viewpoint of business, introducing many of the most widely used procedures in store location studies. Students are urged to evaluate these techniques in terms of the retail chain's strategies and requirements. How much information and model building is appropriate for a new chain that is moving into a rapidly growing market?

Finally, Part four takes a brief look at the policy implications of retail activities and the possible directions for change in the retail system of tomorrow.

The book is generously illustrated with tables, charts, and maps. These are not always discussed in the text because of space limitations, but they give the instructor the flexibility to determine how much time to spend on each topic, or to allocate assignments or tutorial discussions. Some of the examples are based on our experience in Toronto: the environment in which we live and work, and which is most familiar to our students. Others have been adapted from research and planning studies across North America. In our future work, we would like to have a broader representation across the continent, and we need help to locate the studies that describe the retail environment in other cities. Please send suggestions to either one of us. We also hope that the material presented here will be extended by means of locally based case studies and labs, so that this text becomes a catalyst for a more applied approach to geography and marketing studies.

We owe a great deal to our students, who have helped this book into print in a variety of ways. As the reader will note, several examples originated as student theses and class projects. Our students also suffered through years of lectures while we sorted out and articulated the ideas that appear here. They stimulated us to pull this material together by raising questions, voicing their concerns and demonstrating to us what interested them (and what did not!). Those who went on to work within the industry as location analysts, market researchers, real estate managers and consultants became a continuing source of ideas and information.

As our students drew us into the locational issues that concerned the retail and development industry, we turned to practitioners for help. They almost invariably came through by providing case studies, interpreting relationships, and stimulating new questions. We would like to extend particular appreciation to Tony Lea, Professor of Applied Geography, Ryerson Polytechnical Institute, Gord Martin, President of Tipase Consulting, and Kenard Smith of The May Company.

In the process of developing this material we have ourselves rediscovered a kind of old-fashioned geography that tries to discover how part of the local economy works and how landscapes emerge. We have done field work, talked to practitioners, and thoroughly enjoyed the process.

Ken Jones
Jim Simmons

Chapter one

# Why study retail location?

**Without Christmas (or some equivalent social phenomenon), we would have 15 per cent fewer stores.**

**The retail landscape both reflects and reveals the social system in which it is embedded. America is a shopping mall.**

**State governments that depend on sales tax revenues have as large a stake in consumer spending as the K mart Corporation.**

This book describes and explains the spatial pattern of consumption. We will measure the incomes of Americans, examine how they spend their money, and map the locations of the stores and warehouses in which they spend it. Exploring the processes that bring about these patterns will take us back into the past and invite speculation about the future. Again and again we will ask questions about an activity that is usually taken for granted. If governments can sell postage stamps or run museums, why can't they operate drug stores? How can grocery stores operate effectively on such varying scales, i.e. from the roadside stand to the supermarket? Why do some stores cling together while others are widely dispersed? Do we really need so many banks? What if we closed all the stores and sold everything by phone or computer? What level of banking service and food retailing is appropriate for low-income inner city areas?

If we mentally slip behind the desks of major retailers or shopping center developers, other questions emerge. How big must the market be for a store at this site? What kind of sales could be expected at an alternative location? How do the present locations of shops in the retail chain fit into the overall marketing strategy? Where will future growth occur? What will the competition do? Should the store change its mix of products or shift locations?

Land use planners are concerned with the problems that occur as by-products of consumption. How can the need for retail facilities in a neighborhood be reconciled with the traffic and noise that a shopping center will produce? Does a proposed store serve the local community or all parts of the city? Are the new shopping facilities necessary or will they lead to empty stores and business failure in existing centers? How can we create shopping areas that are sufficiently diverse and attractive to draw the recreational shopper?

Not all of these questions will be answered neatly. As travelers soon find out, the world includes a remarkable variety of distribution systems – open-air markets, shopping malls, exotic bazaars, discreet salons, and, in some countries, long queues and empty shelves. Each system works in its own way. The distribution process linking the producer and consumer is such a central economic function and builds so many social networks for individuals that it is a major component of society. Stores and markets color the landscape, and bring variety and human contact into our lives. Retailing is not an activity to be determined by some mechanical model or to be reduced to a minimal level and banished to the outskirts of the community. Choosing, talking, bargaining, and consuming are central to every culture. We want to observe and understand the forms of retail activity in our own society.

## The importance of marketing

We can begin by examining the role of marketing as an economic activity. Here its significance is overwhelming. Table 1.1 suggests that, in terms of employment, almost half of the value of a consumer product derives from distribution activities: transportation, storage, financing, and selling. The primary and manufacturing industries account for smaller and smaller proportions of our gross national product and employment.

This is especially true of urban areas. The employment level in most cities depends less on factories, mines, or sawmills than on providing goods and services for the surrounding region. Cities compete vigorously amongst themselves to expand their trade areas and the range of services they provide. In smaller towns especially, civic leaders know that distribution activities are an important factor in urban growth or decline, as indicated in Figure 1.1. In this example 16 per cent of the jobs created in Texas between 1975 and 1985 were in retailing and these jobs were disproportionately concentrated in the largest centers. Even in areas of declining population jobs in distribution were maintained or increased, partly compensating for the loss of jobs in farming or other primary sectors.

Within the city, retail activities dominate the visual landscape because they locate in high-traffic areas. The first warning to the motorist that a town is ahead may be the scatter of gas stations, car dealerships, and farm implement stores along the highway. The entrance to the community itself is marked by a profusion of fast-food outlets, shopping plazas, and

**Table 1.1** The role of retailing within the United States economy

| Industry | Employment, 1984 (thousands) | Percentage of total employment | |
|----------|------------------------------|-------------------------------|---|
| *Goods production* | | | |
| Agriculture, forestry, fishing | 3,321 | 3.2 | |
| Mining | 957 | 0.9 | 30.5 |
| Manufacturing | 20,995 | 20.0 | |
| Construction | 6,665 | 6.3 | |
| *Distribution services* | | | |
| Transportation, utilities | 7,358 | 7.0 | |
| Trade – wholesale | 4,212 | 4.0 | |
| – retail | 17,767 | 16.9 | 44.8 |
| Finance, insurance, realty | 6,750 | 6.4 | |
| Commercial services | 11,040 | 10.5 | |
| *Public services* | | | |
| Community services | 21,174 | 20.2 | 24.7 |
| Public administration | 4,766 | 4.5 | |
| Total | 105,005 | 100.0 | |

*Source:* Bureau of the Census (annual) *Statistical Abstract of the United States*, Washington

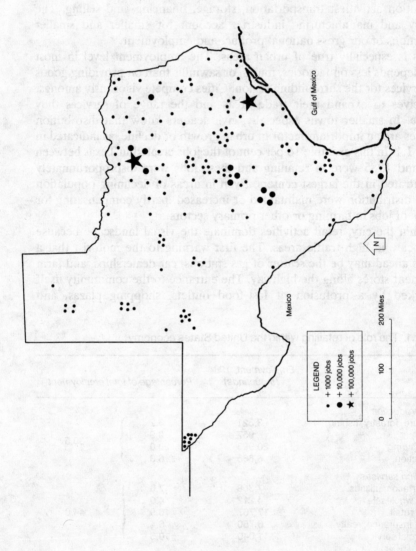

**Figure 1.1** The growth of retail employment in Texas: 1975–85

*Source:* Bureau of the Census (annual) *County Business Patterns*, Washington

discount retailers. One's image of the city is often based on the main street: How wide is it and how busy? How big is the downtown area? Is the street lined with discreet colonial facades, or sprawling cement block buildings with false fronts? The traveler begins to recognize the familiar names of retail chains and brands that are known across the country: Gulf, Sears, Safeway, The Bank of America, and so on. The landscape may vary, but behind the storefronts the products and store layouts are the same throughout the country.

The act of shopping continues to be a major preoccupation of the American household. On average we spend 1.7 hours per day on shopping and personal services. In addition, we know that a certain proportion of discretionary (recreation) time is spent on consumption – window-shopping, eating out, buying souvenirs. Moreover, part of the time spent reading magazines or watching television is devoted to studying the advertisements that support consumption. The purpose of over 10 per cent of household trips is shopping, and as we go through our daily routine we continuously plan and evaluate our purchases and discuss them with our friends. Where did you get those shoes? How can I get a deal on a camera? Do you know a good place for Chinese food? Should I buy a new raincoat? Shopping is as much recreation as it is survival, a means of personal expression for many people.

And why not? Figure 1.2 shows that retail sales absorb from two-fifths to a half of personal income (here we define retail in the narrow sense, excluding such personal services as laundries, hairdressers, and barber shops). But Figure 1.2 also makes another important point: retail expenditures are strongly affected by the social and economic environment in which consumers operate. During the Depression of the 1930s people spent beyond their income and dipped into their savings; during the Second World War they saved their money because there was nothing to buy (and shopped in a frenzy when the war ended). In recent years there have been shifts from retailing to service expenditures.

## The role of location analysis

Marketing is usually defined as the development and efficient distribution of goods and services for consumers. The literature of marketing deals with the seven Ps: people, product, price, place, physical distribution, promotion, and packaging. The location analyst focuses on the subset of these concerns – people, place, and physical distribution – that enter the marketing process after the product has been designed, packaged, and promoted. The mix of products represented by the store and the consumers who buy there defines the location problem.

As the name suggests, the distribution system is concerned with location. It seeks to link the geography of production, which may include areas on

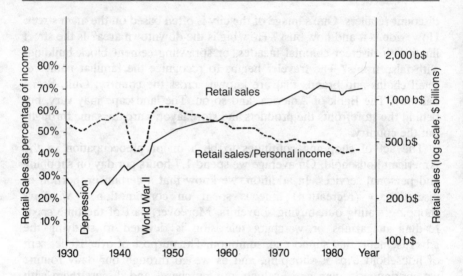

**Figure 1.2** Retail sales and personal income: 1930–present

*Source:* Bureau of the Census (1976) *Historical Statistics of the United States: Colonial Times to 1970*, 2 vols, Washington; Bureau of the Census (annual) *Statistical Abstract of the United States*, Washington

the far side of the globe, with the pattern of consumption which usually falls within a defined market area. The contrast between these two geographies is shown in Fig. 1.3: the production of automobiles in the USA is highly concentrated but the market is widely dispersed. Most production still occurs in the Midwest. In addition, about 30 per cent of the cars sold in the USA are imported from Canada (around the Great Lakes) or Japan. The consumption of cars is far more widespread than production and is roughly proportional to the size of the population and its income level. An elaborate distribution network links the two spatial distributions so that every city receives a share of each product line from each source. The same mix of brand names, styles, and even prices, is displayed in every city, even though the cars may come from Tennessee or Japan or West Germany.

The location of consumers, their numbers, and relative affluence are the starting points in an equation that determines the number and variety of retail outlets. Widely dispersed households result in a restricted variety of stores. Small towns in Nebraska are limited to the basic food, drug, and hardware stores. A concentration of well-to-do shoppers can support the specialized boutiques found on Rodeo Drive in Los Angeles.

From the retailer's point of view, the scale of operation and the variety of product line are directly determined by the spatial distribution of consumers (and competitors). However, as we observe in Figure 1.4, stores also create a geography of their own. Stores attract consumers, channel travel patterns, and ultimately affect the location of other stores. While some retailers in the Seattle region are attracted to highly accessible locations developed at the turn of century (Downtown Seattle, Bellevue), others seek out highway strips (along US 99), or suburban plazas (South-center) that have been created from vacant land within the last 25 years. The latter, in conjunction with the freeways that spawned them, build new patterns of consumer behavior which affect the development decisions that follow.

Retail activities play a growing role in shaping the environments in which we all live. Many of the colors, the smells, and the noises, that make up the atmosphere of a community – the stimuli of different people, new styles, and innovative technology – are contributed by stores, restaurants, shopping districts, and their customers. Inevitably, the quality of our lives partly reflects the quality of this sector. The collective impact of retail facilities grouped in space is difficult to analyse but impossible to ignore. Shopping center developers, once only concerned with the basic consider-ations of location and size, are now trying to find out what makes a landscape, a spatial complex, work. How do retail facilities attract people?

The retail system may vary from region to region, even within a country; the age of retail stock, the land use controls, the characteristics of con-sumers, and the competitive structure may all differ. For example, the map of wine consumption in Figure 1.5 suggests all kinds of explanations. The cultural differences between rural and urban states, or the South and the northeast, produce regional blocks, e.g. New England and the Bible Belt, but why isn't Pennsylvania more northern? Are special taxes or other consumer barriers imposed in that state? Consumption in Utah can be explained by religion; in Washington D.C. by the presence of embassies; in Nevada by Las Vegas; in Alaska by the long winters; and in California by its role as a producer. Location analysts must bring a sensitivity to the effects of these external conditions to the marketing problem.

Every corporate strategy – to expand, diversify, or divest – contains within it a spatial strategy. The strategy must define a spatial market, with a boundary, which in turn requires a certain network of branch facilities. Some of the most interesting location problems arise from these strategic considerations; location decisions are linked to financial considerations such as capital costs, to the degree of specialization of the competition, to the possibility of certain types of technological change. Location decisions become contingent, i.e. dependent on many other considerations.

Most retail problems, then, have a strong spatial component. Thus they require familiarity with the elements of spatial theory and models, a knowledge of expected spatial patterns, and some experience with the data and techniques of spatial analysis: the use of maps, of trade area analysis, and regression techniques.

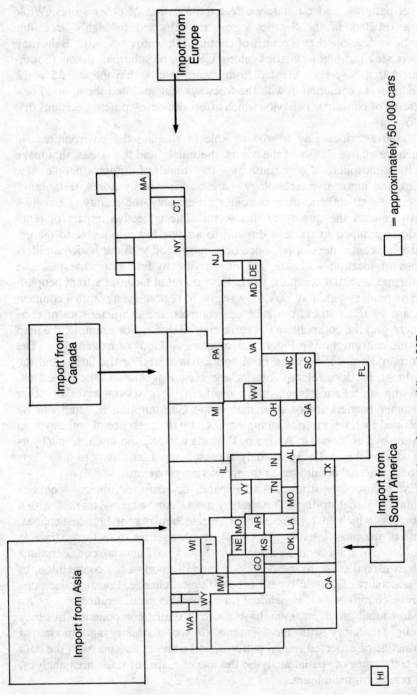

**Figure 1.3** The production and consumption of automobiles: 1987
(a) Consumption. Area proportional to new car registrations

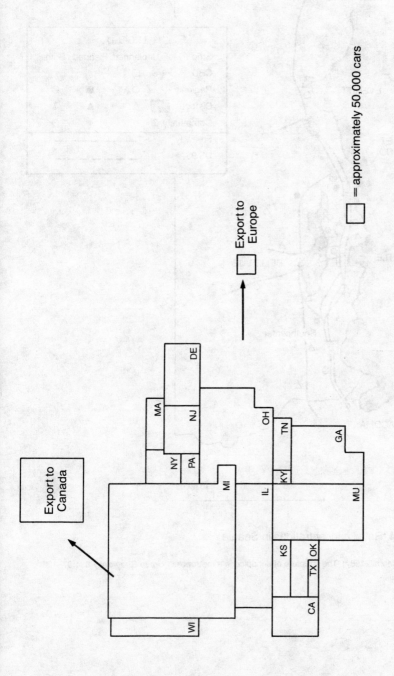

(b) Production. Area proportional to new car production

*Source: Ward's Automotive Yearbook* (1988) Detroit

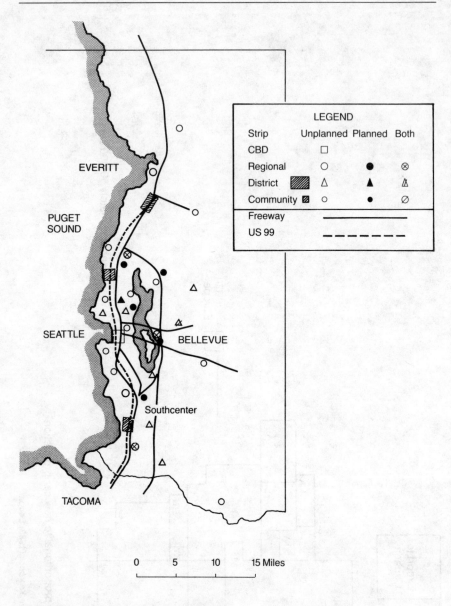

**Figure 1.4** Retail concentrations in Seattle

*Source:* R. Morrill (1987) 'The structure of shopping in a metropolis', *Urban Geography* 8, 1:97–128

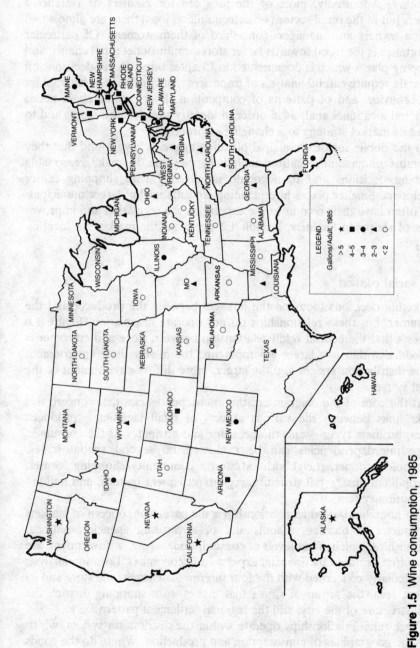

**Figure 1.5** Wine consumption, 1985

*Source:* Bureau of the Census (1987) *Statistical Abstract of the United States*, Washington

Can location analysts get jobs? Table 1.1 shows that more than thirty-three million people worked in retail, wholesale, and private services in 1980. These sectors are the most rapidly growing segments of the economy. Admittedly, most of the jobs are for cashiers or restaurant helpers but in the retail sector (seventeen million jobs) there are almost two million owners and managers (one-third of them women). Of particular importance is the trend towards larger stores, multi-outlet retail chains, and shopping plazas which is documented in Chapter three. Retail decisions on this scale require careful analysis of trade areas, of consumer demographics and behavior, and of patterns of competition. Every major chain needs continual locational analysis in order to identify sites for new stores and to adjust its market strategy to a changing environment.

In the public sector, municipal planning agencies have found that they too must understand location analysis if they are to make reasonable planning decisions and to negotiate intelligently with shopping center developers. Smaller places hire planning consultants, but larger municipalities often have their own in-house experts on the regulation and improvement of shopping facilities. Exhibit 1.1 describes the market for location analysts.

## The social context

Marketing decisions focus on the linkages between the producer and the consumer, but these relationships do not operate in isolation. Figure 1.6 suggests that the central retail relationship between store and customer is embedded within two larger environments: the intermediate environment of the distribution system and the larger, more diffuse environment of the social system.

At the core of the diagram are the interdependencies that concern this book: links between the various aspects of retail facilities – products, stores, business types – and the behavior and attributes of the consumer. These interdependencies can be evaluated on several spatial scales: household/product, neighborhood/store, community/shopping center, metropolitan area/retail structure, region/settlement pattern, and nation/distribution system.

The household/product relationship is the particular concern of marketing courses in business schools and of advertising agencies; national relationships, which affect levels of consumption, saving, or investment, are most often explored by financial experts and economists. Location analysis is particularly concerned with the four intermediate levels: the store and its market area, the group of stores that makes up a shopping district, the retail structure of the city, and the regional settlement pattern.

These retail relationships operate within the distribution system, which links the geographies of consumption and production. Where do the goods

### Exhibit 1.1
## THE MARKET FOR LOCATION ANALYSTS

Paradoxically, the concentration of retail activity in a small number of retail chains and shopping plazas has increased the employment opportunities for retail analysts. Part of the success of these retail giants comes from their ability to hire specialized personnel to analyse markets and identify potential store locations. Most major retail chains and shopping center developers employ several analysts to compile and evaluate a database in the ways described in this book.

•MICHIGAN, BIRMINGHAM 48011.
Market research firm specializing in retail and shopping center research seeks statistically oriented analyst with advanced degree and business orientation.

**MARKET RESEARCH ANALYST WAYNE, N.J.**
Fortune 200 company has oper ...ns for Analyst in Chemical Products Marketing Department.

Duties entail: Assessment tors, forecasting, custom product line assessments, data for capital jobs an preparation of business range strategy.

Technical degree ar analysis experience f degree or equivaler ence preferred. Co excellent benefits. PLEASE SE
i K

**RESEARCH ANALYST TO $75K+**

Major bank seeks a Research Analyst with expertise developing in depth analysis of the Retail Industry. Position requires expertise evaluating major retailers for the Corporate Finance and Lending Division supporting M & A, LBO and Credit deals. Exposure to other service industries ie., Fast Food, Leisure and Transportation a plus. The ideal candidate will have demonstrated experience in Corporate, Credit and Econ... vs. Financial Services in Corporate, I an MBA or CPA. ...us potential.

## RETAIL BANKING EXECUTIVE

Our President & CEO seeks a seasoned executive to direct & enhance the development of our retail banking organization. This aggressive individual will serve as the key manager of our business in terms of products, services, branch locations and operations. As a member of our senior executive team, you will help forge a new organizational culture with direct accountability for sale goals, deposit, loan and fee income, growth and strategic decisions.

The successful candidate will have a proven retail banking track record in a high growth, quick turnaround environment and ...ill have directed

CALIFORNIA, LOS ALTOS 94022.
RETAIL SITE SELECTION ANALYSIS. Several entry-level positions available at both our Los Altos, California and Ann Arbor, Michigan offices. Seeking those with location theory background with a strong interest in applied marked research in a dynamic and fast paced environment. Ideal candidate ...strong working knowledge of micro ...by elementary statistics, ...sions require

FLORIDA, ORLANDO 32859.

and the nation's largest full-service seafood restaurant chain, seeks two motivated individuals to fill positions in our Orlando-based Market Development Department.
Responsibilities include: Conducting in-depth field analysis of markets and trade areas offering potential for expansion; analysis of existing markets for future development; participation in site evaluation; conduct research and evaluate information from secondary sources together with data collected in field analysis to prepare a for... written analysis of market and trad... ecutives; deliver oral pres... on selected mark... communicate re grade the marke industry trends, chographic trend.

Qualifications re in geography, plan Master's degree pre lection experience in unit retail organizat communication skills proximately 40% trav ary, benefits, paid rel potential.

•OHIO, CLEVELAND 44181. METRO MARKET DEVELOPMENT PLANNER. For rapidly expanding retailing division of Cleveland-based Fortune 100 firm. Responsibilities include maintaining metro area economic outlook assessments, prioritizing geographic areas for retail expansion, analyzing growth and evolution of retail trading patterns within metro areas, planning retail site strategy for target markets, developing multiple regression models to evaluate specific retail sites. ...ap- ...excellent sal- ...on, and advancement

## MARKETING PLANNING AND ANALYSIS MANAGER
We're a $130m catalog retailer building to support our rapid growth.

Responsibilities include market planning. sales and order forecasting, statistical analysis. evaluation and analy...
opportunities.
Three years' rel... knowledge of •MINNESOTA, MINNEAPOLIS 55402.
SITE LOCATION ANALYST. The nation's fastest growing major retailer ith nine operating companies in 47 states has immediate opening for a Site Location Analyst assist in the development of corporate and operating company expansion plans through particting company expansion plans through partic...tion in major market studies. Responsibilities lude sales and demographic analysis of retail

locations, development of optimal total marketing strategies, interpretation of study results, and ...aration of final recommendations. 10%-15% ...l. Preferred candidates will have MA/MBA ...ography, business, or related field plus two to four years of related research experience. Excellent research techniques, concise writing skills, and a professional approach in presenting conclusions and recommendations are essential. Send resume and salary history.

*Source:* The authors

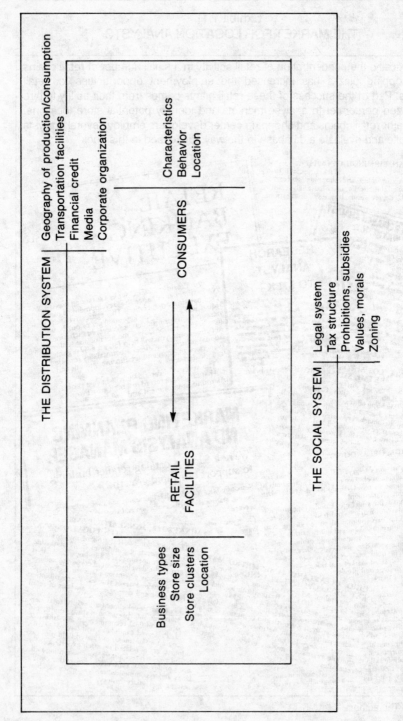

**Figure 1.6** The context of location analysis

*Source*: The authors

come from? Where do they go? What kinds of transportation facilities are available? Trains? Trucks? What is the cost structure? How accessible are competing locations in terms of travel time and costs?

On the corporate side, other issues could be raised. What kinds of financial credit are available? Is it provided through the consumer (the bank card) or the retailer (the store charge card)? What are the relevant advertising media? How are they organized spatially? How do the media define markets? What is the corporate organization of the retailer? Co-operative? Retail chain? Independent? Are the chains linked horizontally with many branches which are all alike, or vertically with different facilities feeding into one another (for example, manufacture – wholesale – retail, as in gasoline retailing)?

These distribution phenomena, in turn, take place within the context of a social system. How does society regard marketing? How do our values, morals, taxes, and regulations shape the market environment? Society has created a whole way of life around the act of consumption in which govern-ment, business, and labor all have a large stake. It has been argued that the mass production of the industrial revolution required the simultaneous development of mass markets and large corporations. Industrial and merchandising interests, along with the media, have promoted a society that puts a high premium on the consumption of personal goods. Our very concepts of market and trade are based on legal institutions and procedures developed to protect property and to encourage the exchange of goods.

In a variety of ways the buying habits of consumers are managed and manipulated to serve some social end. Here are a few examples:

*Governments manage the economy* They stimulate it or deflate it by accelerating or retarding the level of consumer spending. Is the country in a recession? The solution is to remove sales taxes, reduce income taxes and get people buying again.

*Christmas* If marketing were simply the rational and efficient delivery of goods, would retail sales be 20 per cent higher in December (up to 40 per cent of annual sales in some retail sectors), as shown in Figure 1.7? Depart-ment stores make half of their profits in the fourth quarter. The high prices during the Christmas season and the excess retail capacity during the rest of the year suggest a certain madness in our behavior. As people in adver-tising will attest, consumption is a social act as much as an expression of real need.

*Merit and non-merit goods* Societies, and hence governments, have strong feelings about what is good for us (merit goods) and what is not good for us (non-merit goods). They often subsidize our consumption of such merit goods as recreation, opera, medical care, or local wine and

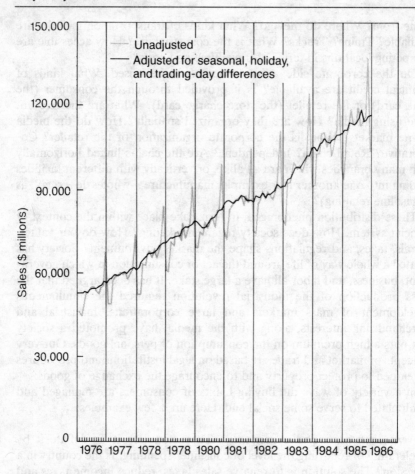

**Figure 1.7** The annual cycle of retail sales

*Source:* Bureau of the Census 'Current business reports: monthly retail trade', Washington

penalize or prevent the purchase of non-merit goods such as prostitution, marijuana, imported wine, and tobacco. Every political jurisdiction debates the process of selling and consuming alcoholic beverages.

*The control of trade* How different might the distribution pattern displayed in Fig. 1.3 be if the United States had not negotiated agreements with Canada about automobile production and trade, and with Japan about the level of imports? The pattern is also affected by taxes on gasoline, emission controls, and investments in highway systems.

The broad social implications of marketing are brought out in the debate about consumer sovereignty: do the household's requirements and preferences determine the products and the distribution system that it receives? Or is the household at the mercy of a massive corporate structure which creates both products and needs and compels the consumer to want, to choose, and to buy. This debate is endless because both sides are partly right.

The concept of consumer satisfaction is an attempt to evaluate the distribution system from the consumer's point of view. Are consumers satisfied with the mix of products, prices, stores, and plazas that are available? Do they enjoy the shopping process? Do they feel that they obtain good value? Some marketing analysts gauge satisfaction by comparing the level of consumption by similar households in different environments. Do people living downtown, with access to a diverse set of shopping options, consume more of certain products than people in the suburbs? Does a household purchase less if it moves to a smaller city, or to a city with a poorly developed retail structure? Is the key element in consumer satisfaction price, accessibility, variety, or the environment of the store or plaza itself?

Some interesting conclusions concerning the pleasure derived from purchasing were drawn by Andrew Hacker in the *New York Times Book Review* when reviewing a book entitled *Money and Class in America* by L.N. Lapham.

It is too easy to dismiss our pleasure in purchasing ... as 'votive ritual and pagan ornament.' Nor is it a failing specific to the yuppie decade. Our founders understood the need for acquisitions and enjoyments, especially in society marked by restlessness and movement; where ... 'all status is temporary'. Throughout most of human history, men and women held settled identities based on religion, class and region, strengthened by family and tribal affiliations going back for centuries. America would weaken those ties, if not sever them altogether. Tocqueville again: 'The woof of time is every instant broken and the track of generations effaced'. In such a setting, individuals – the rich no less than the rest of us – would have to discover who they were, even invent themselves.

And the chief vehicle in this quest would be personal consumption. America became the best-stocked supermarket in the world, from which citizens would select those products and pleasures most expressive of their personalities. Together, our wardrobes, the tapes and records we collect, the vacations we take, combine to establish each of us as unique. This may not be the most elevated approach to individuality, but it is America's way.

(Hacker, 1988)

The various constraints imposed by the distribution system generate a considerable variety of marketing processes to serve Americans, as shown in Figure 1.8. The traditional manufacturer – wholesaler – retailer – household route now plays a smaller role than before. The large retail chains such as Sears or J.C. Penney order appliances made to their own specifications from several different manufacturers. Mail-order shopping via catalogs is making a comeback, but uses upscale advertising media such as the *New Yorker* or the New York *Sunday Times* to appeal to more sophisticated households seeking special goods, rather than to the mass market.

Why do we have the particular mix of distribution activity shown in Table 1.2 at this particular time? How and why is the pattern changing? The share of department stores has declined recently, while franchising and the retail chains are on the increase. Each of these paths from producer to market generates a different locational pattern, a different map of warehouses, stores, and purchases.

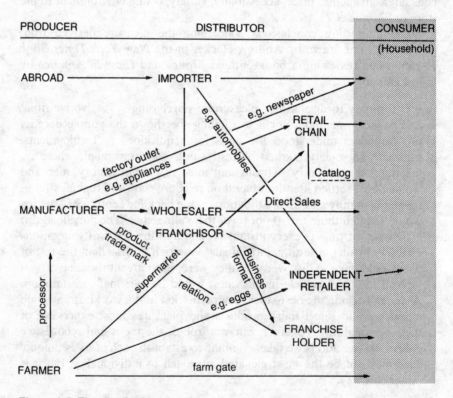

**Figure 1.8** The distribution system

*Source:* The authors
*Note:* Distribution accounts for about half of the cost of a good to the consumer. There are many different routes of distribution. Each route generates a different spatial pattern of distribution activity.

**Table 1.2** The variety of retail activity

|  | $ billions | | % |
| --- | --- | --- | --- |
| *Non-store retailers* | 20 | | *1.9* |
| Mail order | 11 | | 1.0 |
| Vending machines | 5 | | 0.5 |
| Direct (door-to-door) | 4 | | 0.4 |
| *Retail stores* | *1,046* | | *98.1* |
| Department stores | 107 | | 10.0 |
| Other chains[a] | 460 | | 43.2 |
| Franchises[b] | 369 | | 34.6 |
| Independent retailers | 150[c] | (estimated) | 15.0[c] |
| *Total retail sales* (1982) | *1,066* | | *100* |

*Source:* Bureau of the Census (annual) *Statistical Abstract of the United States*, Washington
*Notes:* [a]With two or more establishments. [b]As defined by the Department of Commerce, International Trade Administration. Some franchise operations are retail chains, hence the ambiguity of the estimate of independent retail activity. [c]Estimated values.

## The rest of this book

There are two distinct traditions in location analysis, the theoretical (academic) and the applied (practitioner). The academic tradition dates from the works of Christaller (1933) and Losch (1939) which were concerned with the way retail activities were located in order to serve a regular distribution of demand. They developed arguments to justify the hierarchical distribution of retail activity within a system of urban settlements. Their modern counterparts, such as Berry *et al.* (1988), have extended the theory to fit the complexities of human behavior and the irregular markets found within the metropolitan areas. Other academics look for regularities in aggregate retail structure and land-use patterns and interpret them in terms of economic, geographic, and social processes.

The practitioners (Epstein and Schell, 1982) trace their roots to the work of Applebaum (1966) and his 'how-to-do-it' focus. They are concerned with the problems associated with a location decision by a retail chain. Key elements in this tradition are the delimitation of market areas, the concern for competition and market share, and the development of site selection procedures.

Recently there has been a reconciliation of theory and practice (Davies and Rogers, 1984; Ghosh and McLafferty, 1987; Wrigley, 1988). Academics have become increasingly interested in 'real-world' problems, particularly those dealing with structural change and location strategy. Simultaneously, practitioners have come to recognize the value of general models and frameworks in seeking answers to the complex location decisions that confront large retail units. This book contributes to the reconciliation by extending theoretical discussions to incorporate the concentration of retail activity in chains and shopping centers, and by discussing the techniques of the practitioners within the context of corporate strategy. Both theorists and practitioners are concerned with the sort of issues raised in Exhibit 1.2 on consumer banking. How is this part of the distribution system changing? What are the possible implications for the spatial structure? What decisions have to be made? What information is needed to make them?

This book differs from most other texts in consciously trying to follow the agenda of practitioners within the retail sector. As we will argue repeatedly throughout, developers, location analysts, and policymakers make the decisions that shape this very visible part of our landscape. To understand how that landscape emerges, we must trace through the problems, information, techniques and constraints that result in these choices. Retail decisions and the urban environment are closely intertwined: location decisions made within the context of the present environment help, in turn, to determine the retail environment of the future.

Accordingly, the organization of this book traces the logic of the location sequence. What kinds of information about the urban environment and location procedures are necessary inputs to the process? What kinds of issues and questions are typically raised? This doesn't mean that we unquestioningly support the goals and procedures of retailers or developers: we present many different points of view on these issues. Our stance is simply to try to understand what they do, and why and where they do it. We think that the material will prove useful both to those people who will eventually find themselves working in the industry, and to those who will simply experience, as consumers, the effects of location analysis.

Our book is divided into four parts, as shown in Figure 1.9: Processes, Structure, Strategy, and The Future. The discussions of processes (Chapters two to four) tackle first the demand side (the consumer) and then the supply side (the stores). The two are linked by the behavior patterns of consumers who decide how far they are willing to travel to a store, and what variety of goods they expect when they get there. These three chapters introduce the concepts and perspectives of location analysts; they are supplemented by a glossary of terms frequently used in this literature (Appendix A).

Part two, on structure, describes the geography of the distribution system, both in cross-section (Chapters five and seven) and as it changes over time (Chapters six and eight). Here we emphasize the rapidity of change in retail patterns and the diversity of opportunities created for retailers. We deal with two spatial scales. On the scale of the settlement system, we discuss how the activities of the distribution system are allocated among various towns, cities, and regions. Where are the major wholesale centers? Which villages have bakeries? The two chapters that follow examine the intra-urban patterns, such as the differences between

## Exhibit 1.2
## THE REVOLUTION IN CONSUMER BANKING

The fascination of marketing studies stems from the strategic choices that face the major actors in the system. Entrepreneurs and marketing executives ask 'Is this the time to invest, or to back off, to specialize or to diversify?' In a rapidly changing retail system, with the direction of change inherently uncertain, there are no easy answers and no right answers, but the investment decisions must be made, and made quickly. (*continued*)

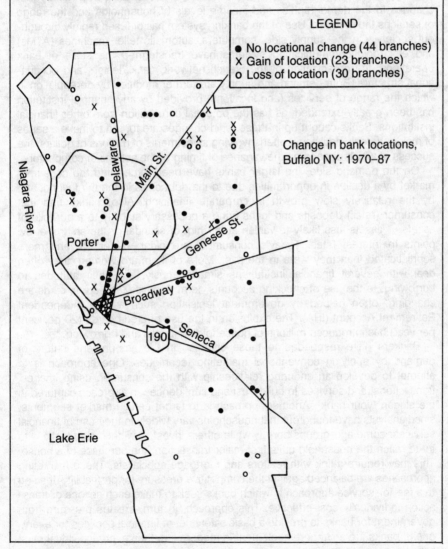

### LEGEND

● No locational change (44 branches)
X Gain of location (23 branches)
o Loss of location (30 branches)

Change in bank locations,
Buffalo NY: 1970–87

*Source: Buffalo City Directory, 1970 and 1987*

Location analysis at this strategic level must be more concerned with the retail structure of tomorrow than that of yesterday. We need to understand the logic that shapes the retailer's options and decisions. The current 'revolution' in consumer banking provides examples of the kinds of change and uncertainty that affect retailers and the types of decision that must be made.

Consumer banking is that part of the financial system that deals with households, and thus household savings, loans, and financial services, by means of a network of bank branches. Consumer banking has been profoundly shaken by three types of change. The demand for financial services has grown rapidly with changes in the demographics and income levels of households and the range of services they require. Use of the banking system has diffused rapidly throughout society. On the supply side, computers, automatic teller machines (ATMs) and electronic communication systems have transformed the scale of bank operations, the organization of the branch network, bank design, and occupational structure. Both demand and supply are further modified by deregulation in which the range of services (and locations) provided by any financial institution has been greatly extended, as has the potential competition from other financial institutions. Banks caught up in these rapid changes are forced to make a series of major strategic decisions, often involving investments of millions of dollars, the success of which depend on the vagaries of timing or the actions of competitors.

On the demand side, the larger banks have been forced into the consumer market by a decline in opportunities due to the debt crisis in the third world, and by the relatively slow growth in corporate financing. Also, banks find that consumer (retail) deposits and loans bring a necessary stability to a portfolio of assets — assets less likely to vanish at the hint of scandal or the shift of a few points in interest rates. Today's consumers are older, better off, and more sophisticated than they were in the past. More of them are women, they often deal with several financial institutions simultaneously, and their attitudes to borrowing, to the use of checking accounts, term deposits, and credit cards are changing, often helped by government legislation such as the Independent Retirement Account (IRA). The explosion in the use of credit cards (20 per cent per year) has introduced millions of households to banks and borrowing.

Bankers have responded to these changes in the amount and nature of demand by applying conventional marketing techniques. One approach is to attempt to develop an enduring relationship with the consumer, using images, transactions, and services to build trust and confidence; an approach captured in the slogan 'your bank'. Another approach is to target certain market segments, since analysts have found out that households vary widely in their use of financial services: some age-groups borrow while others invest. A widely used tactic is to try to reach the household at its first major transaction, the purchase of a house. This may require a link with realtors and mortgage specialists. These marketing approaches are balanced against the competitive pressure for profitability, leading to a fee-for-service approach in which banks seek to make each service or transaction individually cost-effective. This approach, in turn, creates pressure from government for banks to provide a basic safety net of financial services for everyone. If banks are an important element in modern life, then every individual must have access to them, if only to cash welfare checks.

On the supply side, no economic sector has been so transformed by the electronics revolution as the financial industry. First came the internal efficiencies when all the record-keeping was transferred to computers, initiating waves of adjustments to staffing and procedures, and a relentless search for cost-effectiveness. However, better communication systems soon affected the placing of assets as well. Directly or indirectly, every bank could participate in financial markets as far away as Mexico, Poland, or Japan, sometimes with disastrous results. Computers, communications, and charge cards then led inevitably to the ATMs which pared down the major remaining costs of retail banking, but opened up the possibility of consumer banking away from conventional bank premises.

The banking system that has evolved as a result of this technology must use economies of scale in order to recover the substantial investments in these electronic systems. Pressures to permit mergers among banks and links to other locations and financial institutions soon emerged. Banks have developed networks of more specialized branches providing different mixes of services, from ATMs to full service banking. There are now branches specifically oriented to business customers. Consumer banking itself may become a separate division within the financial conglomerate.

Deregulation is intimately linked to changes on both the demand and supply sides as governments respond both to the changing requirements of consumers and to the economies of scale that local and national financial institutions require in order to survive international competition. The spatial scale of competition has increased as a result of the improved communication networks. Regional and national oligopolies have been penetrated by national and international banks, forcing institutions everywhere to offer competitive interest rates and equivalent services and to maintain similar levels of operating expenses. Smaller banks are disappearing or specializing as the competition for consumer banking intensifies.

In addition, the boundaries around the banking component of the financial sector have been broken down. Banks are linking up with trust companies, stock-brokers, realtors, and insurance companies in order to provide cradle-to-grave financial services. At the same time, any financial service that has a network of outlets and a list of customers is now in a position to compete with the banks. American Express, Merrill-Lynch, Sears Roebuck, and various finance companies are all expanding the range of their financial services. The winner may be the institution that can most efficiently support a network of consumer banking outlets. How does a major bank respond to these trends? Each would-be player in the financial services industry must develop a consumer banking strategy, answering questions such as these:

(1) Should we compete for consumer deposits and loans, or turn instead to wholesale banking, buying deposits and loans from other institutions? What is the value of each type of portfolio asset during periods of economic growth/ decline or high/low interest rates?
(2) How large a consumer market is required to justify investments in automa- tion, a network of outlets, etc? How do we trade off the need for rapid growth against the increased risks that it entails? What are the advantages and disadvantages of being a technological innovator within the banking system?
(3) What is the spatial extent of our target market: regional, national, inter-

national? Can it be achieved through mergers with existing institutions or should we select our own locations and types of outlet?

(4) What is the pattern of competition/regulation in the target market? Can it be altered?

(5) What level of operating costs/efficiency is required to achieve profit goals?

(6) What market segments do we target? Young/old? Upscale/middle-class? Can we adopt the techniques of retailers?

(7) What associated services does this market segment require: mortgages, securities, retirement plans, insurance?

(8) What kind of branch network is needed to serve the market: number, size, specialization? Can we substitute direct mailing or telephone service?

(9) What image should be conveyed: personal service? trust? value? range of services?

There is no single right answer to these questions. The right responses will not be known until years later since they depend on future developments in the economy and on the simultaneous strategic choices of other institutions. If several banks choose the same route nobody wins. These are the fascinating challenges that define the context for location analysis.

Although the changes in consumer banking are international in scope, they also penetrate every community within the city. The map on p. 21 shows the redistribution of bank branches in the City of Buffalo between 1970 and 1987. Over that period, while income levels increased and the number of households stayed roughly the same, the city gained twenty-three branches while losing thirty. There is no overall pattern of growth or decline except for the substantial loss of downtown branches, a reflection of the declining role of Buffalo's downtown area. Most of the changes are minor relocations within the same community. What is not apparent is the extraordinary degree of corporate change. By 1987 a series of mergers had changed almost all the main banks and eliminated a number of independent ones.

downtown and the suburban plazas, or the recent specialization of retail districts.

Part three, on strategy, includes four chapters (nine to twelve) that apply the techniques of location analysis to various marketing decisions. The introductory chapter addresses the various uncertainties that surround the decision-maker and the chapters that follow suggest how information can be developed to enable better decisions to be made: to select a site, to delimit a market area, and to develop strategies to serve market segments. Part three is supplemented by Appendix B, which lists data sources commonly used in marketing studies.

Part four looks to the future and how we get there. Chapter thirteen introduces another role in the retail system that of the urban planner or policy-maker who also makes marketing decisions but in the context of the social and political change that may be expected in the metropolitan

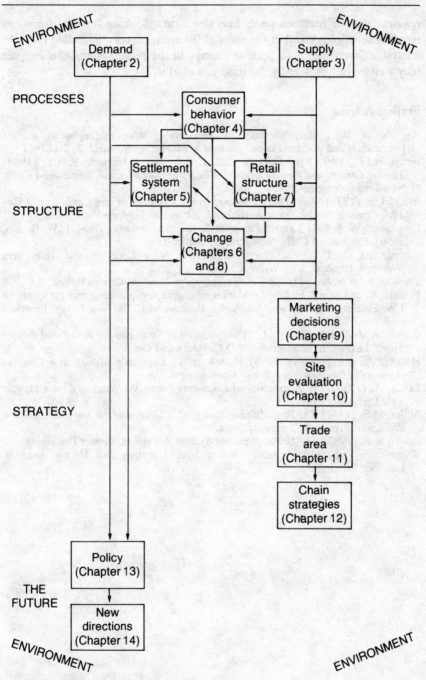

**Figure 1.9** A guide to the book

*Source:* The authors

region. Chapter fourteen peers into the future, looking for new trends in retailing technology and in the roles of different players, including location analysts. Given the rapid pace of change in the retail system, this chapter may well be out of date by the time you read it.

**Further reading**

Applebaum, W. (1966) 'Methods for determining store trading areas, market penetration and potential sales', *Journal of Marketing Research* 3, 2:127–41.

Berry, B.J.L., Parr, J.B., Epstein, B.J., Ghosh, A., and Smith, R.H.T. (1988) *Market Centers and Retail Location: Theory and Application*, Englewood Cliffs, New Jersey:Prentice-Hall.

Braudel, F. (1979) '*The Wheels of Commerce*', *Civilization and Capitalism, 15th–18th Century*. (vol. 2 Trans. S. Reynolds), London: Fontana Paperbacks.

Christaller, W. (1933) *Central Places in Southern Germany* (Trans. C.W. Baskin, 1966), Englewood Cliffs, New Jersey: Prentice-Hall.

Davies, R.L. and Rogers, D.S. (eds) (1984) *Store Location and Assessment Research*, London: John Wiley & Sons.

Dawson, John A. (ed.) (1980) *Retail Geography*, London: Croom Helm.

Epstein, B. and Schell, E. (1982) 'Marketing geography: problems and prospects, in J.W. Frazier (ed.) *Applied Geography*, Englewood Cliffs, New Jersey: Prentice-Hall.

Ghosh, A. and McLafferty, S.L. (1987) *Location Strategies for Retail and Service Firms*, Lexington, Massachusetts: D.C. Heath and Co.

Hacker, A. (14 February 1988) Review of L. Lapham's *Money and Class in America* in the *New York Times Book Review*.

Losch, A. (1939) *The Economics of Location* (Trans. W. Woglom), New Haven: Yale University Press.

Miller, M.B. (1981) *The Bon Marche: Bourgeois Culture and the Department Store*, Princeton: Princeton University Press.

Potter, R.B. (1982) *The Urban Retailing System*. Aldershot: Gower Publishing.

Wrigley, N. (ed.) (1988) *Store Choice, Store Location and Market Analysis*. London: Routledge.

# Processes

The next three chapters introduce three kinds of logic which provide the basis for analyzing the problems of retail location. From geography we extract some principles about the spatial distribution of markets and how to analyze them. Economics contributes the supply side principles that govern the size and location of stores. The literature of psychology describes how individual consumers make choices.

Part one also introduces the reader to some of the major actors in the retail system, their resources, and their goals. What kinds of games are they playing and how much money are they willing to put up? The consumers are described collectively in Chapter two as the most fundamental constraint on the retail system. Every location analysis begins with some kind of market definition. The size (in dollars) of that market can be translated into an upper limit of retail sales. We explore some of the variations among consumers that affect retailers: income level, household composition, and lifestyle. In Chapter four we meet consumers as individuals who travel, shop, and compare, as people with strong likes and dislikes, often unpredictably. How mobile are they? Where do they travel through the weekly routine? What kinds of information do they have about various shopping opportunities? Why do they prefer a particular brand or a particular type of shopping environment? Are these preferences predictable? In this chapter we begin to get a sense of the sources of uncertainty that make retail decision-making so challenging.

Chapter three describes some of the big operators in the retail system, the major retail chains which account for so much of the total retail activity, and the shopping center developers whose decisions and designs create shopping environments. We discuss factors that affect three interdependent aspects of retail structure: the size of an enterprise, the degree of specialization by product or market, and the choice of location.

Demand, supply, and consumer behavior, as interpreted by the various actors, interact to generate five kinds of retail phenomena, each corresponding to a different spatial scale:

(1) The mix of products in a store (the business type): this grouping reflects the purchasing behavior of a single household.
(2) The size and location of a store: the purchasing power of a neighborhood on the one hand and the production function of the store on the other combine to determine this pattern.
(3) The cluster of stores: plazas, retail strips, and boutique areas reflect the interaction among types of stores, as well as the requirements of the neighborhood.
(4) Retail structure: the mix and location of retail clusters that collectively serve an urban area is a fundamental concern of location analysis.
(5) The settlement system: the allocation of retail facilities among urban settlements of various sizes is the other central theme of this book.

# Chapter two

# The geography of demand

**Twenty-five million women in the US wear large sizes (size 16 and over).**

**People who live alone spend more money in restaurants than in grocery stores.**

**The average college student consumes about $300 worth of alcoholic beverages each year.**

**Twenty per cent of the expenditures made by the average American household were allocated to transportation, but only 1 per cent went to public transport.**

The central theme of this chapter is that the consumption patterns of American families are highly predictable and have been very thoroughly described. You do not have to know very much about a neighborhood in order to list its purchases of gasoline or soap or T-shirts in considerable detail. There will be differing preferences among brands – Budweiser or Coors for instance, and local lifestyles may affect the relative consumption of potatoes or pasta or brown rice, but the average supermarket, bank, and gas station will serve the neighborhood very well. We are all deeply immersed in a common technology and culture so that across 1,000 or more households the idiosyncracies disappear into the average pattern.

Every analysis of the distribution system or discussion of a location decision begins with the notion of the market in order to define and qualify the right-hand side of the fundamental retailing relationship:

$$\text{Retail sales} = f\,(\text{market}) \qquad\qquad (\text{eqn } 2.1)$$

$F(x)$ simply indicates some kind of functional relationship involving the variable x. How big is the market? Is it rich or poor? Family-oriented or singles-oriented? Italian or Polish? Central city or suburban? The level of retailing activity will respond appropriately.

Location analysts tend to define markets spatially and usually measure or define the market area early in the study as a basis for the rest of the analysis. This can be done because the factors that determine the market, such as the size of Tucson, or the household income in Waco, Texas, lie outside the analyst's control. They are essentially given.

In contrast, business-based marketing studies treat a market as something more flexible, to be modified as part of the solution to the marketing problem. For example, an advertising campaign aimed at women professionals (the market) could be extended to include college students or clerical workers in the target group. Changing the market becomes one of the strategic options.

In either case, the starting point for discussion is a detailed knowledge of the market: the upper limit that it imposes on sales or its potential for expansion. The sections to follow begin with a very general definition of the market, which is then qualified by discussions of the spatial boundaries, the size, and other characteristics such as income, demographic composition, and lifestyle.

## The market

A market is a set of consumers: for our purposes these consumers must be grouped in some way. The rest of the chapter will address four aspects of describing or segmenting a market that have proven useful for retail location studies:

(1) Location: a market is contained within an area, such as a neighborhood, a metropolitan region, or a nation. The key element here is market size which determines the scale of operation or the degree of specialization possible. Market size is usually defined in terms of population, number of households, or population.
(2) Income: the level of income or the income mix of the market. Because high-income households consume so much more per capita than poor households, the relative share of each group is an important aspect of market size. In addition, different income groups (social classes) become the targets for specialized retailers. Discounters or second-hand stores aim at poor families, fashion boutiques at the well-to-do.
(3) Demographics: the age and sex composition of the market. Certain products and certain retail outlets depend on specific age–sex groups. Record stores, for example, appeal primarily to teenagers and young adults, bars serve singles. A single household or neighborhood may represent many demographic elements so that different advertising media or retail outlets may be required in order to reach all members of the family.
(4) Lifestyle: in larger urban areas the presence of sub-markets with distinct preferences is often evident in clusters of specialized stores. Ethnic identity is particularly important in defining lifestyle groups but there may also be gay, punk, high-fashion, or environmentally conscious communities.

While a market can be defined using any one of these criteria, often several categories occur in combination. Each of the non-spatial markets implicitly defines a spatial market; the Hispanic community, for example, is concentrated in certain neighborhoods. Non-spatial criteria often overlap. Ethnic communities tend not only to cluster in space, but to be concentrated in a specific income class. The term 'yuppie' (young urban professional) implies not only a certain lifestyle but also a particular location (central city), a particular age-group (25–40 years), and a particular income bracket. In Chapter eleven we will tackle the problem of defining spatial markets in a practical way, identifying those households that shop at a specific store or plaza or have specific target characteristics.

## Spatially defined markets

Before beginning our discussion of the ways in which a market is delimited in space, let us introduce the two spatial scales which shape the structure of this book. On the urban settlement scale we deal with national, regional, and urban markets. We treat a metropolitan area, city, or town as a unit, a single market, and talk about its size, growth, and competition with other centers. Atlanta's retail facilities are compared with those of Charlotte, Augusta, or Jacksonville.

The metropolitan scale, in contrast, examines patterns of markets and retail facilities within the urban area, examining communities and neighborhoods as well as non-spatial submarkets: the rich, the old, blue-collar workers, or college students.

This differentiation in scale is carried over from the literature of urban geography which separates the study of settlements or urban systems (e.g. Bourne and Simmons, 1978) from the study of internal urban structure (e.g. Bourne, 1982). Discussions of settlement systems are dominated by the enormous variation in market size, in population density, and in accessibility. New York, for example, has ten times the population of Hartford and one hundred times the population of New London, Connecticut. Consumers in Anchorage, Alaska are hundreds of miles from any shopping alternatives. Discussions of internal structure emphasize the dramatic qualitative differences in income level or age composition that can occur from one neighborhood to another.

On either the urban settlement scale or the metropolitan scale, a spatial market must be delimited in some fashion. Five kinds of boundaries are relevant: (1) institutional, (2) natural, (3) those imposed by the spatial distribution of households (the density of settlement), (4) the spatial decay pattern imposed by transportation costs, and (5) those resulting from the actions of competitors (see Figure 2.1).

Institutional boundaries are imposed by the rules and regulations of organizations. For example, national markets are defined by the federal government, through tariffs or licencing regulations, and by the internal organizations of corporations which designate affiliates to serve a national market. Sub-national boundaries might be statewide (as in the case of liquor sales) or metropolitan, as in the allocation of TV licenses by the Federal Communications Commission.

Firms also designate spatial markets to define the responsibility of

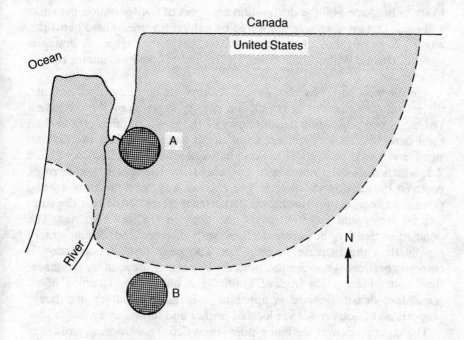

**Figure 2.1** Bounding a spatial market

*Source:* The authors
*Note:* The market served by city A is bounded to the north by an institutional boundary, to the west by a natural boundary, to the south by the trade area of a competitor (B), and to the east by the distance decay effect.

district sales managers, regional distribution centers, and local outlets. Franchises may be given exclusive sales rights within a community or within a given radius of the site. Implicitly, and sometimes explicitly, a retailer signing a shopping center lease expects a restriction of certain kinds of competition within the plaza, and thereby within the community it serves. For particular products or for stores within a retail chain, the size of such spatial markets may be delimited quite precisely, given some estimates about average household consumption of the product and the market share of the brand name (the brand's proportion of total sales of a product).

The spatial pattern of settlement helps to define 'natural' market areas – regions that are reasonably self-contained and isolated from other spatial markets. For example, natural features such as mountains, or the Mississippi River can be used to define regions. The west coast and New England are distinctive regional markets, well-defined by physical features. The South, Midwest, and Great Plains are less obvious regions and are more likely to be shaped by the distribution networks of transportation networks and cities that are themselves affected by natural features. These networks, along valleys and through mountain passes, shape the expansion strategies of retail chains. Within some cities, rivers, harbors, and mountains modify trade areas.

For the most part, however, natural features are now less important than the enormous variations in population density imposed by the settlement system. Urban population densities may be thousands of times greater than rural densities. As a result, each settlement forms a distinct market and significant breaks or boundaries occur between settlements. Consider Figure 2.2, which shows the number of households in Toronto in 1-mile rings, centered on the downtown area. Put another way, how far away are the potential customers for downtown department stores? Note that the rings contain larger and larger areas as the distance (radius) increases. The population density, however, declines with distance and declines more rapidly than the increase in ring size. The peak ring of population is currently between 4 and 5 miles from the city center. Beyond that distance, the density of settlement drops off gradually. A noticeable 'flattening' of the population density surface is apparent over time, as larger and larger proportions of households are located further and further away.

The combination of declining population density with greater distance from the city center (an exponential curve), and increases in ring size with distance (linear), produces the observed pattern. Ultimately, the number of households per ring drops to such a low level that an effective boundary may be drawn. The magnitude of the Toronto market in 1981 is indicated by the area under the curve – about one million households altogether – with three-quarters of the market located within 12 miles of the downtown area.

The pattern of growth over the last 40 years is a useful base for discussing the dynamics of retail structure within the city. Between 1941 and 1961 most of the metropolitan growth occurred within 5–10 miles of the center, while between 1961 and 1981 growth took place 10–15 miles outside the center and, over a 20-year period, added a new market roughly equal in size to the original market of 1941. Where should new activities locate to serve the additional growth? Like other cities located on a waterfront, Toronto is faced with the problem that growth can only occur to the north, east, or west – not to the south. Over time a larger and larger share of the market is located northward so that the downtown core is slowly forced northward, block by block. These pressures to relocate the retail core inland are counterbalanced by the inertia of the downtown office complex which generates its own distribution of customers, and by a transportation system still centered at the old core.

On the spatial scale of the settlement system, the nodes of population density still largely define the extent of markets. Most of the market lies

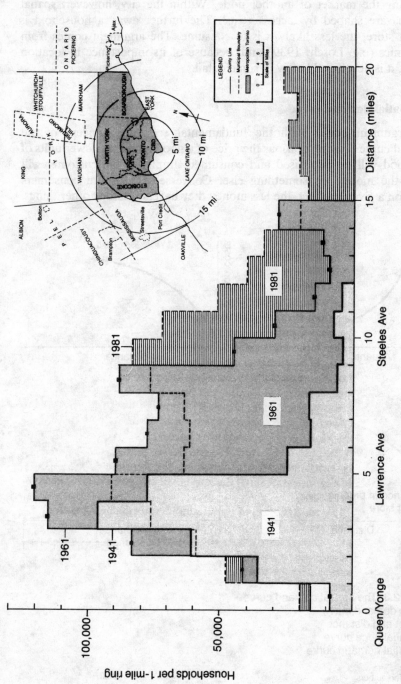

**Figure 2.2** The spatial structure of the Toronto market

*Source:* Statistics Canada (various years) *Census of Canada*

within the node and it is difficult to enlarge the market except by somehow capturing the market of another node. Within the city, however, spatial markets are shaped by 'access costs'. The further away a household is from a store, the less likely it is to consume. The argument comes from economics (e.g. Losch, 1939) and, because of its importance in location theory, it is developed below in some detail.

### The spatial demand curve

The argument begins with the fundamental economic concept of the demand curve (Figure 2.3a): as the price of a good increases, fewer units of that good will be purchased and consumed. Implicitly the customer will spend the money on something else. Conversely, the more consumers spend on a given product, the less money they have left to buy other things.

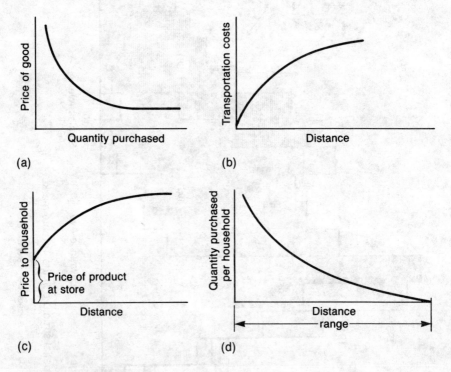

**Figure 2.3** The spatial demand curve
(a) The demand curve
(b) Cost and distance
(c) Spatial price curve
(d) Spatial demand curve

*Source:* The authors

The second concept comes from economic geography: the greater the distance travelled, the greater the transportation costs, whether measured in time or money (Figure 2.3b). In retailing, the costs of travel between home and store (in both directions) are borne by the consumer.

Combining the two ideas (Figure 2.3c), it is apparent that the full cost of a good to the consumer, including travel, increases with distance from the store. The price to the consumer is equal to the sum of the store price plus the travel cost. Since the amount purchased declines as the price increases, the effect of distance is to generate a spatial demand curve (Figure 2.3d) in which the quantity of a good purchased by a household declines with the household's distance from the store. Eventually, of course, as the distance to the store increases, the travel costs become so large that the quantity purchased falls to zero. The distance at which this occurs is called the 'range' of the good (or the store) and defines the spatial extent of the market.

The spatial demand curve is a nice concept, but does it have any empirical application to a real marketing environment? The answer must be yes, if location has any relevance at all. Certainly, one can calculate the costs involved: travel costs at 50c per mile (two-way), time at $10 per hour, etc. The effective price of a $10 item triples for the household located 10 miles away. The effect of the spatial demand curve is observed at every spatial scale: the likelihood of patronage at a given facility declines with distance. On a national scale the decline is observed for tourist attendance, e.g. Floridians are less likely to visit Yosemite than Californians, but the relationship is also modified in other ways. Increasing the price of admission (the cost of the good) will also reduce attendance (the demand curve), but high-income families are less sensitive than poor ones to either distance or cost.

Within a metropolitan area, actual distance is less important than travel time in determining customer patronage; each store or shopping plaza has a distinct spatial demand curve, as demonstrated in Figure 2.4. In this example, drawn from a study in Philadelphia, the number of trips that a customer makes to a shopping plaza is a linear function of travel time to that center from the home.

Market analysts classify all products, stores or plazas into two groups: convenience goods (day-to-day purchases) and shopping goods (department store type merchandise). The former are represented by the smaller community shopping plaza in Figure 2.4; the largest store will be a K mart or Target store. The regional center will have a department store and a large proportion of clothing, jewelry, and gift stores. Market penetration by the community center declines sharply with distance: the range is about thirty minutes travel time. The range of the regional center extends to over an hour's travel away.

Every product or type of store falls somewhere along the continuum

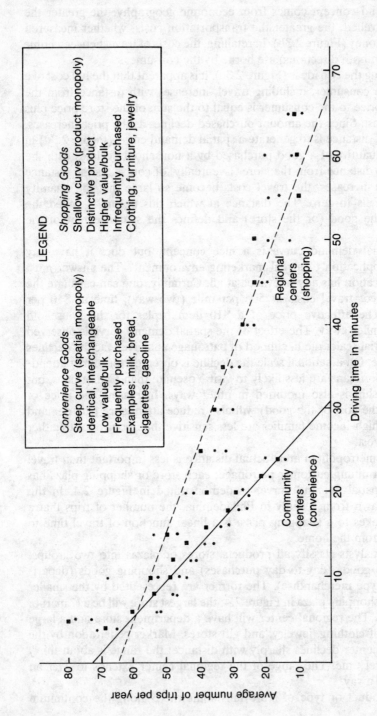

**Figure 2.4** Distance decay curves: convenience and shopping goods

*Source:* Based on data from William Young (1975) 'Distance decay values and shopping center size', Professional Geographer 27:304–9
*Note:* This example looks at shopping frequencies for three regional and three community centers. Symbols on graph represent the number of trips to those centers for customers at given travel times away.

LEGEND

*Convenience Goods*
Steep curve (spatial monopoly)
Identical, interchangeable
Low value/bulk
Frequently purchased
Examples: milk, bread, cigarettes, gasoline

*Shopping Goods*
Shallow curve (product monopoly)
Distinctive product
Higher value/bulk
Infrequently purchased
Clothing, furniture, jewelry

Regional centers (shopping)

Community centers (convenience)

Driving time in minutes

Average number of trips per year

from convenience to shopping goods. Over the decades, however, the various changes in the distribution system have moved products towards the shopping goods end of the spectrum. Cheaper, more widely available transportation (the automobile) tends to make all spatial demand curves flatter and shallower, extending the potential range of a good and reducing the degree of spatial monopoly (a situation in which the cost of shopping at alternative locations is so great that the customer has no real choice). Old people and poor households tend to have steep spatial demand curves and to shop locally for all goods.

The spatial demand curve plays an important role in determining the spatial structure of retailing in the metropolis. If distance were completely irrelevant all purchases could be made at a single huge retail outlet. On the other hand, if spatial demand curves were very steep we would expect a highly dispersed retail pattern with many small shopping clusters and a very modest downtown concentration. For instance, it was not until public transit became widely available that the great downtown department stores like Marshall Field and Macy's became possible.

The effect of distance or access in defining a spatial market is predictable, but the actions of competitors are not. A retail entrepreneur often prefers a small, spatially defined market without competition (e.g., beer sales at the ball park) where there are predictable trade-offs between price and consumption, rather than a spatially extensive market with trade areas largely defined by the location of competing outlets.

Figure 2.5a describes a convenience store A with apparent market range AZ, suddenly faced with competitor store B. As a result of the competition the market range of store A is reduced to distance AY. The rest of the market area is served by store B. A market area cut back in this way is said to be truncated by the competitor. Such a process is continually observed as a city expands in area. Because of the daily travel patterns of households, a typical urban trade area extends towards the outskirts of the city, away from the competition of the city center, but as the city grows outward another competitor may intervene to truncate store B's trade area and divert the trade of the growth area.

Shopping goods, which depend on product differences or prices to distinguish them from competitors, may be less sensitive to spatial competition (although sensitive to competitors trying to penetrate their price and product niche). However, the spatial demand curves of shopping goods may also be eroded, as shown in Figure 2.5c.

Finally, the effects of the spatial demand curve and the distribution of settlement may combine to accentuate the decline in sales with distance. Typically, the main cluster of stores serving a settlement is located near the center of town. As distance from the retail core increases, the density of residential settlement declines (not incidentally, since stores are part of the attraction of the city center). The combined effect (see Figure 2.6) is to

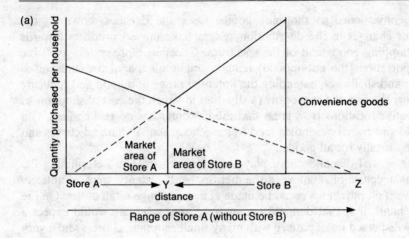

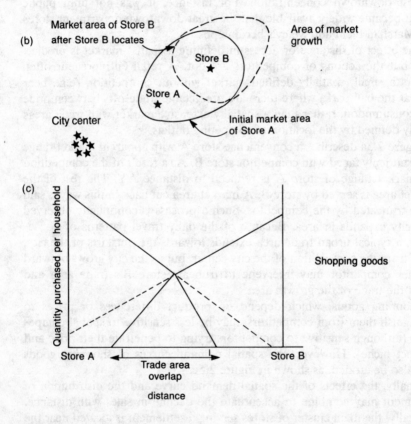

**Figure 2.5** The effect of competition

*Source:* The authors

reduce the level of purchase at the city center for the most distant households and to make a downtown location even more advantageous for the store.

The total number of potential customers, or market size (the hatched area), is the sum of the households in all distance rings that are expected to shop at the location. From another perspective, the question of consumer satisfaction discussed earlier takes on a spatial twist. Suppose initially that there were no stores outside the city center. The addition of facilities at suburban center B would increase the overall consumption of goods within the community by helping to overcome the effects of the spatial demand curve. Is there an optimal location for B? Does the location that maximizes the profit for center B coincide with the location that best increases the overall level of consumption? (see Exhibit 2.1) Entrepreneurs are

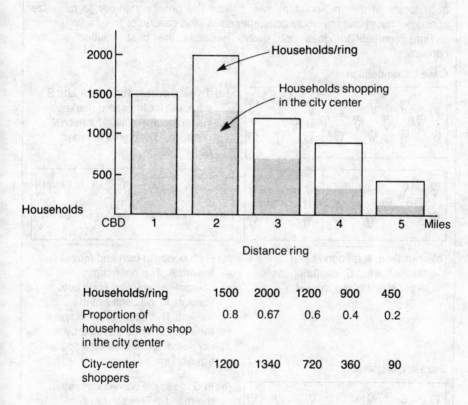

| Households/ring | 1500 | 2000 | 1200 | 900 | 450 |
| Proportion of households who shop in the city center | 0.8 | 0.67 | 0.6 | 0.4 | 0.2 |
| City-center shoppers | 1200 | 1340 | 720 | 360 | 90 |

**Figure 2.6** The combined effects of settlement density patterns and distance decay

*Source:* The authors
*Note:* CBD = central business district.

## Exhibit 2.1
## THE ICE CREAM VENDORS ON THE BEACH

The classic parable about the role of competition in location theory was put forward by Hotelling (1929). Suppose the market consisted of a linear beach, filled with evenly spaced sunbathers. The best location for a single ice cream stand would be at the center of the beach. Now, what if there were two independent ice cream trucks that could adjust their locations: what would the optimal location be for each one?

If one assumes that bathers go to the nearest truck, then each vendor will relocate in such a way as to maximize the length of beach that is closest to his or her truck. After all the competition and relocation is completed, the results are inevitable: the two vendors will both have worked their way back to the center of the beach so that each one serves half the market (Case I). If the two trucks are not independent, but are operated by a single entrepreneur (Case II), they will each locate at the mid-point of their half of the beach, in order to minimize consumer travel and maximize consumer sales (and consumer satisfaction).

Pure competition does not always generate the best solution for the consumer!

Case I: Competition

(a) Two ice cream vendors A and B compete for the same market. Because of A's initial locational decision, B captures a larger trade area.

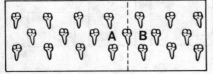

(b) Over time, A responds and moves toward B, capturing the larger share of the market.

(c) B responds in turn and moves toward A. The optimum competitive solution finds both vendors in the center of the market. This strategy maximizes the total distance traveled by the consumers, but creates a spatial equilibrium.

Case II: Co-operation

(a) In Case II, the two vendors split the market. This strategy minimizes consumer travel and the effect of future competition.

*Source:* H. Hotelling (1929) 'Stability and competition', *Economic Journal*, 39: 41–57

concerned with the former, urban planners with the latter. Unfortunately for both planners and entrepreneurs, the optimal decision in 1990 may be less than optimal in the year 2000 or 2010.

## Income

The most important characteristic of a given spatial market, beyond the size of the population or the number of households, is the level of income; first because of the aggregate impact on purchasing power, and second (very much second!) because of variations in purchasing patterns that occur among income groups.

Suppose that we measure market size, not in terms of population or number of households, but in terms of total income (households x average household income). The substantial variations in household income that occur within cities modify purchasing power and market size from one neighborhood to another. Across the United States, from region to region, household income levels in metropolitan areas vary from 10 to 20 per cent around the mean (Table 2.1), with the highest incomes found in larger places and places that have grown rapidly. The growth in market income is particularly important to retailers. It can occur either in population (Phoenix) or income per capita (Washington). Those places where both components have grown (Houston) have substantial advantages over those cities where nothing has changed (Detroit, Cleveland).

Table 2.2 indicates how the national market is concentrated at a small number of locations. Half the country's purchasing power can be reached in only twenty-five markets; three-quarters of the US market can be reached with only 200 outlets. The growth in income is even more concentrated. Seven cities, three in California plus Miami, Denver, Dallas, and Houston, account for 56 per cent of the growth in these major markets and one-fifth of the nation's income growth.

Income variations are much more marked within than among cities. Household income in a well-to-do district may be as much as ten times that of a poorer area. In Miami (Figure 2.7) the wealthy island of Key Biscayne includes 2,500 households (about 7,000 people). With an average household income of $45,000 in 1980, this neighborhood generates a market of $120 million – equivalent to half a dozen census tracts in the inner city neighborhood of Overtown, where the average household income is less than $10,000. In Miami the highest incomes are found near the coast with the lowest incomes just inland from that and the middle income suburbs stretching westward to the swamp. The concentrations of purchasing power strongly shape the location of retail activity.

The relationship between market income and retail sales is very powerful in aggregate. A national retail chain like K mart will find that a 7 per cent increase in consumer income across the country will translate almost

**Table 2.1** Major metropolitan markets

| | | Personal income (1983) ($ million) | Income per capita ($) | Growth rate, 1969–83 | | |
|---|---|---|---|---|---|---|
| Rank | City | | | Population (%) | Income/capita (%) | Total income (%) |
| 1 | New York* | 254,681 | 11,225 | −2.2 | 6.5 | 4.2 |
| 2 | Los Angeles* | 163,104 | 11,100 | 24.0 | 4.2 | 29.2 |
| 3 | Chicago* | 106,201 | 11,175 | 3.3 | 6.3 | 9.8 |
| 4 | San Francisco* | 87,163 | 12,425 | 19.6 | 14.7 | 37.2 |
| 5 | Philadelphia* | 73,032 | 10,125 | 0.1 | 8.5 | 8.6 |
| 6 | Detroit* | 57,957 | 10,900 | −4.4 | 0.5 | −4.0 |
| 7 | Washington | 54,498 | 12,575 | 12.8 | 20.5 | 35.9 |
| 8 | Boston* | 52,516 | 10,750 | 10.0 | 16.3 | 27.9 |
| 9 | Houston* | 48,008 | 11,625 | 64.4 | 28.2 | 110.8 |
| 10 | Dallas* | 45,223 | 10,925 | 42.3 | 19.3 | 69.8 |
| 11 | Miami* | 36,228 | 10,225 | 48.3 | 11.2 | 64.9 |
| 12 | Cleveland* | 35,044 | 10,475 | −7.1 | 3.1 | −4.2 |
| 13 | St. Louis | 30,459 | 10,175 | −1.3 | 14.8 | 13.3 |
| 14 | Minneapolis | 30,428 | 11,125 | 12.6 | 19.0 | 34.0 |
| 15 | Seattle* | 29,200 | 11,200 | 20.2 | 8.7 | 30.7 |
| 16 | Atlanta | 28,795 | 9,800 | 41.3 | 18.3 | 67.2 |
| 17 | Pittsburgh* | 28,366 | 9,975 | −7.2 | 13.5 | 5.3 |
| 18 | Baltimore | 27,353 | 9,900 | 7.5 | 14.3 | 22.9 |
| 19 | Denver* | 25,497 | 11,400 | 44.7 | 29.3 | 87.1 |
| 20 | San Diego | 24,730 | 10,100 | 52.0 | 10.2 | 67.5 |
| 21 | Milwaukee* | 20,254 | 10,800 | −0.4 | 9.6 | 9.2 |
| 22 | Tampa | 20,107 | 8,900 | 63.7 | 18.6 | 94.1 |
| 23 | Phoenix | 19,598 | 11,785 | 76.6 | 14.3 | 101.9 |
| 24 | Cincinnati* | 19,444 | 9,675 | 3.8 | 9.4 | 13.6 |
| 25 | Kansas City | 18,530 | 10,350 | 7.6 | 14.1 | 22.8 |
| | US Total | 2,744,200 | 11,670 | 15.6 | 16.1 | 34.4 |

*Source:* Bureau of the Census (1986) *State and Metropolitan Area Data Book*, Washington
*Note:* *Consolidated metropolitan statistical area (combination of two or more MSAs)

**Table 2.2** Market concentration

| | Total income ($ billions) | Percentage of US total |
|---|---|---|
| 10 largest markets | 942.4 | 34.3 |
| Next 15 largest | 393.8 | 14.3 |

*Source:* Bureau of the Census (1986) *State and Metropolitan Area Data Book*, Washington

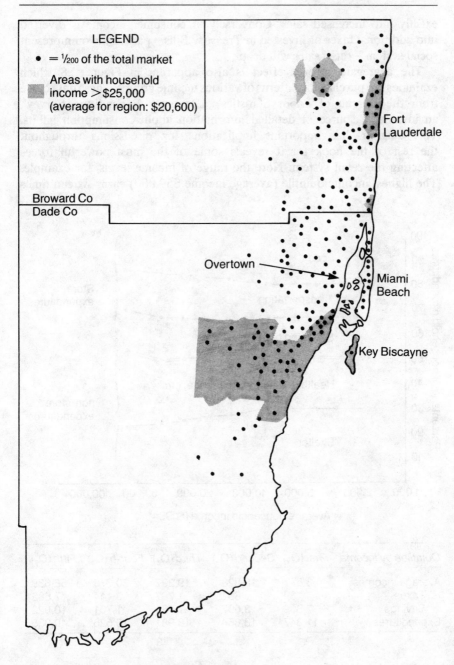

**Figure 2.7** Household income: Miami region

*Source:* Bureau of the Census (1980) *Census of Population*, Washington

exactly into increased sales. Conversely, if consumer income is diverted into additional taxes or invested in Treasury Bills – part of the omnipresent social system – retail sales will drop.

The aggregate income effect is also apparent in Figure 2.8 which examines the purchasing patterns of various income groups. These data come from the Bureau of Labor Statistics' 'Consumer Expenditure Survey', an invaluable source of detailed information about consumption habits. This diagram has important implications for discussions throughout the rest of the book for it reveals some of the most powerful forces affecting the retail system. Note the range of income levels, for example. The highest income quintile (average income $59,000) earns sixteen times

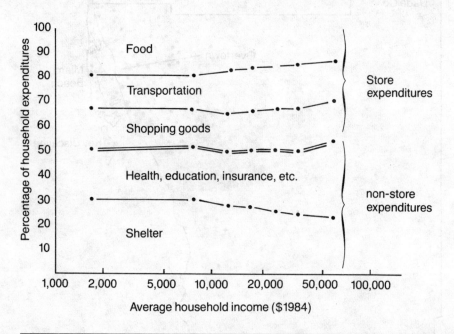

| Quintiles by income | First $(Q_1)$ | Second $(Q_2)$ | Third $(Q_3)$ | Fourth $(Q_4)$ | Fifth $(Q_5)$ |
|---|---|---|---|---|---|
| Average incomes | 3,577 | 10,828 | 19,297 | 30,370 | 58,639 |
| Taxes | 39 | 661 | 1,797 | 3,144 | 7,682 |
| Savings | − 7,809 | − 3,697 | − 1,481 | − 1,701 | 10,022 |
| Expenditures | 11,347 | 13,864 | 18,981 | 25,525 | 40,935 |

**Figure 2.8** Expenditure patterns by income groups

*Source:* Bureau of Labor Statistics (1986) *Consumer Expenditure Survey: Results for 1984*, Bulletin 2267, Washington

as much as the lowest income quintile (average income $3,600). If these households were to spend all their income, this would mean sixteen times as many stores, sales, retail employees, and so forth, in the wealthy neighborhood.

These stark differences are partly ameliorated by the varying ratios of expenditures to income, shown above the graph. First, taxes of various kinds reduce incomes in the higher income groups, but the after-tax income ratio for the highest and lowest income quintiles is still 14 to 1. More important are the differences in the ability to save. Poorer households supplement their income by borrowing or drawing on savings, equivalent to twice the level of income: think of the elderly, students, or the unemployed. Well-to-do households save one-sixth of their income. In terms of expenditure, then, the richest quintile spends four times as much and generates four times as much retail activity as the poorest. As incomes rise the amount spent in stores increases, but not as rapidly as income.

When it comes to the actual pattern of expenditure, the differences are less dramatic. the level of non-store purchases is relatively constant across all income categories at just over 50 per cent, but the importance of shelter declines from 30 to 24 per cent as income increases and there is a greater tendency to spend more money on health, pensions and insurance, and charity.

Food (home and away) accounts for 19 per cent of the lowest income group's purchases, but only 13 per cent for the highest (Table 2.3). Transportation absorbs most of the purchasing power released and the proportion spent on furniture, clothes, and recreation also increases. Goods for which the demand increases disproportionately as income increases are called income-elastic or luxury goods. Insurance and pensions stand out in this regard. Conversely, the shares of expenditures on alcohol and tobacco decline while reading and eating out absorb a constant share of the budget.

To keep things in perspective, the poorest households spend 38.4 per cent of their store expenditures on food, amounting to $2,193 per family; the highest income households spend only 28.5 per cent on food but this amounts to over $5,500 per family – two and a half times as much in dollars. For this reason, the nationwide pattern of preference for goods produced, advertised, and sold – the composite national taste or lifestyle (call it what you will) – is dominated by high-income households. Every dollar has a vote in determining what kinds of goods are designed and displayed in stores, or advertised in the media. The United States, as a result, appears to be more prosperous than it really is, as if everyone had $50,000 a year to spend, because many retailers target the few families which do.

Exhibit 2.2 illustrates the relevance of income level in another context; that of medical care.

**Table 2.3** Differential expenditures among income groups

| Income category | < $5,000 | $5,000–$10,000 | $10,000–$15,000 | $15,000–$20,000 | $20,000–$30,000 | $30,000–$40,000 | $40,000+ |
|---|---|---|---|---|---|---|---|
| Income ($) | 1,783 | 7,288 | 12,427 | 17,343 | 24,608 | 34,417 | 61,231 |
| Taxes ($) | −14 | 214 | 779 | 1,440 | 2,570 | 3,989 | 7,912 |
| Savings ($) | −9,927 | −4,542 | −3,054 | −1,787 | −426 | +2,654 | +11,095 |
| Expenditures ($) | 11,724 | 11,616 | 14,702 | 17,690 | 22,464 | 27,773 | 42,224 |
| Non-store (%) | 51.3 | 52.6 | 50.1 | 51.5 | 51.8 | 51.3 | 54.2 |
| Shelter (%) | 30.1 | 30.8 | 28.3 | 27.5 | 25.9 | 24.4 | 23.8 |
| Health (%) | 4.2 | 6.6 | 5.6 | 5.3 | 4.0 | 3.4 | 3.2 |
| Insurance and pensions (%) | 4.1 | 4.1 | 5.3 | 7.2 | 9.9 | 12.2 | 13.2 |
| Entertainment (%) | 1.6 | 1.1 | 1.3 | 1.3 | 1.4 | 1.5 | 2.0 |
| Personal care (%) | 1.0 | 1.1 | 1.0 | 1.0 | 0.9 | 0.9 | 0.9 |
| Miscellaneous (%) | 10.3 | 8.9 | 8.6 | 9.2 | 9.7 | 8.9 | 11.1 |
| Store (%) | 48.7 | 47.4 | 49.9 | 48.5 | 48.2 | 48.7 | 45.8 |
| Food – home (%) | 13.2 | 14.7 | 12.7 | 11.8 | 10.9 | 10.2 | 8.0 |
| – away (%) | 5.5 | 3.8 | 4.6 | 4.8 | 4.6 | 4.6 | 5.0 |
| Tobacco (%) | 2.9 | 2.8 | 3.2 | 2.7 | 2.6 | 2.3 | 1.9 |
| Apparel (%) | 5.7 | 3.7 | 4.8 | 5.4 | 4.9 | 5.2 | 6.2 |
| Transportation (%)[a] | 14.2 | 14.6 | 11.7 | 16.7 | 17.5 | 17.7 | 16.1 |
| Furniture (%)[b] | 6.6 | 6.1 | 6.1 | 6.4 | 7.0 | 8.0 | 7.9 |
| Reading (%) | 0.6 | 0.7 | 0.7 | 0.7 | 0.7 | 0.6 | 0.6 |

Source: Bureau of Labor Statistics (1986) 'Consumer expenditures: Interview survey, 1984–5', *Bulletin 2267*
Note: [a]Cars, gasoline and repairs. [b]Includes home entertainment.

## Exhibit 2.2
## RICH AND POOR IN CHICAGO

As the map below suggests, the importance of income level is not limited to retailing; access to medical care is directly related to household income. Even if you don't know Chicago, you can guess from the map where the rich and the poor live. Or are the people on the south side simply healthier?

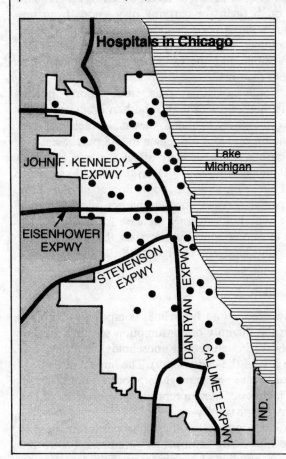

Hospitals in Chicago

JOHN F. KENNEDY EXPWY

EISENHOWER EXPWY

STEVENSON EXPWY

DAN RYAN EXPWY

CALUMET EXPWY

Lake Michigan

IND.

*Source:* Metropolitan Chicago Health Care Service

With household income such a predominant element in determining the level of consumption we can turn the idea around and view the absence of income as the most significant constraint on consumer choice. Because low-income families have so little money to spend on any kind of product, their choices are restricted to one or two of the cheapest brands, or in some cases to the grim choice of going without. Low income levels restrict shopping strategies as well. Without access to credit or savings there is no possibility of stocking up on bargains or carrying over goods from one season to the next. Without a car a poor or elderly household is at the mercy of the nearest retail outlets. The consumption choices available to a large part of the American public, like the variety of goods shown in the stores, may be more apparent than real.

Supermarkets in poor, inner-city areas may stock poorer quality produce and meat or charge higher prices than suburban branches of the same chain. Merchants are not entirely to blame; they make their profit on large orders and expensive items and lose money on the $3 purchases.

These differing expenditure profiles strongly affect the mix of stores found in different types of neighborhoods. Well-to-do areas have many financial institutions, travel agencies, and gift shops. Poorer districts have small food stores and personal services such as barber shops or shoe repairs. In the long run, as household incomes increase for everyone, the whole mix of stores and locations will shift towards the consumption pattern represented on the right-hand side of Figure 2.8.

### Age and household composition

The mixture of age and sex groups and household composition within a market area does not affect the quantity of consumption so much as alter the mix of products purchased (though retired households often have less disposable income than the rest of the community). The impact of demography on retailing is reduced because most neighborhoods do not differ all that much. Fundamental principles of human reproduction keep males and females, children and parents, in proximity.

Nonetheless, a growing tendency to tailor housing to particular types of household has led to some interesting intra-urban variations. Figure 2.9 plots the age-sex profiles of a number of census tracts within the Boston metropolitan area. Males are shown on the left side of the profile, females on the right; the youngest age groups are at the bottom and the oldest at the top. One extreme distribution occurs in the college-age population around Harvard Square which has an enormous concentration of people in the 15–19-year age-group. Suburban areas like Marshfield are weighted toward children and young parents aged 25–34 years.

Older suburbs, like Manchester, have disproportionate numbers of people aged 45–64 years. A black neighbourhood in Roxbury is dominated by young adult females. Some apartment districts in the inner city cater to young singles (Back Bay), others attract older people, especially women. The old working class community of South Boston is top-heavy with older people due to the continual out-migration of young people. Each of these communities requires a different mix of stores, products, and styles.

Relatively little demographic variation exists at the urban settlement scale because the neighborhood differences are aggregated together to produce the city total. None the less, the national demographic composition has changed over time, as Figure 2.10 records. The proportion of older people is increasing while the share (and cultural significance) of young people fluctuates. Community services, such as the education system and recreation activities are particularly sensitive to these ups and downs, but so are those retailers who specialize in serving particular age-groups. The dominant age-group in the population pyramid has shaped the national lifestyle. In the 1940s and 1950s the whole social system adopted the caution of suburban parents, but their children made the 1960s a period of rebellion and innovation. As that baby-boom generation grew into young adults in the 1970s it turned towards consumerism and a more serious consideration of the future. As the baby-boomers grow older in the 1980s, increasingly conservative and materialistic lifestyles are likely to follow.

Table 2.4 examines the variation in expenditure patterns for households in various age-groups. While in reality the age of a household is related to its income (incomes peak in the 40s and 50s), this table controls for income differences. Even so, there are notable differences in the level of store expenditures. Taxes are much lower for the elderly but health care costs are greater and there is a significant life-cycle pattern to the level of saving. The households that spend the most are middle-aged.

As a household ages the pattern of expenditure shifts from food, alcohol, and entertainment toward health care. Consider the implications for the fast-food industry of the preference for eating out by the most rapidly growing segment of the population.

Similar data for household size suggest that smaller families spend more on taxes and save more, so that store expenditures are reduced. Among the store expenditures, the most significant pattern is the increase with family size in purchases of food and clothes, balanced by reduced transportation, recreation, and tobacco/alcohol expenditures. The remarkable decline in household size since the 1960s, then, has reduced the importance of food stores and increased the sales of automobile dealerships and gas stations.

At this level of aggregation, though, the differences due to household composition are not large. It is at the next level of decision-making – choosing the form of recreation, the type of automobile, or the brand of clothing – that the impact of demographic change is felt most intensely.

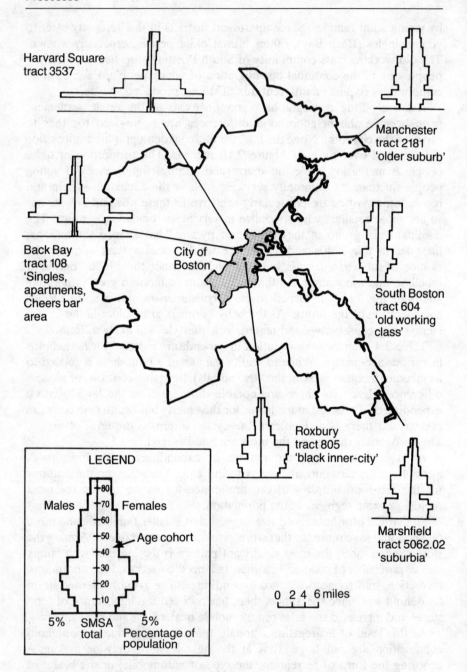

**Figure 2.9** Community demographics: Boston 1980

*Source:* Bureau of the Census (1980) *Census of Population*, Washington

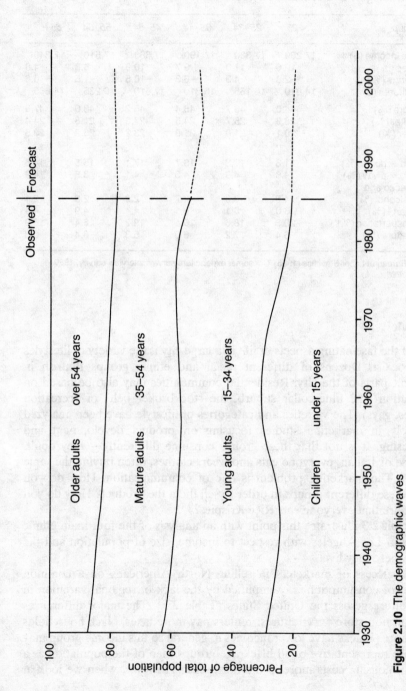

**Figure 2.10** The demographic waves

*Source*: Bureau of the Census (1976) *Historical Statistics of the United States: Colonial Times to 1970*, 2 vols, Washington; Bureau of the Census (annual) *Statistical Abstract of the United States*; 'Population estimates and projections', *Current Population Reports* (1967), Series P-25, no. 952

**Table 2.4** Expenditures by age of household head
(income category $15,000–20,000: 1980)

| Age group | <25 | 25–34 | 35–44 | 45–54 | 55–64 | 65+ |
|---|---|---|---|---|---|---|
| Average income ($) | 17,260 | 17,330 | 17,190 | 17,680 | 17,510 | 17,340 |
| Taxes (%) | 12.6 | 11.0 | 9.7 | 10.9 | 8.8 | 4.8 |
| Savings (%) | +2.8 | −4.3 | −6.3 | −10.5 | −1.5 | +10.6 |
| Expenditures ($) | 14,610 | 16,165 | 16,610 | 17,610 | 16,235 | 14,665 |
| Non-store (%) | 44.0 | 46.7 | 46.4 | 45.2 | 48.0 | 47.9 |
| Shelter (%) | 23.9 | 25.7 | 24.5 | 27.0 | 21.8 | 24.4 |
| Other (%) | 20.1 | 21.0 | 21.9 | 23.2 | 26.2 | 23.5 |
| Store | | | | | | |
| Food – home (%) | 11.3 | 13.3 | 16.7 | 17.1 | 15.5 | 14.6 |
| – away (%) | 4.8 | 4.9 | 4.3 | 4.1 | 3.8 | 4.9 |
| Tobacco and alcohol (%) | 4.0 | 3.3 | 2.7 | 2.9 | 2.6 | 2.1 |
| Apparel (%) | 6.0 | 5.1 | 6.1 | 4.4 | 4.9 | 4.4 |
| Transportation (%) | 20.3 | 18.6 | 16.4 | 19.2 | 16.4 | 16.9 |
| Furniture (%) | 8.4 | 7.2 | 6.0 | 5.3 | 6.4 | 6.8 |

*Source:* Bureau of Labor Statistics (1985) 'Consumer expenditure survey: interview survey, 1980–1',
*Bulletin 2228*

## Lifestyle

One of the fascinating aspects of life in a large city is the variety of lifestyles
that coexist. Dozens of different racial and ethnic groups flourish in
different parts of the city. Residential communities may also be based on
occupation (the blue-collar suburb, the stockbroker belt) or recreation
(singles, gays). The varieties and categories of lifestyle have been analyzed
endlessly in marketing studies focusing on product development and
advertising. It is not that these groups consume differently – they don't.
Chinese or Italian, everyone eats and wears clothes, often buying the same
brands. The marketing problem is one of communication. How do you
reach these different groups in order to sell them the product? How do you
make sure that everyone eats Rice Krispies?

Exhibit 2.3 illustrates this point with an analysis of the four main ethnic
groups in Los Angeles with respect to income, size of population and the
areas where they live.

The success of marketers in selling North Americans on a common
pattern of consumption is exemplified by the lack of regional variation in
expenditure across the United States (Table 2.5). The major differences
occur in non-store expenditures: renters pay more taxes, black households
save more (Blacks have lower incomes in general so this income group may
be more representative of all black age-groups than of the population as a
whole), housing costs more in the north-east. However, when we look at

## Exhibit 2.3
## MAJOR SEGMENTS IN THE LA MARKET

Los Angeles includes four large, culturally distinct markets. Each one displays a distinctive spatial pattern. Can a single retail chain serve them all?

| Segment | No. of households | Average income ($) | Total income ($ billion) |
|---------|-------------------|--------------------|--------------------------|
| White | 1,468,000 | 26,800 | 39.4 |
| Hispanic | 543,000 | 17,200 | 9.3 |
| Black | 335,000 | 16,000 | 5.4 |
| Asian | 143,000 | 24,000 | 3.4 |

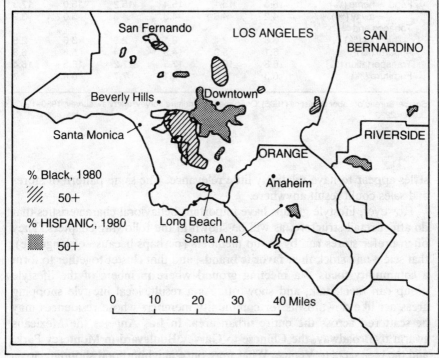

*Sources:* Bureau of the Census (1980) *Census of Population*; W.A.V. Clark (1987) 'Urban restructuring from a demographic perspective', *Economic Geography* 63, 2: 105–25

the expenditures that occur in the retail sector, most of the differences melt away. Blacks eat out less but spend more money on food in the home, westerners spend less on tobacco and alcohol but more on entertainment, the north-central states spend more on transportation. Still, overall, the differences are slight. At the spatial scales that interest marketers then, life-

**Table 2.5** Regional–cultural differences in consumer expenditures
(income category $10,000–15,000: 1980)

| Market segment | North-east | North-central | South | West | Renter | Black |
|---|---|---|---|---|---|---|
| Income ($) | 12,400 | 12,300 | 12,300 | 12,200 | 13,100 | 14,300 |
| Taxes (%) | 9.7 | 8.1 | 8.1 | 8.2 | 11.5 | 10.5 |
| Savings (%) | −14.1 | −9.9 | −15.4 | −20.6 | −5.6 | +2.6 |
| Expenditures ($) | 12,950 | 12,520 | 13,170 | 13,710 | 12,340 | 12,440 |
| Non-store (%) | 45.8 | 45.1 | 45.7 | 45.5 | 46.1 | 46.8 |
| Shelter (%) | 27.7 | 25.1 | 24.7 | 26.0 | 26.9 | 27.3 |
| Other (%) | 12.1 | 20.0 | 21.0 | 19.5 | 19.2 | 19.5 |
| Store | | | | | | |
| Food – home (%) | 16.3 | 15.1 | 16.4 | 15.2 | 15.0 | 17.3 |
| – away (%) | 4.2 | 4.6 | 4.3 | 4.8 | 5.0 | 3.2 |
| Tobacco and alcohol (%) | 3.6 | 3.4 | 3.1 | 2.9 | 3.6 | 2.8 |
| Apparel (%) | 5.1 | 5.0 | 4.9 | 5.4 | 5.8 | 6.3 |
| Transportation (%) | 16.8 | 19.0 | 17.5 | 17.2 | 16.5 | 16.4 |
| Furniture (%) | 6.3 | 6.2 | 6.1 | 7.7 | 6.6 | 5.7 |

*Source:* Bureau of Labor Statistics (1985) 'Consumer expenditure survey: interview survey, 1980–1',
*Bulletin 2228*

styles appear to have relatively little relevance. The same pattern of stores
and sales could result anywhere.

However, lifestyle groups have important behavioral characteristics that
do affect retail structure, as will be shown in the following chapters. They
often prefer stores run by group members (perhaps because of language),
that select and stock their favorite brands, and that cluster together to form
a community focus – a meeting ground where members of the lifestyle
group can meet, talk, and show off. As a result, local lifestyle shopping
areas act like downtowns for community members whose residences may
be scattered across the entire urban area. In Los Angeles the Mexicans
swarm to Broadway, the Chinese to Garvey Boulevard in Monterey Park,
and the teenagers to Venice. What were once neighborhood shopping areas
have become specialized to serve an aspatial market. Customers travel
many miles to visit distinctive food stores or restaurants. The neighborhood
store, offering only accessibility, gives way to a preference for special
goods, often symbolic of community participation and the amenity of
familiar faces and languages. Shopping as a social activity may be more
important than the acquisition of goods.

## Managing markets

We do not want to give the impression that markets are given, fixed, and independent phenomena, the ultimate determinant of a store's success or failure. If this were true the whole advertising industry would disappear, and with it all the communications media.

No. Retailers are able to modify markets in a variety of ways – to extend them spatially, or to modify the levels of penetration into various market segments. These options will be discussed more fully in the chapter on market strategies (Chapter twelve), but at this point let us remind ourselves of some of the ways in which the basic constraints of market size can be overcome.

A retailer faced with a market of given size has three fundamental kinds of adjustment (in addition to relocation): advertising, price changes, and product mix. The simplest of these is advertising. Most studies of consumer behavior (see Chapter four) find that as time and distance and intervening opportunities (competitors) increase, households are less and less aware of a store's existence, or of what it has to offer. In the case of shopping goods, in which a knowledge of the distinctive characteristics of the store is a prerequisite to attracting shoppers, the solution is to increase the 'awareness' range of the store. What does it sell? Where is it? Why is it worthwhile to go there?

For convenience goods the trade-off lies between price and access. Reducing the price at the store extends the spatial range of the good (see Figure 2.2). Is the price difference worthwhile? Does the increase in volume make up for the loss in margin? We will find out in the next chapter.

The third alternative, and one applied with surprising frequency, is an alteration to the mix of products sold in the store. After all, the size of the market depends on the proportion of household income that can be spent in the store. In an effort to increase this proportion food stores carry non-food items, drugstores stock stationery, gas stations sell barbecues and lawn furniture, and lottery tickets, cigarettes, and toothbrushes are almost universally available. Many of these changes, even for retail chains, are incremental and experimental. Success is determined by a match between customers and product mix.

Successful retailers continuously explore these options and adjust their own market as the market itself evolves. Unsuccessful retailers do not adjust, they quickly go out of business and are replaced by an even more radical experiment – a new store.

## Further reading

*American Demographics* (monthly) Ithaca, New York: American Demographics Inc.
Arnold, S.J., Oum, T.H., and Tigert, D.J. (1983) 'Determinant attributes in retail

patronage: seasonal, temporal, regional and international comparisons', *Journal of Research in Marketing* 20, 2: 149–66.

Bourne, L.S. (ed.) (1982) *The Internal Structure of the City*, 2nd edn, New York: Oxford University Press.

Bourne, L.S. and Simmons, J.W. (eds) (1978) *System of Cities: Readings on Structure, Growth, and Policy*, New York: Oxford University Press.

Hall, B.F. (1983) 'Neighborhood differences in retail food stores income versus race and age of population', *Economic Geography* 59, 3; 282–95.

Losch, A. (1939) *The Economics of Location* (Trans. W. Woglom). New Haven: Yale University Press.

United States Bureau of Labor Statistics (1986) 'Consumer expenditure survey: interview survey', *Bulletin 2267*. (See discussion in Appendix B.)

# Chapter three

# The major actors on the supply side

**The richest man in America, Sam M. Walton, runs a chain of discount department stores.**

**Some stores in New York's Trump Tower sell over $3,000 worth of merchandise per square foot per year.**

**Most of the United States retail sales take place in a small number of chains and franchise operations (less than 1,000), operating in a small number of locations (less than 5,000), that are designed and controlled by a small number of development firms (less than 1,000).**

**The most valuable retail sites may occur at the intersection of two expressways.**

Entrepreneurs, retail chains, development corporations, and planners all combine to construct the networks of stores and other distribution facilities that serve a market. An extraordinary diversity of retail systems is possible. Even within a single metropolitan area we observe a wide range of shopping environments, from the regional shopping plaza to the row of classy boutiques, the strident highway strip, or the narrow crowded stores of recent immigrants. Clearly, the economics of retailing do not restrict retail activity to a single optimum size, location, or mix of products. To understand this variation we must look at different participants in the retail system, their diverse goals, and the ways they specialize and compete against each other.

This chapter begins by identifying the major providers of distribution facilities. Both nationally and locally, markets for particular products are dominated by a limited number of retailers. Retail activity is concentrated in large stores, chains of stores, and major shopping plazas. Small, independent businesses are largely window-dressing; they handle only a small proportion of the total sales. The implications of this concentration will emerge throughout the rest of this book.

The sections that follow discuss the activities of each of these major participants and their effect on the retail system. At the level of the store we are concerned with the scale of operation and the degree of specialization. The spatial demand curve, discussed in Chapter two as it applies to the household, can be extended to the firm. Decreasing average cost curves have been demonstrated empirically. In combination, the spatial demand curve and the decreasing average cost curve permit a variety of store sizes and specialties.

The bulk of retail activity is carried out by outlets of large retail chains or franchises operating in multiple locations. The third section of this chapter documents the growth and importance of the retail chain and the megachain. It is followed by a section on franchising. The resulting concentration of control makes the structure of competition a major element in determining a retailer's success. The final section discusses the shopping center developer who now plays a major role in identifying retail locations. The major development firms control many of the key locations in American retailing.

## Who does what in the distribution system?

All of us have some experience as consumers: we can readily identify with the choices that face a household and understand the decisions that result. Few of us, however, have actually been involved in marketing decisions on the supply side: this chapter outlines the issues that confront the independent retailers, retail chains, franchises, and shopping center developers.

The first part of Table 3.1 indicates the overall magnitude of distribution activity. Retail, wholesale and private-sector service activities generate 3.6 million outlets, trillions of dollars in sales, and over 30 million jobs. Financial services, which also deal directly with consumers, account for thousands more outlets and another 1.5 million jobs. Most of the discussion that follows is restricted to retail activity simply because the data are so much better for that sector, i.e. more precisely defined and consistent and available for a longer period of time. Nevertheless, the principles of retail location are equally applicable to banks, dry cleaners, hotels, and medical services.

The second part of the table underlines a central theme of the text. American retailing is dominated by a small number of large enterprises. Over one half of all retail sales are handled by 65,000 retail chains (chains operate two or more fully owned and controlled outlets in the same line of business). Almost half of the sales by retail chains take place in the largest fifty firms. Another third of retail sales takes place within franchise businesses in which a parent company (the franchisor) grants the franchisee the right to do business in a prescribed manner at a specified place for a specified period of time. Service stations and fast-food outlets are typical franchise operations. Unfortunately, the data on franchises come from a different source from the data on retail chains so that we cannot readily distinguish between the two. Some franchisees are also defined as retail chains because they operate more than one outlet.

Chains and franchises are comparative newcomers to the retail sector, both of them emerging in the last hundred years. Our myths, our literature, and most of our theory about retailing still perceive the industry in terms of the independent 'mom and pop' store. Economic theory treats the latter as the archetypal decision makers, as they choose a site, select a product mix and scale of operation, and respond to the market. While there are still over a million stores of this type, they have become increasingly irrelevant to consumers and the distribution system. We estimate that they account for less than 20 per cent of all retail sales.

The most recent innovation in the retail industry is the planned shopping

**Table 3.1** Size and concentration on the supply side

(a) The distribution system: 1982

| | No. of firms | No. of outlets | Sales ($ billions) | Employment |
|---|---|---|---|---|
| Retail | 1,573,000 | 1,923,000 | 1,066 | 15,656,000 |
| Wholesale | 321,000 | 416,000 | 1,988 | 5,401,000 |
| Private Service[a] | 1,154,000 | 1,262,000 | 427 | 12,217,000 |
| Total | 3,048,000 | 3,601,000 | 3,481 | 33,274,000 |
| Banks | 18,000 | 60,000 | — | 1,655,000 |

(b) Retail chains and franchises: 1982

| | No. of firms | No. of outlets | Sales ($ billions) | Percentage of sales |
|---|---|---|---|---|
| Chains[b] | 65,000 | 415,000 | 567 | 53.2 |
| Franchises[c] | 20,000 (est.) | 345,000 | 370 | 34.7 |
| Independents | 1,163,000 | 1,163,000 | 200 (est.) | 20.0 (est.) |

(c) Planned shopping centers: 1987

| Size (sq. ft) | No. of centers | No. of stores | Sales ($ billions)[d] | Percentage of all retail sales |
|---|---|---|---|---|
| <100,000 | 19,700 | 250,000 (est.) | 147 | 12.5 |
| 100,000–200,000 | 7,200 | 130,000 | 129 | 11.0 |
| 200,000–400,000 | 2,200 | 85,000 | 78 | 6.6 |
| 400,000–800,000 | 950 | 75,000 | 66 | 5.6 |
| >800,000 | 580 | 110,000 | 88 | 7.4 |
| Total | 30,630 | 650,000 | 508 | 43.1 |

*Sources:* Bureau of the Census (annual) *Statistical Abstract of the United States,* Washington; *Shopping Center World* (1988) Communication Channels, Atlanta GA; International Trade Administration (annual) *Franchising in the Economy*
*Notes:* [a]Service activities subject to federal income tax. [b]With two or more outlets. [c]Franchises identified by the International Trade Administration. Some overlap exists between chains and franchises. [d]In 1982 dollars.

center, just over 30 years old in most cities. The malls, especially the large regional centers, are now the key locations for many kinds of retail activity. Together they generate over 40 per cent of retail sales and the two largest categories, including only 1,500 centers, control 14 per cent of all retail sales and almost all of the shopping goods activity. Again, these key locations are designed, constructed, and controlled by a much smaller number of development corporations.

The largest consumer market in the world is dominated by a small number of significant retail and development firms. They are the ones that interpret our requirements, stock and price the products, and locate new retail space.

The most familiar way to segment this enormous retail market of over $1 trillion is shown in Table 3.2: the disaggregation by product or kind of business (the retail sector). Note first the variation in size of these different retail sectors, ranging over two orders of magnitude from the largest (groceries, $230 billion; car dealerships, $155 billion) to the smallest (cigar stores or leather goods, $500 million). These numbers impose a limit on the size and growth strategies of retail chains in these sectors: we will observe that America's largest retail chains are department stores and supermarkets, not newsstands.

Average store size also varies widely among sectors, from the department store (almost $10 million per store) to the newsdealer ($60,000). These differences reflect consumer buying habits on the one hand – What kinds of products do they buy, and how much, and how often? – and the production function of the store on the other – economies of scale and service requirements – as we will see later in this chapter.

The role of retail chains and franchises varies considerably from one sector to another; almost 100 per cent for department stores, less than 10 per cent for bars. Once again, the structure of the retail sector limits the marketing strategy of the retailer. Is the competitor an independent store or another retail chain? In some sectors, such as flower shops, the share of the market available for chains is much smaller than the sector as a whole.

In Chapters nine to twelve, we will discuss how retail chains expand using complex clusters of decisions called marketing strategies. A chain may choose to close one site, to develop another, or to carry an outlet at a loss in order to maintain market share. The essential point is that actions taken at each site are interdependent. Closing one site may generate profits elsewhere: closing another might weaken a market strategy that emphasizes dealer networks and service. In the long term as well as the short term, the chain looks to system-wide profit and loss rather than to the profitability of any one outlet.

The importance of the developers in the retail system results from the dominant role of shopping centers in the provision of new retail space for shopping goods, and from their close links with major retail chains. The developer evaluates the retail market, chooses the site, assembles the land, negotiates with the planners and financial agencies, and selects the tenants. Almost overnight, it seems, a city may receive a major increase in retail floor area, a new set of national retailers covering most types of business, and a significant employment- and traffic-generating activity. A neighborhood is suddenly presented with all the retail facilities it will require for a generation. Needless to say, not all the other merchants in town applaud

**Table 3.2** The structure of retail trade: 1982

| SIC No. | Retail sector | Sales ($ billions) | No. of stores | Sales/store ($ thousands) | Threshold[a] ($) | % chain | % franchise[b] |
|---|---|---|---|---|---|---|---|
| 521 | Lumber | 35,144 | 40,100 | 876 | 50,000 | 51.8 | n.a. |
| 525 | Hardware | 8,727 | 25,400 | 344 | 50,000 | 27.3 | n.a. |
| 526 | Garden supplies | 3,120 | 16,500 | 189 | 50,000 | 27.1 | n.a. |
| 527 | Mobile Homes sales | 4,003 | 6,500 | 616 | 50,000 | 34.6 | n.a. |
| 531 | Department stores | 99,170 | 10,000 | 9,917 | 3,500,000 | 99.1 | n.a. |
| 533 | Variety stores | 8,211 | 13,500 | 608 | 100,000 | 86.9 | n.a. |
| 539 | Miscellaneous general | 13,033 | 21,300 | 612 | 50,000 | 75.1 | n.a. |
| 541 | Grocery stores | 230,696 | 168,000 | 1,373 | 100,000 | 74.6 | 4.5 |
| 542 | Meat and fish | 5,652 | 15,500 | 365 | 50,000 | 14.3 | |
| 543 | Bakeries | 3,752 | 22,200 | 592 | 50,000 | 28.9 | |
| 544 | Fruit and vegetables | 1,552 | 6,500 | 239 | 50,000 | 15.1 | 52.1 |
| 545 | Candy and confectionery | 972 | 8,900 | 109 | 50,000 | 47.1 | |
| 546 | Dairy products | 1,531 | 7,100 | 216 | 50,000 | 51.7 | |
| 549 | Miscellaneous food | 1,966 | 13,500 | 146 | 50,000 | 36.8 | |
| 551 | Automobile dealers | 154,726 | 27,200 | 569 | 1,000,000 | 12.9 | 100.0 |
| 552 | Used cars | 8,207 | 34,600 | 237 | 50,000 | 5.7 | 0.0 |
| 553 | Automotive supplies | 21,156 | 48,800 | 434 | 50,000 | 48.2 | 19.0 |
| 554 | Gas stations | 97,440 | 135,500 | 719 | 50,000 | 47.7 | 100.0 |
| 555 | Boats | 2,936 | 5,500 | 534 | 50,000 | 15.5 | n.a. |
| 556 | Recreational vehicles | 2,831 | 3,500 | 809 | 250,000 | 20.5 | n.a. |
| 557 | Motorcycles | 2,930 | 5,600 | 523 | 50,000 | 9.2 | n.a. |
| 559 | Miscellaneous auto | 729 | 4,100 | 178 | 50,000 | 14.7 | n.a. |
| 561 | Men's and boy's clothes | 7,803 | 18,600 | 420 | 75,000 | 55.5 | n.a. |
| 562 | Women's clothes | 20,413 | 47,900 | 426 | 75,000 | 73.8 | n.a. |
| 563 | Women's accessories | 1,851 | 10,900 | 170 | 50,000 | 43.0 | n.a. |
| 565 | Family clothing | 13,360 | 23,700 | 564 | 50,000 | 77.2 | n.a. |

| SIC | Category | | | | | |
|---|---|---|---|---|---|---|
| 566 | Shoe stores | 11,419 | 39,400 | 290 | 100,000 | 74.8 | n.a. |
| 564,9 | Miscellaneous apparel | 8,749 | 18,500 | 473 | 50,000 | 10.2 | n.a. |
| 5712 | Furniture | 17,658 | 38,300 | 461 | 50,000 | 43.5 | n.a. |
| 5713,4,9 | Furnishings | 9,435 | 44,300 | 213 | 50,000 | 33.8 | n.a. |
| 572 | Appliances | 5,855 | 13,900 | 421 | 50,000 | 37.2 | n.a. |
| 573 | Home entertainment | 13,813 | 35,200 | 392 | 50,000 | 56.1 | n.a. |
| 5812 | Restaurants | 95,091 | 301,700 | 315 | 50,000 | 45.6 | 37.4 |
| 5813 | Bars | 9,501 | 80,000 | 119 | 50,000 | 5.3 | n.a. |
| 591 | Drug stores | 36,440 | 52,000 | 701 | 100,000 | 63.3 | n.a. |
| 592 | Liquor stores | 18,146 | 41,500 | 438 | 50,000 | 33.8 | n.a. |
| 593 | Second-hand goods | 4,665 | 59,000 | 791 | 50,000 | 21.4 | n.a. |
| 5941 | Sporting goods | 8,012 | 34,700 | 231 | 50,000 | 43.8 | n.a. |
| 5942 | Books | 3,269 | 14,900 | 219 | 50,000 | 57.7 | n.a. |
| 5943 | Stationery | 1,561 | 6,600 | 237 | 50,000 | 25.8 | n.a. |
| 5944 | Jewelry | 8,829 | 38,700 | 228 | 50,000 | 49.7 | n.a. |
| 5945 | Hobbies, toys | 3,464 | 22,000 | 157 | 50,000 | 68.1 | n.a. |
| 5946 | Cameras | 1,948 | 6,700 | 291 | 50,000 | 43.8 | n.a. |
| 5947 | Gifts | 5,037 | 41,400 | 122 | 50,000 | 38.4 | n.a. |
| 5948 | Luggage | 620 | 3,200 | 194 | 50,000 | 57.6 | n.a. |
| 5949 | Sewing | 2,688 | 21,900 | 123 | 50,000 | 59.3 | n.a. |
| 5961 | Mail order | 11,362 | 12,200 | 931 | 50,000 | 62.8 | n.a. |
| 5962 | Vending machines | 4,924 | 11,800 | 417 | 50,000 | 50.8 | n.a. |
| 5963 | Direct sales | 4,175 | 8,700 | 480 | 75,000 | 42.4 | n.a. |
| 5991 | Fuel and ice dealers | 17,059 | 15,700 | 1,087 | 50,000 | 23.0 | n.a. |
| 5992 | Florists | 3,734 | 34,700 | 108 | 50,000 | 14.9 | n.a. |
| 5993 | Cigar stores | 624 | 3,500 | 178 | 50,000 | 33.2 | n.a. |
| 5994 | Newsdealers | 790 | 13,100 | 60 | 50,000 | 21.6 | n.a. |
| 5999 | Miscellaneous retail | 10,917 | 168,900 | 65 | 50,000 | 19.2 | n.a. |

Sources: Bureau of the Census (1982) Census of Retail Trade; International Trade Administration (1984) Franchising in the Economy 1982–84

Notes: [a] Threshold size is defined here as the estimated sales of the 20th percentile of establishments, ranked by size. Since size data are available only for establishments with payrolls, the other (non-payroll) stores have been allocated to the lowest size group. So many stores are so small that many retail sectors fall below the arbitrary minimum value of $50,000. [b] Sales by franchise are available only for selected retail sectors. For the remainder there is a global estimate of 3.1 per cent. Note that in the case of automotive franchises, chain outlets and franchises can overlap. n.a., not available; SIC, Standard Industrial Classification.

these decisions, and planners and nearby residents may also have reservations.

The developer's tasks include both location analysis – the evaluation of spatial markets and the projection of future growth – and complex financial decisions relating to capital and property costs and to leasing conditions. Unlike the other participants developers move quickly from one market to the next, leaving a trail of retail facilities – good or bad – in their wake.

## The store

Economic theory usually begins with the small, independent producer operating within a competitive market. In effect all stores are assumed to be the same and to operate within identical economic environments. The reality of the distribution system is rather different, however. Retailing is marked by the enormous concentration of activity within a limited number of stores, retail chains and plazas, so that the perceptions and decisions of a small number of people play a disproportionate role in determining the retail structure. There may be thousands of small businesses in the retail sector, but the businesses that count are giants like K mart and Sears; the megachains like Melville Corporation or Campeau, franchisors like Exxon, and developers like Melvin Simon.

We should begin by recognizing that this concentration of retail activity reflects the organization of the American settlement system (shown in Table 2.1). The concentration of buying power in the largest metropolitan markets permits parallel concentrations of retail activity. The largest stores, the largest retail chains, and the largest shopping centers are found in New York, Chicago, and Los Angeles (see Exhibit 3.1), since the size of the market is a major constraint on the growth of any retail activity. These cities could support ten times as much retail activity as Dayton or Hartford.

The initial form of retail concentration is an increase in size of store. As Figure 3.1a suggests, stores vary greatly in size; in 1982 the largest 10 per cent of the stores sold two-thirds of the goods. The smallest 10 per cent sold less than 1 per cent! Since the size of store depends on the size of the trade area, the large department store did not emerge until around the turn of the century when increased consumer income and an efficient transit system led to the mass urban market. The block-size Marshall Field department store, built around the turn of the century to service Chicago's million residents (with an average income in 1982 dollars of $1,000) represented the epitome of market concentration.

Store size is partially determined by the kinds of product sold, as shown in Figure 3.1b. Department stores carry an enormous range of products and are inevitably larger than stores carrying fewer lines, such as pets or bicycles. How big should a store be? The argument below is couched in terms of economic theory and depends on both the shape of the retailer's

Exhibit 3.1
THE GREAT SHOPPING AREAS OF AMERICA

| Rank (sales) | Name of cluster | Metropolitan area | No. of stores | Sales ($m 1982) | Type |
|---|---|---|---|---|---|
| 1 | Midtown Manhattan | New York | 4718 | 4598 | Unplanned (CBD) |
| 2 | The Loop | Chicago | 1112 | 1117 | Unplanned (CBD) |
| 3 | Downtown | Philadelphia | 1705 | 1029 | Unplanned (CBD) |
| 4 | Downtown | San Francisco | 1768 | 1028 | Unplanned (CBD) |
| 5 | Metairie | New Orleans | 664 | 788 | Both |
| 6 | Downtown | Los Angeles | 1711 | 657 | Unplanned (CBD) |
| 7 | Downtown | Boston | 843 | 630 | Unplanned (CBD) |
| 8 | Waikiki Beach | Honolulu | 1082 | 601 | Unplanned |
| 9 | Downtown | Washington | 804 | 556 | Unplanned (CBD) |
| 10 | Cumberland Mall | Atlanta | 275 | 547 | Planned |
| 11 | Oxford Valley Mall | Philadelphia | 235 | 494 | Planned |
| 12 | Downtown | New Orleans | 713 | 494 | Unplanned (CBD) |
| 13 | Beverly Hills (Rodeo Drive) | Los Angeles | 537 | 475 | Unplanned |
| 14 | Downtown | Pittsburgh | 502 | 466 | Unplanned (CBD) |
| 15 | Sharpstown | Houston | 267 | 436 | Planned |
| 16 | South Coast Plaza | Los Angeles | 314 | 430 | Planned |
| 17 | Downtown | Cleveland | 532 | 417 | Unplanned (CBD) |
| 18 | Stephens Creek Blvd | San Jose | 147 | 402 | Planned |
| 19 | Michigan Ave | Chicago | 308 | 395 | Unplanned (fashion) |
| 20 | Downtown | Minneapolis | 524 | 390 | Unplanned (CBD) |
| 21 | Woodfield Mall | Chicago | 228 | 383 | Planned |
| 22 | Glendale | Los Angeles | 485 | 380 | Unplanned |
| 23 | Galleria/Postoaks | Houston | 265 | 377 | Planned |
| 24 | Mountain View | San Jose | 400 | 373 | Both |
| 25 | Walnut Creek | San Francisco | 325 | 372 | Unplanned |
| 26 | Downtown Brooklyn | New York | 477 | 368 | Unplanned |
| 27 | Downtown | Seattle | 492 | 367 | Unplanned |
| 28 | Southdale | Minneapolis | 214 | 350 | Planned |

Source: Bureau of the Census (1982) 'Major retail centers', Census of Retail Trade, Washington
Note: CBD, central business district

cost curves and on the shape of the spatial demand curve (discussed in the previous chapter).

The average cost curve (Figure 3.2a) describes how the cost per unit (box of corn flakes, sweater, or automobile) varies with the number of units sold. If economies of scale are present the average cost curve declines as the number of units sold increases. The logic is simple: the total cost per unit is the sum of the fixed costs and the variable costs. The former are

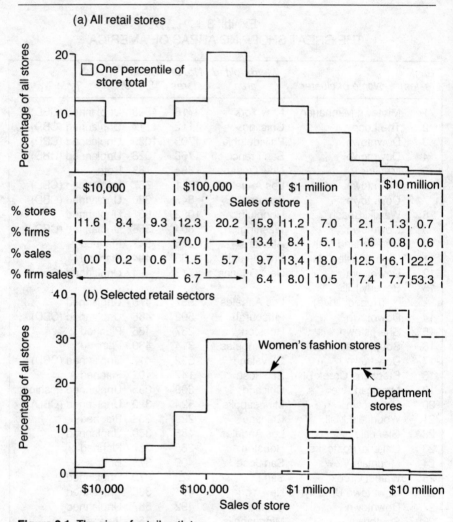

**Figure 3.1** The size of retail outlets

*Source:* The authors

independent of the quantity of goods sold and include such things as rent, wages, and electricity; the latter are calculated on a per item basis and include the wholesale cost of the good plus packaging (see Exhibit 3.2).

A number of studies examining retail costs (e.g. Tucker, 1975; Bucklin, 1978) have shown that retailing is a decreasing cost industry, with an average cost curve shaped as shown in Figure 3.2a. Average cost declines rapidly at first and then flattens out, continuing to slope gently downward indefinitely. Hence the argument that the only limitation to the size of a

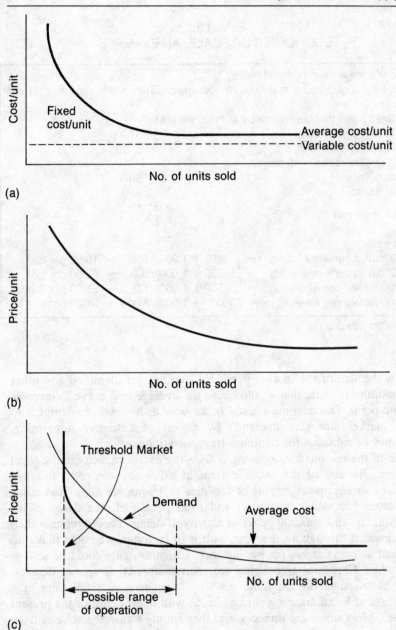

**Figure 3.2** Determining the scale of operation
(a) The declining average cost curve
(b) The sloping demand curve
(c) The range of operation

*Source:* The authors

Exhibit 3.2
## ECONOMIES OF SCALE: AN EXAMPLE

Consider a small neighborhood bakery.
It sells loaves of bread that it buys at 50c apiece. This is the variable cost per unit sold.
It has fixed costs that are shared by all the units sold:

| | |
|---|---|
| Rent ($400 per week) | $400 |
| Equipment/telephone, etc. | $ 80 |
| Wages (2 persons × 40 hours) | |
|    at $8/hour | $320 |
|    at $5/hour | $200 |
| Total overhead | $1,000 |

So if it sells:

| | | | | |
|---|---|---|---|---|
| 100 loaves per week, costs | = | $(50 + 1,000)/100 | = | $10.50 per loaf |
| 500 loaves per week, costs | = | $(250 + 1,000)/500 | = | $2.50 per loaf |
| 1,000 loaves per week, costs | = | $(500 + 1,000)/1,000 | = | $1.50 per loaf |
| 2,000 loaves per week, costs | = | $(1,000 + 1,000)/2,000 | = | $1.00 per loaf |

*Source:* The authors

store is the size of the market itself. No one has yet identified any other diseconomies of scale that would cause the average cost curve to increase at some point. Diseconomies could occur only if the retailer attempted to affect market size (i.e. demand) by means of extensive advertising, discounts, or subsidies for customer transportation costs.

One of the reasons for declining costs is the excess capacity in the retail structure. By any of the usual criteria of efficiency the retail industry possesses an enormous surplus of facilities that generate high fixed costs. Each store's capacity, inventory, and even personnel, are designed for daily, weekly, and seasonal peaks of activity. If demand could be smoothed and regulated throughout the year, as it is in factories, we could make do with half as many stores (if, for instance, Christmas gifts could be sold in July, when Christmas tree lights are manufactured). If spatial demand could be managed in the same way, by concentrating retail sales at a limited set of locations, we would make do with one-quarter of the present facilities. Most stores are unnecessary; they simply transfer purchases from one location to another, saving the consumer a few steps at the expense of the retailer's profit and the overall efficiency of the distribution system.

The overexpanded retail system results from the ease of entry into retailing and its attractiveness as a way of life ('Own your own business; be your own boss' say the advertisements for franchises). Compare the costs of starting up a steel plant to opening a milk store. However, excess retail capacity is also supported by the consumer's interest in variety, innovation, and competition; the desire to 'shop around' rather than to deal with the same store. Also, the strategy of increased 'market share' has pressured the major retail chains into competing in markets that are obviously too small for more than one outlet.

Some indication of how the average cost curve can vary is provided by Table 3.3, which shows the average margin for various store types. The margin is defined as the percentage of the selling price that goes toward the store's overheads, as opposed to the wholesale cost of the goods themselves. Note first that most margins are relatively high – one-third to one-half of the selling price of a good is added by the retailer. Although there is considerable scope for efficiency here – look at the low overheads of supermarkets for instance – the customer is often less concerned with price than with service and the retailing environment. Only farmers buy blue jeans because they need a pair of pants; everyone else is out to make a personal statement.

Stores with high margins typically have high fixed costs, often because they offer accessibility and service. For example, every sale by a florist, garage, or jeweller requires personal attention. Low margins are found in the self-service stores: supermarkets, service stations, and variety stores.

Over time the average cost curve for a business type could change as the relative share of fixed and variable costs change. If the variable cost per unit increases the curve moves upward, if the fixed costs increase the curve becomes steeper and shifts to the right. Over the years, fixed costs have increased because of higher real wages for retailers and because of the more sophisticated fixtures used in stores. Recently, there has been a trend to transfer costs from the fixed side to the variable side by replacing full-time workers with part-time help.

In planning a store it is useful to know the size of the margin because it can be used to estimate the size of market required. If the overheads – rent, wages, interest, etc. – for a drugstore equal $5,000 per month, what level of monthly sales is required? The answer is $5,000/0.30 = $16,700.

Given the average cost curve, what is the appropriate scale of operation of the store? To answer this question we must introduce the spatial demand curve. It was shown in Chapter two that the size of a store's market is restricted by the effect of distance on its customers. Households that live further away are less inclined to shop at the store and the spatial demand curve slopes down to the right. The demand for a good across the entire market area can be calculated for various price levels. The retailer faces a demand curve (Figure 3.2b) in which demand for a good is inversely related to the price charged. This is exactly the same curve with which we began in Figure 2.3, but we now know that the level and shape of this curve is affected by the size and spatial structure of the market. If the size of the local market increases the demand curve shifts to the right (more purchases at

**Table 3.3** Components of the retailer's margin (as a percentage of sales)[a]

| Retail Sector | Gross margin (%) | Wages and benefits (%) | Rent and depreciation (%) | Advertising (%) | Other Operating expenditures (%) | Interest (%) | Sales/sq. ft ($)[b] | Turnover, 1984 |
|---|---|---|---|---|---|---|---|---|
| Building materials | 31.2 | 15.9 | 1.7 | 1.7 | 9.0 | 2.9 | — | 5.6 |
| General merchandise | 33.9 | 19.0 | 2.3 | 3.0 | 7.9 | 1.7 | — | 5.4 |
| Food | 24.1 | 13.5 | 1.4 | 1.0 | 6.5 | 1.7 | 240 | 17.5 |
| Automotive | 20.0 | 10.0 | 0.9 | 1.0 | 4.2 | 3.9 | — | 7.4 |
| Gasoline | 15.8 | 5.9 | 1.1 | 0.2 | 4.4 | 4.2 | — | 39.9 |
| Apparel | 39.9 | 18.3 | 5.7 | 2.4 | 10.3 | 3.2 | 140 | 4.8 |
| Furniture | 37.3 | 16.9 | 3.4 | 3.8 | 10.4 | 2.8 | — | 5.2 |
| Eating and drinking | 59.5 | 29.3 | 4.8 | 2.1 | 19.9 | 3.4 | 150 | 51.2 |
| Drug stores | 30.9 | 16.0 | 2.4 | 1.4 | 7.2 | 3.9 | 155 | 6.1 |
| Liquor stores | 23.1 | 8.9 | 1.8 | 0.5 | 5.6 | 6.3 | 140 | 9.6 |
| All retail sectors | 30.7 | 13.3 | 2.2 | 1.6 | 10.3 | 3.3 | — | 8.4 |

*Sources:* Bureau of the Census (1982) *Census of Retail Trade*; Bureau of the Census (1984) *Current Business Reports*; Urban Land Institute (1987) *Dollars and Sense of Shopping Centers*; Bureau of the Census (1985) *Current Business Reports: Retail Trade*
*Notes:* [a]Only those establishments with payrolls (includes 69 per cent of outlets, 97 per cent of sales). [b]Median sales per square foot ($1982), super-regional centers.

each price), if the market becomes more dispersed in space the demand curve will slope down more steeply.

The retailer can control the scale of operation by changing the price of the good, but the possible range of operation is restricted by the shape of the two curves in Figures 3.2a and 3.2b, as combined in Figure 3.2c. The demand curve, which indicates the number of customers willing to pay a given price, must be at least as high as the average cost curve if the store is to make money and stay in business. If the market is so small that the demand curve is always below the average cost curve there will be no store at all (as is the case for almost any location chosen at random – most city lots do not have a store).

Where the demand curve is higher than the average cost curve, the retailer can stay in business. The next decision is the selection of the most profitable scale of operation. Since the average cost per unit sold rises sharply for small volumes of sales, a threshold store size is defined as the point at which the two curves intersect. The threshold is the minimum size of market in which the store can survive, and thus identifies the subset of locations (markets) that can support the business.

Empirically, threshold markets can be observed at the lower end of the distribution of store sizes. The threshold sizes for a number of business types have been included in Table 3.2, based on the arbitrary cutoff of the twentieth percentile of store size. In other words, 80 per cent of stores are larger than the threshold value given; only 20 per cent are smaller – most of them part-time or otherwise irregular operations. Note first the wide range of operating sizes possible within the retail system. Even when stores of the same type are compared, the threshold is only 10–15 per cent of the average size. In many types of business – antiques, florists, second-hand shops, gift shops – it would be impossible to make a living at the threshold scale, given average mark-up values. Many retail outlets of this type are operated only part-time or as a hobby.

The threshold value varies widely by type of business, from well below $50,000 ($1982) for antiques to over $3,500,000 for department stores. These supply-side thresholds combine with household expenditure patterns (sales per household) to define the population thresholds for each business type. Take shoe stores, for instance. If each household spends $300 per year ($1982) on shoes, the sales threshold of $100,000 requires 333 households to support a store. If there are 2.5 people per household, these requirements suggest a minimum population of 850 people. Alternatively, the average shoe store requires $290,000, or 970 households, or 2,400 people. Perhaps the key question for the retailer is whether he or she wants to live at the threshold wage level (perhaps $15,000 in 1982) or to aim higher.

In this way we can work out whether a small town or a neighborhood plaza can support a hardware store. The type of retail activity in a small

75

town may change over time, depending on whether the local market is able to grow more rapidly than the increase in the threshold size of various kinds of stores. If the town grows quickly, it will attract many new activities; if it grows only slowly some of the stores will be forced out of business or will relocate.

The retailer who operates in a larger market, such as a metropolitan area, may have a much wider range of potential operation, extending from the threshold size to 10 or 100 times larger. How does the retailer decide how large the store should be?

Those of you who have studied economics will recall that a store's profit (the difference between selling price and cost multiplied by the number of units sold) is at a maximum when the marginal cost equals the marginal revenue. The result is a price level and a scale of operation that reflect the characteristics of the market. For the individual retailer, however, the problem may be rather more complex. On the supply side limits may be set by the size of store or site, or personnel or capital needs. What are the costs and benefits of keeping the business within the family? On the demand side, the possibility of competition will cause problems. High prices and low volume leave the market open to competition from new stores that may not play by the same rules. The last thing that the owner of the only grocery store in a small town wants to see is another grocery store.

Within a large city, the configuration of costs and demand permits the retailer to operate over a wide range of sizes. Certainly we observe great differences within every business type. Each retailer attempts to find a niche, a combination of size (hence variety) and specialization that attracts sufficient clientele. In New York Barnes and Noble runs a library-scale operation within a few blocks of small book stores specializing in cooking, French language, travel, law, children's literature, or erotica. Because of the gentle slope of the decreasing cost curve, a large market can be served by a single large enterprise, a number of small, specialized (hence spatially centralized) outlets, or by small spatially dispersed outlets, or a combination of all three. Consumer behavior, not economics, is the final determinant.

## The retail chain

The most important form of concentration in the retail market is the retail chain. In 1982 over 400,000 stores (about 20 per cent of all stores) were controlled by 65,000 chains; they accounted for over 50 per cent of all retail sales. Some chains are larger than others, for example, the 376 chains that each included more than 100 stores collectively accounted for 45 per cent of the chain store outlets and more than half of all chain store sales (Table 3.4). About 350 chain headquarters together control one-quarter of America's retail trade.

**Table 3.4** The importance of large retail chains

| Stores/chain | No. of chains | (%) | Stores | (%) | Sales ($ billion) | (%) |
|---|---|---|---|---|---|---|
| Less than 10 | 60,804 | 94.1 | 148,800 | 35.8 | 141.7 | 25.0 |
| 10–24 | 2,422 | 3.7 | 35,100 | 8.5 | 41.6 | 7.3 |
| 25–99 | 1,031 | 1.6 | 48,400 | 11.7 | 74.5 | 13.2 |
| 100 or more | 376 | 0.6 | 182,800 | 44.9 | 309.0 | 54.5 |
| Total | 64,633 | 100.0 | 415,100 | 100.0 | 566.8 | 100.0 |

*Source:* Bureau of the Census (1982) *Census of Retail Trade*, Washington

The very largest chains are concentrated in the largest retail sectors, department stores (5311) and supermarkets (5411); see Table 3.5. Only the Melville Corporation (shoes, apparel, and drugs) is a truly diversified retailer. Despite the size and the geographical extent of the US market these firms are really big players. Sears Roebuck generates 3 per cent of all retail sales. Even within the economy as a whole they are significant: Sears is the second largest private employer in the country and the ninth largest corporation in terms of sales. Yet, despite their size, many of them are still predominantly regionally based, as indicated by the dispersion of the locations of their headquarters.

The success of the retail chains is not accidental. Compared to independent stores they have many advantages. The chain provides a way of introducing scale economies while avoiding the restrictions of market size. The costs of administration, location analysis, or advertising can be spread over a number of facilities. Market power in purchasing has become particularly important. For example, the major supermarket chains have enormous leverage in negotiating prices with manufacturers who need shelf space to sell their goods. Since chains collectively serve larger markets – a metropolitan area, a region, or even the national market – they are able to use different kinds of media from an independent store. Each communications medium operates on a different spatial scale: you can't advertise a local pet store across a nationwide TV network, but Sears can. Also, because of their greater financial resources, chains are able to carry an unproductive store until the market grows, or to allow the completion of a network of facilities.

Their disadvantage is their inflexibility. They may not be able to respond to specialized local markets such as racial or language groups. Chains have trouble changing image or product mix rapidly because of the enormous investment in existing locations, images, and facilities. The sameness or predictability that attracts some people to eat at McDonald's or Howard Johnson will discourage other customers who are more adventurous, or who want to identify with a distinctive product.

**Table 3.5** America's largest retailers

| Rank in sales | Name | Sales ($ millions) | No. of stores | No. of employees (thousands) | SIC | HQ city | Subsidiaries |
|---|---|---|---|---|---|---|---|
| 1 | Sears Roebuck & Co. | 28,100[b] | 3,457 | 312 | 5311 | Chicago, IL | Sears, McKids, Western Auto Supply |
| 2 | K mart Corporation | 25,600 | 3,934 | 330 | 5311 | Troy, MI | K mart, Waldenbooks, Payless Drug, Bargain Harold |
| 3 | Safeway Stores[a] | 20,312 | 1,681 | 172 | 5411 | Oakland, CA | Safeway |
| 4 | Kroger Co. | 17,700 | 2,206 | 170 | 5411 | Cincinnati, OH | Kroger, King Soopers, Mini-mart |
| 5 | Wal-Mart Stores | 16,000 | 1,200 | 200 | 5311 | Bentonville, AR | Wal-Mart, Sam's Wholesale Club, Hypermart USA |
| 6 | Penney (J.C.) Co. | 15,300 | 1,785 | 181 | 5311 | Dallas, TX | J.C. Penney, Thrift Drug |
| 7 | American Stores | 14,300 | 1,460 | 175 | 5411 | Salt Lake C., UT | Acme Markets, Jewel, Buttrey, Lucky, Skaggs |
| 8 | Dayton Hudson | 10,700 | 577 | 130 | 5311 | Minneapolis, MI | Dayton, Hudson, Target, Lechmere, Mervyn's |
| 9 | May Dept. Stores | 10,600 | 2,989 | 152 | 5311 | St Louis, MO | May Co., Payless Shoe Source, Lord & Taylor, Filene's, Foley's, Caldor, Robinson's |
| 10 | Great A & P Tea Co. | 9,500 | 1,183 | 53 | 5411 | Montvale, NJ | A & P Stores, Family Mart, Super Fresh |
| 11 | Super Value | 9,400 | 9,372 | 172 | 5411 | Minneapolis, MN | Super Valu, IGA, Shopko |
| 12 | Winn-Dixie Stores | 8,800 | 1,271 | 80 | 5411 | Jacksonville, FL | Winn Dixie, Marketplace, Table Supply |
| 13 | Southland[a] | 8,600 (1986) | 7,692 | 67 | 5311 | Dallas, TX | 7–11 Stores, Citgo Petroleum |
| 14 | Federated/Allied St. | 7,200 (1988) | — | — | 5311 | Cincinnati, OH | Bloomingdales, Rich's, Burdines, Maas Bros, Jordan Marsh, Abraham & Straus, Lazarus |
| 15 | F.W. Woolworth Co. | 7,100 | 6,800 | 119 | 5331 | New York, NY | Woolworth's, Kinney's Shoes, Holtzman's, Little Folk (35 formats altogether) |
| 16 | Lucky Stores | 6,900 | 481 | 39 | 5411 | San Francisco, CA | Lucky, Cal-Pharm, Kash'N Karry |

| 17 | Zayre Corporation | 6,200 | 1,187 | 64 | 5311 | Framingham, MA | Zayre, T.J. Maxx, Hit or Miss, Home Club |
| 18 | Albertson's | 5,900 | 465 | 43 | 5411 | Boise, ID | Albertson's |
| 19 | Melville Corporation | 5,900 | 6,117 | 73 | 5661 | Harrison, NY | Thom McAn, Marshalls, Kay-Bee, CVS Drugs, Meldisco, Chess King, Berman's |
| 20 | Supermarkets General[a] | 5,500 (1986) | 627 | 44 | 5411 | Woodbridge, NJ | Pathmark, Angelo's, Purity Supreme, Rickel |
| 21 | Montgomery Ward & Co. | 5,300 | 300 | 71 | 5311 | Chicago, IL | Montgomery Ward |
| 22 | McDonald's Corp. | 4,900 | 10,055 | 159 | 5812 | Chicago, IL | McDonald's |
| 23 | R.H. Macy & Co.[a] | 4,700 | 87 | 46 | 5311 | New York, NY | Macy's Bullock's, I. Magnin |
| 24 | Walgreen Co. | 4,400 | 1,458 | 45 | 5912 | Chicago, IL | Walgreen's |
| 25 | Stop & Shop Cos[a] | 4,300 | 284 | 46 | 5411 | Boston, MA | Stop'n Shop, Bradlees |
| 26 | Tandy Corp. | 3,800 | 7,318 | 36 | 573 | Fort Worth, TX | Radio Shack, McDuff, VideoConcept |
| 27 | Limited, Inc. | 3,500 | 3,095 | 50 | 5621 | Columbus, OH | The Limited, Lerner, Lane Bryant, Henri Bendel, Express, Abercrombie & Fitch |

Source: Fairchild Publications (1988) *Fairchild's Financial Manual of Retail Stores*, New York.
Notes: [a]Private company (buyout); numbers are the latest released. [b]Data for 1987 unless indicated. SIC, standard industrial classification.

One solution is the chains of chains. The last decade has given rise to the megachains such as the Melville Corporation (see Exhibit 3.3), Gap Inc., or The Limited that control dozens of chains selling in different spatial and product niches. The Melville Corporation began with men's shoes (Thom McAn), developed leased shoe outlets within K mart stores (Meldisco), and specialized in outdoor wear (Open Country). It added clothes (Marshall's, Wilson's), drugs (Consumer's Value Stores), furniture, and hobbies, and operates in different regions of the country. The Limited operates a dozen different fashion chains. One phone call from a developer to a megachain can recruit a whole spectrum of tenants for a new shopping mall, or a specific chain can be selected for a specific location: if the market at that location changes, the existing outlet is replaced by a different type of store within the same megachain.

Table 3.6 displays the pattern of concentration within each retail sector by the largest firms. The largest four firms contribute 6 per cent of the total and the top fifty make 20 per cent of all retail sales ($1,066 billion in 1982). The degree of concentration increases to 7 per cent and 26 per cent, respectively, if we exclude the automotive sector with its distinctive franchise structure. However, for particular retail sectors in individual states, regions, or metropolitan areas, the concentration is much higher. Many chains restrict their operations to one region where they compete with two or three other firms to dominate that market. If, for instance, we were to distribute the fifty largest firms among the fifty states, each one would control 20 per cent of their market.

In the state of Mississippi (Figure 3.3), five department stores compete. Three of them are national chains: Sears and J.C. Penney locate in every market in the state, K mart outlets are concentrated in the two metropolitan areas, Jackson and Biloxi. In the last decade a regional firm, Wal-Mart, has emerged as a significant competitor but their network in Mississippi is still incomplete, especially to the South. McRae's is a local chain, operating out of Jackson. Think of the state as being made up of about twenty markets, each of which will support from one to ten stores. Where should the chain go? Which markets are essential?

A situation in which a small number of entrepreneurs compete within a finite market (such as the Mississippi example) is called an oligopoly. Economic theory describes several alternatives open to an entrepreneur. (The discussion of marketing strategy in Chapter twelve will outline these choices in detail.)

The most intense concentration occurs in the retail sectors classified as general merchandising i.e. department stores and variety stores. Women's fashion, drug stores, and book stores show concentration but hardware stores, meat markets, used car dealers, and bars are dominated by independents. There is no obvious logic to this pattern. Both convenience stores (variety stores) and shopping goods (women's clothes) are concentrated.

## Exhibit 3.3
## THE MELVILLE CORPORATION TREE

The megachain combines the chain's advantages of system-wide accounting and purchasing with the flexibility in lines and market segments of an independent retailer. There is an appropriate outlet for every situation and if one merchandising variant doesn't work, a megachain can try another.

The real secret of their success is the bargaining pressure they can exert on both manufacturers and shopping center developers. The Melville Corporation is of the same order of magnitude as a department store chain.

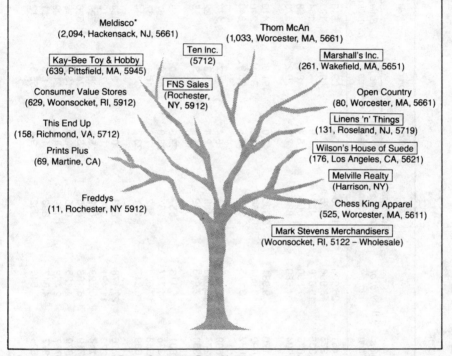

Meldisco*
(2,094, Hackensack, NJ, 5661)

Thom McAn
(1,033, Worcester, MA, 5661)

Ten Inc.
(5712)

Kay-Bee Toy & Hobby
(639, Pittsfield, MA, 5945)

Marshall's Inc.
(261, Wakefield, MA, 5651)

FNS Sales
(Rochester, NY, 5912)

Consumer Value Stores
(629, Woonsocket, RI, 5912)

Open Country
(80, Worcester, MA, 5661)

This End Up
(158, Richmond, VA, 5712)

Linens 'n' Things
(131, Roseland, NJ, 5719)

Prints Plus
(69, Martine, CA)

Wilson's House of Suede
(176, Los Angeles, CA, 5621)

Melville Realty
(Harrison, NY)

Freddys
(11, Rochester, NY 5912)

Chess King Apparel
(525, Worcester, MA, 5611)

Mark Stevens Merchandisers
(Woonsocket, RI, 5122 – Wholesale)

*Source:* Standard and Poor, *Corporate Records*
*Note:* *Jointly owned by K Mart. Parentheses contain no. of stores, HQ, retail sectors (standard industrial classification), respectively. Names in boxes indicate corporate subsidiaries.

So are large sectors (supermarkets) and small ones (toys), and large outlets (department stores) and smaller ones (dairy products). The one shared characteristic of the least concentrated sectors (franchised sectors aside) is a dependence on a variety of local suppliers for commodities such as meat, baked goods, or flowers, and/or a high level of service.

By combining the patterns of concentration and store size we can get a sense of what the retail chains in each sector look like. For example, the four largest supermarket chains average almost $10 billion in sales and run

**Table 3.6** Concentration by retail sector

| SIC | Retail sector | Sales* ($ billions) | No. of stores | Average sales/store ($ thousands) | Concentration of sales Top four firms (%) | Top fifty firms (%) | Average values for the largest four chains Sales ($ millions) | No. of stores | Sales/store ($ thousands) |
|---|---|---|---|---|---|---|---|---|---|
| 521 | Lumber | 31.451 | 25,006 | 1,258 | 10.4 | 29.1 | 818 | 271 | 3,018 |
| 523 | Paint and Wallpaper | 3.375 | 8,996 | 375 | 22.7 | 40.1 | 191 | 306 | 624 |
| 525 | Hardware | 8.335 | 19,870 | 420 | 7.9 | 14.8 | 164 | 43 | 3,814 |
| 526 | Garden supplies | 2.873 | 7,850 | 366 | 8.1 | 18.7 | 58 | 57 | 1,018 |
| 527 | Mobile homes | 3.904 | 4,680 | 834 | 7.2 | 20.2 | 70 | 34 | 2,059 |
| 531 | Dept Stores | 99.170 | 9,981 | 9,936 | 42.0 | 91.8 | 10,410 | 937 | 11,110 |
| 533 | Variety stores | 8.090 | 10,989 | 736 | 61.3 | 84.1 | 1,240 | 763 | 1,625 |
| 539 | Miscellaneous general | 12.687 | 13,175 | 963 | 26.5 | 58.9 | 840 | 140 | 5,995 |
| 541 | Grocery stores | 226.609 | 128,494 | 1,764 | 16.4 | 44.7 | 9,277 | 1,188 | 7,809 |
| 542 | Meat and fish | 5.274 | 10,995 | 480 | 2.4 | 9.3 | 32 | 30 | 1,067 |
| 543 | Fruit and vegetables | 1.330 | 2,943 | 452 | 4.5 | 21.3 | 15 | 2 | 750 |
| 544 | Candy and confectionery | 0.801 | 5,113 | 157 | 23.8 | 44.0 | 48 | 217 | 221 |
| 545 | Dairy products | 1.375 | 4,777 | 287 | 28.0 | 53.9 | 97 | 233 | 416 |
| 546 | Bakeries | 3.543 | 17,580 | 202 | 7.6 | 16.1 | 67 | 311 | 215 |
| 549 | Miscellaneous food | 1.589 | 6,317 | 251 | 23.7 | 38.7 | 94 | 282 | 333 |
| 551 | New car sales | 154.726 | 27,178 | 5,693 | 0.9 | 3.6 | 354 | 27 | 13,111 |
| 552 | Used cars | 6.273 | 11,421 | 549 | 1.2 | 7.2 | 19 | 2 | 8,573 |
| 553 | Auto supplies | 20.714 | 40,729 | 509 | 15.2 | 28.0 | 795 | 1,229 | 639 |
| 554 | Gas supplies | 94.719 | 116,188 | 815 | 6.4 | 24.4 | 1,526 | 965 | 1,581 |
| 555 | Boats | 2.870 | 4,125 | 696 | 2.6 | 13.2 | 19 | 19 | 9,438 |
| 556 | Recreational vehicles | 2.767 | 2,452 | 1,129 | 4.2 | 21.2 | 29 | 4 | 7,231 |
| 557 | Motorcycles | 2.877 | 4,617 | 623 | 1.5 | 8.3 | 11 | 1 | 8,800 |
| 559 | Other auto | 0.525 | 546 | 962 | 9.4 | 55.3 | 12 | 1 | 12,325 |

| Code | | A | B | C | D | E | F | G | H |
|---|---|---|---|---|---|---|---|---|---|
| 561 | Men's clothes | 7.735 | 17,480 | 443 | 9.5 | 26.0 | 184 | 247 | 745 |
| 562 | Women's clothes | 20.248 | 50,961 | 459 | 20.9 | 47.8 | 1,096 | 1,058 | 1,036 |
| 563 | Accessories | 1.740 | 6,798 | 256 | 10.3 | 32.4 | 45 | 137 | 328 |
| 565 | Family clothing | 13.451 | 17,859 | 753 | 23.8 | 52.5 | 800 | 462 | 1,732 |
| 566 | Shoe stores | 11.275 | 36,277 | 311 | 27.3 | 56.3 | 770 | 2,116 | 364 |
| 564 | Children's wear | 1.356 | 5,325 | 254 | 12.8 | 26.3 | 43 | 61 | 711 |
| 569 | Miscellaneous apparel | 1.063 | 6,235 | 1,705 | 6.0 | 20.1 | 16 | 10 | 1,668 |
| 5712 | Furniture | 17.223 | 29,609 | 582 | 5.1 | 17.3 | 219 | 47 | 4,660 |
| 5713 | Floors | 5.015 | 11,125 | 451 | 7.2 | 15.1 | 90 | 166 | 541 |
| 5714 | Drapes | 0.858 | 4,063 | 211 | 4.7 | 19.0 | 10 | 14 | 816 |
| 5719 | Miscellaneous furniture | 2.975 | 9,649 | 308 | 10.0 | 29.1 | 74 | 68 | 1,086 |
| 572 | Appliances | 5.697 | 10,542 | 540 | 7.6 | 19.2 | 109 | 37 | 2,946 |
| 573 | TV, etc. | 13.545 | 28,746 | 471 | 16.0 | 33.5 | 541 | 1,382 | 391 |
| 5812 | Restaurants | 98.158 | 258,584 | 380 | 5.4 | 20.2 | 1,265 | 1,646 | 769 |
| 5813 | Bars | 8.565 | 61,289 | 140 | 0.7 | 2.8 | 15 | 15 | 979 |
| 591 | Drugstores | 34.941 | 49,527 | 706 | 19.2 | 52.5 | 1,695 | 1,048 | 1,617 |
| 592 | Liquor | 17.340 | 34,861 | 497 | 8.6 | 20.7 | 373 | 429 | 869 |
| 593 | Second hand | 3.798 | 17,402 | 218 | 5.6 | 13.4 | 53 | 206 | 257 |
| 5941 | Sports | 7.515 | 20,152 | 373 | 18.5 | 28.6 | 347 | 573 | 606 |
| 5942 | Books | 3.133 | 9,355 | 335 | 26.8 | 45.5 | 210 | 397 | 529 |
| 5943 | Stationery | 1.495 | 4,750 | 315 | 3.3 | 13.7 | 12 | 23 | 519 |
| 5944 | Jewellery | 8.352 | 22,786 | 366 | 17.0 | 32.2 | 355 | 575 | 617 |
| 5945 | Toys | 3.238 | 7,691 | 421 | 51.1 | 65.9 | 414 | 175 | 2,366 |
| 5946 | Cameras | 1.884 | 4,003 | 471 | 6.2 | 29.4 | 29 | 63 | 469 |
| 5947 | Gifts | 4.620 | 22,311 | 207 | 6.4 | 19.5 | 75 | 236 | 315 |
| 5948 | Leather | 0.589 | 1,883 | 313 | 22.5 | 51.8 | 33 | 361 | 387 |
| 5949 | Piece goods | 2.495 | 9,774 | 255 | 31.1 | 53.8 | 194 | 434 | 447 |
| 5961 | Mail order | 11.254 | 7,433 | 1,514 | 26.0 | 57.3 | 731 | 317 | 2,306 |
| 5962 | Vending machines | 4.727 | 5,646 | 837 | 27.0 | 45.8 | 319 | 412 | 774 |
| 5963 | Direct sales | 4.175 | 8,724 | 479 | 14.3 | 36.1 | 149 | 190 | 785 |

**Table 3.6** (continued)

| SIC | Retail sector | Sales* ($ billions) | No. of stores | Average sales/store ($ thousands) | Concentration of sales | | Average values for the largest four chains | | |
|---|---|---|---|---|---|---|---|---|---|
| | | | | | Top four firms (%) | Top fifty firms (%) | Sales ($ millions) | No. of stores | Sales/store ($ thousands) |
| 5982 | Fuel and ice | 0.259 | 788 | 333 | 12.8 | 49.1 | 8 | 263 | 8,263 |
| 5983 | Fuel oil | 11.754 | 6,061 | 1,939 | 6.2 | 20.2 | 183 | 23 | 8,026 |
| 5984 | Bottled gas | 4.805 | 5,898 | 815 | 18.7 | 54.7 | 225 | 217 | 1,039 |
| 5992 | Florists | 3.416 | 22,393 | 153 | 1.2 | 5.1 | 10 | 36 | 288 |
| 5993 | Cigar stores | 0.576 | 2,353 | 245 | 9.5 | 30.8 | 14 | 36 | 381 |
| 5994 | Newsstands | 0.500 | 1,946 | 257 | 16.3 | 37.2 | 20 | 58 | 354 |
| 5999 | Miscellaneous | 7.078 | 32,823 | 216 | 4.7 | 13.1 | 83 | 382 | 217 |
| | All retail | 1,042.721 | 1,337,124 | 780 | 5.9 | 21.3 | 14,613 | 3,410 | 4,285 |
| | (excluding auto) | 757.25 | 1,129,868 | 670 | 7.3 | 26.3 | 14,613 | 3,410 | 4,285 |

*Source*: Bureau of the Census (1982) 'Establishment and firm size, *Census of Retailing*
*Note*: * Firms with payroll only: excludes about 600,000 (30 per cent) of the very small firms. They account for less than 7 per cent of all sales. SIC, standard industrial classification.

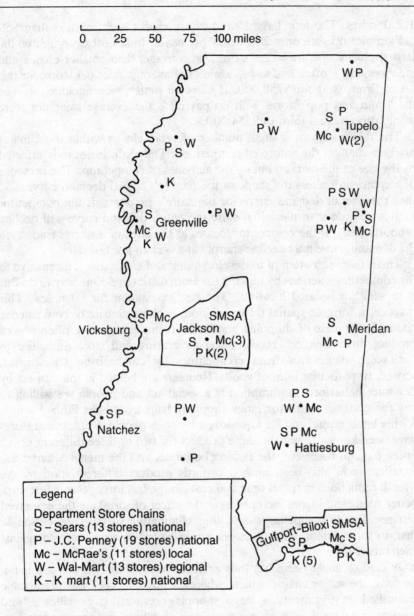

**Figure 3.3** Department store competition in Mississippi

*Source:* 'Market guide' (1987) *Editor and Publisher*

1,200 stores. The four largest candy store chains each sell less than $50 million and operate only 200 stores per chain. In almost every sector the largest chains operate larger stores, on average, than smaller chains and independents – often half as big again. The average sales per store, for this set of firms, is about $750,000. If all retail outlets were included – even the 'mom and pop' stores with no payroll – the average sales per store would drop by one-third to $554,000.

The dominance of a small number of retail chains within most major markets changes the nature of competition. The chain is not only affected by the size of the market, but by the activities of competitors. The presence of a competitor alters the shape of the retailer's spatial demand curve, and thus the overall demand curve for the store's products. If the competitor locates next door to the initial store the entire demand curve will decline proportionally; if the competitor locates at the edge of a store's trade area the demand curve may decline sharply at a certain level of sales.

The retailer can attempt to develop a demand curve that is insensitive to the competitor's actions by making the store distinctive. One way to do this is to seek an isolated location, 'The last gas station for 80 miles'. This practice, a form of spatial differentiation, is characteristic of convenience goods. In the case of shopping goods, the technique is more often one of product differentiation: retailers use advertising and store amenities to distinguish themselves from competitors by emphasizing style, price, service, or particular lines of goods. Retailers are helped in this respect by customer behavior. Consumption is a social act and people are willing to pay for designer jeans, for fancy shopping bags from Saks Fifth Avenue, for the latest music, and for knowledgeable sales people. Department stores have been known to sell the same product for two or three different prices in the bargain basement, the fashion boutique, and the men's department. Retailers have also been pushed towards product differentiation by the overall reductions in travel time and costs in the last forty years. More cars, better roads and higher incomes have the effect of shrinking the perceived distance among competing stores, thus eliminating spatial competition so that, to some extent, all shoe stores within an urban area compete against each other.

A kind of dual system has thus emerged in retailing. On the one hand, we have the major chains, which, wherever possible, seek out predictable controlled environments – large shopping centers, large cities – and innovate very cautiously, after a great deal of debate and experimentation. They learn, and they adapt to new environments. On the other hand, there are still one million independent stores; small, often unprofitable, and located in highly uncertain markets – small towns, older retail strips, ethnic communities. The uncertainty comes both from possible economic decline in the market and from the entry of competitors. The result is a high rate of business turnover and business failure in the latter group. Consider any small retail strip with which you are familiar. From 20 to 25 per cent of the stores will change ownership, location and/or function each year. While some stores remain for decades; over half of the new enterprises disappear within the first year.

It is hard to measure the rate of change precisely because stores go out of business in so many ways: bankruptcy, selling out, retirement, merger, closure, or change in function. Of the 1.8 million retail firms (with payroll) that operated in 1982, over 200,000 were out of business by the end of the year.

### Franchising

The major alternative to the continued expansion of the retail chain is the franchise concept in which an individual entrepreneur operates a business in conjunction with a network of suppliers and other franchises of the same brand. While there are many variants of the franchising relationship, the essential feature is a contract between the parent firm and the franchise-holder which specifies the fee, the location, and the operating rules for the relationship. The fee might be $50,000–$100,000 initially, plus up to 8 per cent of the gross, or perhaps just a committment to buy the products of the parent. In return, the franchise-holder receives exclusive rights within a specified market, plus assistance for advertising and marketing strategies.

Franchising has the advantages of economies of scale in purchasing, marketing, and distribution activities. For instance, gasoline stations and fast-food outlets both need high levels of advertising and sophisticated location analysis. At the same time the manager-owner has flexibility in adapting to local conditions and managing personnel. The larger the service input (i.e. labor inputs) in a retail sector, the better the franchise approach works. Franchising developed first in the automotive sector, in both car dealerships and service stations. In the first case the dealer owns the location and the contract deals primarily with the product. In the second, the parent company may also locate and develop the site. These are called product and trade name franchises. Most of the recent growth in franchising has taken place in business format franchises such as restaurants and convenience stores. Here the franchisee also gets a market strategy and plan, an operating format, and quality control: an ongoing two-way relationship. From the point of view of the consumer, franchise outlets of either kind are just like retail chains: standardized products, locations, decor, and merchandising techniques.

Because of the size and rate of growth of the automotive sector – including about one-quarter of all retail sales – franchising has long been an important element in the retail system. However, as Table 3.7a suggests, the franchise arrangement is now growing rapidly in other areas of retailing. Fast-food restaurants and convenience stores are particularly evident.

**Table 3.7** The franchise phenomenon

(a) Franchise activity: 1985

| Retail sector | Franchise outlets (thousands) | | Franchise sales ($ billions)[a] | | |
|---|---|---|---|---|---|
| | 1975 | 1985 | 1975 | 1985 | Growth (%) |
| Automobile dealers | 31.8 | 27.3 | 169.5 | 248.5 | 46.6 |
| Gasoline stations | 189.5 | 124.6 | 85.0 | 90.2 | 6.1 |
| Automobile products | 47.5 | 36.2 | 9.0 | 9.1 | 1.1 |
| Restaurants | 43.0 | 75.9 | 22.1 | 43.1 | 95.0 |
| Convenience stores | 13.5 | 15.3 | 7.0 | 9.8 | 40.0 |
| Other retail | 49.0 | 59.9 | 18.6 | 23.6 | 26.9 |
| Total | 374.3 | 339.2 | 311.2 | 424.3 | 36.3 |

Note: [a]In 1982 dollars.

(b) Concentration in franchising: Size distribution of non-automotive[a] retail franchises

| Numbers of outlets in chain | Firms | Share (%) | Outlets | Share (%) | Sales ($ millions)[b] | Share (%) |
|---|---|---|---|---|---|---|
| 0–10 | 372 | 31.9 | 2,000 | 1.0 | 800 | 0.8 |
| 11–50 | 426 | 36.6 | 10,700 | 5.7 | 5,700 | 5.7 |
| 50–150 | 193 | 16.5 | 16,400 | 8.7 | 8,200 | 8.2 |
| 150–500 | 107 | 9.2 | 30,500 | 16.1 | 13,600 | 13.6 |
| 500–1,000 | 29 | 2.5 | 24,800 | 13.1 | 13,900 | 13.9 |
| 1,000+ | 38 | 3.3 | 105,400 | 55.6 | 57,500 | 57.6 |
| Total | 1,165 | 100.0 | 189,800 | 100.0 | 99,700 | 100.0 |

Source: Department of Commerce, International Trade Administration (1987) *Franchising in the Economy, 1984–1986*
Note: [a]Excludes automobile dealers and gasoline stations; includes auto parts and tire dealers. [b]In 1985 dollars.

(Unfortunately, the data on franchising are not comprehensive.) While franchise sales were growing at 36 per cent over the decade, the sales of retail chains grew at 29 per cent and the sales of non-chain, non-franchise independents dropped sharply.

Because franchising requires relatively little capital investment and low administrative overheads, the barriers to expansion lie chiefly on the demand side. How big is the market? Who are the competitors? Some franchising firms have grown very rapidly, as Table 3.7b shows. Thirty-eight non-automotive retail franchises have more than 1,000 outlets, amounting to 105,000 stores. Add another fifty automotive franchise firms and you have 250,000 stores and $300 billion in sales, controlled by 100 firms. Now that's concentration!

Table 3.8 lists some of the major non-automotive franchisors (the data are not precise) to give a sense of the scale of these operations. Reading the list of take-out food and restaurant franchises makes you wonder if there's any home cooking left in America.

## The shopping center developer

The final aspect of concentration is location: a small number of planned shopping plazas account for a large proportion of all retail activity. Planned centers are owned, designed, and managed by a single developer or management firm which selects and locates tenants and can determine the goods that the retailer sells. We estimate that they now account for over 40 per cent of all retail sales, and 60 per cent of non-automotive sales, with the share still growing as new types of malls infiltrate older downtown shopping areas and retail strips.

Planned centers vary enormously in size, from the 3,800,000 square feet of the West Edmonton Mall in Alberta to the 25,000 square foot suburban strips. As Table 3.1 indicates, the largest 5 per cent of the malls (the 1,500 that are over 400,000 square feet in area) may account for one-third of all shopping center floor area and sales.

The largest shopping center developers (Table 3.9) are responsible for

**Table 3.8** Major franchise firms

| Firm | Headquarters | No. of stores (S) or franchises (F)* | |
|---|---|---|---|
| *Food* | | | |
| International Dairy Queen Inc. | Minneapolis, MN | 4805 | S |
| Burger King Corporation | Miami, FL | 4635 | S |
| Baskin-Robbins | Los Angeles, CA | 3000+ | S |
| The Southland Corporation (7-11) | Dallas, TX | 2850 | F |
| Hardee's Food Systems | Rocky Mount, NC | 2600 | F (incl. 875C) |
| Wendy's Old Fashioned Hamburgers | Columbus, OH | 4500 | S (incl. 1225C) |
| McDonald's Corporation | Chicago, IL | 1700 | F |
| Dunkin' Donuts of America, Inc. | Boston, MA | 1445 | F |
| Long John Silver's Inc. | Lexington, KY | 1380 | S (incl. 840C) |
| Convenient Food Mart, Inc. | Chicago, IL | 1225 | F |
| Taco Bell | Los Angeles, CA | 2200 | S (1180C) |
| Arby's Inc. | Atlanta, GA | 1550 | S (340F) |
| *Non-food* | | | |
| American Hardware Supply | Butler, PA | 3865 | F |
| Radio Shack | Fort Worth, TX | 3000 | F |
| Ben Franklin (variety) | Chicago, IL | 1300 | F |
| National Video | Portland, OR | 1125 | F |
| Coast to Coast Stores (hardware) | Minneapolis, MN | 1025 | F |

*Source:* Department of Commerce, International Trade Administration (1987) *Franchise Opportunities Handbook*, Washington
*Note:* * As estimated by franchise firms for 1985. There is some confusion between number of stores (S) and franchise-holders (F), between company-owned (C) outlets and franchise outlets, and between US and foreign outlets.

**Table 3.9** America's top shopping center developers

| Rank | Name | Headquarters | Total floor area (millions of sq. ft) | No. of centers | Average size (thousands) | No. of large centers | Spatial reach | Size | Theme |
|---|---|---|---|---|---|---|---|---|---|
| 1 | Edward J. DeBartolo Corp. | Youngstown, OH | 66.1 | 130 | 508 | 62 | National, OH, FL | Sup. reg. | Mass mkt |
| 2 | Homart (Sears) | Chicago, IL | 56.9 | 60 | 948 | 56 | National | Sup. reg. | Mass mkt |
| 3 | Melvin Simon & Associates | Indianapolis, IN | 54.7 | 230 | 238 | 62 | National, mid-west | All size | Mass mkt |
| 4 | The Hahn Co. | San Diego, CA | 43.9 | 61 | 720 | 49 | CA | Regional | Upscale |
| 5 | Jacobs, Visconsi & Jacobs | Cleveland, OH | 34.3 | 41 | 836 | 39 | East, OH | Sup. reg. | Mass mkt suburban |
| 6 | Corporate Property Investors | New York, NY | 34.1 | 30 (est.) | 1100 | 30 (est.) | East coast | Sup. reg. | Mass mkt |
| 7 | The Cafaro Co. | Youngstown, OH | 30.8 | 58 | 531 | 16 | Mid-west, OH | All size | Small city |
| 8 | The Taubman Co. | Detroit, MI | 30.0 | 27 | 1111 | 23 | National | Sup. reg. | Mass mkt |
| 9 | The Rouse Co. | Columbia, MD | 27.6 | 64 | 431 | 13 | National | 200–300k | Upscale, theme mall |
| 10 | National Property Analysts | Philadelphia, PA | 26.9 | 209 | 129 | 3 | National | Community | K mart |
| 11 | General Growth Companies | Des Moines, IN | 24.9 | 38 | 655 | 29 | National, IA | Regional | Mass mkt |
| 12 | The Macerich Co. | Los Angeles, CA | 20.7 | 37 | 559 | 13 | National, CA | Sup. reg. | Mass mkt |
| 13 | Equity Properties & Dev. Co. | Chicago, IL | 20.5 | 48 | 427 | 13 | National | All size | Mass mkt |
| 14 | Crown American Corp. | Johnstown, PA | 20.0 | 34 | 588 | 22 | PA | Regional | Small city |
| 15 | May Centers Inc. | St Louis, MO | 19.5 | 25 | 780 | 23 | CA, MO | Sup. reg. | Upscale |
| 16 | CBL and Associates Inc. | Chattanooga, TN | 18.9 | 89 | 212 | 16 | South | All size | Small city |
| 17 | Southmark Comm. Mngt. | Dallas, TX | 16.5 | n.a. | n.a. | n.a. | — | — | — |
| 18 | Leo Eisenberg Co. | Kansas City, MO | 16.4 | 231 | 71 | 2 | National, MO | Neighborhood | Small city |

| | | | | | | | | | |
|---|---|---|---|---|---|---|---|---|---|
| 19 | Cambridge Shopping Centres | Toronto, Canada | 15.6 | n.a. | n.a. | n.a. | — | — | — |
| 20 | Ramco-Gershenson | Southfield, MI | 15.3 | 82 | 187 | 6 | Community | K mart | — |
| 21 | Developers Diversified | Cleveland, OH | 15.2 | 117 | 130 | 1 | Community | K mart | — |
| 22 | Kravco Co. | Philadelphia, PA | 15.0 | 36 | 417 | 24 | Sup. reg. | Metro. | — |
| 23 | The Goodman Co. | West Palm Beach, FL | 15.0 | n.a. | n.a. | n.a. | — | — | — |
| 24 | Forest City | Cleveland, OH | 14.1 | n.a. | n.a. | n.a. | — | — | — |
| 25 | Urban Inv. & Dev. Co. Development | Chicago, IL | 14.0 | 13 | 1077 | 9 | Sup. reg. | Chicago suburbs | — |
| Total | | | 666.9 | 1,660 | 365 | 511 | | | |

Source: Communications Channels, Shopping Center World (1988), Atlanta, Georgia

Note: * Over 400,000 sq. ft. sup. reg., super regional; metro, metropolitan; n.a., not available.

667 million square feet of shopping space, about 20 per cent of the total floor area in shopping centers. (Shopping centers now account for about 25 per cent of all shopping space.) Perhaps more important, these developers control one-third of the largest regional and super-regional locations which are the most important outlets for department stores and fashion goods. These centers have become the critical locations in America retailing: without access to them, a retailer cannot reach the market.

Each developer has carved out a special niche within the industry. Perhaps the most distinctive is the Rouse Company, which has created an historic theme mall approach that has been repeated in redevelopments across the country: an enclosed mall of about 250,000 square feet, with no anchor tenant. Examples include South Street Seaport (New York), Faneuil Hall (Boston), and Union Station (St Louis). Other developers have a strong regional base (Hahn, Ramco-Gershonen, Kravco), or a distinctive size and design format. Developers Diversified and National Property Analysts operate dozens of community scale plazas built for K mart or Wal-Mart. In Pennsylvania Kravco has concentrated on the metropolitan suburbs while Crown American has been more predatory, attempting to replace the town centers of smaller communities. Some, e.g. May Centers or Homart (Sears), have close links with department stores. Taubman owns John Wanamaker and Woodward & Lothrop. Campeau, the Canadian developer who bought Allied and Federated Department Stores (with the help of De Bartolo), hoped to dominate the development of new regional shopping plazas across the country.

Some developers are innovative, some imitative, some specialize, others just try to grow, but collectively they provide an essential access to the United States market. Melvin Simon and Associates control malls of every size in every market of the country. The Rouse Company penetrates upscale markets in every major city. With the aid of the right developer a European clothing store can quickly arrange outlets in fashion centers across the United States.

Close ties between the shopping center developers and the major retail chains have encouraged the rapid growth of both institutions in recent years, as the case study in Table 3.10 suggests. Seventy-five to 90 per cent of the tenants in a regional shopping mall may be outlets of national chains, using almost all the floor space and generating over 90 per cent of the sales. On the other hand, local stores still dominate downtown retailing, accounting for 75 per cent of the floor space. The majority of retail chain outlets are found in plazas. Whereas independent retailers grow or go broke over a period of time in the uncertain environment of the unplanned retail center, both chains and shopping plazas try to reduce the uncertainty by controlling all aspects of the shopping environment. For the chain this means exposure to a known, regular traffic flow with a fixed quantity of competition. The shopping center developer in turn looks for retailers whose

**Table 3.10** The role of chains within planned centers
(regional shopping centers in Winnipeg)

| | Number (%) | | Floor Area (thousands of sq. ft) (%) | |
|---|---|---|---|---|
| | Local stores | National chains | Local stores | National chains |
| Polo Park | 17  (25.8) | 49  (74.2) | 22.1  (3.1) | 689.2  (96.9) |
| Grant Park | 3  (15.0) | 17  (85.0) | 24.9  (8.2) | 277.9  (91.8) |
| Garden City | 12  (22.6) | 41  (77.4) | 15.8  (4.8) | 315.4  (95.2) |
| Unicity | 8  (13.8) | 50  (86.2) | 10.6  (2.4) | 432.2  (97.6) |
| St Vital | 15  (18.1) | 68  (81.9) | 16.4  (2.7) | 589.7  (97.3) |
| Kildonan | 7  (9.9) | 64  (90.1) | 11.7  (2.7) | 416.2  (97.3) |
| Total | 62  (17.7) | 289  (82.3) | 101.5  (3.6) | 2,720.6  (96.4) |
| Downtown | 287  (74.9) | 101  (25.1) | 626.9  (27.5) | 1,652.2  (72.5) |

*Source:* A. Honigman *et al.* (1985) *Downtown and Regional Shopping Centre Retailing in Winnipeg*,
report no. 7, Institute for Urban Studies, University of Winnipeg
*Note:* Includes only retail activities.

product mix and type of operation are known and successful with a
predictable ability to extract sales from traffic flow.

A side effect of the close link between major retail chains and shopping
center developers is the barrier to entry created by the leasing patterns in
major regional centers. Independents, new retail chains, and rapidly
expanding ones find it difficult to gain access to the important regional
centers once the latter are committed to existing chains. The only way a
new chain can enter the market quickly is to buy out another chain for the
sake of its network of leases.

The importance of the link between retail chains and development
corporations is underlined by the emergence of several leasing agencies
that operate as go-betweens (e.g. Williams, Jackson, Ewing, The Round
Table). These brokers can put together a package of stores from various
smaller retail chains to suit a new plaza, providing an alternative to megachains. They may help a retailer to enter a new market, or to negotiate
leases in different centers. Brokers may lease as many as 10 per cent of the
outlets in a major mall on behalf of the small chains that they represent.

### The value of location

Given the size of store and degree of specialization, what is the appropriate
location? While the decision whether or not to penetrate a particular
market (Oklahoma City, for example) depends on the relationship between
average cost and demand, as described in Figure 3.2, the problem of where to
locate within Oklahoma City is complicated by the presence of competing
retailers who are interested in the same sites. The retailer is faced with a

map of possible locations with different prices attached to each. How much can the store afford to pay?

The argument presented below applies to an urban downtown situation in which many different types of stores compete for locations that are allocated in a reasonably independent fashion. A competitive market situation, such as occurs on a downtown street, creates a pattern of land values centered around the most accessible point (Figure 3.4a), usually a main intersection with a high density of traffic, including cars, public transit, and especially pedestrians. In the marketing literature it used to be referred to as the 'hot corner' or the '100 per cent corner'. State Street and Madison in Chicago is an example, Fifth Avenue and 57th Street in New York is another. In today's city it may be the intersection of two interstate highways. Variations in urban land value reflect differential access to the market, as represented by the travel patterns of consumers.

The map of land values represents the composite wish-list of all the different kinds of retail stores. Each type of store values accessibility differently and is able to pay a different amount for a site. In the diagram (these are actual recorded rents) the fashion retailer is most sensitive to pedestrian

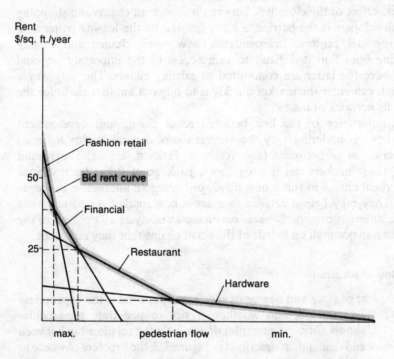

**Figure 3.4** The bid rent curve
(a) Bid rent curves for street retailing in a major metropolitan area

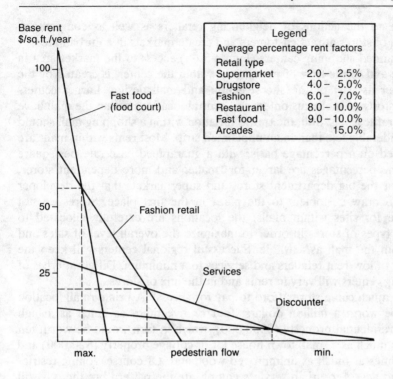

Legend
Average percentage rent factors

| Retail type | |
|---|---|
| Supermarket | 2.0 – 2.5% |
| Drugstore | 4.0 – 5.0% |
| Fashion | 6.0 – 7.0% |
| Restaurant | 8.0 – 10.0% |
| Fast food | 9.0 – 10.0% |
| Arcades | 15.0% |

**Figure 3.4** (*continued*)
(b) Bid rent curves in a regional shopping center

*Source:* The authors

access, paying the highest rice for high levels of pedestrian flow, but with the ability to pay declining sharply with distance. Hardware stores, in contrast, are not interested in highly congested sites. Gas stations may be willing to pay more than other stores for specific patterns of automobile traffic but place a negative value on pedestrian flow. Rent values are defined by the highest bidder at each distance and access level. When the highest bidders are sorted out on the ground the fashion store is usually found on the 'hot corner' with the bank nearby.

The differing rents paid by different stores according to location complicate the retailer's choice of site by further reducing the potential for high profit levels. Some of the store's profit must now be shared with the landlord who always has the opportunity to rent to a competitor. Within the city then, the potential for profit that is conferred by spatial monopoly is eroded by location costs. Also, because access to pedestrians is partially created by the presence of other nearby stores, the retailer is highly sensitive to the actions of neighboring retailers as well as competitors. Clusters of stores attract customers and create markets in an urban area.

In planned shopping centers (Figure 3.4b) access to the market area in general, and to the flow of pedestrians within the center, is created by the developer as part of the site selection and mall design. Larger centers expose stores to more customers and central locations within the mall have higher traffic levels. Still, the traffic variation within a shopping mall should be considerably less than in an unplanned strip. Most rents within malls are calculated on a percentage basis, with a guaranteed base rate per square foot. The percentages are larger for smaller and more dependent stores, lower for the big department stores and supermarkets that the developer needs to draw customers to the plaza in the first place. Stores do not compete for sites within malls: the locations are carefully allocated to various types of stores in order to maximize the overall level of sales and rent from the mall as a whole. Successful regional centers will keep the number of low-rent retailers and services to a minimum. Different types of shopping centers will vary in rents and in the mix of stores.

How much can a store afford to pay for access? A prime retail location might be worth a million dollars: four or five times as much as a high quality residential property ($200,000), which in turn would be worth ten times as much as a small town house lot or cottage property ($20,000) and 1,000 times as much as unimproved woodland. Of course, zoning restrictions and access to urban services complicate the pattern but there is still considerable variability in the location choices and costs for retailers. One of the very highest rental rates occurs in the Trump Tower in Central Manhattan, reputedly as much as $500 per square foot. This would be regarded as a very high level for sales, let alone rent, in most malls. Exhibit 3.4 illustrates how certain factors affect the ability of department stores to pay rent.

The retailer decides how much rent can be paid according to the sensitivity of store sales to location (the spatial demand curve, here defined at a very local level). We can begin with the key variable in retail location – sales per square foot. Sales per square foot depend on the price-density of stock (varying with the product and store design) and especially on the turnover, the number of times per year that the stock is sold and replaced. Retail analysts claim that a turnover of 6–8 times per year is required for a successful department store.

The retailer, then, must compare the location rent for a store site with the site's ability to generate sales by increasing the turnover of stock. Table 3.3 suggests how this ability varies between different kinds of stores. The proportion of retail sales allocated to rent and real estate varies among retail sectors, ranging from 0.9 to 8.9 per cent. The highest proportionate rents are paid by small stores selling shopping goods: shoes, clothes, jewelry, and flowers. The lowest rents are paid by automobile-oriented activities

Exhibit 3.4
THE ABILITY TO PAY RENT

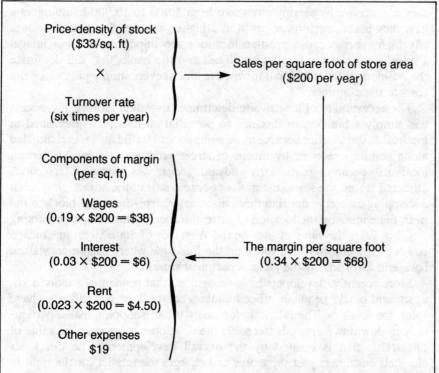

Price-density of stock
($33/sq. ft)

×

Turnover rate
(six times per year)

Sales per square foot of store area
($200 per year)

Components of margin
(per sq. ft)

Wages
(0.19 × $200 = $38)

Interest
(0.03 × $200 = $6)

Rent
(0.023 × $200 = $4.50)

Other expenses
$19

The margin per square foot
(0.34 × $200 = $68)

If the turnover rate increased by 25 per cent, so would the margin, most of which would be available for increased rent. $5 per square foot rent is roughly equivalent to $50/square foot in land value, or approximately $5,000 per front foot.

*Source:* The authors

that require large amounts of space and attract their own customers: fuel oil dealers, service stations, and new car sales.

If the turnover rate increased by 25 per cent, store sales and the store's margin would increase as well. Most of the gain would be available for increased rent. An annual rent of $5 per square foot is roughly equivalent to a land value of $50 square foot, or approximately $5,000 per front of footage.

The ability to pay for location is not so much a question of market threshold as of the characteristics of the store's production function that enable the retailer to translate turnover into profit. For example, certain exotic kinds of stores with very large market requirements (e.g. model train stores) are able to attract their customers to any location within that market, so improved pedestrian flow would not improve their sales at all. The highest bidders for location are fast-food franchises. They have low market thresholds but are able to take advantage of scale economies. Although they can survive by serving anywhere from 1,000 to 10,000 hamburgers a day, they make much more profit at a higher volume. Some retail sectors pay high rents because prestige locations are important to their image. Typical examples are fashion boutiques and the banks that still dominate the business districts of small towns. Prestige seekers simply pass along the costs to the customer.

The accessibility of a retail site determines its value. Historically, access was simply a function of distance to potential customers, as described in Figure 2.3, but as cities became more complex and traffic flow was channeled along certain streets or by means of street-car lines or subways, certain locations became particularly advantageous. As these intersections attracted stores, the stores themselves became part of the attraction. Within a shopping district pedestrian flows may vary sharply from one block to the next, depending on the location of store entrances, transit stops, or parking lots. For years the value of sites on the West side of State Street in Chicago has been much lower than those on the East side where customers walked back and forth among the great department stores.

More recently, developers have recognized that residential subdivisions, apartment blocks or major office buildings create flows of traffic that have value for retailers. The rationale for many urban shopping malls, particularly in downtown areas, is to enable the developer to capture the value of this traffic that is created by the overall development. The developer channels customers past the stores and charges the retailer for the right to serve those customers. Everyone is happy.

The linkages among stores and other activities created by the flow of customers are called externalities – benefits created by one store that also assist another store. Positive externalities, such as flows of customers are good things; negative externalities, such as traffic congestion or pollution are bad. Retail analysts differentiate between stores that create positive externalities – generative stores – and those that depend on these externalities – suscipient stores. Examples of the former are department stores or supermarkets which through their size and advertising budget, attract large numbers of shoppers. Suscipient stores, typically smaller outlets oriented to the impulse buyer, such as news stands and fast-food outlets, are attracted to high-traffic sites near the generative stores.

At this point we can finally respond to the question raised in the frontispiece. 'Is Fifth Avenue and Central Park the best location in the world?' Only if you own a store that is able to convert that location into sales. For a classy jewelry store, yes, for a discount supermarket (or almost any other store you can think of), no.

## Further reading

Bolen, W.H. (1982) *Contemporary Retailing*, Englewood Cliffs, New Jersey: Prentice-Hall.

Bucklin, L. (1978) *Productivity in Retailing*, New York: American Marketing Association.

Davidson, W.R., Sweeney, D.J., and Stampfl, R.W. (1988) *Retailing Management* 6th edn, New York: John Wiley & Sons.

Dawson, J.A. (1983) *Shopping Centre Development*, London: Longman.

Lloyd, P.E. and Dicken, P. (1977) *Location in Space* 2nd edn, London: Harper and Row.

Sternlieb, G. and Hughes, J. (eds) (1981) *Shopping Center: USA*, New Brunswick, New Jersey: Rutgers University, Center for Urban Policy Research.

Tucker, K.A. (1975) *Economies of Scale in Retailing*, Westmead: Saxon House.

Wrigley, N. (1988) 'Retail restructuring and retail analysis', in N. Wrigley (ed.) *Store Choice, Store Location and Market Analysis*, London: Routledge.

Chapter four

# The mystery of consumer behavior

**Inveterate bargain-hunters tend to be insecure people.**

**Much of the variety and apparent inefficiency in the retail sector stems from our need to be somehow distinguishable from our peers.**

**Americans make seven billion trips a year to shopping malls – about twenty-five per person.**

The key to transforming several square miles of residential landscape and household requirements – neighborhoods, roads, and houses – into a map of stores and retail centers of various kinds and sizes, lies in the mysterious combination of travel patterns, information, preferences, and shopping decisions called consumer behavior. We call it mysterious because these choices are not necessarily logical nor predictable; who can say why some people prefer strawberry ice cream to vanilla? We have already noted the irrational temporal phenomenon of Christmas and the unpredictable spatial phenomenon of Chinatown. Marketing analysts probe and describe consumer decisions and attempt to alter them by means of advertising, but they cannot explain them in a series of graphs or equations.

The study of human behavior incorporates all the various approaches of the social sciences (Table 4.1). Chapters two and three introduced notions of 'economic' man – rational, well-informed, and maximizing the benefits from each shopping trip. Economic man is most relevant, however, on the supply side of retailing; particularly for the study of groups of enterprises – the economy as a whole. Studies of consumer behavior, in contrast, look beyond economics to the disciplines of psychology, sociology, anthropology, and geography. Consumer studies have at various times incorporated every social theorist from Freud to Pavlov to Marshall McLuhan: a measure, perhaps, of the frustrating complexity of the topic.

However, whether one takes a rational, an empirical, or a psychological approach three major themes emerge (Table 4.2). The first is the importance of the opportunities provided by the consumer's daily and weekly travel patterns; activity space as it is sometimes called by the empiricists. What retail locations will be visited, bypassed, or observed during the week? A distance-minimizing logic suggests that this weekly path will generate most of the consumer's shopping trips, although the mode and time of travel may also be important. The second theme is cognition: what shopping opportunities are known to the consumer? Knowledge (let's call it awareness) is closely related both to experience and to the consumer's exposure to various advertising media. Researchers have found out that for specialized purchases (automobiles, for instance) the awareness space changes very rapidly over time. Once ready to buy, consumers accumulate new information very quickly.

The third theme, preference, embraces all the peculiarities that remain in the choice of goods. Some explanations are psychological (automobiles

**Table 4.1** Approaches to consumer behavior

|  | Rational | Empirical | Psychological |
|---|---|---|---|
| Theory | 'Economic man' | Decision-making literature | Freud 'Sub-conscious' Pavlov: 'Conditioning' Veblen: 'Conspicuous consumption' Lewin: 'Micro-behavior' McLuhan: 'Media-technology' Piaget: 'The learning of children' Riesman: 'Inner- and outer-directed' Maslow: 'Hierarchy of needs' |
| Information (awareness) | Fully informed | Observed awareness space | Selective, overwhelmed by preference |
| Spatial interaction (activity space) | Gravity model, minimum distance | Observed activity space | A minor constraint |
| Preferences | Utility assumptions | Observed trade-offs | Based on chosen theory |
| Outcome | Central place theory | Observed store clusters and trends | Exploratory, oriented to advertising and design |

Source: The authors
Note: The implication of the three different viewpoints is reflected in the lower line 'outcome', which indicates how a store location might be arrived at. A 'rational' study of the market ordains that the store should be located at the center of the area. The 'empirical' analysis might incorporate the location of existing stores or traffic flows, plus the customer's perception of the market and sources of information. An 'attitudinal' approach might dispense with both theory and observation in favor of a massive advertising campaign to convince consumers that a 30-mile side trip to a certain store will make their friends envious and restore sexual vigor.

as sex symbols or reflections of personality), others anthropological (conspicuous consumption), and still others deal with the minutiae of behavior, such as a consumer's response to a salesperson or to different selling procedures.

Marketing techniques are available to help location analysts gain more information on each of these topics. Location analysis is at ease with the more empirical notions of activity space and awareness space, but less so with theories about preference. The latter are primarily important at the level of product and store design.

We will begin with a discussion of the basic consumption unit, the household, and then examine the household's weekly travel pattern and the variety of information that consumers can apply to the purchasing decision. We will examine consumer decision-making on three scales: first, the links

**Table 4.2** Obtaining data on consumer behavior

|  | General | Retail activity | Specific store |
|---|---|---|---|
| Activity patterns | Transportation studies Traffic flows Travel diaries | Traffic counts Street or mall interviews Parking lot surveys Credit card use | Customer lists Contest entries Store-front interviews Point-of-sale records |
| Awareness Information, choices available | Media distribution and penetration Phone interviews | Mapping the alternatives, content analysis of advertisements | Test information sources (e.g. coupons) Shopper interviews (e.g. Figure 4.1) |
| Preferences Attitudes | – | In-depth interviews by phone or in the home, using the full range of survey techniques. | |

Source: The authors

among the consumption of different goods that determine product mix within a store; second, the links among stores that result in various kinds of retail clusters; and third, the fundamental consumer trade-off, i.e. the choice between distance (in time and cost) to the store and the variety of goods (including amenity and price). Convenience or variety? Bargains or fancy labels? Is shopping a necessity or a recreation? Finally, we ask how the consumer's preferences affect the development of the distribution system.

Probing the mysteries of consumer behavior has been one of the major research interests of the last decade. However, because interviews are expensive and the local context (the set of choices available to a particular household) is so important, it is difficult to identify many hard and fast relationships.

**The household as a decision unit**

Most consumption decisions are made by household units. Households are defined as one or more people sharing the same dwelling space. In households of more than one person, individual members of the household may choose their own clothes or decide where to buy lunch separately, but overall budget constraints operate on the household as a whole – the food budget, the recreation budget, etc. Decisions about shelter and transportation affect the entire household and often certain members of the household are delegated the role of shopping for specific items.

The paragraph above is worded rather carefully. During the last two decades American households have become much more diverse. The traditional family-based household with Mom and Dad, two kids, and a dog has given way to half a dozen variants: the elderly couple, the single parent, the one-person, and the two-income household. The roles of individuals may be fundamentally different within each type of household. All these households have in common is that each contains fewer people than the traditional household. Table 4.3 suggests, in fact, that the man–wife–child family is now in the minority, constituting only 27 per cent of all households. Single mothers account for 8 per cent, and single-person households are now up to 23 per cent with one-half of the latter aged over 65 years. Another 15 per cent of family households are headed by a senior citizen.

Three aspects of the household as a consumption unit are significant. Who in the household buys? How much do they buy? Where do they buy? The demographic characteristics shown in Table 4.3 give clues to the possible allocation of consumption roles. How many adults? Are they all mobile? Do they have separate incomes? What purchases are likely to be pooled? Which goods are consumed individually? Is it likely that one household member will purchase certain goods for the rest? For example, mothers may buy children's clothes; it is usually males who buy power tools. This knowledge is important to marketers because, while the whole family may eat the same breakfast food, each member has different sources

**Table 4.3** The variety of American households

| Household category | Number | % | Average income ($) |
|---|---|---|---|
| All households | 86,788,000 | 100.0 | 27,460 |
| Family households | 62,706,000 | 72.3 | 31,280 |
| Married couples | 50,350,000 | 58.0 | 34,230 |
| Children under 18 | 24,210,000 | 27.8 | 34,390 |
| No children | 26,140,000 | 30.2 | 33,940 |
| Single parent | 12,357,000 | 14.2 | 18,424 |
| Children under 18 | 6,902,000 | 8.0 | 24,350 |
| No children | 5,454,000 | 6.3 | 10,930 |
| Male-led | 2,228,000 | 2.6 | 28,400 |
| Female-led | 10,129,000 | 11.7 | 17,270 |
| No earners | 9,221,000 | 10.6 | 15,490 |
| One earner | 17,949,000 | 20.7 | 24,880 |
| Two or more earners | 34,760,000 | 40.0 | 36,770 |
| Households 65 or over | 9,687,000 | 11.2 | 24,230 |
| Non-family households | 24,082,000 | 27.7 | 17,510 |
| Single person | 20,602,000 | 23.7 | 15,330 |
| Under 65 years | 12,491,000 | 14.4 | 18,200 |
| 65 or over | 8,111,000 | 9.3 | 10,910 |
| Two or more persons | 3,480,000 | 4.0 | 30,460 |

*Sources:* Bureau of the Census (1986); 'Money income of households, families and persons in the United States: 1984', *Current Population Reports, Series P-60*, no. 151

of information: different social contacts, exposure to different media, different associations.

Household composition is closely linked to disposable income. Single-parent households and the elderly tend to have small income streams and their consumption choices are severely restricted. Urban households with two wage-earners are surprisingly affluent, in contrast, with excess income either saved or allocated to luxury items such as travel, clothes, and cars. (By 1980 there were more families with two wage-earners than with one.) The differences in consumption induced by the variation in both household composition and income suggest how complex the study of consumer behavior has become.

The location of the household's purchases is determined by the weekly round of travel. Where do various members of the household have to be at various times of the day? Do they work? Go to school? Go to the movies? Go to the cottage? A knowledge of this travel behavior gives insight into the spatial mobility of household members, and hence their choices of places to shop and the amount of time devoted to shopping. Is it work or fun? Which family members are involved in the shopping process?

Gasoline retailers are especially concerned with household travel patterns because their location strategies are designed to serve people engaged in particular types of travel: in town or out of town, the route to work or trips around the neighborhood. A number of transportation studies have gathered data on weekly trip patterns through travel diaries that describe how family members spend their time and where they go on each journey within the urban area. For example, about 10 per cent of all urban trips are shopping trips and about 15 per cent of non-work time out of the home is spent on shopping. Shopping is an important element in the city's spatial fabric and travel patterns.

Bunting (1980) examined the variations in household activity patterns in a sample of households from a small city in Ontario, Canada. She was interested in how different households spend their discretionary time (that is, time not spent on work, school, sleeping, and personal care). She categorized households into eight types, approximately equal in number, shown in Table 4.4. Three family types stand out as particularly significant consumers: Group 8, the 'harried leisure class', spends relatively high proportions of time on both food and non-food shopping. Groups 2 and 7, church and home-oriented, respectively, also spend large amounts of time on shopping, but the latter is largely composed of low-income households which will spend less money than the other groups.

Bunting points out that these activity groups are not easily predicted by conventional economic and demographic measures. Their lifestyles and activity patterns reflect work situations, personal mobility, and choice of recreation, and will probably evolve as the household's size and age composition changes. A woman's decision to enter or leave the workforce

**Table 4.4** Household behavior groups

| Group label | Things they do | Things they don't do | Time spent on | | Socio-economic status | Demographics |
| --- | --- | --- | --- | --- | --- | --- |
| | | | Grocery shopping | Other shopping | | |
| Grasshoppers (1) | Family activities, organized social events, home-centered activities | None | Average | Average | Average | Young |
| Good-bodies (2) | Organized social events | None | High | Above average | High | Slightly older; wives at home |
| Gad-abouts (3) | Family activities | Organized social events | Low | Average | Average | Young single adult |
| Blahs (4) | None | Family activities, out-of-town trips, in-home activities | Low | Below average | Low | Old; working wives |
| Good timers (5) | Entertainment, organized social events | Family activities | Average | Above average | High | Older |
| Home-bodies (6) | Home-centered | Family activities, organized social events | Average | Low | Low | Older |
| Videos (7) | Family activities | Entertainment | High | Above average | Low | Wives at home |
| Go-getters (8) | Trips out-of-town, entertainment, organized social events | None | High | High | High | Working wives |

*Source:* Adapted from T. E. Bunting (1980) 'Styles of living in the city: a study of household behavioral systems', in L. Russwurm and R. Preston (eds) *Essays on Canadian Urban Process and Form*, vol. II, Waterloo, Department of Geography, University of Waterloo, Research Publication no. 15

is particularly important. Marketers will be interested in how well these behavior-based groups predict the choice of shopping location. If getting out of the house is in itself an effort, the distance to a shopping facility will probably prove to be a significant barrier. If shopping is an important, family-oriented recreation, the household may range far afield to seek out new shopping areas.

Bunting's typology differs from the other lifestyle classifications in that it is based on time budgets rather than questions about values and attitudes (see Exhibit 4.1). Advertisers argue at length about which characteristics of a household are most effective in predicting consumer decisions.

## The pool of information

What the retailer or shopping center manager really wants to know is 'Will they come to my store?' Shopping decisions begin within the consumer's head, in accumulated information about where stores are (including a sense of how far they are from other points) and what they offer. What kind of mental map of shopping choices does a consumer carry around? How can the store best use its advertising budget to alter this map?

Advertising aside, the consumer's information begins as the accumulation of past shopping experience, often built up over many years. It includes memories of visits to stores and an impression of their product mix, of window-shopping at nearby stores, and of stores glimpsed from a car during the daily round. The mental map is often distorted and full of holes. It may include stores that are now defunct or substantially changed while omitting newer places. Extensive sections of the city (anything off the main roads) are seldom visited or observed. Some retail activities may be misread or forgotten. Few consumers, in short, could draw a comprehensive map of retail opportunities in a city (see Exhibit 4.2).

Nonetheless, most people can direct you to a place to buy the basic products such as milk, newspaper, or gasoline, and can probably provide specific information about prices and opening hours as well. The greatest uncertainty, and thus most of the variation in knowledge from one person to another, concerns shopping goods activities. It is not only that these purchases occur less frequently, there is also a greater variance in stock carried, prices, brands, and service from store to store, as well as in the requirements of individuals. Parents and their teenagers, for instance, seldom shop in the same clothing stores if they can avoid it.

Incomplete knowledge about alternatives leads to poor decisions, so both consumer and retailer benefit from improved awareness. The consumer in search of a specialized, seldom-used retail activity may turn to the yellow pages, and in many cases the information gaps are filled by advertising.

In an urban environment where there are many alternative locations, a

## Exhibit 4.1
## CONSUMER BEHAVIOR SEGMENTS

The advertising industry, concerned as it is with symbols and images, likes to classify consumers according to preferences and attitudes rather than demographics or activity patterns. This may well be the best approach for those products that reflect lifestyles, such as restaurants or clothes. The two studies summarized below are based on questionnaires from nationwide samples. Consumers were asked how they felt about a wide range of consumption (and other) issues and these responses were used to identify groups of similar individuals.

The VALS (Values and Life Styles) study suggests that American consumers can be grouped into eight categories, combining attitudes to consumption with economic and demographic characteristics. The survey of Canadian women identifies five groups, and places a stronger emphasis on retail shopping behavior. Some common threads are apparent in both studies: 'belongers' (A2) and 'traditionalists' (B2); 'emulators' (A4) and 'strivers' (B5); 'sustainers' (A9) and 'insecure' (B4).

Interpreting and applying information about these market segments is an art form in itself. How do we translate these segments into advertising or location strategies? Whom do we target? How do we reach them? How, for example, can these groups be located in space?

## THE VALS CLASSIFICATION

| Group | Size (%) | Name | Characteristics |
|---|---|---|---|
| A1 | 2 | Integrated | Creative, prosperous, together |
| A2 | 33 | Belongers | Patriotic, stable, traditional, content, all ages |
| A3 | 25 | Achievers | Prosperous, self-assured, materialist, middle-aged |
| A4 | 10 | Emulators | Ambitious, believe in the system, young |
| A5 | 5 | 'I am me' | Unconventional, narcissistic, impulsive, experimental |
| A6 | 7 | Experiential | People-oriented, looking for inner growth |
| A7 | 9 | Socially-conscious | Mission-oriented, looking for causes, mature, successful, non-materialist |
| A8 | 4 | Survivors | Old, poor, not optimistic |
| A9 | 7 | Sustainers | Poor, resentful |

*Source:* A. Mitchell (1983) *The Nine American Life Styles*, New York: Macmillan

## SURVEY OF CANADIAN WOMEN

| Group | Size | Name | Attitude | Shopping behavior |
|-------|------|------|----------|-------------------|
| B1 | Independents | 44 | Equality of sexes, attached to work-force | Convenience buyers, less price sensitive, less brand loyalty, not attracted by coupons, give-aways, samples |
| B2 | Traditionalists | 28 | Women's place is in the home | Price conscious, read grocery ads, not attracted by convenience, brand loyalty |
| B3 | Shoppers | 10 | Budget sensitive, rural? | Pay cash, but not price sensitive, brand and store loyal, quality, accept no-names |
| B4 | Insecure | 9 | Lonely, unhappy | Bargain hunters, look for sales |
| B5 | Strivers | 9 | High personal expectations, self-confident, want to make money | Fashion oriented, experimental, try special offers, accept advice, use coupons |

*Source: Globe and Mail,* Toronto

change in a potential customer's perception about a store or shopping center (that it exists, has a wide selection of goods, is inexpensive, or whatever) may affect purchasing decisions more than modifications to the actual facilities, stock, or price structure. The customer's decision begins with the image, not the reality. The rewards to retailers or shopping center managers of manipulating this image are enormous, particularly for new stores that are trying to elbow their way into a competitive market. A new convenience store will often offer milk or cigarettes at a cut price for the first three months so that local residents will seek out the store and write it into their mental geography of the neighborhood.

Researchers have recently identified 'market mavens': consumers who spend enormous amounts of time and energy on the shopping experience – reading advertisements, comparing prices, exploring new stores – and telling other consumers (Feick and Price, 1987). Mavens may be key personalities in the diffusion of new shopping information.

A store's advertising campaign is often preceded by extensive marketing research that explores how well the shopping plaza is known and how it is compared to other places (Figure 4.1). The subsequent campaign may build on strengths (a quality image), or try to overcome weaknesses ('expensive'). Ideally, a retailer can supplement this information about shopping perceptions with hard data about actual behavior, such as the study of cross-shopping reported in Exhibit 4.3. Stores that are perceived in the same way ought to be visited by the same set of people with the same frequency.

Families with small children may be satisfied with the nearest supermarket, but as the families grow up and become more affluent they may look for more adventure in their shopping. The retailer may have to add a deli to the supermarket, or feature an Italian week, or organize a craft show. Chapter seven will discuss some of the strategies that have been developed to convert the bland standardized community shopping plaza into a center that can compete over a larger area or appeal to certain market segments.

Most households visit three or four shopping centers or retail strips periodically, and will explore new shopping opportunities as they become available. If one can make any generalization about urban life, it is that urban residents try to maintain a wide range of choice.

Exhibit 4.4 examines advertising as a marketing strategy, and the differences in advertising expenditures between department stores, retail shops, and supermarkets.

Exhibit 4.2
STUDENT PERCEPTIONS OF RETAIL OPPORTUNITIES:
TORONTO

Consumers make their choices from the set of shopping alternatives that exist within their minds. Retailers want to know what these images are. The maps shown below are the result of a class exercise in which college students in downtown Toronto were asked where they would go to shop for clothes, and their impressions of different shopping areas.

In each response, only three or four shopping districts are identified (Yonge and Queen, Eaton Centre), and often these alternatives are very far apart – including both downtown and a suburban mall, for example. Images of a retail district are shaped by experiences at a limited number of stores: for example, the Holt Renfrew store symbolizes Bloor Street to one student. Some people know one store intimately, others generalize about half a dozen. As a retailer, your problem is how to reinforce or modify these images and the shopping patterns that result from them. Do you want to win over those people who see an area as 'too expensive' or to attract those who see it as 'mass trendy'?

*Source:* The authors

Exhibit 4.2 *(continued)*

YONGE ST.

**YORKVILLE AVENUE**

HAZELTON LANES – EXPENSIVE
- GREAT FOR · HOMOGENEOUS FOR RICH
  IDEAS
EDDIE BAURER · TOO BRIGHT FOR MY TASTE

- BIG DECISION
- SPORTY
- FUN
- EXPENSIVE
- QUALITY

LE CHATEAN    BRA
BRAGUE    SHIRT HOUSE

- TRENDY    – FUN
- RIGHT-ON    – FAST
- QUALITY    – IMPULSIVE SHOPPING
- ME

**BLOOR ST.**

PIAGO (SHOES)
- QUALITY
- MODERN
- TRENDY
- WATCH OUT
  FOR GARBAGE

**DUNDAS ST.**

EATON CENTRE

- EXPENSIVE
- WIDE VARIETY
- TIRING TO SHOP IN
- LOOK FOR SALES
- MAIN STREAM

GLUE – GREAT
SKY

**QUEEN ST.**

(QUEEN ST. E. IN GENERAL)
- LOOK FOR DEALS
- LOTS OF POOR QUALITY,
  OLD GOODS WITH HIGH PRICE TAGS
- GOOD TO SHOP IF YOU HAVE
  LOTS OF TIME

FLYING
DOWN
TO
RIO

MY HOME

SCARBOROUGH
TOWN
CENTRE

- BRIGHT
- HOMOGENEOUS
- PREDICTABLE
- MIDDLE PRICED
- MASS TRENDY
- VARIETY

LIVED IN SAME HOME
FOR 22 YRS.

HARRY MANTTARI

Exhibit 4.2 (continued)

Christina Smit

```
Section A                1. Residence _____  2.  Apt. [ ]  House [ ]

Consumer                 3. Age  15-20 [ ]  20-30 [ ]  30-50 [ ]  50+ [ ]
Characteristics
                         4. Sex     M [ ]  F [ ]

                         5. Household size  1 [ ]  2 [ ]  3-4 [ ]  5+ [ ]

                         6. Household Income

                            Under $15K [ ]  15-25 [ ]  25-40 [ ]  40+ [ ]


Section B                Where would you most likely buy

Information              7. Milk      _____  _____  _____

                         8. Groceries _____  _____  _____

                         9. Clothing  _____  _____  _____

How many shopping plazas can you name?

1. _____        2. _____         3. _____

If not Jonesville
(Prompt) Any others _____  _____

If not Jonesville
(Prompt) Have you heard of Jonesville Plaza? Yes [ ]  No [ ]

If yes, have you ever shopped there? Yes [ ]  No [ ]


Section C
Image
Which of the following words do you associate with Jonesville Plaza?

                                 Yes      No     Perhaps
                    Expensive?   _____   _____   _____
                    Friendly?    _____   _____   _____
                    Attractive?  _____   _____   _____
                    Convenient?  _____   _____   _____
                    Unusual?     _____   _____   _____
```

**Figure 4.1** Questionnaire on shopping center image

*Source:* The authors

## Exhibit 4.3
## CROSS-SHOPPING IN LOS ANGELES

Most American urban households regularly frequent several shopping areas, department stores, supermarkets, etc. By asking which of the other locations a shopper visits we get a behavioral measure of similarity of stores or malls, from the consumer's viewpoint. This study of Los Angeles evaluated twenty-six different shopping areas, excluding downtown. A telephone sample of shoppers was asked where they had shopped within the last month. Virtually all customers had visited more than one location.

The study area is Los Angeles, spread over 60 miles with many barriers (mountains) and channels (the freeway system). The circles on the map represent the shopping centers, ranked by size (floor area). The arrows link each shopping center to the next most likely center that its patrons will visit. Note the effect of size. The largest center (South Coast Plaza) attracts most of the arrows. There are also distance effects, especially in the more isolated pockets such as the San Fernando Valley to the north-west, and there are lifestyle links – the line of affluent northern suburbs and Latino east Los Angeles. Finally, note the impact of the Santa Monica Freeway which makes South Coast Plaza the main alternative to a mall 30 miles away near Beverly Hills.

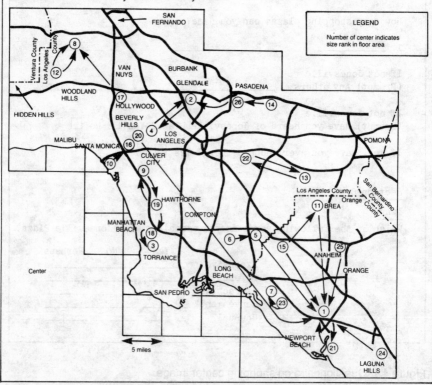

*Source:* Los Angeles Times Marketing Research Department (1987) *Regional Shopping Centers: Shopper Traffic and Duplication*

114

Exhibit 4.4
## ADVERTISING AS A MARKETING STRATEGY

Retailers are doubly concerned with consumer perceptions, i.e. how the products are viewed as well as the store. Yet retailers spend only 2.5 per cent of sales revenues on advertising, slightly less than the 3.1 per cent of the average for all US corporations. However, Sears Roebuck still spends $925 million per year, second only to Proctor and Gamble in total advertising expenditures.

### ADVERTISING RETAIL SALES

| Retail sector | | Supermarkets | | Department stores | |
|---|---|---|---|---|---|
| Restaurants | 3.8% | Kroger co. | 1.11% | Sears Roebuck | 2.38% |
| Apparel | 2.1% | Lucky Stores | 0.94% | K mart | 2.60% |
| Building products | 2.2% | Household Int. | 1.87% | J.C. Penney | 3.46% |
| Dept stores | 3.1% | Winn-Dixie | 1.23% | Federated Stores | 2.97% |
| Drug stores | 1.6% | A & P | 2.03% | Dayton-Hudson | 2.44% |
| Food | 1.4% | Supermarkets General | 1.15% | Montgomery Ward | 5.01% |
| Furniture | 6.5% | Stop and Shop | 1.92% | May Stores | 3.33% |
| Specialty | 5.6% | First National | 1.10% | Associated Stores | 3.96% |
| Variety | 2.2% | Cullum | 1.25% | Allied Stores | 3.66% |
| | | Pantry Pride | 1.71% | Carter Hawley Hale | 2.99% |

Note: Stores ranked by total sales

The differences in advertising expenditures among retail sectors largely reflect their positions along the spectrum from convenience (food, variety) to shopping goods (furniture). The less frequently we purchase a good, the less we know about where to find it and the more we look for additional information. All supermarket chains keep advertising at a low level, but in shopping goods sectors, such as department stores, the level of advertising expenditure is an important strategic option, hence the observed variation. Changing the customer's perception of the store may be a more cost-effective way to attract customers than reducing prices or hiring more staff, or it may not.

Source: Standard and Poor (1985) 'Special report-advertising', *Industry Surveys*, October 3

## The product mix of a retail sector

Although few stores stock exactly the same mix of products, the resemblances among them are sufficiently strong that 'drugstore' or 'bakery' immediately brings to the consumer's mind a list of expected goods. This expectation obliges the retailer to sell aspirin or bran muffins, respectively. We call these typical mixes of product 'kinds of business types', or 'retail sectors'. The Bureau of the Census goes to a great deal of trouble to identify stores according to their Standard Industrial Classification. The *Census of Retail Trade, 1982* distinguished eighty-six retail business types, along with ninety-six commercial consumer services, with aggregate data provided for each one (see Table 3.2).

How do these distinct business activities emerge? They reflect certain patterns of behavior and preference on the part of both the retailer and the consumer. Stores sell products that have similar spatial demand curves, that appeal to the same spatial set of households, and that have similar frequencies of purchase. Goods that appear in the same part of the spectrum between convenience goods and shopping goods are sold at the same store, e.g. milk, bread, newspapers, cigarettes.

The retailer also likes to stock goods that require the same kinds of sales or processing expertise. Butchers, beauticians, fashion experts, and interior decorators each take advantage of their own skills. It has taken a long time, but we have finally witnessed the separation of gasoline sales (which requires a minimum-wage, part-time employee) from automobile repair (which calls for a $25 per hour mechanic). All these jobs have in common is cars: the supply-side skills and consumer purchasing patterns are markedly different, but for years a mechanic would haul himself out from under a car in order to fill your tank. Sometimes retailers are pressured to sell entire lines of goods – plumbing fixtures, cosmetics, or outdoor clothes – by a manufacturer who insists on a certain product mix.

As retail analysis becomes more concerned with the bottom line of profits and growth, other aspects of product complementarity may be important. Is the rate of stock turnover comparable? Is the advertising target group the same? Do the seasonal fluctuations in the sales of different goods compensate for each other? Are the security problems and sales procedures sufficiently alike?

Exhibit 4.5 illustrates some of the decisions involved in stocking the shelves of a supermarket.

A central concern in determining product mix is the set of goods that a customer purchases at one time. What products are linked together (hamburgers, buns, and relish, hammer and nails, or shirts and ties for example?) The same question shapes the layout of the internal geography of the store. What products should be located side by side? Is there a rhythm or logic to purchasing? One of the most useful recent developments in retail analysis is point-of-sale monitoring. Computerized cash registers read and record product labels, providing a record of both products and brand names purchased by each customer (see Figure 4.2). If the customer uses a store charge card, the retailer also has access to a record of frequency of purchases, as well as an opportunity to map the spatial extent of the market.

Some advertising agencies are trying to correlate the purchase record

## Exhibit 4.5
## STOCKING THE SUPERMARKET

A supermarket may stock over 10,000 different products and brands and is faced each year with 2,000 new candidates, even though the shelf space stays the same. The problem is to give each product enough space to maintain the level of turnover, while introducing new ones and dropping those that don't sell. As many as 80 per cent of new products fail.

Can customers adapt as quickly as the mix of products changes? Do they want a product because it's new? Or because they've used it for 30 years?

What happens when the store adds a whole shelf of in-house brands? Which other products get pushed aside? The relationship between major supermarket chains and manufacturers' representatives involves some hard bargaining.

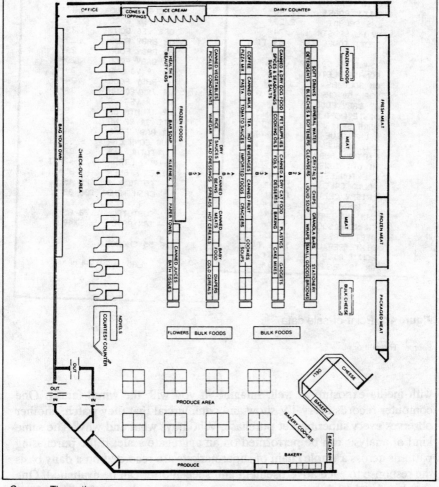

*Source:* The authors

```
                              GROCERY          . 63*
                         DHINE CK MIX        1. 06*
                         BAKED BEANS          . 61*
                         SCR N SPGE           . 51 TI
        "KASH-N-KARRY"    GLD MDL FLR          . 88*
    DISCOUNT SUPERMARKETS LL TUNA WTR          . 65*
 3/01/88  2:50PM STORE    880  LL TUNA WTR     . 65*
   CUST 150 REG  7 OPR    106  CHOC CREAM      . 67*
                               CAM CKN GMBO    . 51*
     PARSLEY BUCH      . 39*    SWANSON SOUP   . 47*
     GREEN ONION       . 35*     GROCERY       . 45*
     DAN BANANA        . 67*    5LB WHT POT    . 89*
     LL CREAM CHS      . 89*    GR BABY FOOD   . 29*
     HUB BUB COLA      . 33*TI  GR JR T/R HM   . 39*
     YOPL 150 STW      . 59*    HAW PCH ASCP   . 85*TI
     MORN SCRAMBL     1. 35*    WHITE GP JCE  1. 85*
     PK BL CHOPS      3. 95*    GG SWT PEAS    . 50*
     VITA HERRING     3. 75*    C CURLY NOOD   . 47*
     CHUCK ROAST      7. 40*    HZ BABY FOOD   . 24*
     L/S SALAMI       2. 29*    GRB VEG BCN    . 39*
     NY PL BRDSTK      . 74*    GR BABY FOOD   . 29*
     SCOTT TOWEL       . 69 TI  GR BABY FOOD   . 29*
                               GR BABY FOOD   . 29*
     . 54LB @ . 59/ LB          GR JR VG LMB   . 39*
     ROMAINE LETC      . 32*    HZ BABY FOOD   . 24*
     ON BOLO BF       1. 59*    GR JR VEG HM   . 39*
     YOP 150 CHRY      . 59*    GR JR VEG BF   . 39*
     HZ BABY FOOD      . 24*    GR JR MTM BF   . 39*
     DIXIE REFILL     1. 16 TI  GRB JR BF ND   . 39*
     BARB SEN SKI      . 99 TI  HZ BABY FOOD   . 24*
     L L TISSUE        . 95 TI  HUG CONN LAR  9. 68 TI
     L L TISSUE        . 95 TI      TOTAL  $  67. 87
     LIPTON SOUP       . 95*    7-UP 2 LTR    1. 42*TI
     HI DRI TOWEL      . 63 TI  HIRES RTBEER  1. 95*TI
     L L TOWELS        . 48 TI      TOTAL  $  71. 45
     POUND CAKE       1. 79*        CASH TEND 100. 00
     CRISPY CRITR     1. 89*
     HZ BABY FOOD      . 24*        SUBTOTAL   70. 05
     CAM CKN GMBO      . 51*        TAX PAID    1. 40
     SWANSON SOUP      . 47*
     DIET PEPSI       1. 42*TI  28. 55 CHANGE
     DIXIE REFILL     1. 16 TI
     BCNUT RICE C      . 63*        "LADY LEE VALUE"
     GR JR VEG TK      . 39*
```

**Figure 4.2** Point-of-sale data

*Source:* The authors

with media exposure as well. Imagine, if you will, the wired family. One computer records every TV show and commercial that they watch, another observes every supermarket purchase. Who buys what and why? The same kind of analysis can be performed on an aggregate scale: if the purchasing patterns across a whole chain of supermarkets are recorded on a daily basis the response to each advertisement and special offer can be evaluated. One firm has developed the capacity to give customers an instant feedback from their current purchases, in the form of coupons for future shopping trips: buy Pepsi now and they may give you a chance to try Coke, buy a large box of detergent and get a coupon for some other laundry item (e.g. Fluffy or bleach), buy cosmetics of a certain style and they give you a chance to sample another product linked to your age and gender.

The full implications of point-of-sale monitoring for simulating marketing decisions have not yet been realized. Enormous amounts of data are generated by these procedures – billions of transactions each year – and the output cannot be simplified until the marketing questions are defined more precisely. Each product has thousands of possible associations. A certain amount of experimentation is required on the supply side as well. How can you identify the purchasing link between power saws and band-aids until the customer has the opportunity to buy them jointly?

For large chains, a shift in product mix involves major investments in stock, layout, and promotion. You can bet your shirt that they would like to be able to simulate the possible costs and benefits of opening snackbars or selling lawn furniture ahead of time, instead of having to set up a test market.

The potential for analysis is choosing a product mix is illustrated in Exhibit 4.6.

## The retail cluster

Location analysis is particularly concerned with the retail cluster and the variety of retail clusters that make up the retail structure of an urban area. What mix of business types (hence of products) is appropriate for a given market? What business types require similar markets?

In this section some economic arguments are relevant. Chapter two described how the demand for a good declines with distance from the store, as the cost in time and money of consumer travel is effectively added to the selling price of the product. One way that this cost can be minimized is to share the costs of transportation among several products. This occurs when different stores are close enough together to enable the customer to buy a variety of goods in one stop. The clustering of stores in space increases consumption as a whole and benefits all retailers. In addition, many suscipient retailers depend on the traffic flow attracted to generative stores.

Store clustering is limited by the different market thresholds required by various business types. If the threshold market for an activity is small enough to support a store on every block, why should the consumer travel 5 miles to a shopping center? As the discussions of central place theory will argue in the next chapter, the solution has been to form a hierarchy of retail clusters of different threshold size; appropriate groups of stores to serve the neighborhood, the community, and the region.

## Exhibit 4.6
## PROFITABILITY AND PRODUCT MIX

The potential for analysis in choosing a product mix is shown in this data from the National Retail Merchants Association which describes production functions for various product groups within a department store. All numbers are median values for a sample of eighty department stores. These data lead to a kind of a bid rent curve study within the store. As a result, major department stores are increasing their emphasis on soft goods over hard goods, and expanding their lines of cosmetics and women's accessories and giving them more space on the main floor. Because of their high level of inventory per square foot, these goods generate more sales and more profitability per unit area. 'Each department must have a logic.' Those that don't measure up are eliminated or franchised.

| | Share of dept store sales (%) | Turnover | Gross margin (%) | Markdown (%) | $ per sq. ft | | | |
| --- | --- | --- | --- | --- | --- | --- | --- | --- |
| | | | | | Sales | Inventory | Margin | Profit |
| Women's clothes | 35.2 | 3.6 | 43.9 | 24.3 | 153 | 45 | 70 | 55 |
| Women's accessories | 8.5 | 3.1 | 46.2 | 12.0 | 222 | 68 | 107 | 112 |
| Men's clothes | 14.6 | 2.7 | 41.1 | 20.1 | 173 | 61 | 79 | 63 |
| Children's clothes | 5.8 | 3.0 | 42.4 | 22.2 | 106 | 34 | 47 | 77 |
| Shoes | 4.8 | 2.1 | 40.2 | 24.6 | 170 | 96 | 113 | 67 |
| Cosmetics/drugs | 6.1 | 2.3 | 38.7 | 1.9 | 238 | 131 | 185 | 94 |
| Recreation | 3.8 | 2.2 | 31.5 | 12.0 | 179 | 59 | 106 | 37 |
| Furnishing | 14.3 | 1.9 | 36.7 | 14.7 | 87 | 44 | 72 | 33 |

*Source:* National Retail Merchants Association (annual) *Merchandising and Operating Results*, New York
*Note:* Profit = Margin − direct operating expenses

Regardless of the economic logic for retail clusters, most consumers accept the existing network of retail facilities and build them into their weekly travel rounds. Originally, retail location theory was based on studies of dispersed farmsteads whose residents wished to minimize the number of trips required to neighboring towns: nowadays we deal with a multi-person, multi-trip household in which shopping may be linked to work trips (e.g. gasoline purchase), recreation (restaurants, gift shops) or social activity. The particulars of the household's travel pattern have become even more important in forming a store cluster. Should the stores be open in the evening? On Sundays? How valuable is a retail site near the workplace of 2,000 people, compared to one that is next to a large apartment building?

Today's households are more diverse than ever and shop under a variety of conditions. As we will discuss in Part two of the book, the response has been to make retail facilities more specialized. The basic community shopping center is the place to buy the weekly groceries and the kids' shoes, but for recreational shopping the family may seek an ethnic or lifestyle district, a tourist-oriented facility, or a boutique area. Individual retailers in these shopping areas depend on the size, variety, and attractiveness of the district as a whole in order to make the household's trip worthwhile.

The advent of the planned shopping center in the 1950s, with carefully selected tenants and a floor plan designed to manipulate customer flows and maximize sales, stimulated a number of studies of the behavior of shoppers within a retail cluster. These studies built on a long tradition of concern with pedestrian flows in the downtown area. Retailers have always linked their sales, rents, and land values to the number of people passing by the store, and city planners are aware of how sensitive these pedestrian flows are to changes in transit stops, or the locations of parking lots, or to new buildings or demolitions.

The first extensions to this approach involved interviews with shoppers on the street or in the mall, as shown in Figure 4.3. (Careful attention must be given to the spatial distribution of the sample since the location of the interviews will affect the results.) The answers to the question 'Which stores did you intend to visit at this center?' indicate the significant generative activities, while the responses to 'Which stores have you visited so far?' may suggest the suscipient activities, but also the significant linkages of activities for various kinds of shoppers. For example, a teenager might mention a record store, a video arcade, and a pizza stand; a business person might list a bank, a drugstore, and a delicatessen. Over the years shopping center developers have learned how to fine-tune the mix of activities; often combining a number of different price ranges and shopping amenities for popular retail activities.

More sophisticated studies of consumer behavior within shopping districts actually trace the customer's path from entry point (parking spot or transit stop) to exit, permitting store-to-store links to be identified. Which stores are most frequently visited? Which pairs of stores are visited in succession? Does anyone ever go to the bank after shopping? What about window-shopping? Where do people pause? Hurry past?

Pedestrian flows through a regional shopping mall are shown in Figure 4.4. Note the reasonably even contribution of each of the access points from outside (ranging from 1.1 to 4.2 per cent of the total), the balanced attraction of the two department stores; and the imbalance between the two supermarkets and the intensification of flow in the central mall. Electronic devices are now available to monitor flows at any location at any time.

Studies such as these provide the raw material for the design of large shopping plazas (see Figure 4.5). Most designs incorporate some common principles:

Customer Profile:

1. Employed? 77%; Unemployed 4%; Housewife 9%; Retired 5%;
   Student 5%

2. Type of Job? Man.-Prof. 30%; Sales/Clerical 26%; Trades 11%;
   Other 9%

3. Place of Work? City/Downtown 35%; Rest of Metro 14%; Other 28%

4. Income Range? $40K+ 17%; 30-40 15%; 20-30 28%; 10-20 25%;
   under 10K 10%

5. Sex? Male 42%; Female 58%

6. Married? Married 46%; Single 43%; Formerly married 11%

7. Age? 18-19 7%; 20-24 17%; 25-29 17%; 30-39 16%; 40-49 15%;
   50-64 17%; 65+ 6%

8. Household Size? 1 24%; 2 30%; 3 16%; 4 14%; 5 10%; 6+ 5%

9. Residence? Downtown 20%; Rest of City 9%; N. York 12%; Rest of
   Metro 16%; Rest of CMA 6%; Rest of Ont. 13%; Rest of Can. 6%;
   USA 12%

Travel

10. Mode? Subway 47%; Walk 28%; Car 23%; Bus 23%; Train 3%

11. Subway Station? Dundas 26%; Queen 16%; Other 1%

12. Starting Place? Downtown 56%; Rest of Metro 29%; Extended
    Suburbs 7%; Other 7%

13. Travel Time? 10 mins. 28%; 10-20 23%; 20-30 19%; 30-45 14%;
    45+ 17%

Shopping Patterns

14. Have you been in a store yet? Yes 61%; No 39%

15. Bought anything? Yes 33%; No 67%

16. Planning to Buy Anything? Yes 45%; No 32%; Maybe 23%

17. Did you eat, drink here? Yes 36%; No 64%

18. Planning to? Yes 43%; No 40%; Maybe 11%

**Figure 4.3** Shopping mall survey results

*Source:* The authors

GROUND FLOOR

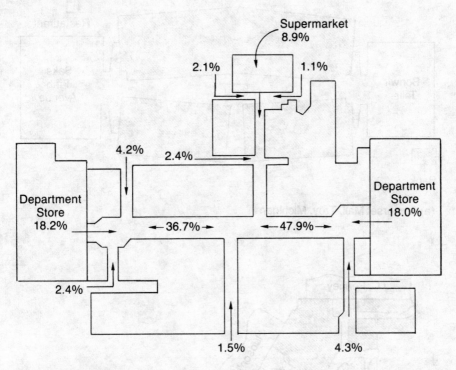

SECOND FLOOR

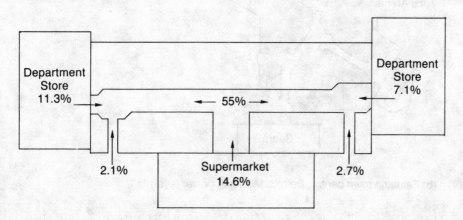

**Figure 4.4** Pedestrian flows in a regional shopping center

*Source:* The authors
*Note:* Flow values equal the percentage of shoppers entering the mall. Flows within the mall are related to the same base.

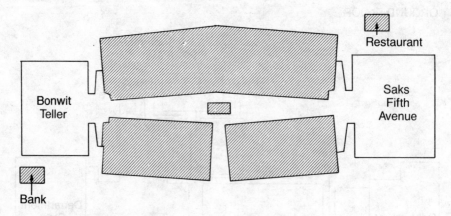

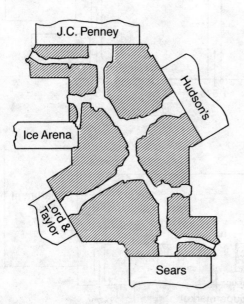

(a) Somerset Mall, Troy, Michigan

(b) Fairlaine town center, Detroit, Michigan (lower level)

**Figure 4.5** Examples of mall layouts

*Note:* Shaded areas refer to the retail selling areas occupied by mall tenants.

(c) World of Shops, Renaissance Center, Detroit, Michigan (street level)

1. The large anchor (generative) tenants are placed at the ends of an internal mall, so that customers will visit both ends and pass by the smaller suscipient stores in the process.
2. Access is strictly controlled to minimize the number of mall exits at intermediate locations, so that customers cannot escape. Downtown malls try to create an internal street parallel to the real one.
3. This 'street' is often curved or zigzagged, in order to extend the street length and increase the number of store-fronts.
4. Clusters of closely related or competitive activities may provide subfoci in their own right. Food stores are grouped near the supermarket. Fast-food outlets form a 'gourmet court' with communal tables and seating facilities. Retailers serving different age or income groups are kept

125

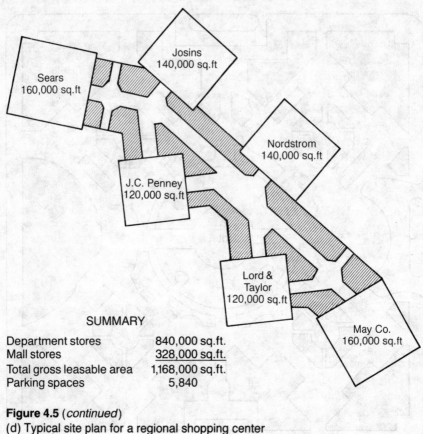

Sears
160,000 sq.ft

Josins
140,000 sq.ft

Nordstrom
140,000 sq.ft

J.C. Penney
120,000 sq.ft

Lord &
Taylor
120,000 sq.ft

May Co.
160,000 sq.ft

SUMMARY

| | |
|---|---|
| Department stores | 840,000 sq.ft. |
| Mall stores | 328,000 sq.ft. |
| Total gross leasable area | 1,168,000 sq.ft. |
| Parking spaces | 5,840 |

**Figure 4.5** (*continued*)
(d) Typical site plan for a regional shopping center

separate; stores catering to teenagers, for example, are segregated from upscale retailers. In the very largest centers the fashion stores and the mass market retailers may be located on different floors or in different wings.

In unplanned retail clusters, particularly outside the central area of the city, retailers and planners may wish to know which stores actually interact and which simply share an accessible location. The latter are readily relocated, the former may require special parking facilities and traffic arrangements. Such a study, carried out in Edmonton, Alberta, is reproduced in Figure 4.6. The Whyte Avenue retail cluster has two anchor stores: the Army and Navy department store and the supermarket. Other retailers show strong linkages with the department store but some are surprisingly isolated. Gas stations, it turns out, have very few local linkages but banks have many.

We will argue in Chapters seven and eight that several new forms of retail cluster are emerging in urban areas to serve markets which are often spatially dispersed, catering to the Hispanic community, for example, or to the tourist trade. Each specialized district will have its own characteristic internal linkages and pedestrian flow, and urban planners will have to give considerable attention to the impact on pedestrian flows of such things as parking spaces, non-retail activities (a fire hall?) and high-traffic streets. As within the suburban plaza, the goal should be to spread pedestrian flow evenly, without barriers to movement, perhaps channelled in a mall or loop to permit optimal location of the participating activities. How do we retain the charm and vitality of a Chinatown as it expands along a major traffic artery?

## Distance and variety

The spatial distribution of retail activity – the central concern of the location analyst – depends on the customer's preference for one shopping area over another. While the household's information about opportunities (awareness space) and weekly travel pattern (activity space) are clearly important in these decisions, the ultimate issue is how people trade off distance against variety or amenity.

Consider family C, living in an older suburb of a medium-sized metropolitan area such as Seattle (see Figure 1.4). Dozens of shopping areas are available to them: a couple of older downtown retail clusters and many plazas and retail strips. During the weekly round perhaps a half-dozen of these areas are visited by various members of the household, but over a year another dozen or more special stores or shopping districts are explored. Distances are short; the options are many; the household uses several locations within a short period. The relative frequencies of visits – hence volume of sales – to these shopping alternatives is the central concern of retailers, developers, and planners who wish to forecast and manipulate sales at any one location. How does the household decide?

The simplest, most mechanical solution combines distance and variety concepts into a mathematical relationship:

Trips (or sales) from household i to center j =
$f$ (distance$_{ij}$, floor area$_j$) (eqn 4.1)

where floor area is a surrogate measure for the variety of stores and products at the shopping center. When specified more precisely as

$$(\text{Trips/household})_{ij} = K \times (\text{Area}_j)^{b1} / d_{ij}^{b2} \qquad \text{(eqn 4.2)}$$

the relationship is called a gravity model. $K$, $b_1$ and $b_2$ are constants to be evaluated in specific situations, usually by means of the statistical technique called regression analysis. Such a model, when applied to a series of

# Processes

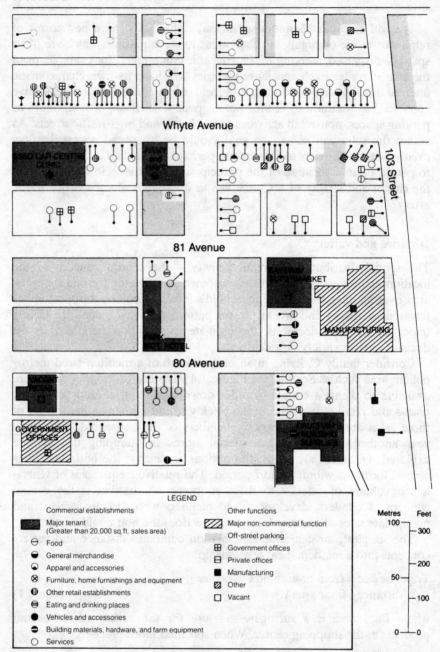

Whyte Avenue

81 Avenue

80 Avenue

LEGEND

**Commercial establishments**

Major tenant
(Greater than 20,000 sq.ft. sales area)

⊖ Food

◗ General merchandise

◔ Apparel and accessories

⊗ Furniture, home furnishings and equipment

❶ Other retail establishments

⊜ Eating and drinking places

● Vehicles and accessories

⊜ Building materials, hardware, and farm equipment

○ Services

**Other functions**

⊘ Major non-commercial function

Off-street parking

⊞ Government offices

⊟ Private offices

■ Manufacturing

▨ Other

□ Vacant

Metres   Feet

100 ——
           —— 300

           —— 200

50 ——
           —— 100

0 —— 0

**Figure 4.6** Links among stores in a retail strip

*Source:* D.B. Johnson (1978) 'Unplanned commercial nucleation as a regional shopping center', in P.J. Smith (ed) *Edmonton: The Emerging Metropolitan Pattern*, Western Geographical Series, vol. 15, pp 59–91. Reproduced by permission of the author and the Western Geographical Series

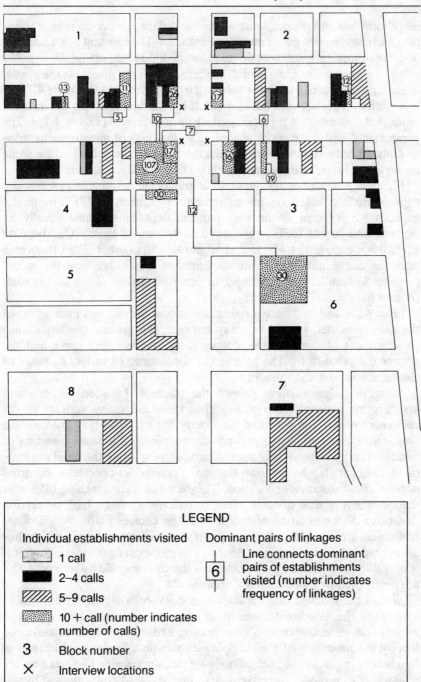

LEGEND

Individual establishments visited

Dominant pairs of linkages

░░░ 1 call

■ 2–4 calls

▨ 5–9 calls

▒▒ 10 + call (number indicates number of calls)

3 Block number

X Interview locations

Line connects dominant pairs of establishments visited (number indicates frequency of linkages)

**Figure 4.6** (*continued*)

neighborhoods and plazas, summarizes the distance decay curves for shopping and convenience goods shown in Figure 2.4. The constant $b_2$ is a measure of the customer's sensitivity to distance for this kind of shopping: the larger its value, the greater the friction of distance. Similarly, $b_1$ measures the appeal of center size. In urban areas the values of $b_2$ range from 1.00 (Figure 4.7a) to 2.00 with $b_1$ lying between 0.5 and 1.0. If $b_2 = 2$ then doubling the distance reduces the number of trips (and sales) to one-quarter (Figure 4.7b). The parameter K scales the result according to the units of measurement (trips or dollars per household) and permits the model to be calibrated for some aggregate of households (a neighborhood), or for different time periods.

Figure 4.8 describes the input to a gravity model analysis of bowling trips in Buffalo based on phone interviews (Lieber, 1977). The model explains 81 per cent of the map pattern, depending almost equally on distance and size of facility (measured as number of lanes). One bowling alley, it appears, is virtually interchangeable with another. For other retail activities one might incorporate measures of social class into the model (well-to-do families travel further), or other properties of the facility itself (does it have a bar? restaurant?).

Over time, and in different spatial situations, the two key parameters of the gravity model, $b_1$ and $b_2$, may change. The greater the importance (cost? time?) of distance, the steeper the distance decay curve and the greater the value of $b_2$. The greater the significance of variety or range of choice, the greater the value of $b_1$.

Some investigators have probed the trade-off between distance and diversity more deeply, recognizing that there are many variants in the response pattern. The poor and the elderly, for example, may not have the time, money, or mobility to expend on shopping, while some members of middle-class households take great pleasure in exploring the retail environment. Other studies have shown that many consumers operate on distorted notions about distance or location. They are not truly weighing off center size or variety against distance, time, or cost but against a hazy perception that plaza X seems to be further away. The choices made by individual consumers are also affected by the particular spatial structure in which they are embedded. If they live next door to a large shopping center no trade-off is necessary and their response obscures the choice made by shoppers who are confronted by more complex situations.

Within the modern metropolitan area distance is rapidly giving way to variety as the dominant element in shaping consumer behavior. The variation in shopping choices is increasing and attractiveness is measured less by the sheer size of the shopping district than by its specialization in function or in market segment. Shopping plaza managers, like retailers, are attempting to project distinctive images that will lead consumers to bypass other shopping opportunities.

In part, such a response reflects the decline in travel time and the

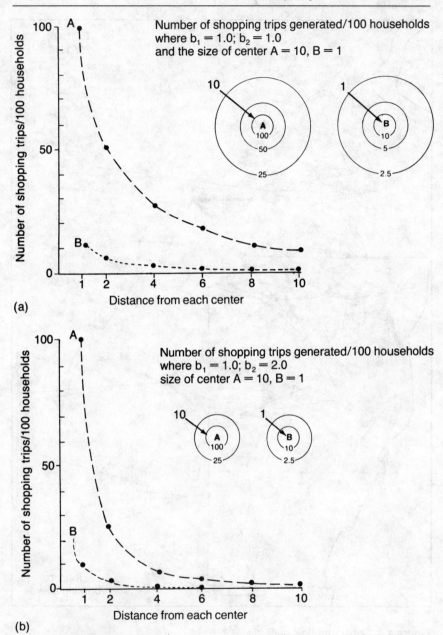

**Figure 4.7** The gravity model
(a) Low friction of distance
(b) High friction of distance

*Source:* The authors

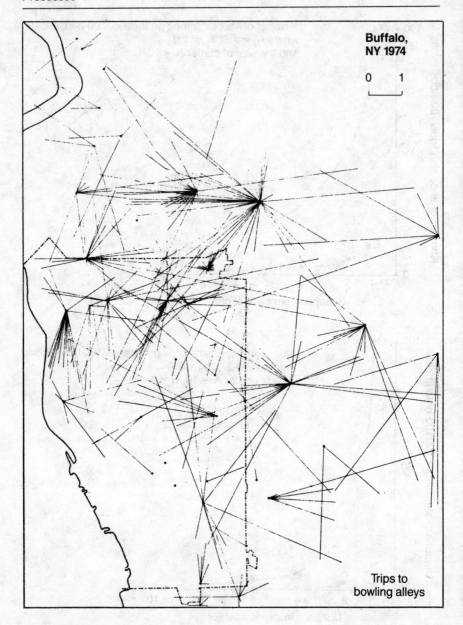

**Buffalo, NY 1974**

0      1

Trips to bowling alleys

**Figure 4.8** Consumer flow patterns

*Source:* S. Lieber (1977) 'Attitudes and revealed behavior: a case study'. *Professional Geographer* 29,1 53–8. Reproduced by permission of The Association of American Geographers

increased mobility (more cars per household) of urban life, but it is also part of the continuing shift away from the necessities of life towards luxury goods as North Americans become more affluent. Variety and diversity are part of the attraction of the urban lifestyle. Money and leisure transform a trip to the store from a frustrating drudgery to a pleasant self-indulgence. Contrast the single mother with three kids and a tight budget, counting her pennies in a no-frills supermarket, with the elegant matron in a gourmet food store, filling her baskets with all the world's delicacies. The well-to-do have always been less sensitive to distance than the poor and in major cities the shops of the downtown area have largely catered to the elite. A variety of products, architecture, and shopping environments has a powerful attraction. It is not just simple size: small towns with picturesque main streets, old mill buildings, and new boutiques attract customers from as far as 50 miles away.

As a final note, we should point out that some customers go to the other extreme in the distance/variety trade-off: they may refuse to travel at all and shop at home by means of direct sales or catalog shopping. Both techniques have been around a long time, from the days of the pedlar, the Fuller Brush Man and the Sears Roebuck catalog, but both have been transformed in recent years. Direct sales firms such as Amway, Tupperware, and Avon Products account for over 2 per cent of all retail sales. Although catalog sales still account for less than 1 per cent of all retail sales, a trend towards upscale merchandizing by catalog is apparent. Everyone wants those New York Fifth Avenue labels or the chance to buy from the Neiman–Marcus Christmas catalog. Upmarket magazines (*Atlantic Monthly, Harper's*, The *New Yorker*) and newspapers (Sunday NY *Times*) aimed at affluent suburbanites across the country, are heavy with advertisements for mail-order merchandise.

## Consumer preference and the retail landscape

The great debate in marketing economics revolves around the role of consumer preference, the idea that the actions and choices of consumers determine the stores and goods and services that they receive. 'I'm only giving the customers what they want', has been the cry of sellers of dubious goods since long before Christ cleared the Temple.

Modern economic theory takes up this point of view, arguing that all market transactions must begin with a demand curve of some kind and that a growth in sales of a product probably reflects some kind of growth in demand. People buy T-shirts with little animals on them because the animal symbols are important to their psychic well-being. Arguments in favor of consumer preference emphasize the level of competition for the consumer's dollar. There are a myriad of competing goods, from flowers to liquor to trips to the Caribbean; there are hundreds of stores competing to sell these goods and clusters of stores exist in different parts of the city. The enormous surplus of retail facilities guarantees that the consumer is king.

Those on the other side of the debate take these same arguments and twist them around. They argue first, that consumption is just as much shaped by the supply side as by demand. At the ball-park people pay high prices for lousy hot dogs because that's all there is. If health-food stores replaced taverns we would all live longer. Consumers are constrained to buy the goods available at the locations available.

However, the main thrust of the arguments about the manipulation of the consumer, as laid out by Leiss (1976), is that the widespread availability of goods and services and the intensive advertising of their merits has created a culture of consumption in which information about new products and prices is as important to newspaper readers as the news itself, and in which new demands are continuously created. A stunning example of this ability to create new demands is the achievement of the international diamond cartel. The cartel decided to boost the size of the world market by convincing Japanese brides that their happiness depended on the gift of a diamond. After 15 years of diligent promotion by an advertising agency the proportion of Japanese brides who wore diamonds increased from 5 per cent to over 60 per cent, creating the second largest market in the world.

The size of the advertising industry and the associated media activities are the strongest evidence in support of the manipulated consumer. Expenditures on various forms of advertising amounted to almost $90 billion in 1984, the equivalent of 5 per cent of all retail and service sales. A sizeable proportion of the value of a product is devoted to convincing consumers that it is what they really want.

Both sides of the debate contain some truth. Over a long period North Americans have created a juggernaut of consumption: a combination of expectations and lifestyles that drive the entire economy. New products are created and old ones revised to create new needs. However, it is not only the product that is sold: every beer advertisement sells beer as a way of life as much as it sells a brand name and every TV situation comedy shows viewers how they should live and what they should buy.

In the short-term, however, consumers do choose – even if only between different advertising campaigns. Because of the oversupply of retail facilities, most households can take their pick among several brands of stores or plazas. The constant turnover of product lines, the opening and closing of chain outlets, and the high failure rate of new retail enterprises testify to the uncertainty of retail planning – uncertainty created partly by the fickleness of the consumer, who looks for something new, if not necessarily better.

To sum up then, in an affluent, highly mobile world, with an excess of retail facilities, the consumer has considerable influence in determining the variety and form of retail activity. Unfortunately for retailers and planners, these choices are not easily predictable. Consumers are not really irrational, but they operate within a web of other non-retailing activities and preferences that interact with the choices that have been discussed here. If pay television or videocassette recorders absorb large amounts of leisure time, then shopping is relegated to a weekly chore. If work activity becomes more meaningful, there may be less pressure (and time) to consume. Despite their undoubted importance, shopping trips and shopping time are still overshadowed by family, community, and workplace. Hence the mysteries.

## Further reading

Bacon, R. W. (1984) *Consumer Spatial Behaviour: A Model of Purchasing Decisions over Space and Time*, London: Oxford University Press.

Bunting, T.E. (1980) 'Styles of living in the city: a study of household behavioural systems', in L. Russwurm and R. Preston (eds) *Essays on Canadian Urban Process and Form* vol. II, research publication no. 15, Waterloo: Department of Geography, University of Waterloo, pp. 367–392.

Darien, J.S. (1987) 'In-home shopping: are there consumer segments?' *Journal of Retailing* 63, 2: 163–186.

Feick, L.F. and Price, L.L. (1987) 'The market maven: a diffuser of marketplace information', *Journal of Marketing* 51, 1: 83–7.

Johnson, D.B. (1978) 'The unplanned commercial nucleation as a regional shopping centre', in P.J. Smith (ed.) *Edmonton: The Emerging Metropolitan Pattern*, Western Geographical Series vol. 15: 59–91.

Leiss, W. (1976) *The Limits to Satisfaction*, Toronto: University of Toronto Press.

Lieber, S. (1977) 'Attitudes and revealed behavior: a case study', *Professional Geographer* 29: pp. 53–8.

Lloyd, R. and Jennings, D. (1978) 'Shopping behavior and income: comparisons in an urban environment', *Economic Geography* 54, 2: 157–67.

Lord, J.D. (1986) 'Cross shopping flows among Atlanta's regional shopping centers', *International Journal of Retailing* 1, 1: 33–54.

Lynch, K. (1960) *The Image of the City*, Cambridge, Mass.: MIT Press.

Mazursky, D. and Jacoby, J. (1986) 'Exploring the development of store images', *Journal of Retailing* 62, 2: 145–65.

Mitchell, A. (1983) *The Nine American Lifestyles: Who We Are and Where We Are Going*, New York: Macmillan.

Potter, R.B. (1982) *The Urban Retailing System: Location, Cognition and Behaviour*, Aldershot: Gower Publishing.

Settle, R.B. and Alreck, P.L. (1986) *Why They Buy: American Consumers Inside Out*, New York: John Wiley & Sons.

Shepherd, D. and Thomas, C.J. (1980) 'Urban consumer behaviour', in J. Dawson (ed.) *Retail Geography*, London: Croom Helm.

Stanley, T.J. and Sewall, M.A. (1976) 'Image inputs to a probabalistic model: predicting retail potential', *Journal of Marketing* 40, 1: 48–53.

# Retail structure

The four chapters which follow explore the landscape of retail facilities that has emerged from the processes described in Part One. How do the decisions of the various participants – consumers, retailers, and developers – combine to produce the patterns that we observe: the stores, the retail clusters, and, to a considerable degree, the entire settlement system?

The primary goal of this part of the book is to describe, i.e. to identify, classify, and map various retail phenomena. Two different spatial scales are used. Chapters five and six consider the allocation of retail activity among different kinds of urban settlements: metropolitan areas, cities, towns, and villages. What mix of retail facilities can we expect in each of these? How does the size of each market translate into sales in the various retail sectors, and how do retail sales shape a combination of stores of different types and sizes? Very powerful regularities in retail structure exist at this spatial scale because of the great differences in market size. For retail chains the need to administer and supply a network of outlets imposes an additional distance constraint. The branch stores must all be linked to the headquarters of the chain in some fashion. As a result, we observe a number of different strategies for the location and expansion of chain activities.

Chapter six extends the discussion of location problems at this spatial scale to the processes of change. We note the contributions of population and income growth to changes in retail structure, as well as the effect of greater consumer mobility. On the supply side, we observe the shifts toward larger stores with fewer sales personnel. The processes examined in Part one are applied to the interpretation of changes in the retail landscape.

Within the metropolitan area, the problem is more complex. In addition to variation by size of market, opportunities exist for all kinds of specialized facilities, e.g. ethnic shopping areas, boutique districts, used car strips. Chapter seven first identifies the variety of these retail clusters and then examines their magnitudes, locations, and functions. How big is downtown and what role does it play within the metropolitan area? Where do regional shopping centers locate? Chapter eight examines the patterns of change within the metropolis. Within the metropolitan region, distinctive new retail elements have emerged as planned centers, introduced to most cities less than 40 years ago, now dominate much of the city. Downtown malls have sparked the redevelopment of the city center. There is continuing competition between the suburban mass retailers and the specialized retail districts in the older part of the city. The retail structure at any point in time is a transient phenomenon, a delicate balance between demand and supply. How quickly does it adjust to changing conditions?

Any observed change in the pattern of distribution activity may reflect changes in demand (the market size) or supply (the retailing technology), or in both. The first is the province of the location analysts and the second is tackled in marketing studies by the business school, but neither can be interpreted without some knowledge of the other. For example, a cluster of vacant stores in a town center could be a sign of slow or negative growth in the surrounding area but is more likely to reflect the construction of a shopping center on the periphery or shifts in cost structures that favor larger stores.

Much of the emphasis in this descriptive part of the book necessarily falls on the aggregate pattern of retail activity in shopping centers and various retail clusters, but these spatial distributions also define the environment in which the individuals in the retail system operate. The retail chain or shopping center developer needs to understand these patterns in order to make locational choices. What set of cities comprise the bulk of the west coast market? Where should the next outlet be? How much can the chain afford to pay for a lease in a new shopping mall?

These shopping locations – aggregates of stores – represent distinct markets as well as patterns of competition. Within a metropolitan area, for instance, there may be dozens of alternative locations: high/low income, Black or Hispanic areas, central/suburban. How does a chain choose between these options? Each retail chain appears to define a different niche, a different combination of market characteristics, which imposes a distinct set of location requirements. We will look at a few examples of these decisions as a way of setting the stage for the discussion of location analysis in Part three.

# Retailing and the settlement pattern

**The twenty-five largest urban areas constitute half of the American market.**

**All other geographical variation pales in comparison with the extraordinary differences in the size of cities.**

**Only a few hundred retail chains are truly national in the sense of operating in every region of the country.**

**Des Moines, Iowa is the most popular market research test location in America.**

This chapter describes how retail and service activities are sorted out among settlements. These local markets are defined by the rapid decline in the density of consumer households as one moves out from the city center into the countryside. These villages, towns, and cities are as much a product of the distribution system as they are its cause. Stores serve the spatial markets represented by settlements, but settlements are also built around retail and service activities.

The settlement system poses some interesting marketing problems. The individual retail entrepreneur is concerned both with market potential – the likelihood of population growth and increased income – and with market profile – the details of income and demographic composition. The retail chain is also interested in these issues but within a larger context, that of location strategy. What is the most appropriate location for the next store given the existing network of stores? Is the firm's goal to maintain market share across the spatial system so as to be represented in all settlements? To maximize the return at the outlet in question, i.e. to choose the best city? To increase sales for the chain as a whole? Each of these goals could lead to a different choice of settlement in which to locate the next store.

The sections below explore the retail hierarchy, defined as the variation in retail and service activity with city size. Two complementary arguments interpret these patterns: the extensive literature on Central Place Theory examines the place-to-place variation that results from the pattern of demand, while Vance (1970) and Brown (1981) look at the locational logic imposed by access to source of supply.

The retail complexes of neighboring settlements may compete with, or complement each other. Places that are the same size and that serve approximately the same size of market possess the same kinds of stores and services and compete against one another for the trade of the intervening region. However, centers that differ in size include different mixes of stores in their retail hierarchy and can coexist in uneasy harmony, since each performs different tasks for the nearby region. The larger city may provide wholesale and business services for both centers while the small city provides less specialized retail activity for a local trade area.

## The settlement pattern

The location decisions of retailers occur at two levels: on the settlement scale the entrepreneur selects the city or town which the store will serve, on the retail structure scale a particular neighborhood and site are identified. Two essential differences distinguish these two levels of location decision. At the settlement level the market size and trade area are determined by the size and spatial structure of the settlement. A location in Peoria gives access to 150,000 people while a site in Chicago is potentially accessible to twenty times as many people. A Peoria retailer has little chance of modifying the market size since the secondary trade area, extending into the countryside, is severely constrained by distance. In contrast, within the larger metropolitan area, local markets are often determined by the location of a competitor or by the size of an urban market segment defined by income, age, or ethnicity, and they can be substantially modified by the retailer (or by a competitor).

Also, decisions to locate in one settlement instead of another are relatively unaffected by the actual site cost of the land or the land rent which will not vary greatly from one city to the next. However, within the urban area these costs may vary greatly and play an important role in site selection. A downtown Peoria location probably costs much the same as one in nearby downtown Springfield, but a downtown Chicago location costs more than one in suburban Cicero and excludes many retailers because of the high cost.

The primary market is bounded in space by the decline in population density at the edge of the settlement (remember Figure 2.1). In this chapter, these primary markets will be treated as separate units (metropolitan statistical areas, cities, towns) and sometimes in combination with the surrounding secondary trade area of the settlement (urban regions, service areas). Within a nation or state the variation in the population or income of settlements, hence in market size, is described by an asymmetric histogram, often treated as a log-normal distribution (see Figure 5.1). Because of the enormous range in population of settlements, from perhaps twenty households in a hamlet with a population of seventy-five to three or four million in major markets like New York and Los Angeles, market size, i.e. total income from all households, is the overwhelming consideration in a firm's market selection. It is evident from Figure 5.1 (see also Table 2.1) that the settlement size distribution means that much of the US market is concentrated in a few locations. For example, by locating twenty-five stores in the twenty-five largest markets a chain gains access to half the country's consumption. The 200 largest markets provide the goods for three-quarters of the country's total consumption. In practice, retailers are torn between the benefits and costs of market size. On the one hand, they are aware of their minimum market size requirements or thresholds, on the other, they

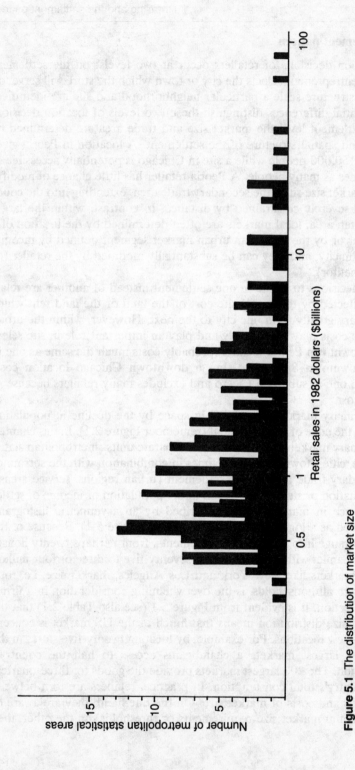

**Figure 5.1** The distribution of market size

*Source:* Bureau of the Census, *Census of Retail Trade 1982*, Washington

know that the degree of competition, specialization, and fragmentation (in terms of lifestyle, for example) represented in large markets may lead to a different set of merchandising problems.

Wholesalers and managers of retail chains may also be concerned with the spacing and interaction between a number of settlements (Figure 5.2). The map reveals a powerful regionalization. California and the Northeast Corridor are the most intensely urbanized, with a density of cities five to ten times greater than the rest of the East – that part of the nation lying east of the 100° longitude. Between Kansas City and the coast lies only Denver, in the 'Great American Desert'. When the sheer distance is complicated by mountain ranges and cultural differences it is apparent why the west coast is treated as a distinct market by many retailers. Exhibit 5.1 illustrates the attractions of the Californian market for retail chains. It may be easier to go to Canada, or even Europe, if you run a chain in New York. The south is now less isolated physically than it was a generation ago, but it is still culturally distinct. Hispanic areas in South Florida, Texas, and California may also be treated as distinct markets for certain products.

The relationships between nearby settlements are expressed in terms of trade areas. Where does the district served by one center end, and the service area of the next center begin? Figure 5.3 looks at the country in this way, using newspaper circulation as an indicator of the spatial extent of each urban market. Newspapers are the major means of communication between retailer and consumer: people shop at the place where they get their news.

The map displays a complex overlapping pattern of trade areas as the largest centers surround and override smaller cities. Trade areas are more extensive on the side of the city towards the frontier and away from the competition. State boundaries may be important to the media because of the preoccupation with political news. Small isolated places (such as Great Falls, Montana) have more extensive service areas than larger places that are near major markets (such as Baltimore). Salt Lake City serves one of the largest regions but it ranks forty-third in retail sales.

Aside from the problems introduced by market size and the varying degree of spatial isolation, metropolitan areas are relatively homogeneous. The differences between them in income, demography, and lifestyle are less than the variations that occur within a metropolitan market, as Figure 5.4 indicates. In 1983, the national median household income was $17,000 and the median for most metropolitan areas lay within $5,000 of that figure. Demographic differences between cities are even smaller, with the exception of the concentration of older people in places like Sarasota. As noted in Chapter two (Table 2.4), lifestyle differences across the country do not appear to affect aggregate consumption patterns.

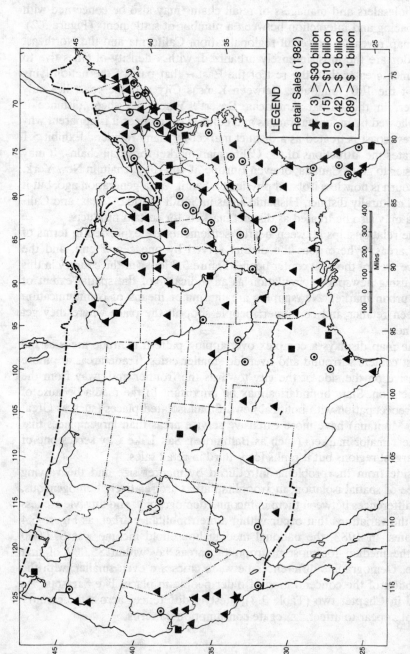

**LEGEND**

Retail Sales (1982)

| | |
|---|---|
| ★ | ( 3) > $30 billion |
| ■ | (15) > $10 billion |
| ⊙ | (42) > $ 3 billion |
| ▲ | (89) > $ 1 billion |

**Figure 5.2** The major markets in the USA (metropolitan statistical areas)

*Source:* Bureau of the Census, *Census of Retail Trade 1982*, Washington

## Exhibit 5.1
## THE CALIFORNIA MARKET

The map in Figure 5.2 reveals the isolation of the California market. As we will see later, this market is served by its own retail chains, restaurants, and banks. Nonetheless, it offers a tempting target for retail chains based elsewhere in the country because of its size and rate of growth. The table below suggests why it is so attractive. California contains 10 per cent of the population but 12 per cent of the income of the US, and it is growing almost twice as fast as the rest of the country. It generated 16 per cent of the nation's population growth during the 1970s. All of this has occurred in a relatively compact market, sheltered from many potential competitors.

| | Characteristics, 1980 | | | | | Population growth 1970–80 | |
|---|---|---|---|---|---|---|---|
| | Population (millions) | Income ($ billions) | Per capita ($) | % Black | % Hispanic | (millions) | % |
| California | 23.7 | 259.3 | 10,930 | 7.7 | 19.2 | 3.7 | 18.5 |
| Rest of the country | 202.8 | 1,901.3 | 9,510 | 12.2 | 5.0 | 19.4 | 10.6 |

*Source:* The authors

### The retail hierarchy

The spectacular differences in market size from place to place are mirrored by systematic variations in retail and service facilities. Larger centers generate more sales, more retail floor area, more stores, more retail employment, and a greater variety of stores. In 1982 950,000 retail employees worked in the New York metropolitan statistical area, the largest market in the country. This is almost 7 per cent of the total number of retail employees in the country. While the amount of retail activity in a town or city is very closely related to the market size, the relationship is nonlinear since the share and characteristics of the retail production function are different in larger places. The nature and cause of these size relationships will be discussed in this section.

The fundamental relationship between retail sales and market income for metropolitan statistical areas in 1982 (see eqn 2.1) is shown in Figure 5.5. A simple log-linear regression model, i.e. $\log_{10}(y) = A + B \log_{10}(x)$, generates the following equation:

Retail sales $= -2.767$ (market income)$^{0.941}$, $r^2 = 0.981$.          (eqn 5.1)

The $r^2$ value for the equation is very close to 1.0, and indicates that the relationship is strong and consistent for all places. The intercept suggests that 58 per cent of income is turned into retail sales. The fact that the

147

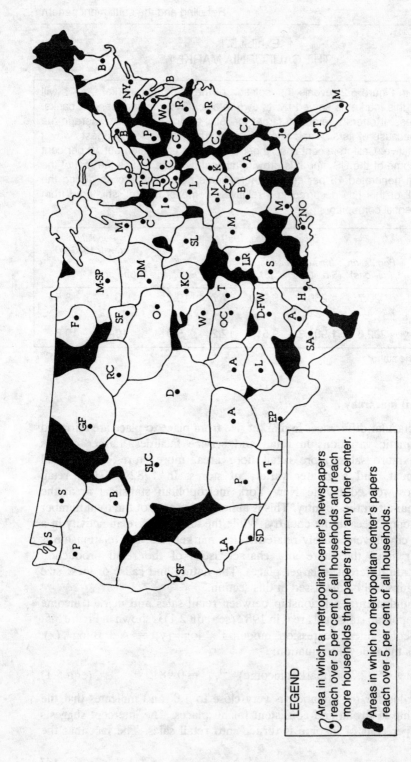

**LEGEND**

Area in which a metropolitan center's newspapers reach over 5 per cent of all households and reach more households than papers from any other center.

Areas in which no metropolitan center's papers reach over 5 per cent of all households.

**Figure 5.3** Metropolitan newspaper circulation hinterlands

*Source:* M.P. Conzen and P.D. Phillips (1982) 'The nature of metropolitan networks', in C.M. Christian and R.A. Harper (eds) *Modern Metropolitan Regions*, Columbus, Ohio: Charles E. Merrill

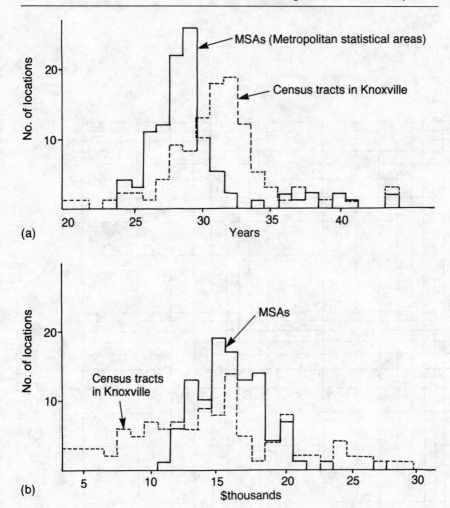

**Figure 5.4** Income and demographic variation among urban markets
(a) Median age
(b) Median household income

*Source:* Bureau of the Census (1980) *Census of Population*; Bureauy of the Census (1986) *State and Metropolitan Area Data Book*, Washington

exponent for market income (0.941) is less than 1.0 suggests that the ratio of sales to income declines slightly in larger markets because of income effects. Higher-income households spend a lower proportion of their income in stores and, on average, the households in the large markets in Figure 5.5 receive 20 per cent more income per capita than those in the smallest places.

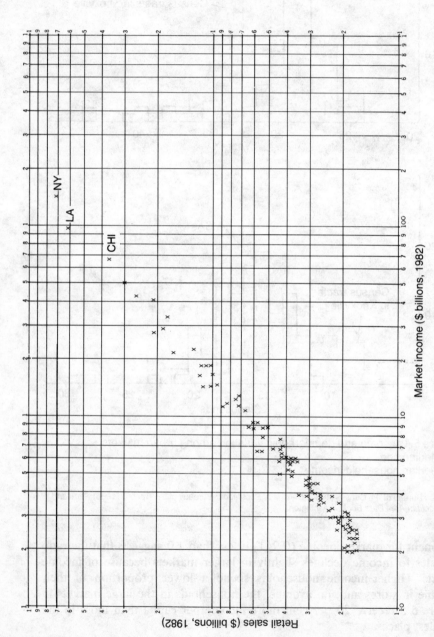

**Figure 5.5** Retail sales and market income (100 largest MSAs)

Market income ($ billions, 1982)

Retail sales ($ billions, 1982)

*Source:* Bureau of the Census (1986) *State and Metropolitan Area Data Book,* Washington

The more interesting variations in the retail hierarchy occur at the very lowest end of the settlement scale, for places smaller than those shown in Figure 5.5. Table 5.1 provides an example drawn from rural Iowa. In this region and at this scale, the income differences from place to place are quite small and the functional specialization of centers of different sizes shows up clearly. In smaller places, the ratio of sales per person declines sharply with declining population, from about $7,000 per person in a settlement with a population of 15,000 to $2,000 per person in rural areas and villages with a population below 2,500.

At the lower end of the retail hierarchy a household can choose between several different centers of differing sizes within daily travel distance and the centers become specialized to provide daily, weekly or occasional shopping facilities. The larger centers serve extensive areas while small centers provide convenience goods for nearby residents. The nature of the shopping experience will also differ according to the size of the community: small places have smaller stores.

Table 5.1 also describes how sales of various kinds of products are affected by this trade-off between distance and range of choice. The rural areas sell little more than food and gas. In small towns (3,000–4,000 population) farm supplies and auto sales become important; slightly larger places add a variety of shopping goods. At the level of the small city (15,000–20,000) department stores become important.

**Table 5.1** At the lower end of the retail hierarchy: Iowa

| | Rural areas[e] | Small towns[f] | Towns[g] | Small cities[h] | Cities[i] | Metropolis[j] |
|---|---|---|---|---|---|---|
| Average population | | 3,500 | 7,100 | 17,500 | 95,400 | 267,200 |
| Sales/capita ($) | 1,855 | 4,750 | 5,135 | 6,855 | 5,895 | 7,155 |
| Sales/store | 182,000 | 285,000 | 394,000 | 559,000 | 549,000 | 642,000 |
| *Share of sales by retail sector (%)*[a] | | | | | | |
| Builder's supplies (%)[b] | 6.5 | 10.8 | 5.3 | 5.4 | 5.4 | 4.6 |
| General (%)[c] | n.a. | n.a. | n.a. | 11.4 | 15.0 | 14.3 |
| Food (%) | 31.9 | 26.6 | 26.2 | 23.3 | 21.5 | 23.1 |
| Automotive (%)[d] | 15.5 | 20.7 | 26.2 | 20.8 | 18.2 | 17.7 |
| Gasoline (%) | 26.5 | 17.2 | 8.4 | 13.2 | 8.8 | 9.5 |
| Apparel (%) | 2.9 | 4.6 | 7.6 | 5.9 | 5.6 | 5.3 |
| Furniture (%) | 1.6 | 4.4 | 6.2 | 2.8 | 4.5 | 4.6 |
| Restaurants (%) | 11.7 | 6.1 | 8.2 | 7.7 | 9.4 | 9.9 |
| Drugs (%) | n.a. | n.a. | 5.3 | 3.7 | 3.7 | 2.5 |
| Miscellaneous (%) | 5.5 | 8.2 | 5.9 | 8.5 | 8.1 | 8.5 |

*Source:* Bureau of the Census (1982) *Census of Retail Trade*, Washington
*Note:* [a]Establishments with payroll only. [b]Includes farm supplies. [c]Dealers and parts. [d]Liquor, sports, jewelry. [e]Less than 2,500 population in Page, Ringgold, and Taylor counties. [f]Approximately $15 million sales: Clarion, Eagle Grove, SocCity. [g]Approximately $35 million sales: Jefferson, Knoxville, Pella. [h]Approximately $100 million sales: Carroll Newton, Ottumwa. [i]Approximately $500 million sales: Dubuque, Sioux City, Waterloo. [j]Des Moines.

Consumers are attracted to shopping in a larger market because of the diversity and specialization that occur there. As the size of the market increases retailers counter their competition by expanding the size of their store to take advantage of economies of scale, or by becoming more specialized in a limited number of products or clientele. Researchers (e.g. Berry *et al.*, 1988) have observed that the number of different kinds of businesses found in a city or town is related to the logarithm of the number of stores or retail sales, as illustrated in Exhibit 5.2. These regularities result from the sequential appearance of various business types as markets increase in size, from the country store or gas station at the lower end of the retail hierarchy to the store specialized to sell candles or model boats at the upper end. Another aspect of market size operates throughout the retail hierarchy. Larger markets permit retailers to increase the sales per store. Access to a large number of customers brings into operation all the

## Exhibit 5.2
## THE REGULARITIES OF THE RETAIL HIERARCHY

Marketing analysts and planners base their strategies on a sequence of relationships between markets and consumer behavior, illustrated below for the 100 largest metropolitan statistical areas. Together these places make up two-thirds of the US market. The general relationships hold for any settlement system at any point in time, but they have been calibrated for 1982 in this example, using data from the *Census of Retail Trade*.

Market income = population × income per capita (by definition)

Retail sales = 0.5843 (market income)$^{0.941}$ (by regression), $\quad r^2 = 0.981$

Retail stores = 2.287 × (retail sales, \$millions)$^{0.959}$, $\quad r^2 = 0.918$

Retail employment = 14.32 (retail sales, \$millions)$^{1.022}$, $\quad r^2 = 0.982$

Retail payroll = 0.1338 (retail sales)$^{1.020}$, $\quad r^2 = 0.982$

No. of business types = A ($\log_{10}$ retail stores)$^B$ $\quad$ – not calibrated

A set of relationships like these provides a means of forecasting future retail requirements. For example, a new factory creates x jobs and y additional income; each dollar of income, in turn, generates sales, stores, and retail employment according to the equations of the model. Between 1972 and 1982, for instance, about two-thirds of the change in retail employment could be explained simply in terms of changes in market income. In cross-section, as shown here, the models fit even better.

The fact that for each equation the exponent on the right-hand side does not equal 1.0 suggests that there are systematic differences in store operations by size of market.

*Source:* The authors

benefits of economies of scale, as outlined in Table 5.2 higher sales per store, more employees per store, and higher sales and wages per worker. Lower margins and greater profitability result in a fundamentally different operating environment in larger metropolitan areas. Take a store from Manhattan and exchange it with a store in Boise, Idaho; neither would survive in its new environment.

## The logic of central place theory

About half a century ago, two German scholars formulated their theories about the location of settlements in independent, but each justly famous studies (Christaller, 1933; Losch, 1939). The village or town that emerged in rural areas, they argued, depended precisely on the demand for goods and services that was generated in the surrounding area, and therefore one could predict the spatial pattern of retail activities. We have already introduced part of the theory in the discussion of the range of a good in Chapter two, and of threshold in Chapter three. This section describes how a central place system works with actual business types in the real world. To put it more precisely: which of many possible models of a settlement system is actually observed?

The theory has been widely elaborated and applied but almost always in a partial form. Some researchers (e.g. Berry et al., 1988) emphasize the characteristics of the markets and the close correlation between the size and composition of retail facilities and the size of the markets they serve, as outlined in the previous section. Others (e.g. Berry and Garrison, 1958) focus on the systematic variation in retail composition with city size. Which business types are most frequently observed (ubiquitous) and which ones serve only the largest markets? Still others (e.g. Rushton, 1969) are concerned with the behavioral choices that were discussed in Chapter four, particularly the trade-off between distance and size or diversity.

**Table 5.2** Store operating ratios by city size

|  | Market size (retail sales $ millions) | Population (thousands) | Sales/ store ($) | Workers*/ store | Sales/ worker ($) | Wages/ employee ($) |
|---|---|---|---|---|---|---|
| Chicago, IL | 33,082.2 | 7,104 | 702,000 | 10.7 | 65,900 | 8,920 |
| Omaha, NE | 2,872.7 | 570 | 646,000 | 10.2 | 63,300 | 7,960 |
| Dubuque, IL | 434.6 | 94 | 572,000 | 8.7 | 60,500 | 8,010 |
| Sioux Center, IA | 33.5 | 4.6 | 523,000 | 7.4 | 70,800 | 6,950 |
| Rock Valley, IA | 6.4 | 2.7 | 220,000 | 5.1 | 43,200 | 5,425 |

*Source:* Bureau of the Census (1982) *Census of Retail Trade*, Washington
*Note:* *Workers = paid employees + proprietors.

Central place theory begins with some assumptions about the market: suppose that customers with equal incomes are spread evenly over a plain with no significant physical features (Figure 5.6a), so that distance is the only restriction on a customer's travel. On the supply side, assume that there are a fixed number of store types, each with a characteristic average cost curve that determines its threshold size of operation, and each with a distinctive spatial demand curve that determines range, given spatial pattern of demand. Recall that the threshold is the minimum size of market that will support a given type of store. The result is a spectrum of retail activities that can be ranked by threshold market, from the smallest (e.g. service station) to the largest (e.g. art gallery specializing in modern sculpture).

Consider the retail activity with the smallest threshold, the gas station. With no restrictions on entry, competition forces all such stores to operate at the smallest possible scale (the threshold size), and to spread evenly across the landscape (Figure 5.6b). Suppose that the store with the next largest threshold (perhaps the general store) locates independently of the gas stations, creating a similar facility network with stores slightly further apart. Each succeeding retail type adds another layer of stores at a different distance apart (Figure 5.6c).

The result is chaos. Stores of any type could theoretically be placed at any location, on any farm road. A major department store might be found in a small hamlet. There is no necessary starting point in such a space: any site is acceptable for a store and the independent location decisions do not generate groups of stores.

Suppose, instead, that the location of one set of stores of a particular type affects the location of other business types. In Chapter four it was argued that retail clusters reflect the customer's desire to visit several different stores in one trip, thus reducing total travel costs significantly while increasing the potential distance travelled (the range). In addition, it is apparent that once one set of stores (the gas stations) is located, the people who operate them also become part of the market for other retail activities. The market is no longer distributed evenly in space.

Once the assumption of the independent location of store types is set aside and replaced by the notion of the multiple purpose trip, a retail hierarchy emerges (Figure 5.6d). Customers prefer to visit several different stores on each trip. Those activities with similar thresholds and service areas group together for the convenience of their customers: the retail activities with the smallest thresholds operate at a slightly larger scale so that their locations coincide with store types with larger thresholds. Retail clusters emerge around the stores with the largest thresholds, including all those activities with smaller thresholds. Stores with small thresholds can operate on a larger scale but stores with large thresholds cannot operate below that level. Settlements grow up around the retail cluster.

In this way the lowest threshold size in the retail spectrum determines

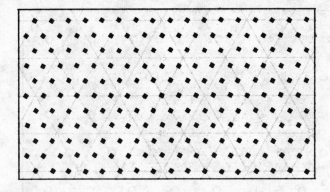

(a)

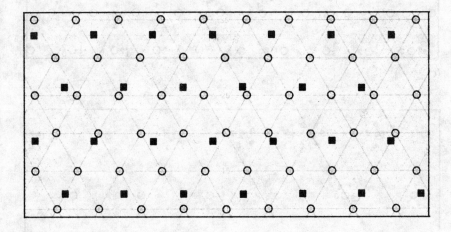

(b)

**Figure 5.6** The logic of central place theory
(a) The evenly dispersed market
(b) Location of stores with the smallest threshold (gas station, 0); and with a
     slightly larger threshold (the general store, ■)
(c) Location of five different business types, each independent of the rest
(d) Location of business types, assuming multiple purpose trips

*Source:* The authors

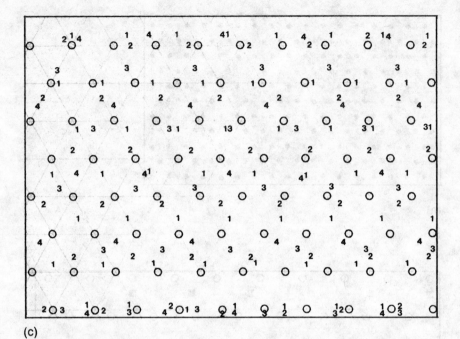

(c)

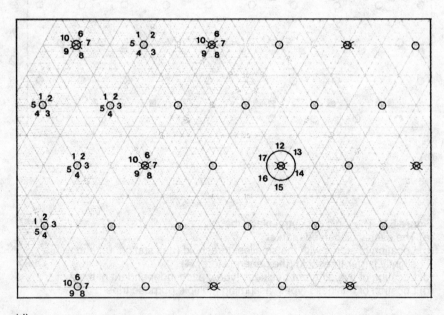

(d)

the lower and upper limits of the lowest order retail cluster: larger than the lowest threshold but still small enough to exclude competition from gas stations locating between the settlements. The upper limit of this retail cluster (call it the hamlet) becomes the lower limit for the second order of settlement (the village), and so on until the highest order activities are grouped in a single metropolitan center that serves the entire district. Because the metropolitan activities also have limitations due to range, the settlement should be located in the most central location over all. Once this location is identified, the location of other, lower order centers is specified as well. Each higher order center contains all the activities of lower order centers so that the variety of goods available is purely a function of level in the retail hierarchy.

The ordering of retail activities as predicted by the theory is readily observed. Table 5.3 is taken from a study by Berry and Garrison (1958) which was conducted in a rural county in the state of Washington, hence the predominance of the very lowest-order activities. The number of stores of each central place activity was counted in each settlement in the county, there were thirty-three in all. The very lowest-order activities – gas stations and food stores – were found almost everywhere but were not heavily concentrated in larger centers. The higher-order activities, such as drug stores, were disproportionately found in the larger centers. The relationship to settlement size also reflects the possibilities of economies of scale which are greater for automobile dealerships than for barber shops.

A settlement is attractive to a consumer because of the variety of functions that it offers, known as 'centrality' in the theoretical literature. Centrality, rather than population or market income, affects consumer behavior. It also affects the store locations because of the positive externalities that stores exert upon each other. In a small town every business depends on the existence of other stores – the drugstore, the liquor store, the hospital – to help draw customers to the community.

The great debates in the central place literature concern the patterns of spatial interdependence among centers of different orders, i.e. the geometry of the settlement system. Figure 5.7 a, b, and c illustrates some of the alternative theoretical structures for settlement systems. In the 'market' model the trade area served by a lower-order center is subdivided among three higher-order centers so that a second-order place serves $1/3 \times 6 = 2$ first-order centers + 1 (its own first-order trade area). K (the ratio of first-order to second-order centers) = 3. This was the original theoretical model put forth by Christaller as that most efficiently serving a region.

The 'transportation' model where K = 4, is an efficient alternative that has the additional merit of aligning major settlements on a road network. It has been widely observed in many different cultures but particularly in those parts of North America served by grid road systems. As 'administrative' model 'nests' each lower-order trade area completely within the next

**Table 5.3** Order of entry of central place activities

| Activity | Number of activities | Number of places | Threshold population (A)* | Elasticity (B)* |
|---|---|---|---|---|
| Gas station | 42 | 30 | 196 | 1.35 |
| Food store | 57 | 20 | 254 | 1.74 |
| Church | 78 | 21 | 265 | 1.29 |
| Eating place | 66 | 19 | 276 | 1.33 |
| Tavern | 50 | 21 | 282 | 1.65 |
| Elementary school | 43 | 26 | 322 | 1.67 |
| Physician | 32 | 10 | 380 | 1.42 |
| Real estate agent | 31 | 9 | 384 | 1.40 |
| Appliance store | 29 | 12 | 385 | 1.46 |
| Barber shop | 32 | 18 | 386 | 2.39 |
| Automobile dealer | 28 | 8 | 398 | 1.35 |
| Insurance agent | 23 | 8 | 409 | 1.32 |
| Bulk oil distributor | 26 | 8 | 419 | 1.56 |
| Dentist | 24 | 9 | 426 | 1.57 |
| Motel | 23 | 8 | 430 | 1.56 |
| Hardware | 26 | 12 | 431 | 1.90 |
| Garage | 20 | 11 | 435 | 1.72 |
| Fuel dealer | 23 | 9 | 453 | 1.78 |
| Drugstore | 23 | 15 | 458 | 2.23 |
| Beauty parlor | 20 | 10 | 480 | 1.89 |
| Auto parts | 21 | 10 | 488 | 1.94 |
| Meeting hall | 18 | 13 | 525 | 2.01 |
| Feed store | 13 | 5 | 526 | 1.79 |
| Lawyer | 18 | 9 | 528 | 2.12 |
| Furniture | 13 | 7 | 546 | 1.85 |
| 5 and 10c store | 18 | 10 | 549 | 2.30 |
| Trucking | 16 | 7 | 567 | 2.04 |

*Source:* B.J.L. Berry and W.L. Garrison, (1958) 'A note on central place theory and the range of a good', *Economic Geography* 34: 304–11

*Note:* *For each activity (k) the number of stores (N) in each town was regressed against the town's population in the equation: population $= A_k \times N^B k$. $A_k$ and $B_k$ are the constants recorded above. If the value 1 is substituted for N in the equation, the value $A_k$ is equivalent to the threshold population as estimated over all the settlements in the sample. The elasticity, $B_k$, indicates the non-linear size effect, i.e. how rapidly the number of stores of type k increases as the population increases.

higher-order, resulting in a value of K = 7. While such a model provides insufficient high-order activity for most distribution systems, the clarity of spatial responsibility for delivering services is appealing for public and institutional activities: churches, schools, the postal service, and municipal governments.

Which of these models (or combination of models) is most appropriate in a given region will depend on the local economic base and its distribution in space, the transportation pattern, and the history of the region, particularly its administrative history. A number of studies have been undertaken with the Corn Belt particularly favored because of its agricultural economy. The map in Figure 5.8, however, has the advantage of

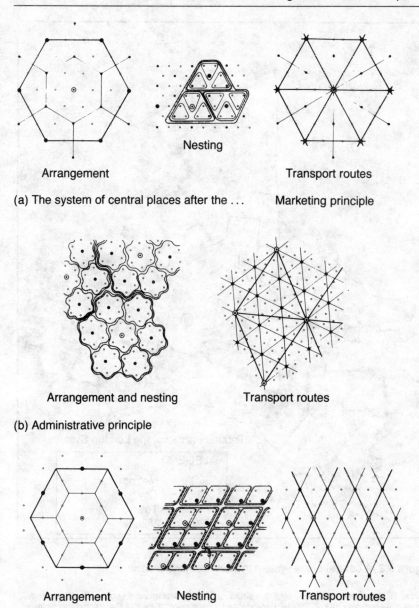

(a) The system of central places after the ...     Marketing principle

(b) Administrative principle

(c) Transportation principle

**Figure 5.7** Central place settlement patterns

*Source:* B.J.L. Berry and A. Pred (1961) *Central Place Studies: A Bibliography of Theory and Applications*, Philadelphia, Regional Science Research Institute. Reproduced by permission of the authors

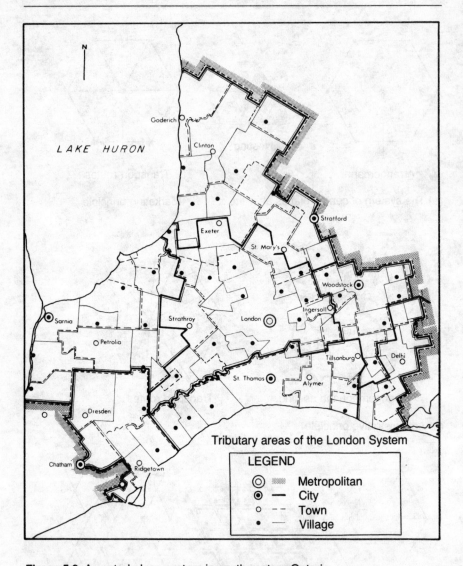

**Figure 5.8** A central place system in southwestern Ontario

*Source:* R. Muncaster (1978) 'The empirical structure of urban systems: the London, Ontario example', *Canadian Geographer* XXII, 4:306–18. Reproduced by permission of the The Canadian Association of Geographers

incorporating actual trade areas, based on an origin–destination questionaire: 'Where are you going? For what purpose? Where did you come from?' The highest-order place is London, Ontario (the 'Metropolis'), bounded to the west by Lake Huron, the US border, and Windsor, to the south by Lake Erie, and to the east and north-east by the trade areas of Kitchener and Hamilton. For the most part the cities that surround London, such as Stratford and Woodstock, are found on the boundaries of its service area, while the towns, such as Ingersoll and St Mary's, are found on the boundaries between the city and the metropolis. Low-order trade areas are not nested within the larger ones.

The ratio between the numbers of centers of each of the four orders is 1:3.5:11:39 (giving half value to Stratford, Woodstock, and Chatham); a K ratio of about 3.5:1. While in reality the places mapped here make up a size continuum from the very smallest to London itself, each household's shopping options are based on the set of nearby places and are usually restricted to quite distinct choices, depending on the nature of the trip, i.e. village, town, or city.

## The distribution system

Central place theory is based largely on the location of consumer demand and pays little attention to the supply-side of retail operations. An alternative point of view, argued most strongly by Vance (1970), emphasizes the locational constraints imposed by the sources of goods, the transportation networks, and the pattern of warehouses and markets serving retailers that together make up the distribution system. While Vance developed his argument as part of a study of wholesale activity, it also has relevance for the locational choices of financial firms and retail chains, as we will argue below. Brown (1981) spells out the supply-side requirements of retailers in some detail.

Each node along the distribution route between producer and consumer has potential for growth. When these supply-side advantages and constraints are combined with the market segmentation of the retail chain – a focus on a particular region or city size – some characteristic spatial patterns result. The retail chain combines sensitivity to the location of consumer demand with an awareness of the cost implications of various store network configurations.

Consider a retail chain looking for a new location. The key factor is the profitability of each new outlet which can be broken down into revenue and costs. Revenue is directly related to market size and can occur anywhere where there is sufficient demand, in any part of the country. However, the costs of delivering goods and services, and those of administration, transportation, and financing are related to distance from headquarters, warehouses, and the locations of other outlets. Thus, while sales potential permits the chain to expand in any location with a market above a certain threshold, logistics costs restrict expansion to those opportunities within a certain distance.

As an example, Brown (1981) describes the expansion of Friendly Ice Cream shops, a chain of restaurants with headquarters near Springfield, Massachusetts. This chain's outlets are basically identical and thrive in markets that satisfy a series of threshold requirements: population of community over 12,000 and growth rate and family income above average – a family, kids, and dog image. It is not difficult to satisfy these require- ments and the chain grew rapidly, spreading into nearby towns and cities (see Figure 5.9). The more important constraints on expansion came from the logistic requirements of the chain. Friendly's runs a highly centralized operation, owned and closely controlled from the head office and provid- ing all foods from the central processing plant. All outlets had to be located within the 400-mile overnight range of delivery trucks and accessible to supervision from management based at the head office. As a result, further expansion was channelled along the expressway routes up and down the east coast. In the mid-1970s they overcame this constraint by setting up another processing plant and regional headquarters in Ohio, generating a new cluster of outlets.

Logistics costs will vary widely from one chain to another. They may result from the nature of the product: is it bulky or perishable? Does it require high turnover, rapid price changes, or a high level of service? Is the administration centralized? Are the outlets uniform with close adminis- trative control or is the chain vertically integrated, with production, wholesale, or packaging requirements that restrict the possible sources of goods?

A chain's system of retail outlets implies an invisible network of flows of finance, information, merchandise, and authority that increase in cost with distance and restrict future growth. At each new location the chain trades off the benefits of growth and economies of scale against the marginal costs of extending the distribution network in space. For some chains with high levels of turnover or service, it may be impossible to operate in an isolated region with less than a certain number of stores. The chain may try to open a number of outlets simultaneously, in order to justify a complete distribution system, or it may simply try to buy out an existing regional chain.

## Retail chains at the settlement scale

From the point of view of a retail chain or a shopping center developer, the settlement system of the United States represents an extraordinarily diverse set of opportunities. The selection of target markets will be restricted by the product mix, the market threshold, the pattern of competition, and the

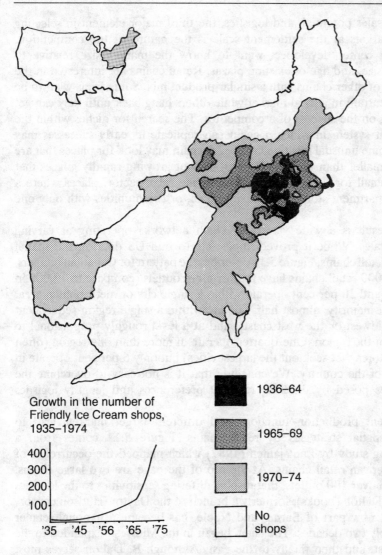

Growth in the number of
Friendly Ice Cream shops,
1935–1974

400
300
200
100

'35  '45  '56  '65  '75

1936–64

1965–69

1970–74

No
shops

**Figure 5.9** The spatial dispersion of Friendly Ice Cream shops

*Source:* L.A. Brown (1981) *Innovation Diffusion: A New Perspective,* New York: Methuen

distribution requirements of warehousing, delivery, and servicing. Even then the number of opportunities may still exhaust the growth potential of the enterprise; the retailer must use a market strategy, based on the firm's organizational structure, experience, and corporate goals to choose the high priority locations. (Market strategy will be discussed more fully in Chapter twelve.)

After sales potential, and logistics, the third major element in selecting target markets at the settlement scale is the nature of the competition. Shopping center developers want to know the market size relative to number, size, and age of existing plazas. Retail chains are interested in the presence of other chains with a similar product mix. Some firms want to be the first entrant in a local market while others hang back until they can get a reading on the success of a competitor. The search for niches within the settlement system in which a chain can replicate its early successes may lead to some unusual location criteria. A chain may look for places that are slightly smaller than the store's threshold but growing rapidly, places that are too small for the dominant chain in the retail sector, places where a major department store has just withdrawn, or communities with only one mall.

The result is a wide variety of chain networks operating at varying spatial scales. While it proved impossible to find US data on the spatial reach of retail chains, Figure 5.10 describes the pattern for Canadian retailers. About 1,000 retail chains have four or more outlets (compare to 12,000 in the US), and 30 per cent operate within a single city or metropolitan area. The great majority, almost half, operate within a single region (equivalent to the Midwest or the west coast); and at a level roughly proportional to the size of the region. One-quarter operate in more than one region (often fashion stores that seek out the largest cities) but only 6 per cent operate in all parts of the country. We conclude that it is not easy to overcome the challenges posed by differing regional preferences and lengthy logistics networks.

Different production functions and different target markets lead to diverse spatial strategies by retail chains. Figure 5.11 comes from a fascinating study by Laulajainen (1987) which mapped the occurrence of fifty American retail chains. At the top of the page are two large chains, each with over 100 outlets, that display differing sensitivities to the logistics costs. B. Dalton (books), formerly a branch of the Dayton-Hudson corporation but now part of Barnes and Noble, has become a national retailer within only two decades. The chain began in the Midwest, expanded to the west coast, and then finally to the east. Although B. Dalton serves most urban places above a certain size threshold, it prefers college and white-collar communities to blue-collar cities. Its main competitor is found in the same kind of communities as are many other national chains or speciality stores: the fundamental requirement is the amount of market income. Exhibit 5.3 illustrates the spatial structure of competition for convenience stores.

Caldor is a discount/mass market retailer that expanded from the New York suburbs into Connecticut and Massachusetts. Its spatial strategy centered on access to chain headquarters and warehouses, and because of the low market threshold required there were plenty of potential sites in the

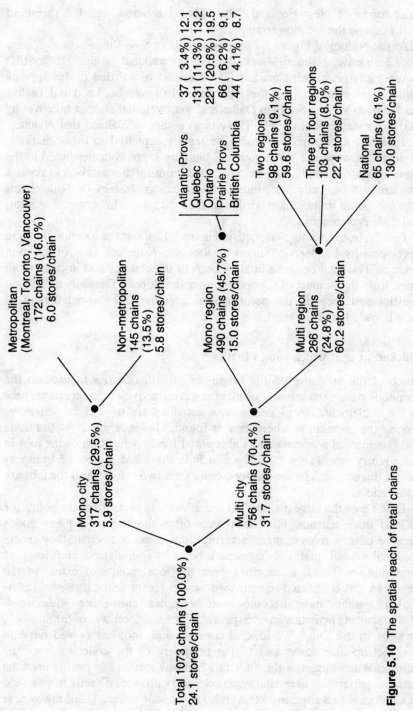

**Figure 5.10** The spatial reach of retail chains

*Source:* J. Simmons and B. Speck (1988) 'The spatial imprint of business strategy', *Discussion Paper no. 35*, University of Toronto, Department of Geography

small towns of New England. The type of business and the threshold market shape the location strategy.

At the bottom of Figure 5.11 are two chains whose site requirements are more restrictive. Neiman-Marcus typifies the national fashion retailer that requires a large, affluent market. The same set of a dozen places appears on the list of every chain of this type: Saks Fifth Avenue, Lord and Taylor, etc. Neiman-Marcus began in Dallas and went national after its takeover by Carter Hawley Hale in 1969. The parent company realized that Neiman-Marcus had a prestige that could be readily exploited in other markets. Payless Cashways is a 'do-it-yourself' building supplies dealer based in the west. In contrast to Neiman-Marcus it seeks out smaller markets in regions that are still basically agricultural. The location strategy of both chains depends on an intimate knowledge of their target markets, their behavior, and their preferences.

Finally, from another perspective, Figure 5.12 shows the locations of retail developments by Melvin Simon Associates. Note the lack of location strategy. This firm operates in all regions of the country and in cities of all sizes: truly the K mart of shopping center developers. Developers have no logistics costs beyond the occasional airfare; they are restricted only by their knowledge of the market.

**Chicken or egg: which comes first?**

Much of the literature on the origins or growth of cities focuses on the economic base – the primary or manufacturing activities that create income in the settlement. Retail and service activities are treated as derivative, serving the population wherever it is found. However, by 1984 the trade and commercial services sectors accounted for 31.4 per cent of the jobs in the country (see Table 1.1). If we include the allied sectors of transportation, finance, and public services, more than two-thirds of all the jobs are non-basic.

In the past the largest cities had the advantage as distribution points for at least three reasons. First, they were often the source of many goods because of their roles as manufacturing cities or ports. Second, they generated substantial markets, measured both by population and level of consumption. Third, these cities were the focal points of extensive rail networks that connected regions together. In recent years, however, distribution systems have become more complex and more widespread. Manufacturing activities have dispersed to the small centers of the sun-belt, or even to the Third World, and consumption, too, has moved out into non-metropolitan areas and to the periphery of the country. Also, the enormous investment in the interstate highway system has restructured the national patterns of accessibility. Trucks carry produce directly from a field in California to a supermarket warehouse in Milwaukee. Small towns near

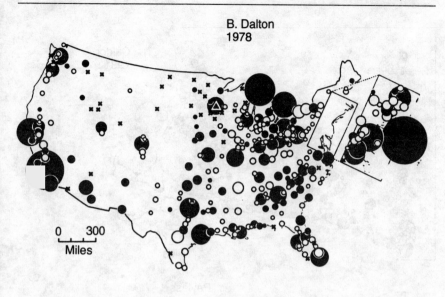

B. Dalton
1978

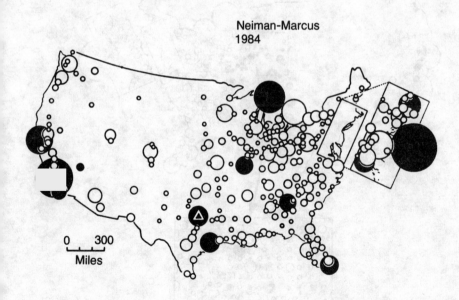

Neiman-Marcus
1984

**Figure 5.11** Location strategies on the settlement scale. Major retail chains

*Source:* R. Laulajainen (1967) Spatial Strategies in Retailing, Dordrecht D. Reidel

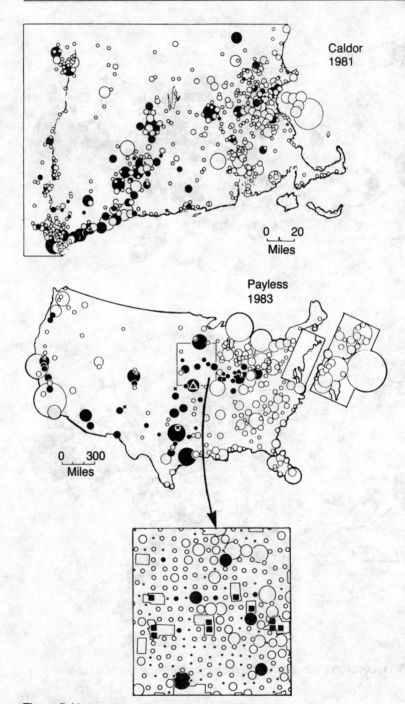

Caldor
1981

0    20
Miles

Payless
1983

0    300
Miles

**Figure 5.11** (*continued*)

## Exhibit 5.3
## THE SPATIAL STRUCTURE OF COMPETITION:
## THE CONVENIENCE STORE

One of the fastest growing retail phenomena of the last decade is the convenience store. In 1975 there were 25,000, by 1985 there were 45,000 and over 60 per cent of stores were controlled by the top fifty firms. Within any one region, however, the competitive structure is reduced to a battle among a much smaller number. In New England, for example, Cumberland Farms dominates, competing with three local chains and one from Florida. None of the other 'big five' firms have tackled this region yet. In New York, Southland and Cumberland Farms compete with a number of local chains but in Miami Circle K is also involved. Out on the Coast, Southland dominates but a local chain, Arco, is important. Each major chain is strong within certain regions. None are truly national.

|  | No. of stores | City/state |
|---|---|---|
| *Major national chains* |  |  |
| Southland (7–11) | 7,440 | Dallas |
| Circle K | 2,660 | Phoenix |
| Cumberland Farms | 1,200 | Boston |
| Convenient Food | 1,120 | Chicago |
| National Convention | 1,100 | Houston |
| All stores | 42,950 |  |
| *New York chains* |  |  |
| Southland | 179 | Dallas |
| Dairy Stores | 152 | New York |
| Cumberland Farms | 151 | Boston |
| Qwikcheck | 71 | New York |
| Dairy Barn | 58 | New York |
| All stores | 912 |  |
| *Los Angeles chains* |  |  |
| Southland | 799 | Dallas |
| ARCO | 262 | Los Angeles |
| Circle K | 260 | Phoenix |
| National Convention | 152 | Houston |
| Kayo Oil | 58 | TN |
| All stores | 1,703 |  |
| *New England chains* |  |  |
| Cumberland Farms | 481 | Boston |
| Charter Marketing | 92 | FL |
| Christy's Markets | 76 | MA |
| Dari Mart | 65 | CT |
| Richdale | 65 | MA |
| All stores | 1,286 |  |

Exhibit 5.3 (*continued*)

| South Florida chains | | |
|---|---|---|
| Southland | 263 | Dallas |
| Circle K | 131 | Phoenix |
| Farm Stores | 114 | Miami |
| Cumberland Farms | 96 | Boston |
| Mister Grocer | 71 | FL |
| All stores | 991 | |

*Source:* Progressive Grocer (annual) *Directory of Convenience Stores*, Stamford, Connecticut

an interstate intersection have become central places at the national or regional scale.

The logic of retail location at the settlement scale has become a powerful determinant of urban growth in its own right. If, among a number of small centers of similar size and economic role, one or two places are singled out because of their locational advantages for distribution activities, these centers will grow more rapidly than other places since distribution activities are among the most rapidly growing sectors of the economy. Any internal reorganization or shift in the locational determinants of these sectors will affect all cities in the settlement system. Rather than simply tracking the growth in income due to new mines or factories, the retail, service, and financial sectors are increasingly important determinants of urban growth.

What kinds of location are favored for specialized roles within the tertiary economy? Figure 5.13 shows the headquarters for the 151 leading retail chains (all those that sold more than $500 million worth of goods in 1985) – hence the best places from the point of view of the logistics of distribution. These headquarters are almost as widely dispersed as retail sales. New York leads with 16 per cent of the headquarters (twenty-four), followed by Los Angeles and Chicago with 7 per cent. The rest are scattered in seventy different places. Once again we can see the importance of regional structure in American retail organization. Regional chains serve regional markets. The important role of smaller centers such as Benton-ville, Arkansas (Wal-Mart Stores) suggests that the starting point of a chain may be more significant than the size or situation of a city.

This chapter has explored the two-way relationship between retailing and the settlement system: a system that simultaneously generates markets for stores and stores to serve markets. Because it is relatively easy to sort out trade areas at the settlement scale and to allocate trade areas to retail facilities, we can begin to examine the effects on retailing of different kinds of changes in the distribution system.

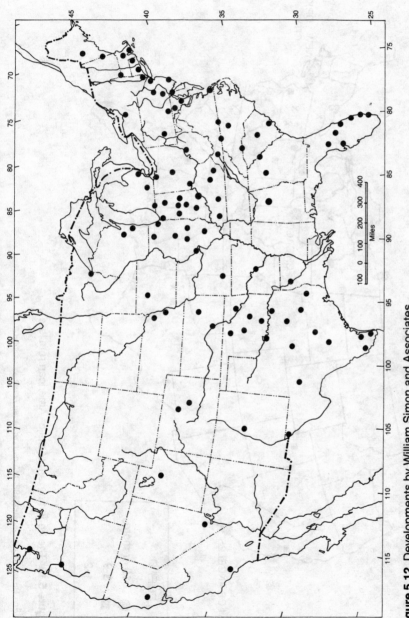

**Figure 5.12** Developments by William Simon and Associates

*Source:* The authors

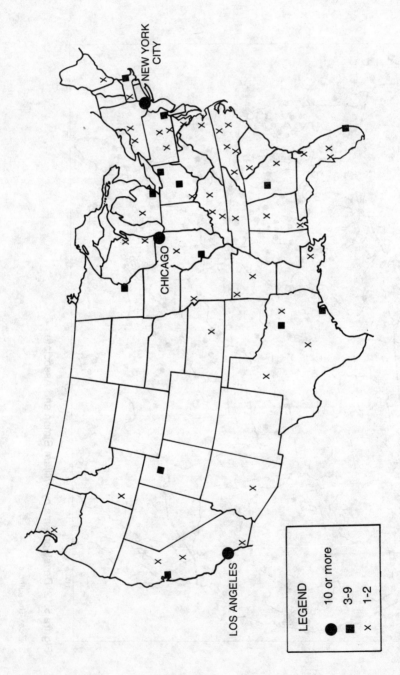

**Figure 5.13** The headquarters of major American retailers

*Source:* Bureau of the Census (1982) *Census of Retail Trade,* Washington

## Further reading

Archer, C.J. and White, E.R. (1985) 'A service classification of American metropolitan areas', *Urban Geography* 6, 1: 122–51.

Berry, B.J.L., Parr, J.B., Epstein, B.J., Ghosh, A., and Smith, R.H.T. (1988) *Market Centers and Retail Location: Theory and Application*, Englewood, New Jersey: Prentice-Hall.

Berry, B.J.L. and Garrison, W.L. (1958) 'A note on central place theory and the range of a good,' *Economic Geography* 34: 304–11.

Brown, L.A. (1981) *Innovation Diffusion: A New Perspective*, New York: Methuen.

Christaller, W. (1933) *Central Places in Southern Germany* (trans. C.W. Baskin, 1962), Englewood Cliffs, New Jersey: Prentice-Hall.

Conzen, M.P. and Phillips, P.D. (1982) 'The nature of metropolitan networks', in C.M. Christian and R.A. Harper (eds) *Modern Metropolitan Regions*, Columbus, Ohio: Charles E. Merrill.

Ghosh, A. (1986) 'The value of a mall and other insights from a revised central place model', *Journal of Retailing* 62, 1: 79–97.

Hudson, J.C. (1984) *The Plains Country Towns*, Minneapolis: University of Minnesota Press.

Ingene, C.A. (1984) 'Structural determinants of retail potential', *Journal of Retailing* 60, 1: 37–64.

King, L.J. (1984) *Central Place Theory*, Beverly Hills: Sage.

Laulajainen, R. (1987) *Spatial Strategies in Retailing*, Dordrecht: D. Reidel Publishing.

Losch, A. (1939) *The Economics of Location* (Trans. W. Woglom), New Haven: Yale University Press.

Muncaster, R.B. (1978) 'The empiricial structure of urban systems: the London, Ontario example,' *Canadian Geographer* 23: 306–18.

Preston, R.E. (1971) 'The structure of central place systems', *Economic Geography* 47, 2: 136–55.

Rushton, G. (1969) 'The scaling of locational preferences', in K. Cox and R. Golledge (eds) *Behavioral Problems in Geography: A Symposium*, Studies in Geography No. 17, Evanston, Illinois Northwestern University, Department of Geography.

Vance, J.E., Jr (1970) *The Merchant's World: The Geography of Wholesaling*, Englewood Cliffs, New Jersey: Prentice-Hall.

# Chapter six

# The changing distribution system

**The sales of women's clothes have grown almost twice as fast as the sales of men's clothes over the last half century.**

**Most of the expansion of retail facilities since the Second World War has been due to increases in real income per capita.**

**Differences in the kinds of goods available in big cities and small towns have almost disappeared.**

Because retail and service activities are so central to the economic function of cities and towns, the evolution of the settlement pattern and that of the distribution system are inextricably linked. In an agricultural region like the Corn Belt, 50 per cent of the jobs occur in the tertiary sector; and as the share of retail sales shifts away from nearby hamlets and catalogue sales to the city down the highway, the settlement system must surely respond. Good years or bad years for agriculture directly affect the economic health of stores and retail chains throughout the region, while the introduction of new crops or some other spatially differential pattern of economic growth may require a reorganization of the entire distribution system.

This chapter examines the various forces that are involved in redrawing the retail component of settlement patterns. We raise again the questions posed in Chapter one about the relationship between consumer demand and retail facilities. Does the basic economy of the region force the distribution system to adjust? Or do changing economies of scale and new forms of retailing relocate employment from one type of location to another? On the demand side, there have been substantial shifts away from jobs in the old economic staple of farming towards energy-linked activities, and manufacturing jobs have dispersed to smaller centers in the south and south-west. Relative income levels across the country can change rapidly but the significant, long-term trend has been a closing of the income gap between the smallest and the largest places. Since the distribution system is inherently dependent on transport, the transition from dependence on railways to dependence on roads has transformed the relative accessibility of many locations. Finally, the distribution system itself has evolved. Stores have become bigger and greater horizontal and vertical integration is evident. However, before we tackle the thorny question of the primary determinant of distribution patterns, let us examine the overall growth of the retail system.

## The magnitude of change

The Bureau of the Census has been collecting detailed records about retail, wholesale, and service activities since the *Census of Retail Trade* in 1929. It is not surprising, perhaps, that this half century has witnessed an extraordinary level of growth in these sectors (see Table 6.1). The number of retail stores has increased by 30 per cent but the level of sales, in constant

**Table 6.1** Changes in retailing: 1929–82

| | 1929 | 1939 | 1948 | 1958 | 1967 | 1977 | 1982 | Growth 1929–82 (%) |
|---|---|---|---|---|---|---|---|---|
| Number of stores (thousands) | 1,476.0 | 1,770.0 | 1,688.0 | 1,788.0 | 1,763.0 | 1,855.0 | 1,923.0 | 30.3 |
| Sales ($ billions, 1982 dollars) | 272.2 | 291.9 | 523.3 | 666.3 | 896.8 | 1,151.8 | 1,065.9 | 291.6 |
| Percentage of chains* | 20.3 | 21.7 | 29.6 | 33.7 | 39.8 | 47.1 | 53.2 | 162.1 |
| Employment (thousands) | 5,722.0 | 6,438.0 | 8,661.0 | 9,731.0 | 11,005.0 | 14,552.0 | 15,976.0 | 179.2 |
| Staff/store | 3.9 | 3.6 | 4.9 | 5.4 | 6.2 | 7.8 | 8.3 | 114.2 |
| Sales/store ($ thousands, 1982 dollars) | 184.0 | 165.0 | 296.0 | 373.0 | 509.0 | 621.0 | 554.0 | 201.1 |
| Sales/staff ($ thousands, 1982 dollars) | 47.6 | 45.3 | 60.4 | 68.5 | 81.5 | 79.2 | 66.7 | 40.1 |
| Turnover (sales/inventory) | n.a. | 8.0 | 9.2 | 8.2 | 8.1 | 9.3 | 10.0 | 25.0 |
| Population (millions) | 121.8 | 130.9 | 146.6 | 174.1 | 198.7 | 220.2 | 232.5 | 90.9 |
| Personal income/Capita ($ dollars) 1982 | 3,970.0 | 3,865.0 | 5,750.0 | 6,930.0 | 9,155.0 | 11,145.0 | 11,120.0 | 180.1 |

*Sources:* Bureau of the Census (1976); *Historical statistics of the United States: Colonial Times to 1970; Statistical Abstract of the United States* (annual), Washington

*Note:* *Retail firms with two or more establishments.

dollars, has increased fourfold and employment has almost tripled (despite the fact that the end-point for this table, i.e. 1982, was a recession year).

This growth largely reflects the 90 per cent growth of population and the 180 per cent increase in real income per capita over the study period, but the differential growth rates of stores, sales, and employment suggest that the overall rate of growth obscures significant changes in the nature of retail operations. The average size of stores, for instance, tripled in terms of sales, while the number of employees per store doubled and the efficiency of the employees (measured by sales per worker) increased by half. The typical retail establishment of 1982 was quite different from that of 1929. It covered a much larger floor area, sold a greater variety of products, emphasized self-service, and served a larger trade area, based on a wealthier clientele.

Such dramatic patterns of growth and change could not fail to generate striking spatial patterns of change. Figure 6.1 looks at the growth in retail employment over fifty years, using the largest metropolitan statistical areas introduced in Chapter five. Not one of the 100 regions shows a decline in retail employment. Even where population growth was zero or negative, income levels rose sufficiently to support a growth in retailing. During this period, employment in farms and other primary activities was slowly replaced by jobs in retailing and services.

The map also suggests a number of issues that will be discussed in greater detail in the rest of the chapter. Regional variations in income growth contribute to the much higher growth rates in retail employment per capita in the south than in the Midwest or East Coast. The equalization of rural and urban income levels has helped smaller places to grow more rapidly than larger ones. New York, Los Angeles, Chicago, and San Francisco are all in the slowest growth group. The most dramatic increases have occurred in smaller places in the south: Knoxville, Charlotte, Greensboro, Raleigh, etc.

Improved accessibility due to changes in transportation and increases in income has altered the roles of the smallest settlements. The general store has been replaced by the gas station. The appearance of larger stores with larger thresholds and the growth of retail chains has led to different choices of location and altered the relative attractiveness of places. Exhibit 6.1 details the sources of change in the distribution system and explores their implications. Figure 6.2 plots the sequence of growth in three important factors: population, per capita income, and automobile ownership. While the long-term trend to growth is powerful and has been consistent since the early 1950s, the events of the last few years remind us that growth and progress are not inevitable. A reduction in the rate of growth of real income severely threatens the distribution sectors. Without continued income growth retailers merely compete among themselves for slices of the same pie.

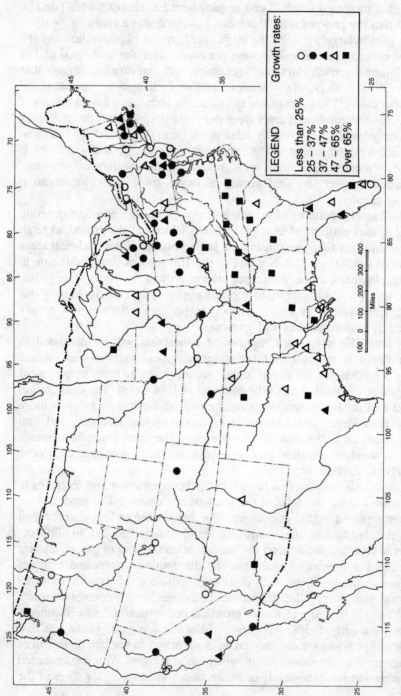

**Figure 6.1** Growth in retail employment per capita: 1939–82

*Source:* Bureau of the Census (various years) *Census of Retail Trade*, Washington

Exhibit 6.1
## THE SOURCES OF CHANGE IN THE DISTRIBUTION SYSTEM

| | Implications | |
| --- | --- | --- |
| *Source of change* | *On the settlement scale* | *Within metropolitan area* |
| *Population growth* Highly concentrated in space | Requires reorganization of retail hierarchy. Accentuates growth differences among competing places | New facilities concentrated in suburbs and downtown (redevelopment) |
| Regional rather than hierarchical variation | Some retailers get lucky! | |
| Unpredictable | | |
| Suburbs grow as central city declines | | CBD loses ground to suburbs |
| *Increased income per capita* Higher expenditures per household, everywhere | Universal growth in retail sales and employment | Maintains the number of stores |
| Shift toward luxury goods | Most rapid growth occurs in smaller urban centers, as big city purchasing pattern is extended throughout the retail hierarchy | Larger shopping malls grow more quickly than smaller convenience stores |
| Increased size of store | Fewer, but more varied stores in smaller places | Specialization increases. The chains thrive, as do inner-city specialty areas |
| Greater leisure activity | | Shopping linked to recreation facilities |
| *Greater use of automobiles* Decline in transportation costs extends range of spatial demand curve | Greater choice at low end of retail hierarchy produces decline in smaller centers | Lower residential densities. Shift away from mass transport. Planned centers with parking dominate suburbs |
| Greater proportion of expenditures in automotive group | Gas stations dominate sales in smallest places | Automotive group (franchises) remain the major non-plaza, non-chain retail activity. Arterial ribbons remain important |

*Source:* The authors
*Note:* CBD, central business district.

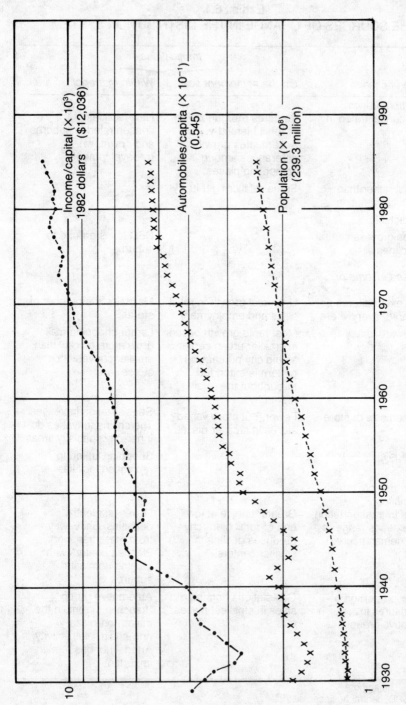

**Figure 6.2** The changes in demand (1985 values in parentheses)

*Source: Bureau of the Census (1976) Historical Statistics of the United States and Statistical Abstracts of the United States, Washington*

Although we will discuss each of these factors in retail change separately, Figure 6.2 reminds us that they are not independent of each other. The modifications that we observe daily in the retail facilities in our neighborhood reflect the interaction between complex changes in housing, demography, and income structure. When households are smaller and people have higher incomes they tend to own more cars; retail employees demand higher wages. Higher wages and greater personal mobility lead retail chains to invest in larger stores with a higher degree of automation and thus, fewer workers.

The point of examining change in the past is to anticipate what may happen in the future. The new forms and locations for retail facilities are not entirely accidental; they are logically related to continuing patterns of social and economic change.

## The effect of population growth

Population growth leads to the most dramatic spatial changes in the retail fabric. A city grows, extending hundreds of acres of subdivisions into the countryside, and within every suburb sits a shopping mall. A new express-way intersection is constructed and a major regional shopping plaza emerges almost at once. Every symbol of population growth, from a suburban tract to a new downtown apartment building, is accompanied by new retail facilities. As we saw in the previous section, the rate of population growth is only half the rate of growth in real income per capita but the place-to-place variation in population growth makes it important to retailers. Income levels increase everywhere but population growth has a powerful geography of its own. Exhibit 6.2 describes the growth of regional markets.

Exhibit 6.2
### THE GROWTH OF REGIONAL MARKETS

The pattern of growth of a spatial market, hence the rate of investment and the opportunities for new retailers, is often more spatially dispersed than the pre-existing pattern of retail activity (as shown in Figure 5.2). The following map depicts the growth of the US market between 1963 and 1985. Each dot represents one-hundredth of the total growth ($537 billion in 1985 dollars). Unlike Figure 5.2 this map balances the growth along the northeastern seaboard with growth in California. The 'Rustbelt' of the Midwest gives way to the 'Sunbelt'. Within the apparent dispersion, however, there is some remarkable concentration. Three states: California, Texas, and Florida, account for almost one-third of all growth in the country; including the growth in retail sales, floor area, and stores. These growth areas will generate the retail giants of tomorrow.

*Source:* Bureau of the Census (1963) *Census of Retail Trade*; Bureau of the Census (1988) *The Statistical Abstract of the United States*

Exhibit 6.2 (*continued*)

LEGEND

Percentiles of national growth ●
Retail sales (US) grew by 62.6%
= $537 billion
One dot = 1% of that growth

Pacific

HAWAII

0   100   200 MILES

ALASKA

0   200   400 MILES

0   200   400 MILES

*Source:* The authors

In Figure 6.3 the growth in the local market is related to the expansion of shopping centers. The relationship is not exact, because the size of planned centers varies greatly, there is a time-lag between urban growth and putting a center in operation, and the initial shopping capacities of markets vary. However, the graph suggests that for every billion dollars growth in the market another twelve centers are generated. New York and New Jersey appear to lag behind.

At this point we can turn back to equation 5.1 which describes the fundamental retail relationship between income and sales. If income at any one point in time explains the amount of distribution activity, then an increase in income should lead to an increase in retail activity:

Retail sales* $= -0.218 + 0.714$ market income*, $r^2 = 0.662$.     (eqn 6.1)

Note: *rate of growth for retail sales, 1972–82; for market income, 1970–80, using 100 metropolitan statistical areas.

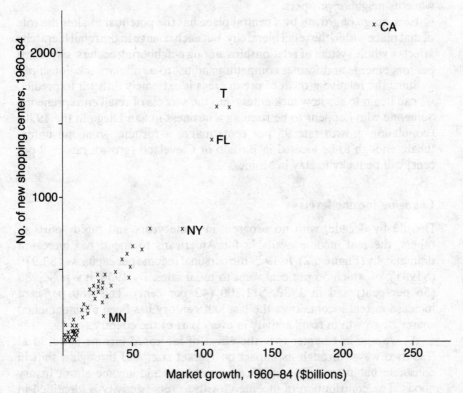

**Figure 6.3** Market growth and shopping center development

*Source:* Bureau of the Census (1976) *Statistical Abstract of the United States*; and *Shopping Center World*

The equation indicates an overall decline in retail sales of 21.8 per cent (the intercept), due in part to a statistical aberration. Between 1979 and 1980 incomes were high but 2 years later incomes and retail sales dropped sharply as the country plunged into recession. In addition, Americans shifted expenditures away from retail goods into services, housing, and taxes, but this decline was compensated by the continued growth in population and income. Of the growth rate for market income, 71.4 per cent is translated into retail sales. This simple model explains two-thirds of the place-to-place variance.

In some cases, the expansion of retail activity grows even more rapidly than the rate of growth of the local market. The retail function of the city expands because the city can better compete within the settlement system. Delicately balanced competitive structures are typical of the retail hierarchy. If the advantage shifts toward one of the two competing towns, rapid changes in retail functions may occur. In small centers, a fire, or the loss a of single large enterprise, can start a village down the road to decline while its neighbor prospers.

Each surge of growth by a central place has the potential to alter the role of that place within the retail hierarchy, but each change in the retail hierarchy affects a whole system of relationships among neighboring centers: new competitors emerge and former competitors adjust to a tributary relationship.

Since the relative growth of urban areas is extremely difficult to predict, we can begin to see how luck enters into the success of retail entrepreneurs. Someone who happens to be running a business in San Diego in the 1970s (population growth rate 95 per cent) makes a fortune; someone unfortunate enough to be located in Buffalo or Cleveland (growth rate − 9 per cent) will be lucky to stay in business.

## Changing income levels

Decade by decade, with no progress in some years and rapid spurts in others, the real income available for Americans to spend has increased dramatically (Figure 6.2). In 1929 the personal income per capita was $3,970 ($1981), of which 56 per cent went to retail sales. By 1958, it was $6,930 (56 per cent) and in 1982, $11,100 (42 per cent). This 180 per cent increase in real income over the last half century has been a fundamental source of growth in retail activity in every part of the country.

As we saw in Chapter two, the effect of increased income is felt in at least two ways: through its impact on market size, and through a shift in consumer habits towards non-store expenditures and income-elastic luxury goods. The contribution of income growth to retail activity is identified in equation 6.2, which determines the rate of growth in retail employment using three independent variables: population growth rate, income per capita growth rate, and ($\log_{10}$) size of urban region.

Retail sales* = −0.253 + 0.818 Population* + 0.936 Income/capita*,
  $r^2 = 0.700$.                                                                                    eqn 6.2

Note: *rate of growth for retail sales, 1972–82; for market measures, 1970–80.

While this model suggests that retail sales are highly responsive to population growth, almost all the per capita income growth is also translated into new retail activity. In any spatial market, then, the retailer can expect a gradual increase in sales due to the increasing affluence of the clientele, and over an extended period (a decade or so) substantial growth will result which may be as high as 30 per cent. Unfortunately, retailers, too, wish to increase their own real income and that of their employees. The result is an inexorable pressure to increase sales per store and sales per employee.

While income levels have grown everywhere, they have one notable spatial pattern. Over the last five decades there has been a substantial reduction in the place-to-place variation in income levels across the country. One reason for the greater spatial equality of income has been the substantial increase in programs that redistribute income by various levels of government, such as revenue sharing and social security benefits. Also important, and often overlooked, has been the continuing urbanization of our society. It is well known that larger urban centers generate higher levels of income with particularly dramatic differences occurring between farming and non-farming and non-farming populations. As the number of farmers declines the whole country becomes better off and the differences between urban states such as Massachusetts and rural states such as Mississippi decline.

As a result, the mix of retail activities in smaller centers has become more and more like that of the largest cities. People in Dubuque are eating the same imported foods, drinking the same wines, and buying the same labels as the sophisticates in Manhattan. While the threshold size of retail stores has been rapidly increasing, the market incomes in smaller cities have grown even more rapidly and business types have moved steadily down the retail hierarchy. Some developers have made a point of seeking out small markets for shopping centers, aware of the growth in market size that reflects higher incomes rather than population growth.

As seen in Chapter two, however, the increase in income per capita does not affect all sectors of the retail system equally; it tends to direct the customer's purchases towards the shopping goods carried by fashion stores, automobile dealers and such specialty stores as sports, pets, gifts, and antiques. The results of these changes in purchasing habits are shown in Table 6.2. Some kinds of stores have grown rapidly while others have declined. The most rapid growth has taken place in the restaurant and automotive groups (see next section), while the slowest growth has

**Table 6.2** Retail sales by business type: 1929–82 ($1982)

| | 1929 ($ billions) | 1939 | 1948 | 1958 | 1967 | 1977 | 1982 | Growth Rate, 1929–82 (%) |
|---|---|---|---|---|---|---|---|---|
| Lumber/Building materials (52. .) | 11.16 | 10.27 | 20.55 | 23.78 | n.a. | 43.20 | 35.14 | 214.9 |
| Hardware | 3.98 | 4.37 | 9.99 | 9.07 | 8.13 | 9.78 | 8.73 | 119.3 |
| Farm and garden | 2.92 | 2.39 | 9.57 | 10.63 | 13.97 | 2.86 | 3.12 | 6.8 |
| Total | 21.67 | 19.00 | 44.68 | 47.76 | 49.73 | 58.80 | 50.99 | 135.3 |
| Department stores (5211) | 24.51 | 27.63 | 37.82 | 44.59 | 43.51 | 113.18 | 99.77 | 307.1 |
| Variety stores (5331) | 5.09 | 6.78 | 10.04 | 12.09 | 15.63 | 11.13 | 8.21 | 61.3 |
| Other general | 6.71 | 4.96 | 15.48 | 16.35 | 16.73 | 15.58 | 13.03 | 94.2 |
| Total | 36.31 | 39.37 | 63.34 | 73.03 | 125.87 | 139.89 | 120.41 | 231.6 |
| Grocery stores | 41.43 | 53.67 | 99.17 | 145.86 | 188.13 | 252.37 | 246.12 | 444.1 |
| Meat markets | 7.06 | 4.87 | 6.58 | 7.77 | 5.29 | 6.14 | 5.65 | −20.0 |
| Fruit, vegetables | 1.74 | 1.54 | 1.58 | 1.69 | 1.30 | 1.74 | 1.55 | −10.9 |
| Candy stores | 3.22 | 2.05 | 2.35 | 1.76 | 1.56 | 1.04 | 0.97 | −69.9 |
| Bakeries | 1.13 | 1.17 | 2.90 | 3.03 | 3.87 | 3.75 | 3.75 | 231.9 |
| Total | 61.07 | 70.65 | 117.12 | 163.64 | 203.10 | 252.40 | 246.12 | 303.0 |
| Automobile dealers | 36.10 | 34.77 | 73.75 | 94.50 | 140.59 | 205.15 | 162.94 | 351.4 |
| Tires and accessories | 3.38 | 3.63 | 54.46 | 8.09 | 12.25 | 20.86 | 21.16 | 526.0 |
| Gasoline stations | 10.07 | 19.61 | 25.94 | 47.33 | 65.65 | 90.22 | 97.44 | 867.6 |
| Total | 49.75 | 58.17 | 106.55 | 153.50 | 226.43 | 329.38 | 290.96 | 484.1 |
| Shoes | 4.54 | 4.29 | 5.85 | 6.33 | 8.68 | 11.24 | 11.42 | 151.5 |
| Women's apparel | 6.13 | 7.01 | 13.14 | 16.39 | 15.55 | 19.97 | 20.41 | 233.0 |
| Men's apparel | 6.72 | 5.37 | 8.69 | 8.67 | 10.08 | 23.10 | 18.60 | 176.8 |
| Other apparel | 6.50 | 5.97 | 11.28 | 10.42 | 13.89 | 16.77 | 18.19 | 37.6 |
| Total | 23.89 | 22.64 | 38.96 | 41.81 | 48.20 | 59.20 | 57.82 | 142.0 |

| | | | | | | | | |
|---|---|---|---|---|---|---|---|---|
| Furniture | 8.89 | 6.76 | 13.69 | 15.97 | 18.98 | 22.40 | 17.66 | 98.6 |
| Appliances | 5.35 | 3.70 | 9.66 | 11.68 | 17.40 | 7.53 | 13.90 | 159.8 |
| Electronics | n.a. | n.a. | n.a. | n.a. | n.a. | 13.03 | 13.81 | n.a. |
| Total | 15.52 | 12.04 | 26.43 | 33.63 | 42.04 | 53.08 | 46.76 | 201. |
| Restaurants (5812) | 11.97 | 14.84 | 25.82 | 36.84 | 54.58 | 88.68 | 95.09 | 694. |
| Bars (5813) | 0 | 9.63 | 16.86 | 13.90 | 14.35 | 12.27 | 9.50 | −1.* |
| Total | 11.97 | 24.47 | 42.68 | 50.74 | 68.93 | 100.95 | 104.59 | 773.8 |
| Drugstores | 9.52 | 10.86 | 16.08 | 22.63 | 31.60 | 37.25 | 36.44 | 282.8 |
| Liquor stores | 0 | 4.07 | 10.33 | 14.03 | 19.26 | 20.76 | 18.15 | 345.9* |
| Fuel, ice dealers | 5.71 | 7.04 | 9.72 | 11.59 | 10.40 | 16.20 | 17.06 | 198.8 |
| Jewelry stores | 3.02 | 2.51 | 4.85 | 4.99 | 6.38 | 9.10 | 8.83 | 192.4 |
| Cigar stores | 2.31 | 1.44 | 1.54 | 0.78 | 1.02 | 0.75 | 0.62 | −73.2 |
| Florists | 0.99 | 1.03 | 1.50 | 2.13 | 3.19 | 3.84 | 3.73 | 276.8 |
| Gifts | 0.34 | 0.37 | 0.74 | 1.30 | n.a. | 4.10 | 5.04 | 1382.4 |
| Second-hand stores | 0.83 | 0.96 | 1.19 | 1.84 | n.a. | 4.54 | 4.67 | 462.7 |
| Other | 29.44 | 17.57 | 30.97 | 42.82 | n.a. | 57.45 | 53.73 | 96.3 |
| Total miscellaneous | 52.16 | 45.85 | 76.92 | 102.31 | 132.49 | 153.99 | 148.27 | 184. |
| All Retail | 272.00 | 292.00 | 517.00 | 666.00 | 897.00 | 1,148.00 | 1,066.00 | 291.9 |

Source: Bureau of the Census (1976); Historical Statistics of the United States: Colonial Times to 1970; Bureau of the Census (1982) Census of Retail Trade, Washington

Note: *Prohibition in 1929; growth rate calculated from 1939.

occurred in the building materials and clothing groups. Many of the shifts are directly attributable to higher income levels, the increased sales of liquor, flowers, and gifts, for example. Others are indirectly affected by the technological innovations that depend on consumer income: refrigerators doomed the ice dealers and butcher shops; home appliances and home entertainment generated a variety of new furniture stores. Others reflect new lifestyles: women working outside the home buy more clothes, but fewer hats. The joint growth of supermarkets and bakeries reflects changes in consumer behavior as well as changes in income and mobility.

The enormous overall growth of retail sales – almost 300 per cent in the study period – contrasts with the rather slow growth in the number of stores – just under 40 per cent. Because we know that large numbers of new outlets have located in shopping plazas and suburban strips, by implication there are far fewer stores in small towns and inner cities. For example, the number of drug stores in America has declined by over 10 per cent while sales have increased fourfold. Think of the implications for changes in the size of stores and their location requirements.

## Transportation and other technology

As consumers become better off they can afford to buy automobiles, and they do so. Figure 6.2 showed that the ratio of automobiles to people has increased from 2:10 just after the Second World War to more than 5:10 at present. As society has more financial resources it spends more on roads. As cars and highways are better designed they carry us further, faster, and more efficiently. The effect of all these improvements is to increase the mobility of the consumer, who is no longer limited to walking distance (about half a mile) or transit distance (3–5 miles), but has an effective shopping range of up to 15 miles. This increase in mobility has been somewhat offset by the accompanying dispersal of residential and retail activity, reflected in reduced population and land-use densities. Nonetheless, every household has access to far more shopping alternatives than it did 10, 20, or 50 years ago. Following the arguments of Chapter two, this reduction in the relative costs of transportation should increase overall levels of consumption.

Transportation changes affect retail location by changing the slope of the spatial demand curve (Figure 6.4). Over time the attractiveness of store A to nearby households has declined because of greater competition from distant stores, while its attractiveness to more distant consumers may have increased. The spatial monopoly conveyed by a store's location within a residential market has given way to product monopoly, based on mix of products, brands, or special services. Direct competition among stores has increased: the effective range of a store's trade area is now shaped not by the spatial demand curve but by the actions of its competitors. Exhibit 6.3 illustrates the effects of changing mobility.

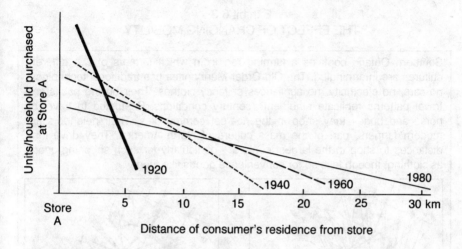

**Figure 6.4** The changing spatial demand curve

*Source:* The authors

These changes have resulted in some dramatic sorting out among the smaller settlements in the retail hierarchy, though paradoxically, increased spatial competition has been partly offset by the spectacular growth of the automotive group. In 1929 the latter accounted for 18 per cent of all sales; by 1982 this figure had reached 27 per cent. While automotive dealerships are a classic comparison-shopping activity, service stations and garages just as clearly provide convenience goods and have now become the main retail activity in many of the smallest settlements.

Still, the overall effect of transportation improvements has been to reduce the role of the smallest places in the retail hierarchy. Table 6.3 shows the pattern of change in the province of Saskatchewan in Canada. In this wheat-growing region (much like the Dakotas) settlements provide services for farmers – just as in central place theory. However, over 20 years improved accessibility has changed the retail hierarchy significantly. The number of centers at each of the intermediate levels has declined while the number of activities provided at each level has increased. The result is fewer, but more complex service centers. The spatial structure has also changed, as two-thirds of the level four centers have disappeared. The surviving centers are more widely spaced as only one center remains from each pair of competing settlements. Overall, increased mobility has shifted the trade-off between variety and accessibility toward the larger, more distant centers.

To put it another way: retailers in even the smallest hamlets now face

## Exhibit 6.3
## THE EFFECT OF CHANGING MOBILITY

Southern Ontario contains a farming region in which farmers of two different cultures are intermingled. The Old Order Mennonites use traditional technology: no cars, no electricity, no appliances or fancy clothes. Their buying habits and travel patterns replicate nineteenth century conditions. Restricted to travel by horse and buggy they shop in the nearest communities. Their neighbors are modern farmers, part of the mass culture of North America. They drive long distances to shop in the largest centers – particularly for such shopping goods as clothing, though less so for convenience goods like food.

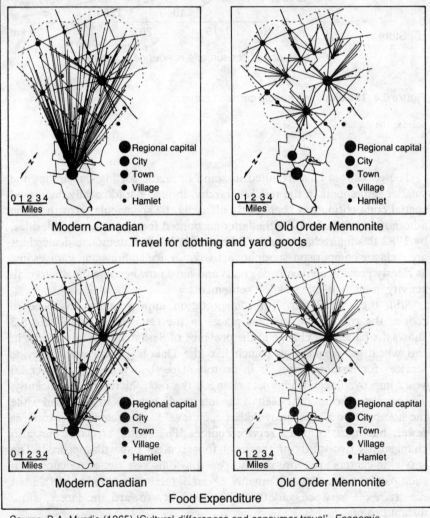

Source: R.A. Murdie (1965) 'Cultural differences and consumer travel', *Economic Geography*, 41: 211–33

**Table 6.3** Changes in the retail hierarchy: Saskatchewan

| Level in the Retail | Number of Places | | Population (thousands) | | Number of activities * | |
|---|---|---|---|---|---|---|
| Hierarchy | 1961 | 1981 | 1961 | 1981 | 1961 | 1981 |
| Largest center | | | | | | |
| (e.g. Regina) | 2 | 2 | 103.8 | 158.4 | 1525 | 3438 |
| Second level | | | | | | |
| (Moose Jaw) | 8 | 8 | 14.2 | 16.7 | 287 | 544 |
| Third level | 29 | 22 | 2.2 | 3.0 | 78 | 134 |
| Fourth level | 99 | 30 | 0.7 | 1.3 | 33 | 57 |
| Fifth level | 189 | 136 | 0.3 | 0.5 | 17 | 21 |
| Sixth level | 271 | 400 | 0.1 | 0.1 | 6 | 5 |

Source: J.C. Stabler (1987) 'Trade Center Evolution in the Great Plains', Journal of Regional Science 27, 2:225–44
Note: *Activities include all businesses reported in Dun and Bradstreet (see Appendix B).

competition from larger, better stocked stores in the neighboring towns. As discussed in Chapter three, retailers may respond to this intensification of competition in different ways. One approach is to increase the scale of operation, using economies of scale to compete with other retailers. Large markets with high levels of accessibility permit a very wide range of operating scales, as will be shown in the following section.

Another frequently observed option is specialization, leading to a diversification of business types. By focusing on a different product mix or a specialized target audience, the retailer avoids direct confrontation with a competitor. Both of these trends – larger stores and greater specialization – are also encouraged by the increased incomes of consumers. The result is a much higher ratio of business types to number of stores. A small town that used to have four grocery and two hardware stores may now have a single larger version of each but may also possess a deli, a bakery, an appliance dealer, and a paint and wallpaper store.

Sometimes the whole town develops a specialized niche. L.L. Bean turned Freeport, Maine into a major tourist attraction. There is a town near Winnipeg that has developed a specialization in automobile dealerships and people come from miles around to compare models and prices. Also, large numbers of places now depend on recreational activities. As Exhibit 6.4 suggests, tourists increase retail sales as well as the takings of hotels and restaurants. Many travellers seem to be motivated by shopping.

**The organization of enterprise**

A retailer who had opened a business in the 1920s would have to make some major adjustments in order to pass a thriving business on to his

## Exhibit 6.4
## RECREATIONAL RETAILING

Real estate developers have found that any land use activity that attracts a crowd also has value as a retail location. Even people in a hurry will buy things, see, for example, the souvenir stands outside the stadium or the news-stands at a commuter station. The very best customers are people on vacation – away from the usual distractions, slightly bored, looking for a way to stretch out an experience. 'We've stared at Niagara Falls: now what do we do?' Think of it this way: each hotel room is the equivalent of an extra household with a $100,000 income.

Shopping linked with recreation has grown explosively, at both the settlement and metropolitan scale. The map on p. 195 shows the retail sales per capita of the Florida counties. Note that the six main resort areas have sales levels that are twice as high as the median, and for special subareas – like Palm Beach, Key West, Sanibel, or Naples – the ratios are much higher.

If we take into account the income of Florida residents we find that in 1982 each additional hotel or motel room generated about $10,000 in retail sales for its county. These expenditures are highly skewed towards certain kinds of retail activities, especially shopping goods, from clothes to the miscellaneous specialty shops. You've probably seen some of the more excessive concentrations, like Gatlinburg in the Great Smokies, or a large beach resort.

### PERCENTAGES OF INCOME GENERATED
### BY VARIOUS GOODS AND SERVICES

|  | Building materials | General | Food | Auto | Gas | Clothes | Furniture | Res-taurants | Drugs | Miscel-laneous |
|---|---|---|---|---|---|---|---|---|---|---|
| Florida | 4.8 | 11.0 | 22.8 | 20.6 | 8.8 | 5.0 | 5.0 | 10.2 | 3.7 | 8.2 |
| Naples | 4.3 | 11.2 | 25.5 | 13.4 | 6.1 | 8.0 | 7.9 | 10.5 | 3.9 | 9.2 |

*Source:* Bureau of Economic and Business Research, University of Florida (1987) *Florida Statistical Abstract*, Gainesville, Florida

grandchild in the 1980s. Many of the changes have been suggested above: a shift in product mix to suit higher household incomes, an increase in the scale of operation to reflect higher incomes and higher wages, relocation to take advantage of greater household mobility, and/or expansion into a planned center in order to compete with the chains.

Few stores survive such changes. For the most part, stores don't adjust; they go out of business and are replaced by new activities more suited to new conditions. Sometimes the store is absorbed by a chain. Figure 6.5 outlines some of the major changes in the organization of retail activity over time. Note first the long-term impact of changes in consumer spending. Since 1948 there has been relatively little growth in non-

Exhibit 6.4 (*continued*)

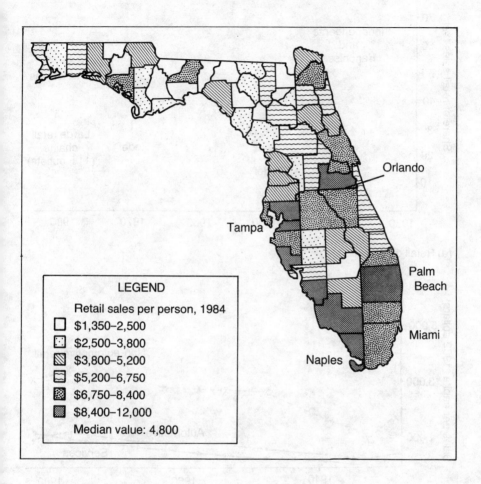

LEGEND

Retail sales per person, 1984

☐ $1,350–2,500
▫ $2,500–3,800
▨ $3,800–5,200
⊟ $5,200–6,750
▩ $6,750–8,400
▦ $8,400–12,000

Median value: 4,800

automotive retailing on a per capita basis, and within retailing the shares of the various groups have remained essentially the same. The major shift, aside from the expansion of automobile-related activity, is the even more rapid growth in private services. Superimposed on these changes is the linkage of stores into retail chains and franchise operations. The role of the chains did not really expand until the mid-1950s when planned shopping centers began to spread across the landscape. Chains and malls were made for each other, but with the decline in the rate of construction of new malls and the growth of franchising, the growth of chain activity has flattened out. At the same time, the spatial reach of retail chains is expending. The very largest chains become larger, local chains expand

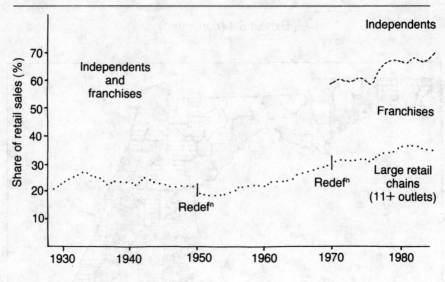

(a) Retail organization

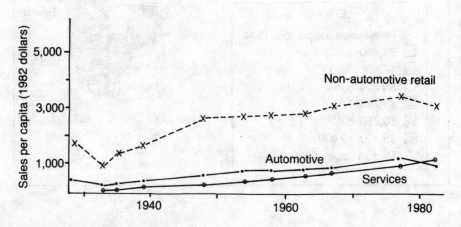

(b) Sales/capita by sector

**Figure 6.5** The reorganization of the retail system

*Source:* Bureau of the Census (1976) *Historical Statistics of the United States* and *Statistical Abstract of the United States* (annual)

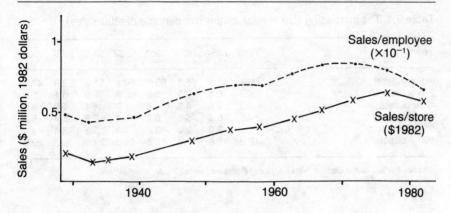

(c) Changes in store characteristics

*Source:* Bureau of the Census (various years) *Census of Retail Trade*, Washington

to nearby cities, regional chains become national, and national chains go international.

Inevitably, the retail chains and the shopping center developers impose uniformity on the retail landscape across the country. From Portland, Maine to Portland, Oregon, shopping plazas are designed by the same architect, using universal materials, and leased to the same set of national chains. The prices may very slightly but the products are all the same: the same paperbacks and candy bars, the same colors for sweaters or shoes, the same records and movies.

A measure of how this has occurred is given in Table 6.4 which records the growing concentration of retail activity in the very largest chains, the ones that serve national or regional markets. As the role of the chains has expanded, the importance of the largest (100 + outlets) has expanded even more rapidly, until these 376 organizations now account for over 60 per cent of chain sales. While new local chains keep emerging, the larger ones grow even faster or swallow up the smaller ones.

Laulajainen's (1987) study gives us an insight into how retail chains expand in space. He differentiates convenience type stores with low market thresholds, low markups, and high logistics costs from shopping goods chains. Chains of the first type must build strong local and regional networks before they attempt to expand nationally. Consider three super-market chains (Figure 6.6). A & P is a predominantly eastern chain with temporary western outliers while Safeway is a West Coast chain which is moving eastward. Kroger's (including Dillon's) is a Midwest chain. Each one expands into contiguous areas: the occasional attempt to break into a distant market is often disastrous, in part because the competition is so

**Table 6.4** The increasing size of retail chains (percentage of retail sales)

| Year | 1948 | 1954 | 1958 | 1963 | 1967 | 1972 | 1977 | 1982 |
|---|---|---|---|---|---|---|---|---|
| Independents | 70.4 | 69.9 | 66.3 | 63.3 | 60.2 | 51.8 | 52.9 | 47.7 |
| 2–3 outlets | 6.9 | 6.4 | 6.9 | 6.5 | 5.8 | 5.9 | 6.1 | 6.8 |
| 4–10 outlets | 4.2 | 3.8 | 4.5 | 4.6 | 4.7 | 4.4 | 4.9 | 4.9 |
| 11–50 outlets | 4.6 | 5.3 | 5.7 | 6.5 | 6.5 | 5.8 | 6.4 | 6.8 |
| 51–100 outlets | 1.6 | 2.0 | 2.3 | 3.2 | 4.2 | 3.3 | 3.4 | 4.1 |
| 100 + outlets | 12.3 | 12.6 | 14.3 | 15.8 | 18.6 | 24.6 | 26.3 | 29.5 |

*Source:* Bureau of the Census (various years) *Census of Retail Trade*, Washington

strongly entrenched. The Federal Trade Commission watches acquisitions closely. The real battles occur at the margins of the service areas shown here.

The great department stores chains, as exemplified by Allied Department Stores (Figure 6.7), have grown by acquiring existing stores in distant markets. The spatial strategy is serendipitous, depending on the acquisition alternatives and the corporate financial situation. Some obvious markets – Chicago, California – are not covered and some peculiar outlets remains as traces of earlier acquisitions. Since this map was drawn the pace of restructuring has accelerated (See Chapter twelve).

One of the most fascinating recent stories in American retailing is the explosive growth of Wal-Mart Stores from a single outlet in 1962 to more than 1,000 outlets in 1988 (Figure 6.8). This growth occurred in the most unlikely markets, i.e. in small, low-income communities in the South, but there is some logic to the store's success. Thanks in part to the massive investment in interstate highways and the rapid industrialization of this region, income levels in this area have risen (See Exhibit 6.2). Wal-Mart insists that new outlets be accessible to headquarters and warehouses for close supervision and cost-cutting inventory controls.

The diversity of retail chains and the spatial strategies that they practice largely defy generalization. Still, Laulajainen indicates in Figure 6.8 the routes followed by retail chains as they expand from local to regional to national organizations. Many chains begin in the great market concentrations: the New York region, Chicago and the Midwest, or southern California. New York is still the leader in fashion goods speciality chains, with close links to New England, the east coast (especially Florida), and the Midwest. Midwest firms expand to the south (down the Mississippi) and the southwest (Route 66). From southern California retail chains expand northward along the coast and back to the southwest. Growth in the target regions accelerates expansion and competition; stagnation or decline frustrates expansion.

Exhibit 6.5 makes the point in another way, showing how a national

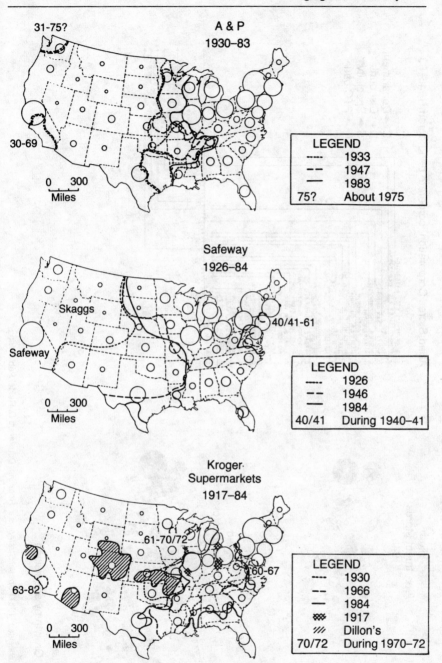

**Figure 6.6** Spatial expansion by supermarket chains

*Source:* R. Laulajainen (1987) *Spatial Strategies in Retailing*, Dordrecht: D. Reidel Publishing

## Allied Stores Corporation, corporate dendrogram 1945–83

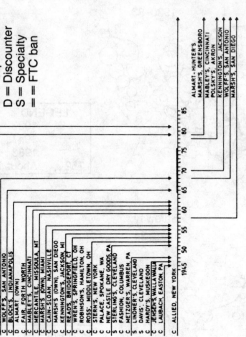

C = Department
D = Discounter
S = Specialty
= = FTC ban

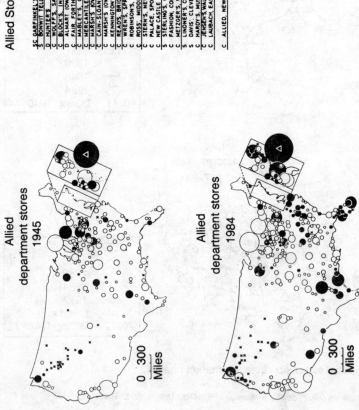

**Figure 6.7** Growth by acquisition

*Source:* R. Laulajainen (1987) *Spatial Strategies in Retailing*, Dordrecht: D. Reidel Publishing

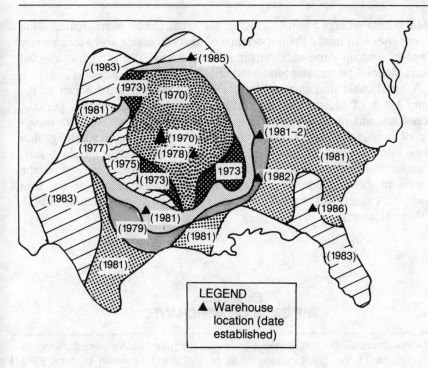

**Figure 6.8** The growth of Wal-Mart (southeastern United States)

*Source:* R. Laulajainen (1987) *Spatial Strategies in Retailing*, Dordrecht: D. Reidel Publishing

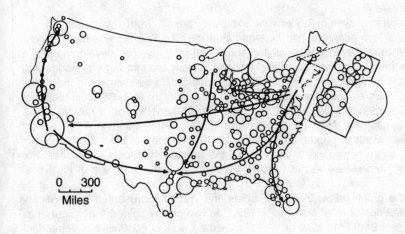

**Figure 6.9** The routes for expansion

*Source:* R. Laulajainen (1987) *Spatial Strategies in Retailing*, Dordrecht: D. Reidel Publishing

retail system emerged before most of the retail chains were created. One cannot over emphasize the importance of Sears Roebuck and Montgomery Ward in shaping America's consumption patterns. The catalogue created wants, defined prices, and pioneered new retailing procedures.

A retail chain that survives for over half a century must adjust to the many kinds of radical changes outlined in this chapter: boom periods, recessions, and variations in patterns of urban growth and in the consumption of various products. In addition, the chain must develop a strategy that takes into account its own strengths and weaknesses – product mix, financial base, management ability, and market share – as well as the actions of its competitors. The market environment changes: the firm changes. A successful strategy requires some creative combination of both of these elements.

## Exhibit 6.5
## THE CATALOG MERCHANTS

No innovations in the retail system have had such far-reaching implications as the creation of the great catalog firms in the late nineteenth century. First Montgomery Ward (1872), and then Richard Sears (1886) initiated retail systems in Chicago that penetrated into every community in the nation, creating new demands and shaping the stock and prices of local merchants. Eventually they were both to grow into great department store chains and Sears Roebuck, in particular, has continued to innovate as it has grown into America's greatest retail empire.

The catalog system underwent explosive growth from the beginning. An enormous farm economy had emerged after the Civil War but was badly served by small town merchants of varying ability and integrity. The development of a national rail service and an efficient postal system brought big city goods and prices within reach, with minimal time and cost. Each improvement in the postal system, such as the introduction of rural free delivery in 1896 or parcel post in 1913, expanded the market. By 1893 Ward's handled half a million orders per year and by 1899 its catalog was 1,000 pages thick. In 1900 it sold $8 million worth of goods, but Sears sold $100 million. As the catalog services thrived, angry newspaper stories reveal the threat to the local merchants. The catalogs were mailed in plain brown wrappers to avoid sabotage at local post offices.

As the graph below indicates, Sears and Ward's represented extraordinary concentrations of retail activity. By 1920 the two chains shared 1 per cent of all retail sales. Both firms built up a widespread network of controlled or dependent suppliers, plus huge distribution centers throughout the country. Ward's built warehouses in Kansas City, St Paul, and Portland: Sears went to Dallas, Atlanta, and Los Angeles. However, by the 1920s the small towns and agricultural econ-omies were no longer growing. The children who had grown up with the cata-log were moving to the expanding cities. In 1925 Sears opened its first retail store in Evansville; Ward's followed suit soon after. By 1930 each firm had more than 300 retail outlets. Again, the local merchants protested and state govern-ments imposed special taxes on the chain outlets.

The map on p. 202 shows Sears' penetration of the market across the country in 1939. The pattern is quite irregular and must reflect the local competitive situation. By this time the department stores had been open for more than a decade and Sears was doing best in urban markets: the Midwest, of course, but also the north-east and parts of the south. They did very poorly in the sparsely settled rural areas west of the Mississippi. Outside the Midwest the best state was Mississippi where their share was twice the national level.

The growth of Sears and Ward's more than kept pace with the nation. Sears became one of the largest firms in the country with sales equal to 2.5 per cent of national retail sales in 1970. A spectrum of retail outlets was developed. Thousands of catalog outlets simply delivered shipments from the distribution centers. 'C' stores retailed hard goods as well, 'A' stores carried the complete range of Sears goods, and smaller 'B' stores about 60 per cent of the range. Each store format targeted a certain kind of market. As the population of the country became more and more urban, Sears focused on the big stores for urban consumers. They established a new retail form – free-standing, auto-mobile-oriented, on the major arterial roads that served the growing suburbs. In the post-war period Ward's dropped back from Sears, to be replaced by a revitalized J.C. Penney (another catalog firm!) and the upstart K mart. In the late 1980s Sears and K mart are neck and neck.

The story of Sears and Ward's represents the whole thrust of chain retailing. The catalog created national markets by transmitting images, wants, needs, and fashions to every part of the United States. By 1910 Sears sent out over four million catalogs, providing the only reading material in many homes. Its 50,000 items far exceeded the stock of any but the largest stores. These firms also imposed national prices everywhere, placing severe constraints on the pricing policies ('the village tyranny') of local stores. Catalog prices seldom varied by more than 3 or 4 per cent across the country. Also, they introduced new ways of distribution, purchasing, and administration, bypassing traditional wholesalers to develop their own sources of supply. One of the results was a transfer of retail activity (i.e. employment) for smaller places into the key nodes in the catalog system.

*Sources:* F.B. Latham (1972) *A Century of Servicing Consumers: the Story of Montgomery Ward*, Chicago, Montgomery Ward; B. Emmet and J. Jeuck (1950) *Catalogues and Counters: a History of Sears Roebuck and Company*, Chicago: University of Chicago Press

Exhibit 6.5 (*continued*)

(a) SEARS MARKET PENETRATION, 1939
(PERCENTAGE OF TOTAL RETAIL SALES IN STATE)

0.34

0.28

0.34

0.08

0.04

0.07

0.14

0.11

1.29
1.60

0.62

0.74

0.19

0.10

0.81

1.31
2.27
2.31

0.66

1.43

2.06

0.61

0.44
1.28
1.07

0.53

0.59
1.04

1.20

1.27

0.87
0.46
1.27
1.43

1.65

0.96
0.51
0.41

Exhibit 6.5 *(continued)*

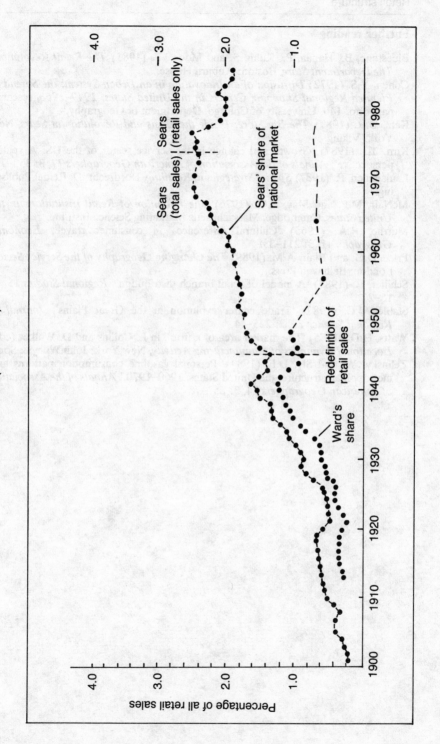

# Further reading

Bluestone, B., Hanaa, P., Kuhn, S. and Moore, L. (1981) *The Retail Revolution: The Department Store*, Boston: Auburn House.

Cohen, Y.S. (1972) *Diffusion of an Innovation in an Urban System: the Spread of Planned Regional Shopping Centers in the United States, 1949–1968*, research paper no. 140, University of Chicago, Department of Geography.

Katz, D.R. (1987) *The Big Store: Inside the Crisis and Revolution at Sears*, New York: Viking.

Kirn, T.J. (1987) 'Growth and change in the service sector of the US: A spatial perspective', *Annals of the Association of American Geographers* 77, 3: 353–72.

Laulajainen, R. (1987) *Spatial Strategies in Retailing*, Dordrecht: D. Reidel Publishing.

McNair, M.P. and May, E.G. (1976) *The Evolution of Retail Institutions in the United States*, Cambridge, Massachusetts Marketing Science Institute.

Murdie, R.A. (1965) 'Cultural differences in consumer travel', *Economic Geography* 41, 3: 211–33.

Price, D.G. and Blair, A.M. (1989) *The Changing Geography of the Service Sector*, London: Belhaven Press.

Schiller, R. (1981) 'A model of retail branch distribution', *Regional Studies* 15, 1: 15–22.

Stabler, J.C. (1987) 'Trade center evolution in the Great Plains', *Journal of Regional Science* 27, 2: 225–44.

Watts, H.D. (1975) 'The market area of a firm', in L. Collins and D. Walker (eds) *Locational Dynamics of Manufacturing Activity*, New York: John Wiley & Sons.

Zelinsky, W. and Sly, D.F. (1984) 'Personal gasoline consumption patterns and metropolitan structure: the United States, 1960–1970,' *Annals of the Association of American Geographers* 74, 3: 257–78.

# Chapter seven

# Commercial structure within the metropolis

> Over half the retail sales in Chicago take place in small plazas, retail strips, and free-standing stores along major arterial streets.

> You can tell a neighborhood by the retail chains it attracts.

> 'The shopping mall completed the link between the highway and television' (Kowinski, 1985).

> The proliferation of speciality retail clusters increases the complexity of the retailer's location decision.

The diversity of lifestyles within a large metropolitan area, the neighborhoods stratified by social class, race and ethnicity, and the relatively short distances between consumers and shopping facilities, have led to a bewildering variety of retail groupings. The junk food arterial strip, the automobile row, the flashy boutique area, Chinatown or Greektown, the utilitarian suburban plaza, the theme mall, and the linear retail strip of the inner city are all familiar variants of the metropolitan retail structure.

This chapter describes the various components of the urban retail landscape. First, we will examine the contemporary retail hierarchy as it has developed within the city, and second, the structure and development of the planned shopping center, a relatively recent innovation that now dominates suburban retailing. In the final two sections we will discuss the responses of the inner city: the emergence of specialized retail environments in older residential areas and the role of downtown. The following chapter will describe some of the current trends and the forces behind these changes.

Before we examine the spatial organization of retailing within the city, let us take a brief look at the pattern of demand that must be served. Figure 7.1 describes some of the important features of the Atlanta metropolitan market – about two million people in total, with an average income per capita of $7,800 in 1980. Three significant elements are apparent in this map and in almost every metropolitan area. First, the population (and market income) is still distributed around a central node, but less so than 2 or 3 decades ago. Although the street and mass transit system focus on downtown, major investments in expressways have created important secondary nodes around the periphery of the city. Second, the railroads and expressways subdivide the city into natural residential communities that shape retail trade areas. In the 1960s and 1970s the expressway system generated three spatial extensions along major access routes into the city, to the northwest, the northeast, and the south. Third, high- and low-income households are strongly segregated into distinct sectors of the city, divided by a line that cuts through the city just north of the central business district. South of the line incomes are less than half the metropolitan average, while to the north incomes are over twice the average figure. Suburban income levels vary less sharply. These income groups are further

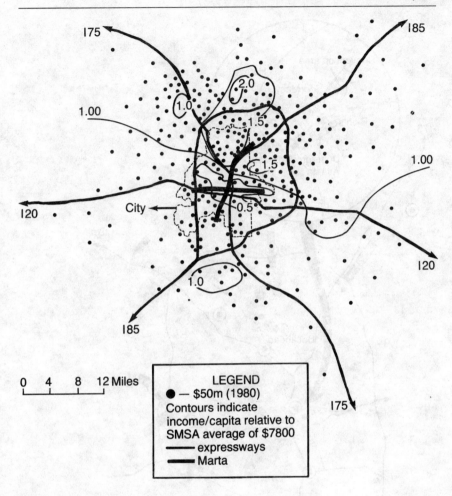

**Figure 7.1** The urban market: Atlanta

*Source:* The authors

subdivided by race (there is relatively little ethnic variation in Atlanta). Blacks are concentrated in the inner city and in an east–west band extending to the suburbs.

These spatial variations in the market help to shape the retail response, shown in Figure 7.2. The stores are clustered together in groups that range in size from isolated stores to the 400 retail outlets of downtown. A number of unplanned strips can be linked to the distinct spatial submarkets within the metropolitan area, but the bulk of the shopping goods retailing is found in the eight super-regional plazas, three unplanned centers, and downtown.

207

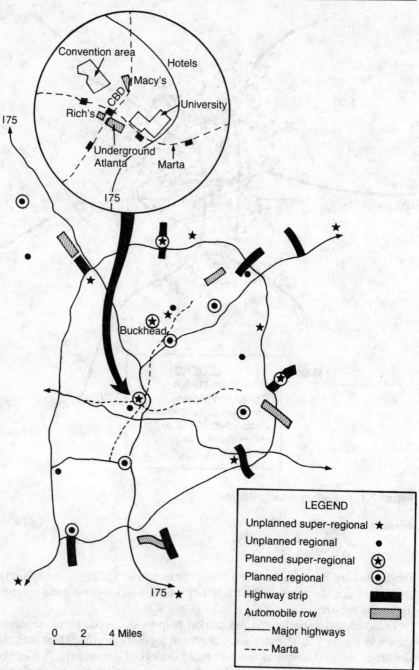

**Figure 7.2** The retail response: Atlanta

*Source:* The authors

Hundreds of smaller plazas fill out this hierarchy. In addition to this size variation the map indicates various specialized clusters of functions. Near downtown is the entertainment/tourist complex called Underground Atlanta, currently under renovation, and towards the high-income sector an up-market shopping and entertainment center has emerged called Buckhead. Around the perimeter highway are automobile rows and other highway shopping strips.

To what degree are these patterns unique to Atlanta? How can we generalize about all metropolitan areas?

## The variety of commercial clusters: a taxonomy of taxonomies

The great variation in the size of settlements and in the distance to alternative centers imposes some strict regularities on the retail patterns observed within a regional settlement system. The size and spacing of central places is severely restricted. When these two constraints are removed, as they are within a large metropolitan region, retailing activities take on an amazing variety of forms. Much research in retail geography has been devoted to describing these patterns. This section will review the various categories of retailing.

Given the variety of retail and service activity within the city – stores of all sizes and descriptions, clustered in a variety of ways from downtown locations to the neighborhood convenience store to shopping malls – how can we describe and generalize these patterns? The fundamental concern of this chapter is the grouping of stores. This leads to a discussion of their interdependence, scale, and functional variation. Four different approaches have been taken to this taxonomic (i.e. classification) problem. These are the (1) morphology or the spatial form of the cluster, (2) the functional composition of the business types in the cluster, (3) the composition of the market that they serve, and (4) the ownership patterns that differentiate planned and unplanned centers. Most taxonomies include each of these characteristics to some degree.

The visibility and familiarity of retail and service clusters led early researchers to focus on their shapes and boundaries, i.e. their morphology. Were shopping districts within the city nodal (with centers, cores, and edges) and focused on a major intersection? Or were they linear, stretching along a major street or transit line with no apparent internal organization, or dispersed, with free-standing stores dotted intermittently along an arterial street? How were the boundaries of the retail cluster determined or defined? These concerns produced the basic variants of nodes and strips but also implied that differences existed among retail clusters with respect to the internal organization of stores and the intensity of interaction.

Functional composition considers the kinds of businesses within the retail cluster. The central place hierarchy suggests a regular ordering of activities within retail nodes with large centers containing more specialized activities. At the other extreme, specialization implies clusters of identical or closely related shopping activities that serve that same market segments or clientele. Again, some kind of interdependence is implied. Consumer behavior binds the stores together, as shown in Chapter four.

Market composition differentiates those specialized clusters, with apparently similar functions (bars, restaurants, and gift shops), that serve specialized markets such as Italians, Blacks, gays, or punks. In terms of store types, or Standard Industrial Classification (SIC) categories, a discount shopping mall may be indistinguishable from a fashion mall but their roles within the overall retail structure will be quite different.

Ownership distinguishes unplanned retail clusters from the major postwar innovation in retail structure, the planned shopping center, in which the centralized control of tenant composition, size, layout, and rent permit the coordination of externality effects among the stores. As will be shown below, planned centers are quite distinct from their unplanned counterparts in terms of size and layout.

These four different dimensions of variation permit over 100 possible combinations of characteristics, many more kinds of retail clusters than could be identified in any real metropolitan area. Clearly, some combinations are irrelevant: there are no examples of planned retail strips at the regional scale, for instance. Other category pairs reinforce each other; for example, most specialized clusters are unplanned. Table 7.1 draws on

**Table 7.1** The varying morphology of the metropolitan retail cluster

| | Unplanned nodes | Strips | Planned centers |
|---|---|---|---|
| Market size | **Metropolitan** (a) Central business district (b) Specialized product area e.g. furniture, fashion | (a) Downtown pedestrian mall (b) Specialty retail strip, e.g. entertainment (b) Ethnic shopping street | (a) Super-regional (b) Downtown fashion mall (b) Theme mall |
| | **Regional** (a) Arterial intersection (a) Downtown of older suburb | (b) Automobile row (b) Furniture strip | (a) Regional mall (a) Pedestrian mall at major intersection (b) Superstore (b) Discount mall |
| | **Community** (a) Street intersection | (a) Shopping street (a) Fast-food strip | (a) Community mall |
| | **Neighborhood** (a) Corner cluster | (a) Suburban strip mall | (a) Neighborhood plaza |

Source: The authors
Note: Items marked (a) serve spatial markets, (b) serve specialized markets.

recent research in Toronto (Jones, 1984) but also derives from earlier studies (e.g. Berry, 1963; Potter, 1982) and field research in a number of US cities. As it stands it is simply a list: the proportions of retail activity in the different categories will vary widely from place to place, and over time, as new groupings and combinations become significant.

Table 7.2 indicates the relative importance of different kinds of retail clusters in Atlanta. Note that the level of detail is restricted by the procedures of the Bureau of the Census (see Exhibit 7.1) which only records values for larger clusters and does not differentiate planned centers from their unplanned surroundings. In this table planned centers are distinguished by the presence of a major regional mall, as indicated in the *Directory of Shopping Centers.* Still, an important part of the story is the continuing significance of smaller (undefined) retail clusters and strips which account for 70 per cent of sales and 80 per cent of stores. For example, there are over 300 neighborhood and strip malls in metropolitan Atlanta (*Atlanta Journal and Constitution*).

The importance of the centers, both planned and unplanned, lies in their concentration of floor area, hence retail sales. The regional centers have more stores and average higher levels of sales per store than smaller centers or strips. In Atlanta the Central Business District (CBD) behaves more like a non-center in this regard. It now contains only 2.4 per cent of the stores in the Standard Metropolitan Statistical Area (SMSA), and only 2.2 per cent of the sales. The average sales per store are only half those of the outlying regional centers with which it competes.

A striking feature of the Atlanta retail structure is the marked bias of retail activity toward the affluent northern end of the city. Seven of the eight most productive retail clusters in terms of retail sales are located north of the CBD, because they serve customers whose incomes are two to four times higher.

The functional significance of these different types of retail structure is outlined in part (b) of Table 7.2. The central business district is oriented toward shopping goods – department stores and apparel – but also provides convenience goods (notably bars and restaurants) for office workers. The planned centers are more sharply focused on shopping goods than the unplanned centers, especially department and apparel stores, but have fewer restaurants. Smaller centers, strips, and independent stores provide non-convenience, non-shopping goods that are often automobile oriented – car dealerships, gas stations, and hardware and building supply dealers.

## The intra-urban retail hierarchy

In the built-up part of the pre-Second World War city, levels of automobile ownership were relatively low and many households shopped daily for their

**Table 7.2** The relative importance of different retail clusters: Atlanta

(a) Size of the retail cluster

| Type of cluster | No. of stores | Average sales ($ millions) | Sales/store ($) |
|---|---|---|---|
| Downtown (tracts 19, 27, 35) | 400 | 246 | 619,000 |
| *Super-regional* | | | |
| Primarily unplanned[a] (3) | 232 | 268 | 1,156,000 |
| Primarily planned (8) | 150 | 207 | 1,382,000 |
| *Regional centers* | | | |
| Primarily unplanned (6) | 66 | 66 | 998,000 |
| Primarily planned (6) | 75 | 71 | 941,000 |
| Total centers (24) | 3,059 | 3,456 | 1,130,000 |
| Smaller centers and strips[b] | 12,543 | 7,240 | 577,000 |

*Source:* Bureau of the Census (1982) *Census of Retail Trade*
*Notes:* [a]Includes all the centers not classified as major regional centers, within the inner counties of the standard metropolitan statistical area: Buckhead, Memorial Drive, Sandy Springs. [b]Includes all the centers not classified as major regional centers, within the inner counties of the standard metropolitan statistical area: Clayton, Cobb, DeKalb, Douglas, Fulton, Gwinnett, Henry, Rockdale. There are about seventy-five community centers and 200 neighborhood centers in this area.

### (b) Functional composition

| | Sales (%) | | | Stores (%) | | | | | | | | | |
|---|---|---|---|---|---|---|---|---|---|---|---|---|---|
| | Convenience[a] | Shopping[b] | Other | Hardware[c] | General | Food | Auto | Gas | Apparel | Furniture | Restaurants | Drug | Misc. |
| CBD | 33.9 | 58.0 | 8.1 | 0.3 | 3.1 | 7.1 | 0.3 | 1.4 | 23.2 | 5.7 | 28.3 | 3.4 | 27.2 |
| *Super-regional* | | | | | | | | | | | | | |
| Unplanned (3) | 35.0 | 39.1 | 25.9 | 3.2 | 0.9 | 7.4 | 5.1 | 6.9 | 10.1 | 12.0 | 24.9 | 3.2 | 26.7 |
| Planned (8) | 18.1 | 66.3 | 15.6 | 0.7 | 3.3 | 6.0 | 2.0 | 2.7 | 36.0 | 9.3 | 14.0 | 1.3 | 24.7 |
| *Regional* | | | | | | | | | | | | | |
| Unplanned (6) | 35.3 | 44.4 | 20.3 | 3.0 | 3.0 | 9.1 | 6.1 | 4.5 | 12.1 | 10.6 | 27.3 | 3.0 | 19.7 |
| Planned (6) | 21.0 | 64.2 | 14.8 | 2.7 | 5.3 | 5.3 | 6.7 | 4.0 | 21.3 | 0.7 | 12.0 | 2.7 | 23.2 |
| Remainder | 36.6 | 10.5 | 52.9 | 5.4 | 1.8 | 13.9 | 8.0 | 11.5 | 5.6 | 6.8 | 24.0 | 4.6 | 18.4 |

Source: Bureau of the Census (1982) Census of Retail Trade
Notes: [a] Convenience includes food, restaurants, and drug stores. [b] Shopping includes general merchandise, apparel, furniture, and miscellaneous shopping. [c] Hardware, automotive, and liquor. CBD, central business district.

## Exhibit 7.1
## THE MAJOR RETAIL CENTER

Data about retail sales and operating characteristics of 1,500 planned and unplanned centers within metropolitan areas have been provided by the Bureau of the Census as part of the *Census of Retail Trade*. A major retail center (MRC) is

A concentration of at least twenty-five retail stores located inside an SMSA but outside a CBD (downtown). At least one of the twenty-five stores must be a general merchandise store (SIC 53) with a minimum of 100,000 square feet of total under-roof floor space. MRCs include planned suburban shopping centers as well as unplanned centers such as older 'string streets' (continuous businesses along a thoroughfare with few cross streets containing any businesses) and combinations of planned and unplanned centers. Where the MRC is unplanned, each block within the boundaries should have at least one general merchandise store (SIC 53); apparel store (SIC 56); furniture, home furnishings and equipment store (SIC 57); or miscellaneous shopping goods store (SIC 594).

MRCs are defined with the help of local census committees. The Bureau has announced that MRCs will not be used in 1987. We will lose a valuable tool for comparing the effectiveness of various retail clusters

For the largest 100 metropolitan statistical areas (MSAs), the average number of MRCs was fifteen; the central business district accounts for 3.5 per cent of all retail sales and the MRCs for another 21 per cent. The threshold level of MRC sales for inclusion in the 1982 census appears to be about $20 million and the largest one (in New Orleans) was $788 million. In two-thirds of these cities the largest MRC is bigger than downtown. While the number of MRCs and their total sales can be closely related to the size of city, their share of MSA sales cannot.

*Source:* Bureau of the Census (1982) *Census of Retail Trade*, Washington
*Note:* CBD, central business district; SMSA standard metropolitan statistical area; SIC, standard industrial classification.

food. Nearby food stores were a necessity. At the same time, low overall mobility led to relatively steep, and often asymmetric, travel–time gradients around each household as networks of public transit facilities along major arterial streets defined nodes of higher accessibility within the metropolis. The result of these behavioral constraints was an intra-urban retail hierarchy, similar in many ways to the one observed in a settlement system.

A number of retail nodes could be identified, ranging in size from the corner store to the downtown shopping district. The mix of stores was directly linked to the size of the center, as measured by the number of stores and volume of sales. Each node served a relatively well-defined spatial market proportional to its size and the centers (and their markets) were ordered into a rough hierarchy, with downtown being the area of highest rank. In the pre-war period many of the outlying, unplanned retail centers were large and important. In Chicago, for instance, the shopping district around 63rd and Halsted was equivalent to the downtown of a small city, with two department stores, a movie theater, and hundreds of smaller stores. Some of these clusters had served as centers for towns and villages that were later absorbed into the urban fabric, while others benefitted from the peculiarities of the residential spatial structure and/or the local transportation system.

A very plausible analogy could be made between intra-urban retail structure and the settlement system, but there are several anomalies. First, because of the finite, circular extent of the built-up area as a whole, market accessibility tends to be greater towards the center of the metropolis. As in the parable of the two ice cream vendors on the beach (Exhibit 2.1), competing stores attempt to enlarge their trade areas by moving closer to one another. Across the metropolis as a whole, then, the density of stores and store clusters is higher at the center than at the periphery. Second, as we have seen, neighborhoods within the city are strongly differentiated in terms of income and social class, so much so that a market of a thousand households in a wealthy section of town purchases four or five times as much as a market of the same size in a low-income area. As in Atlanta, the map of purchasing power may be quite asymmetric. The neighborhood around 63rd and Halsted is now so improverished that the retail function has almost disappeared. Berry's (1963) study of Chicago identified two different retail hierarchies with poor areas generating a 'truncated' hierarchy with only two levels of center and much fewer business types.

However plausible the intra-urban retail hierarchy appears to be, it actually accounts for a relatively small proportion of urban retail facilities. Typically, the downtown area constitutes less than 3 per cent of stores in the metropolitan region and the major regional centers constitute perhaps 15 per cent (see Table 7.2), although these nodes, with their larger stores, may together account for as much as one-third of the total sales. The majority of urban retailers still operate relatively independent stores in a variety of retail strips, or less structured districts that serve specialized submarkets. In Atlanta, retail strips, planned and unplanned, account for over 80 per cent of stores and over 70 per cent of sales. Most older, middle-class, residential areas are also served by long strings of lower-order activities along major urban arterials. Suburban communities are supplied with similar developments, although oriented to the car rather than to the bus or to pedestrians.

## The shopping center

The dominant element in the process of retail change in North America over the last forty years has been the planned shopping center (Dawson,

215

1983). The growth rate of suburban shopping centers is documented in Table 7.3. Since 1960 they have accounted for almost all of the growth in shopping goods activities.

Shopping centers have altered consumer spatial behavior, changed the patterns of access within the city, contributed to the growth of the large, multi-unit retail chain, affected the roles of both central areas and retail strips, and spurred the development of alternative forms of specialty shopping facilities. Shopping centers themselves have evolved as they have participated in the revitalization of the downtown core, in major, mixed-use projects, and in specialty retail districts.

The importance of planned centers does not lie simply in their central-ized control and free parking space. In size, form, location, internal struc-ture, and occupancy cost they differ fundamentally from the older retail hierarchy. Over the last two decades the two innovations – shopping centers and retail chains – have developed strong complementary bonds. Table 7.4 summarizes some of the important differences between planned and unplanned centers, and Figure 7.3 portrays some of the differences graphic-ally. It is apparent that planned centers are overwhelmingly concentrated in the smallest categories, i.e. those less than 100,000 square feet in floor area, while the retail strips and unplanned centers extend across a con-tinuum of sizes. A comparison of the slopes of the two lines indicates that the average store size in a planned center is 2,650 square feet, compared to 1,100 square feet in a retail strip. The ancillary malls (i.e. downtown malls within office buildings) lie between the extremes.

Unplanned centers, downtown for instance, evolve over time as their markets fluctuate in size. Adjustments are made incrementally as stores and activities are added or deleted. Planned centers, in contrast, are designed to serve a certain market size for all time (Table 7.5). The site is appropriate to the size of center and is located at the intersection of streets with appropriate traffic levels. Store size is predetermined, as is the internal layout of the plaza and access to parking. A neighborhood center can never become a regional shopping mall. Any growth in the market requires the addition of another planned center. As a result, shopping centers are vulnerable to competition and to new innovations over time. As we will see in the next chapter the trade areas of shopping malls are eventually trun-cated by malls located further out. The innovation of the regional mall in the 1960s challenged the community plaza of the 1950s, and the regional mall, in turn, was replaced by the super-regional plaza of the 1970s. In most places income growth has been sufficient to maintain both old and new centers, but in a few cities older shopping centers have been closed.

It is the predictability and degree of control over the shopping environ-ment that makes planned centers so attractive to retail chain outlets and vice versa. Planned centers generate specified levels of traffic and their mix of tenants is known ahead of time. Chain retailers know how to convert a

**Table 7.3** The growth of shopping centers

| | 1955 (total) | 1955–60 | 1960–5 | 1965–70 | 1970–5 | 1975–80 | 1980–5 | 1985 (total) |
|---|---|---|---|---|---|---|---|---|
| Number (change) | 1,300 | +3,200 | 4,700 | 3,300 | 3,900 | 5,650 | 6,450 | 28,500 |
| Gross leasing area (millions of sq. ft) | 150 | +450 | 650 | 250 | 650 | 810 | 690 | 3,650 |
| Average size (area in sq. ft) | 115 | 140 | 138 | 76 | 167 | 143 | 107 | 128 |
| Population (millions) | 165.3 | +15.4 | 13.8 | 10.5 | 10.4 | 11.8 | 11.5 | 239.3 |
| Income/capita ($1982) | 6,780 | +450 | 1,240 | 1,320 | 700 | 630 | 900 | 12,040 |
| Floor area/capita (sq. ft) | 0.9 | 3.3 | 6.4 | 7.3 | 10.0 | 13.0 | 15.3 | 15.3 |

*Sources:* Communications Channels (1988) *Shopping Center World*; Bureau of the Census (annual) *Statistical Abstract of the United States*, Washington

**Table 7.4** Differences between planned and unplanned centers

| | Unplanned | Planned |
|---|---|---|
| Center size | Flexible, growing (or declining) with trade area and competition. | Essentially fixed to serve a finite market size. |
| Location | Accessibility must evolve as center grows. Transit system may become necessary. | Level of automobile traffic (road capacity) determines market size and scale, often isolated from pedestrian traffic. |
| Store size | Varies greatly; no correlation with center size. | Highly structured; average store area depends on specialization. |
| Business types | Number increases (log-linearly) with number of stores. High-order centers contain all low-order activities. | Relatively little duplication; low-order activities drop out of high-order centers. Chain stores dominate. |
| Occupancy cost | Declines with distance to central intersection (rent gradient). | Largely aspatial; depends on store size and store's ability to generate traffic. Per cent of gross sales. |
| Internal structure | High traffic, shopping goods activities at high value intersection. | Often bimodal with connecting mall between largest tenants. Parking is controlled and access carefully planned. |
| Competition | Primarily among similar stores in same center. | With competing planned centers across metropolitan region. |
| Renovation | Evolves as stores are replaced. Individual adjustments. | Systematically, after 5–10 years; often involves changes in tenant mix and format. |

*Source:* The authors

given level of traffic into sales in the most effective manner. Urban planners prefer planned centers too, because they solve the traffic, parking, and noise problems that are inherent in the growth of unplanned centers or retail strips. Since the scale of the planned center is known, municipal services and traffic access can be provided ahead of time.

The management of the planned shopping center exemplifies a new form of retail collective. The developer selects tenants carefully and negotiates long leases (typically five years or longer) with each one. (Exhibit 7.2 describes the negotiation process). Offers to lease from a strong representation of reputable tenants are required to put together the initial financing package, hence the close ties between planned centers and major retail chains described in Chapter three. Both the developer and the tenants depend on the ability of the plaza to attract customers away from competing malls. Internal cooperation is required to meet external competition since each tenant depends on the total retail mix and the center's total attractiveness to the consumer. If a few stores falter, than all may fail.

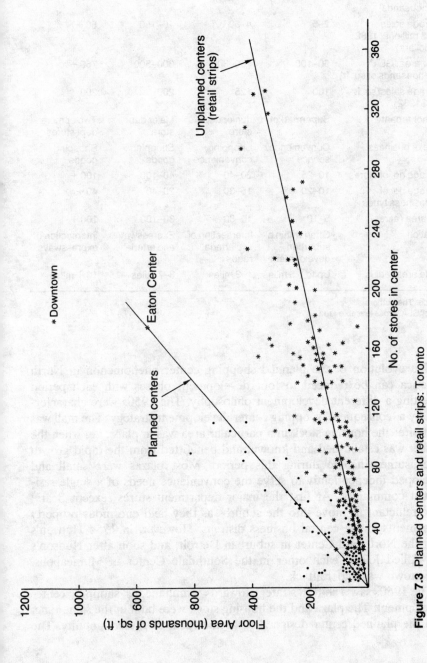

**Figure 7.3** Planned centers and retail strips: Toronto

*Source:* Metropolitan Toronto Planning Department (1983) *Retailing in Regional Municipalities and Metropolitan Toronto, 1983*, Toronto

**Table 7.5** The hierarchy of planned shopping centers

| | Neighborhood | Community | Regional | Super-regional |
|---|---|---|---|---|
| Market size (population, thousands) | 20–40 | 40–200 | 100–500 | 500 + |
| Average sales ($ millions, 1982 dollars) | 2–5 | 4–30 | 10–150 | 50 + |
| Floor area: GLA* (thousands of sq. ft) | 50–100 | 100–300 | 300–500 | 750 + |
| Average sales/sq. ft ($1982) | 100 | 125 | 200 | 200 |
| Anchor tenant | Supermarket | Junior dept store | Major dept store | Two or more dept stores |
| Type of business | Convenience, service | Shopping, convenience | Shopping goods | Shopping goods |
| Average no. of stores | 10–25 | 20–40 | 40–100 | 100 + |
| Average no. of business types | 10–20 | 15–30 | 20–40 | 40 + |
| Site area (acres) | 5–10 | 10–30 | 30–100 | 100 + |
| Location | Often within a suburban development | Intersection of two arterial roads | Expressway and arterial | Intersection of expressways |
| Trade area radius | Up to 1.5 miles | 1–3 miles | 3–7 miles | 10 + miles |

Source: The authors
Note: *GLA, gross leasable area.

The evolution of the planned shopping center phenomenon in North America can be reduced to four development phases with each period reflecting a different development philosophy. The 1950s were characterized by a 'consequent' shopping center development strategy. The mall was built after the housing stock in a particular area was in place, i.e. when the market was established and known, and benefitted from the rapid growth in consumer income during this period. Most plazas were small and developed independently to serve the convenience needs of a single residential community. At first the major department stores (except Sears) were reluctant to move into the suburbs as they held enormous property investments in the central business districts. However, in 1954 Hudson's built the Northland Center in suburban Detroit, and soon after Hudson's and Allied joined each other in the Southdale Center in Minneapolis. Downtown was under attack.

The 1960s saw a shift in strategy towards 'simultaneous' shopping center development. The plaza and the housing stock were built at the same time, with the planned center designed to be the focus of the community. The

Exhibit 7.2
## NEGOTIATING THE LEASE

Because of the intense concentration of retail activity within a few hundred retail chains and a few dozen shopping center developers, much of the spatial pattern, variety, and competition in retail facilities is determined by negotiations among a small number of leasing and location specialists who represent the various chains and developers. The discussions are based on considerable experience and knowledge of consumer behavior: most of the participants have dealt with each other before, know each other's operating requirements, and work within industry-wide limits of acceptable rents or leasing conditions. They know that any special deals will quickly become known throughout the industry and affect future negotiations. No one can afford to be seen as too heavy-handed or too soft.

When a new regional center is planned the leasing manager for the developer is given the store layout and the anchor tenants (who may own a piece of the center). He or she then designates the internal variations in marketing mix – the fashion center, gourmet food bar, or lifestyle center (which may have been built into the design) – and begins to identify possible locations for stores of different types. The manager knows that all the major chains want and expect to be part of this market and that the center needs them because they are good merchandisers, i.e. able to convert traffic into sales in the most efficient manner. The tenant pays a base rate of so much per square foot, plus a percentage of sales – typically between 5 and 7 per cent, with another 2 or 3 per cent required to pay for taxes, promotions, and other extras.

The manager, who has probably visited half the malls in the region, knows what store size the chain prefers, what sales volume it requires, its major competitors, and the kinds of stores with which it feels comfortable and can predict its requirements accurately. The chain's location analyst, in turn, has read the traffic reports and sales projections for the center, looked at the design and made calculations based on personal experience within the local market. The negotiations revolve around the selection of particular sites within the center and the choice of chains within the megachain. The retailer may want to try out a new chain outlet or line of goods while the developer's representative would prefer a tried and tested money maker. Sometimes the solution to renting the new plaza may involve a decision about another plaza 500 miles away. A little log-rolling keeps both sides happy. As the concentration of control in the retail industry increases and the shared experience grows, both sides avoid complex leases that build long-term commitments to exclusive rights or required product mix.

A chain's clout in these negotiations depends on the number of stores it controls (hence the potential relationships in other malls) and its ability to outsell competitors on a square footage basis. Mall owners look for chains that deliver consistently, even if they have to fire managers and adjust product lines to make a location perform. The developer's clout comes from overall size, hence the number of other negotiations ongoing, and from the attractiveness of the market represented by the center. Chains with a good market share in a given city can afford to be choosy. Chains that are late entries to the market, or that have been shut out of other shopping centers may be desperate.

link between residential and commercial development activities helped to foster the emergence of the large development companies such as De Bartolo and Melvin Simon & Associates. The philosophy of simultaneous development soon became accepted at all scales, from the large regional developments to the small neighborhood plazas in the center of a community. The large regional plaza flourished as downtown department stores everywhere began to develop suburban branches in response to the success of Sears and the new retailers such as K mart and Korvette that were explicitly oriented to the community plaza. During this period shopping center development became an institution with established policies and procedures, such as common area maintenance. A host of specialists sprang up within the industry to deal with shopping center architecture, landscaping, traffic control and parking, tenant mix, energy conservation, and lighting.

The end product of this process was a series of homogeneous shopping environments. One shopping center at any one level of the hierarchy looked much the same as the next. The size and layout were the same, the plaza felt the same, and it offered the same goods and services in the same 'sterile' environment. The major challenge for the development industry was to reduce the sameness that drove more affluent shoppers to seek distinctive unplanned environments.

The early 1970s saw a gradual shift toward a third stage – the 'catalytic' shopping center. The large mall was viewed as a growth pole that would stimulate future residential construction. In a typical case, a super-regional shopping center was built in a 'green field' at the intersection of two major expressways, preceeding residential construction by three to five years. The attraction was the size of the center, which was often twice as large as alternative facilities. In part, these developments were in keeping with the 'bigger is better' philosophy that characterized North American business decision-making in that period. Because tenants needed sufficient resources to wait for the market to develop, these centers became the sole preserve of the national retail chain. In some cities the commercial revitalization of central areas provided a second major focus of shopping center development in this period. The process typically involved the construction of a major enclosed shopping facility in the downtown core or a nearby upscale shopping area.

By the end of the 1970s, the shopping center industry in North America appeared to have reached a point of market saturation, except for the high growth cities of the Sun Belt. Developers pursued a series of alternative growth strategies. First, a number of selected shopping centers were rejuvenated. This process generally involved the enclosing and 'remixing' of first-generation regional centers that had been constructed in the 1960–5 period. Second, through a strategy termed 'infilling', a number of smaller cities became targets for enclosed regional or community malls on the edge of town. As a consequence, the downtown cores in these smaller communities experienced severe decline. Third, developers began to compete with unplanned shopping areas by building strip malls along arterial roads and renting space to low-rent retailers and services.

Finally, the 1980s saw the emergence of a fourth form of shopping center development – the shopping mall as entertainment center or tourist attraction. By far the most ambitious example of this format is the 3,800,000 square foot West Edmonton Mall, with its dozens of tourist and recreation facilities to attract people who come only incidentally to shop (see Exhibit 7.3). South Coast Plaza in Los Angeles includes a variety of architectural features, plus a sculpture court and museum. A mall of this scale and diversity can challenge the attractions of any downtown. Other developers are experimenting with the entertainment format, introducing waterslides, children's villages, or architectural features that attract tourists. The Eaton Centre is Toronto's most popular tourist attraction. South Street Seaport (New York) and Ghiradelli Square (San Francisco) are mentioned in every guidebook.

## The specialized retail environments

Berry (1963) pointed out that there have always been specialized retail clusters within metropolitan areas, providing alternatives to the hierarchy of unplanned centers and plazas. It is the growth in the importance and variety of these districts that is new. Several reasons may be put forward: the sterility of the suburban plazas has been mentioned already, but there are expanding demands as well. The most rapid areas of growth in retailing include restaurants and bars and specialized shopping – boutique goods, gifts, etc. The demographics and lifestyles of the 1980s have led to expanded, leisure-based shopping. Ethnic communities are growing again and their retail districts attract weekend shoppers from all over the metropolitan region.

Specialty retailing can be spatially dispersed or concentrated. The former includes merchants who offer a highly specialized product (e.g. kites, postage stamps for collectors, militaria, model trains, feminist books) for a small number of widely dispersed customers. These retailers have no need for spatial concentrations since they offer 'one-of-a-kind' merchandise. The consumer is willing to travel long distances and the purchase is not linked directly with other retail expenditures.

Other specialty retailers cluster because their customers overlap and can combine their visits. Five types of shopping environments are identified in Table 7.6: each type can be found in planned or unplanned form. Specialty product areas attract comparison shoppers interested in a limited range of shopping goods. Fashion centers and factory outlet malls focus on the two extremes of the income range – or the same households on different

## Exhibit 7.3
## WEST EDMONTON MALL

West Edmonton Mall (WEM) is one of the more important shopping center innovations of the 1980s. While there is widespread debate about whether it is too big, about its economic viability, and about its impact on the rest of the city, many features of the mall are being widely copied. Developers and retailers have been impressed by the way the management has combined design features, recreational attractions, and skillful promotion to attract enormous numbers of potential customers.

With 600 stores and 3.5 million square feet of retail space, WEM is the largest shopping center in North America. It has almost twice the retail floor area of downtown Edmonton, and it's climate-controlled (Edmonton is Canada's northernmost metropolitan area). In size alone the mall dominates the city's retail environment but the developer (Triple Five Corporation, run by the Ghermazian family) has provided further attractions. Recreational facilities (1.4 million square feet) attract tourists from all over western Canada. Visitors come by bus and plane from as far away as Saskatchewan and British Columbia to see Fantasyland (the amusement park), the Deep Sea Adventure (aquarium), the National Hockey League scale ice rink (where the Oilers practice on occasion), and the 5-acre indoor Water Park. Many of them stay in the on-site hotel.

Needless to say, the mall does a lot of business: the Edmonton Planning Department estimates that it accounts for one-third of the city's retail sales and generates 15,000 jobs. The mall cost almost $1 billion and pays $11 million per year in municipal taxes. Central Edmonton, aside from the downtown planned centers, looks devastated. Other major plazas in the city are feeling the pinch as the mall lures away their tenants, and all over western Canada merchants complain that local shoppers are taking their money out of town to the mall.

But is the mall a success? Does it generate sufficient retail sales per square foot to cover the investment? At this point in 1988 the jury is still out. West Edmonton Mall was not originally planned to take this form: it grew in three distinct jumps, from 1.0 million to 2.4 million to 3.5 million square feet. The scope of the last addition, completed in 1986, pushes it into the twilight zone beyond our knowledge and prediction of retail behavior. Is there an upper limit to shopping center size, a point where scale diseconomies set in? For instance, are certain kinds of store types (supermarkets, for example) unable to operate there because of access and parking problems? Are all those visitors really shoppers, or are they simply sightseers? Is the cost of the recreational attractions offset by the extra sales they generate? Has the mall exhausted the list of potential tenants? Some of the stores such as Canadian Tire (auto accessories), Ikea (furniture) and Hometown (building supplies) are unlikely occupants for a regional scale plaza. A concerted effort to develop an upscale 'theme' street within the mall, based on European fashion boutiques (Europa Boulevard) has not succeeded. That segment of the fashion market is not interested. Also, while the mall has enjoyed the benefits of the Alberta boom until recently, the City of Edmonton is no longer growing in population or income. Will there be enough market to go around?

Exhibit 7.3 (continued)

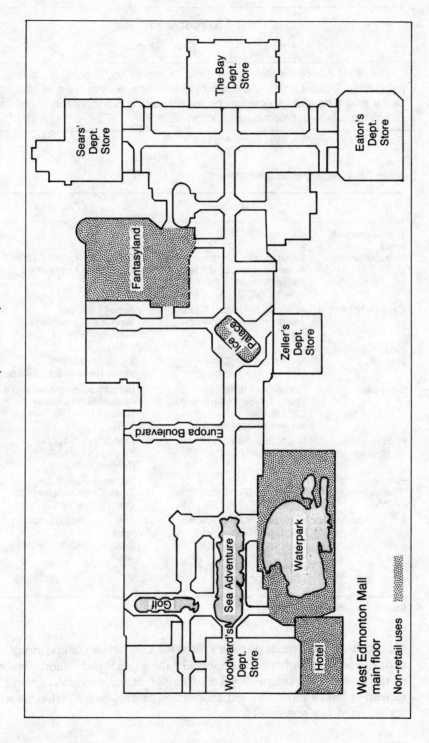

The Bay Dept. Store

Sears' Dept. Store

Eaton's Dept. Store

Fantasyland

Ice Palace

Zeller's Dept. Store

Europa Boulevard

Golf

Sea Adventure

Waterpark

Woodward's Dept. Store

Hotel

West Edmonton Mall
main floor

Non-retail uses

## Exhibit 7.3 (*continued*)

The West Edmonton Mall format (and its impact on other retail centers) is being hotly debated in Minneapolis, where the same developers plan to build a similar mall (The Mall of America) on the site of the old Minnesota Twins ballpark in the suburb of Bloomington (Exhibit 13.3).

*Source:* Brochure for the West Edmonton Mall

**Table 7.6** Specialty retail environments

|  | Unplanned | Planned |
| --- | --- | --- |
| *Special product areas* | | |
| Metropolitan-wide | Entertainment, Broadway (NY) Automobile row, Skid row Farmer's market Jewelry, Hill St (LA) or 47 St (NY) | Pike Street Market (Seattle) Mercado de Los Angeles |
| Neighborhood | Antiques, N. Halsted (Chicago) Telegraph Ave. (Berkeley) | Airport gift shops Malls in office building Auto service malls |
| *Fashion centers* | | |
| Inner city | North Michigan (Chicago) Madison Ave. (NY) | Trump Tower (NY) Water Tower Place (Chicago) |
| Suburban | Rodeo Drive (LA) Worth Avenue (Palm Beach) Carmel (CA) 5th Ave. (Scottsdale, AZ) | Bal Harbour Shops (Miami) Phipps Plaza (Atlanta) Newport Island Fashion Center (CA) |
| Factory outlet/ off-price center | Lower East Side (NY) North Conway (NH) | Fairfax Mall (VA) Factory Outlet Mall (Niagara Falls) |
| Historic/theme developments (NY) | Georgetown (DC) Stockyards (Fort Worth) | Ghiradelli Square (SF) South Street Seaport (NY) Union Station (St Louis) |
| Ethnic/lifestyle | Calle Ocho (Miami): Cuban Chinatown, Greektown Broadway (LA): Mexican Castro (SF): gay Greenwich Village (NY) H Street (DC): black | Evergreen Plaza (Chicago): black Crenshaw/Baldwin Hills (LA): black |

*Source:* The authors

afternoons. Ethnic streets provide a focus for a particular cultural group but may also attract tourists and members of the general population. Historic or theme retail environments take advantage of the enormous growth in recreation-linked retailing – gift shops or restaurants – by customers who are attracted to a non-retail focus.

Specialty product areas provide an environment for comparison shopping in which customers are attracted by the variety offered by a group of stores selling similar goods. Some areas serve the entire metropolitan market, others a smaller portion of it. The usual examples are automobiles, furniture, and entertainment. Antiques and lifestyle clothing stores are more recent variants. Those areas that serve the whole metropolitan market tend to locate near the city center, although automobile and furniture districts, because of their floor area requirements, may locate on the edge of the built-up area in low-rent districts. The neighborhood specialty strip is typically found in older, residential areas that have experienced recent gentrification. It provides higher quality food and fashion products and new forms of personal services.

Fashion and factory outlet centers: the former deliver designer products in an upscale environment; the latter similar products, perhaps last year's models or imitations, in a low-overhead store. Both types of center attract recreational shoppers. Fashion streets are often the most expensive and visible shopping locations within the metropolis, with close links to the high-income residential sectors, or to executive employment locations. They have proven to be particularly attractive to foreign labels and European chains (see Exhibit 7.4, Georgetown Park). In a number of

### Exhibit 7.4
### GEORGETOWN PARK

One of the most rapidly growing forms of retailing in recent years in every major city is the fashion cluster, in which designer boutiques – often international – compete for the dollars of the newly affluent. Georgetown Park, 'your destination for world-class shopping', is typical.

This is a new building that looks old, located on the Chesapeake and Ohio Canal in the exclusive Washington suburb of Georgetown. Four floors of shops provide 200,000 square feet of retailing for eighty-three shops (an extension will increase the size by 60 per cent). The architectural feature is the lavishly appointed atrium cum courtyard. While the major tenants are Garfinckel's (a DC department store), Ann Taylor, and Abercrombie and Fitch, most of the smaller boutiques have more exotic names: Uozzola, Alfred Sung, Linea Pitti, Godiva Chocolatier, Antonio Buttaro, Crabtree and Evelyn.

The target market is diverse: it appeals to upscale shoppers from all over the metropolitan area (if they can find a place to park), as well as the nearby townhouses. However, it also provides recreational shopping: the streets of Georgetown are crowded every night with bored residents of the Washington suburbs and the tourists who have spent all day lining up in the museums. They have time and they have money and this is perceived to be the only area in Washington where you can walk around at night.

*Source:* Brochure for Georgetown Park

## Exhibit 7.4 (*continued*)

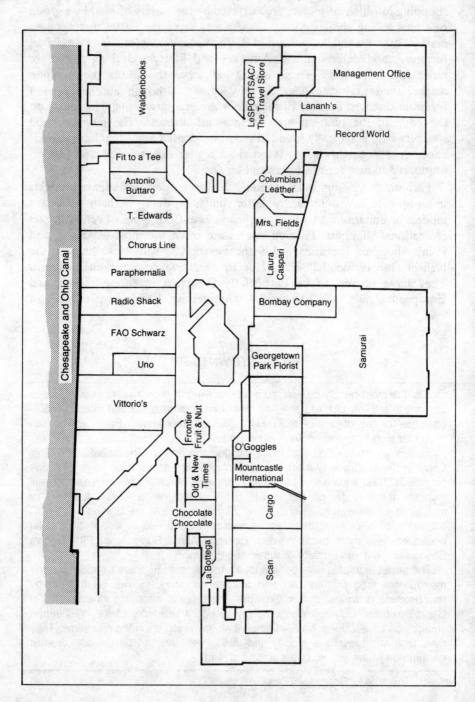

instances the fashion street has been incorporated into mixed-use projects that integrate offices, hotels, and entertainments, e.g. the Trump Tower on Fifth Avenue near 57th Street, or Water Tower Place in Chicago.

The factory outlet mall or off-price center is the most recent variant in the evolution of the planned suburban mall, deriving in part from the discount center, but including a number of specialty stores that pursue the same, low-price strategy. Costs are reduced by devices such as less glamorous mall design, reduced customer service, minimal store fixtures, and a reliance on products that are ends-of-line, over-runs, or factory seconds. These malls have proven particularly attractive to vacationers and can often be found along the major interstate highways in both new malls and old factory buildings.

The ethnic strip, founded at the point of entry for the ethnic group within the city, first expands to serve the immediate neighborhood but eventually evolves to cater to members of the ethnic community throughout the metropolitan area. In time, these areas may also become tourist attractions. The stores provide food, personal services, and restaurants. These areas have proven to be the most enduring parts of the inner city retail fabric (Greektown in Detroit, Astoria in New York) in some cities. In other cities waves of recent immigrants have helped to rejuvenate older shopping streets. The Cubans have their Calle Ocho in Miami, and Mexicans, Chinese, and other East Asian communities are building new retail foci in Los Angeles.

Historical redevelopment and theme malls are another feature of the revitalization of older parts of the city, particularly in waterfront and warehouse districts. Almost every major city in the country has developed such a project and the Rouse Corporation has participated in dozens of these developments: Boston (Faneuil Hall), New York (South Street Seaport), Baltimore (Harborplace), St Louis (Union Station). Historic or unusual buildings and waterfronts provide the focus. Often federal or state funding is provided for land assembly, parking, or renovations. Sometimes existing building stock is used and sometimes new structures are created. In either case, the explicit institutional coordination gives the development some of the characteristics of a planned center. Unplanned versions of these recreational retailing clusters have also emerged in smaller communities, from Key West to Provincetown. L.L. Bean has single-handedly made Freeport ME into a tourist attraction.

The rapid growth of specialty retailing areas has added a new aspect to the competition within the metropolitan retail environment. The addition of a shopping goods role to the older retail strip presents the upscale consumer with an alternative to the conventional plazas. Independent merchants and some of the more specialized retail chains are taking aim at the market niches that such environments provide. In response, the conventional malls try to develop more distinctive images. Location analysts find that a new level of complexity has been added to the location decision.

Exhibit 7.5 describes the shopping facilities in Manhattan, and why it is different to most other cities in this respect.

## Downtown

The central business district of a city combines almost all the retail clusters that have been described above: it is the highest order of unplanned center – the node that represents the city within the larger settlement system – and it serves the entire metropolitan region. Usually it also incorporates a variety of specialized retail areas, from skid row (bars, cheap restaurants, hotels) to the financial, fashion, and entertainment districts. Also, in the last decade, many downtown areas have added planned shopping centers of various kinds, both regional centers and small ancillary malls integrated into office development.

Downtown is a distinct shopping environment. In some cities, such as Detroit, this environment has almost disappeared under the pressure of

### Exhibit 7.5
### MANHATTAN IS DIFFERENT!

In number and variety of stores and intensity of retail specialization, no other American city approaches New York, and especially Manhattan Island. Here, within about 10 square miles, are dozens of different retail clusters embedded within miles of shopping streets, each one fascinating in its own right. The shopping facilities in other cities are finite: eventually you come to the end of the street or the mall, but this is not true of Manhattan – turn a corner and there's another shopping opportunity.

Facilities vary, from the most elaborate shopping complex – the Trump Tower – to the sidewalk merchants who operate out of a suitcase; from the Orthodox Jewish jewelers of 47th Street to the sleaze of 42nd Street. South Street Seaport serves the tourists and suburbanites, the East Village caters to the avant-garde. There are Chinese streets, Greek streets, Jewish streets, Puerto Rican streets, and dozens of other nationalities. 57th Street is reputedly the most expensive shopping street in the world, Fifth Avenue and Madison Avenue are close behind. Macy's is the world's biggest department store. Bloomingdale's is an international symbol of American affluence.

The greatest concentration of stores – in the Manhattan central business district – accounted for $4.6 billion in retail sales in 1982. That's more than all of Omaha or Las Vegas, and most of the sales are shopping goods ($708 million worth of jewelry, $827 million worth of clothes, but only $3 million worth of gasoline).

*Source:* The authors

Exhibit 7.5 (*continued*)

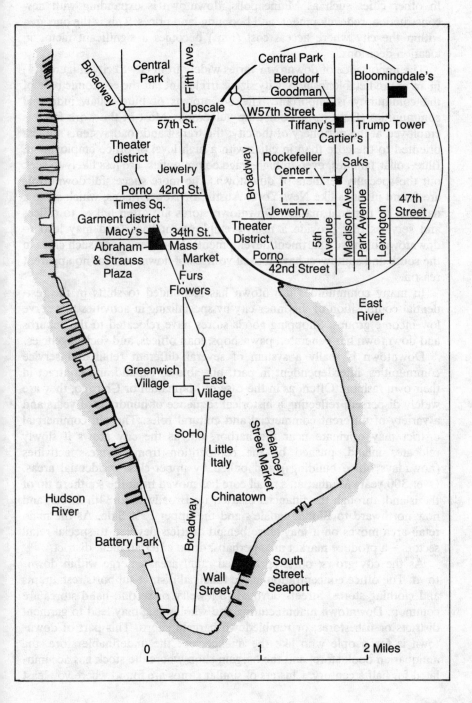

continued development of suburban facilities within a no-growth market. In other cities such as Minneapolis, downtown is expanding with new construction, redevelopment, and booming land prices. This is the one area within the city where access cost (rent) becomes a significant factor in location decisions.

The importance of downtown varies widely from city to city (Figure 7.4) in an unpredictable fashion. City size is irrelevant but the economic base of the community is important. The downtowns of blue-collar, industrial communities (Detroit, St Louis) are vulnerable. Most of the work force is employed at the periphery of the city; the transit and road systems are less oriented to the core than in cities with a high level of office employment. Blue-collar families, even in high-wage communities, are less likely to seek out the specialty retailers of downtown. The more successful downtowns are found in cities like New York, Austin, or New Orleans, which serve a national or regional market. Downtown stores are often linked to offices and services that provide a nearby employment base (and may lead to downtown highrise apartment development). However, many such cities in the south and southwest have lost all vestiges of downtown for no apparent reason.

In many communities downtown has responded to shifts in the residential composition of the inner city by specializing in activities that serve low-income groups. Shopping goods stores have relocated to the suburbs and downtown has generated pawnshops, loan offices, and social agencies.

Downtown is really a system of several different retail and service communities, interdependent in part, but able to expand and contract in their own fashion. Often, as in the case of Manhattan or Chicago, they are widely dispersed, reflecting a historical sequence of hundreds of years and a variety of different commercial and cultural roles. The old commercial district may originate near the harbor, but as the city grows it slowly relocates inland, pushed by the competition from business activities (nowadays office buildings) and pulled by upper-class residential areas. Over 300 years Manhattan's retail core has moved from the southern tip of the island, through the financial district, up Broadway to 34th Street, and now northward to Bloomingdale's and the upper East Side. As the main retail area moves on it may leave behind districts devoted to special retail sectors – a produce market area perhaps, or an entertainment district.

As the city grows, other specialized retail areas emerge within downtown. The office concentration in the financial district supports restaurants and clothing stores. Streets devoted to jewelry or second-hand stores are common. Downtown manufacturing and wholesaling may lead to garment districts or fish stores, or tumbledown bargain shops. This part of downtown is for people who like the unexpected: the undefinable store, the antiquarian book store, and the bargain shop where the stock has accumulated for half a century. Clusters of similar stores are found where you least

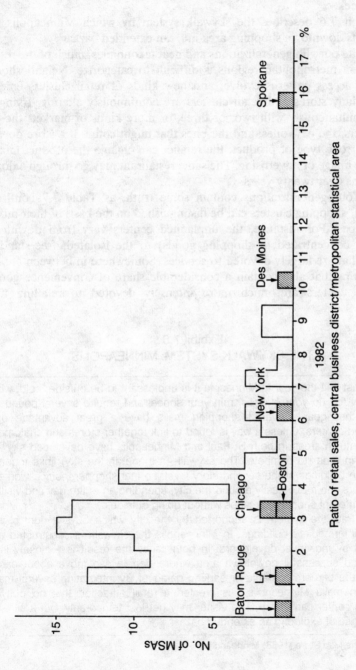

**Figure 7.4** The role of downtown

*Source:* Bureau of the Census (1982) *Census of Retail Trade*, Washington

expect them, remnants of a neighborhood or marketplace now gone. Downtown stores often lack the rational logic of shopping malls: they serve markets that are not clearly visible, and their accounts are not monitored every week.

Exhibit 7.6 describes the skywalk system by which Minneapolis has turned its downtown shopping area into 'an extended bazaar'.

Despite our glib generalizations and neat taxonomies, much of the retailing within metropolitan regions is difficult to categorize. Neighborhoods change, access patterns evolve, and new kinds of retail clusters emerge daily. Many stores and retail clusters are continuously altering, trying to deal simultaneously with two, or three, or more kinds of market: the old customers, the new ones, and the ones that might come. If a store doesn't work for one type of product, the retailer can change the product mix or alter the image or advertising. The same restaurant may go through a dozen variations over twenty years.

Still, our generalizations contain some truth, as Table 7.7 confirms. Different shopping clusters can be distinguished on the basis of their mix of store types. For instance, the unplanned centers vary from downtown (heavily concentrated in shopping goods) to the isolated, free-standing outlets that are largely devoted to services. Somewhere in between are the retail strips that also contain a considerable share of convenience goods. Planned centers are much more intensely devoted to retailing than

Exhibit 7.6
## THE SKYWALK SYSTEM: MINNEAPOLIS

For at least half the year in Minnesota it is unpleasant to be outside: cold, wind, and snow fog up your glasses, ruin your shoes, and require several pounds of cold-weather gear. Covered shopping malls have a great advantage over unplanned centers, unless a way is found to link together stores and customers. The downtown areas in both St Paul and Minneapolis have developed skywalk systems in order to compete. The skywalk (a tunnel in the sky) links together downtown buildings at the second story level, so that shoppers, office-workers, and visitors can move easily around the city, spending an entire day and visiting several different shopping arcades without going outside.

In St Paul the system is supported by the city which buys a right-of-way through intermediate buildings. In Minneapolis the skywalk is constructed and managed by individual developers. In both cases the result is a closely integrated and successful downtown area where people can move about easily, ignoring the barriers of traffic or parking garages. By integrating several major downtown malls Minneapolis has created a retail attraction that no outlying shopping center can match. The visitor may get lost temporarily, but it all adds to the sense of exploring an extended bazaar.

*Source:* The Map Store (1988) Minneapolis

Exhibit 7.6 (*continued*)

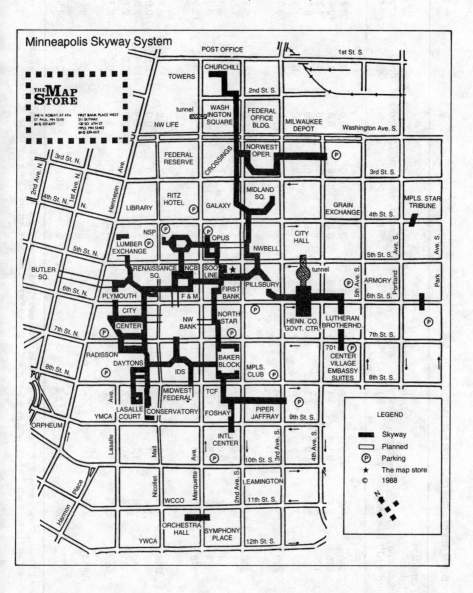

unplanned centers, and the ratio of shopping to convenience goods increases dramatically with the size of the center. The largest plazas resemble downtown; the smallest act like traditional retail strips. Even at this most aggregate level then, each kind of retail cluster has a specific role within the retail environment. If we were to break down the functional categories further (as in Table 3.2) and to introduce variations in quality or

**Table 7.7** The functional mix of retail clusters: Edmonton

| | Edmonton total floor area (m² × 10³) | Percentage | Downtown[b] (%) | 23 retail strips (%) | Industrial areas (%) | Other unplanned locations (%) | All unplanned (%) | Regional (7; %) | Community (8; %) | Neighbor-hood (5; %) | All planned[c] (%) |
|---|---|---|---|---|---|---|---|---|---|---|---|
| **Shopping Goods** | | | | | | | | | | | |
| General | 500 | 20.5 | 41.5 | 2.7 | 0.3 | 5.5 | 8.9 | 62.0 | 50.6 | 0.0 | 56.4 |
| Clothing | 138 | 5.7 | 9.1 | 3.4 | 2.4 | 1.8 | 3.2 | 15.9 | 8.4 | 4.3 | 13.4 |
| Furniture | 102 | 4.2 | 1.2 | 8.7 | 4.2 | 5.3 | 5.2 | 0.2 | 3.6 | 0.0 | 1.2 |
| Automobile | 83 | 3.4 | 1.2 | 4.7 | 6.0 | 4.7 | 4.5 | 0.0 | 0.0 | 0.0 | 0.0 |
| Other | 173 | 7.1 | 7.1 | 15.8 | 6.9 | 4.5 | 7.1 | 6.9 | 7.2 | 8.7 | 7.0 |
| Total | 996 | 40.9 | 60.1 | 35.3 | 19.8 | 22.8 | 28.9 | 85.0 | 69.9 | 13.0 | 78.0 |
| **Convenience** | | | | | | | | | | | |
| Food | 200 | 8.2 | 0.0 | 15.4 | 1.2 | 9.9 | 8.1 | 5.6 | 10.2 | 52.2 | 8.7 |
| Drug | 41 | 1.7 | 1.2 | 3.7 | 0.3 | 1.5 | 1.6 | 1.2 | 3.0 | 4.3 | 1.8 |
| Hardware | 114 | 4.7 | 0.0 | 6.0 | 12.3 | 5.1 | 5.4 | 0.7 | 7.2 | 0.0 | 2.5 |
| Other | 23 | 0.9 | 0.8 | 1.3 | 3.0 | 0.6 | 1.3 | 0.0 | 0.0 | 0.0 | 0.0 |
| Total | 378 | 15.5 | 2.0 | 26.4 | 16.8 | 17.1 | 16.4 | 7.6 | 20.4 | 56.5 | 13.0 |
| **Services** | | | | | | | | | | | |
| Restaurants | 239 | 9.8 | 17.0 | 7.0 | 12.0 | 11.8 | 11.9 | 2.7 | 4.2 | 13.0 | 3.5 |
| Hotels | 496 | 20.4 | 7.1 | 15.4 | 29.3 | 34.4 | 27.0 | 0.0 | 0.0 | 0.0 | 0.0 |
| Personal | 143 | 5.9 | 8.7 | 9.1 | 3.0 | 7.2 | 7.0 | 1.7 | 2.4 | 17.4 | 2.5 |
| Other | 181 | 7.4 | 5.0 | 6.7 | 18.6 | 7.3 | 9.0 | 2.7 | 3.0 | 0.0 | 2.7 |
| Total | 1,059 | 43.5 | 37.8 | 38.2 | 62.9 | 60.7 | 54.9 | 7.1 | 9.6 | 30.4 | 8.7 |
| Grand total | 2,433 | 100.0 | | | | | | | | | |
| Share of floor area by cluster | | 100.0 | 9.9 | 12.2 | 13.7 | 40.1 | 75.0 | 16.8 | 6.8 | 0.9 | 24.5 |

*Sources:* City of Edmonton, Planning Department (1983) 'Retail Space: Its Use and Distribution,' and 'Service Space: Its Use and Distribution,' Edmonton, Alberta
*Notes:* [a]One square meter equals 11 square feet. [b]Includes Edmonton Center and McCauley Plaza. [c]Excludes Edmonton Center and McCauley Plaza.

service, the differences would become even more apparent. Both urban retailers and urban consumers have an extraordinary range of choice.

## Location choices by retail chains

The diversity of retail environments within the metropolis intensifies the need for explicit spatial strategies on the part of the retail chain. Each prospective retail site serves a distinctive market and represents a major investment, but which site is most appropriate to the chain's product mix, threshold, and operating characteristics? While in general the retail chains have flourished within the predictable environments of the suburban shopping plaza, a new generation of chains is seeking out more specialized shopping environments. Entrepreneurs who have succeeded in serving Mexican or Chinese communities expand as their markets grow. Fashion houses and discount centers that flourish in specialized retail strips attempt to replicate their success in similar environments throughout the metropolitan region.

The sprawling Los Angeles metropolitan area, containing over 7.5 million people and extending over 2,000 square miles, provides ample variation in location choices. There are physically isolated canyons, sprawling retail strips that serve communities of Blacks, Hispanics, and Asians, upscale shopping streets, and mass-market regional plazas. A network of regional centers (Figure 7.5) blankets the built-up area; only the low-income Black community of Watts to the south of downtown is excluded. None of the major retail chains, even the discount houses, venture there. Blacks are forced to 'out-shop' at plazas in the surrounding districts. We begin to understand why when we look at the distribution of sales per square foot. Most of the inner city shopping centers are below the regional median. Centers in the wealthier areas do well, as do those in the more distant suburbs to the south. The highest level of sales intensity occurs in the mall at Santa Monica. The sales per square foot tell the retailer the level of customer traffic and the rent that can be expected in a given center.

Figure 7.6 contrasts three different department store location strategies. Sears, oriented to the mass market, pioneered the free-standing department store. A number of the latter remain in the older suburbs of Los Angeles, but most of the new outlets occur in regional and super-regional malls. Although Sears penetrates every part of the market, they favor the low-income areas to the southeast. Bullocks is an upscale department store, with a spin-off fashion version called Bullocks Wilshire (ironically the very first free-standing department store in Los Angeles). While this chain is represented in the wealthier fringes of Orange County to the south, it is strongest in Beverly Hills and the San Fernando Valley. Target Stores, a discount chain, represents the mirror image of Bullocks. All the stores are

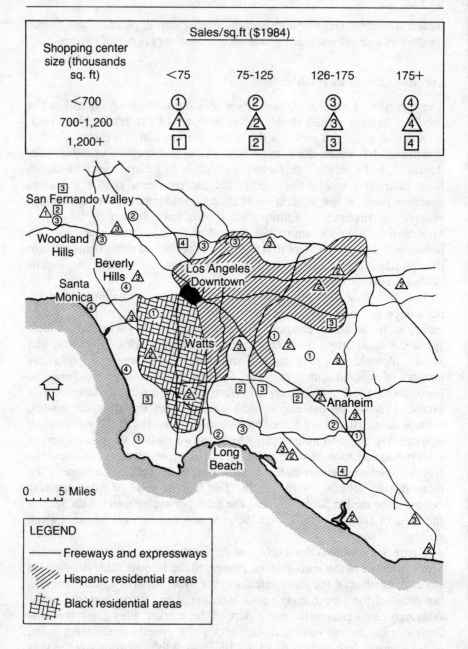

| Shopping center size (thousands sq. ft) | Sales/sq.ft ($1984) | | | |
|---|---|---|---|---|
| | <75 | 75-125 | 126-175 | 175+ |
| <700 | ① | ② | ③ | ④ |
| 700-1,200 | △1 | △2 | △3 | △4 |
| 1,200+ | □1 | □2 | □3 | □4 |

**Figure 7.5** Major plazas in Los Angeles

*Source:* Los Angeles Times Marketing Research Department (1985) *Southern California Shopping Center Directory*

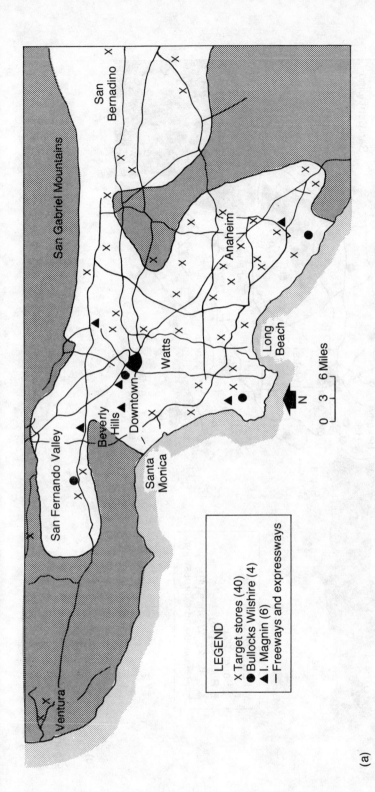

**Figure 7.6** Department store location strategies

*Source:* Los Angeles Times Marketing Research Department (1985) *Southern California Shopping Center Directory*

(a)

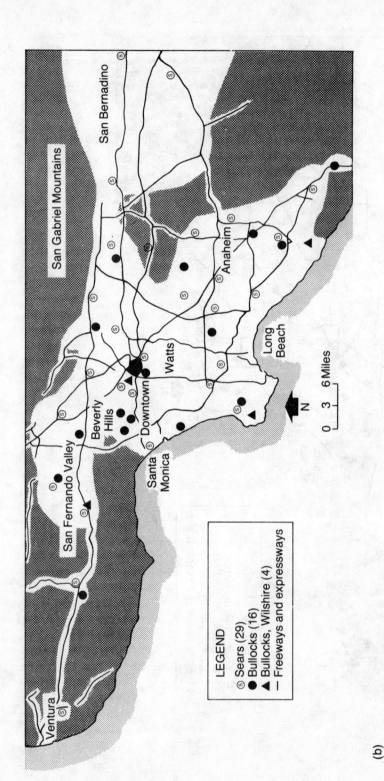

**Figure 7.6** (*continued*)

free-standing: they circle the Black community, serve the Hispanics of east Los Angeles, and thrive in the working-class areas to the southeast.

The maps in Figure 7.7 show the variation in retail chain locations among a more limited set of alternatives: the set of forty-six regional and super-regional centers depicted in Figure 7.5 Benetton is a Europe-based fashion store which serves carefully selected centers in the high-income periphery of the metropolitan area, especially to the north. Payless Shoes has identified the shopping centers that are closest to the low-income population.

This chapter has underlined the complexity of the retail environment within the city. The explosion in accessibility has extended the spatial scale

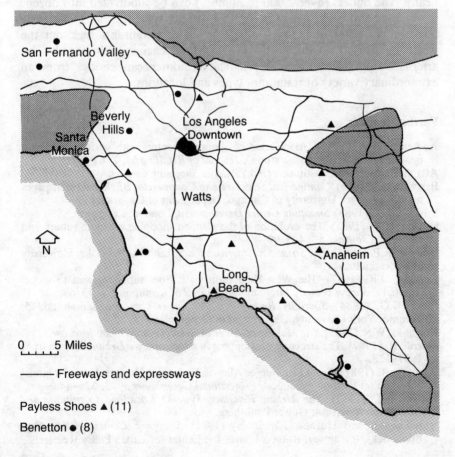

0 ⌞⌟⌟⌟⌟ 5 Miles

——— Freeways and expressways

Payless Shoes ▲ (11)

Benetton ● (8)

**Figure 7.7** Other retail chains

*Source:* Los Angeles Times Marketing Research Department (1985) *Southern California Shopping Center Directory*

of competition. Shopping districts, both planned and unplanned, are unable to depend on a spatial monopoly. Instead they attempt to distinguish themselves from the competition by being bigger, or cheaper, or more exclusive. The result is variety of distinctive retail environments or niches. These environments, in turn, have led to the evolution of more specialized retail and service chains. Crabtree and Evelyn, a gift shop specializing in Victorian-style English goodies, is found in every upscale historical redevelopment. With a little experience you can classify the shopping districts by means of the chains, or vice versa. To reposition a chain (or a mall) to suit a different clientele may involve substantial location (leasing) adjustments.

Pillsbury's (1987) study of Atlanta restaurants illustrates the point neatly. The outlets (over 2,000 in number) can be subdivided into dozens of variants, and each variant occupies a distinct spatial niche. Full-service restaurants cluster downtown, ethnic specialty restaurants seek out the wealthier districts on the north side, fast-food chains group together on arterial strips (hamburger alleys). The customer can choose from an extraordinary variety of restaurant types and locations.

## Further reading

Anderson, P.M. (1985) 'Association of shopping centers with performance of a non-anchor specialty chain's stores', *Journal of Retailing* 61, 2: 61–74.

Atlanta Journal and Constitution (n.d.) *Atlanta Shopping Centers.*

Berry, B.J.L. (1963) *Commerical Structure and Commercial Blight,* research paper no. 85, Chicago: University of Chicago, Department of Geography.

Dawson, J.A. (1983) *Shopping Centre Development,* London: Longmans.

Gillette, H. Jr (1985) 'The evolution of the planned shopping center in suburb and city', *APA Journal* 51: 449–60.

Horwitz, R.P. (1985) *The Strip: An American Place,* Lincoln, Nebraska: University of Nebraska Press.

Johnson, D.B. (1987) 'The West Edmonton mall: from super-regional to mega-regional shopping centre', *International Journal of Retailing* 2, 2: 53–69.

Jones, K.G. (1984) *Specialty Retailing in the Inner City,* monograph no. 15, Toronto: York University, Department of Geography.

Kowinski, W.S. (1985) *The Malling of America,* New York: William Morrow.

Morrill, R. (1987) 'The structure of shopping in a metropolis', *Urban Geography* 8, 1: 97–128.

Pillsbury, R. (1987) 'From Hamburger Alley to Hedgerose Heights: toward a model of restaurant location dynamics', *Professional Geographer* 39, 3: 326–44.

Potter, R.B. (1982) *The Urban Retailing System: Location, Cognition, and Behaviour,* Aldershot: Gower Publishing.

Sternlieb, G. and Hughes, J.W. (eds) (1981) *Shopping Centers, USA,* New Brunswick, New Jersey: Rutgers University, Center for Urban Policy Research.

# The changing retail structure

**Between 1972 and 1982 the average downtown shopping district lost
one-quarter of its retail sales.**

**The average floor area of stores in large shopping centers is declining.**

**Rapid growth accelerates the rate of change in location, function, and quality of retail activity.**

**Two-thirds of America's largest cities have an outlying retail center that is bigger than downtown.**

Within the city, the various forms of locations of retail activity continually adjust to new conditions: new apartment buildings are constructed, neighborhoods age, freeways or bridges are built. As a result, some stores go out of business, some commercial buildings are torn down for redevelopment, other stores expand or change the mix of services that they provide. A new shopping center affects the sales of all the nearby retail clusters.

The same forces of change, from both the supply and demand sides, that affect the distribution system on the settlement scale (Chapter six) also operate on the retail system within the metropolis. However, just as the retail structure is more complex within the city, the pattern of response to change is also more complex. Because the metropolis is an aggregation of many markets – some spatial and some sectoral – simple increments in the size of market due to increased population, income, and mobility may be less important than the changes in composition or characteristics of these markets, both locally and across the city. Thus, the various forces of retail change may have contradictory effects.

Figure 8.1 shows that the three elements of retail structure – consumer demand, functional mix, and retail cluster – are subject to a variety of changes in the social and economic environment which operate through many processes and people. A change in household composition alters the relative importance of different segments of the market and modifies the mix of store types. It also affects consumer behavior by changing mobility and personal schedules, thus altering preferences in shopping environments. For example, we can use the diagram to trace the implications of a widely recognized trend: the increasing proportion of households made up of senior citizens. This segment of the market is characterized by low discretionary income, small households, and a preference for living in inner-city, residential areas. While these households have plenty of time to shop, their spatial mobility is restricted and most of their shopping will be done within the neighborhood. The retail landscape will shift towards smaller neighborhood stores, emphasizing price and service rather than fashion and rock music. The overall effect is to move the retail environment back to the stores and store groupings of the past – the traditional shopping street.

Table 8.1 lists some of the other important socio-economic trends of the 1980s and the ways in which they affect retail structure. The pattern of residential growth extends the city outward so that much of the population growth occurs at the periphery of the urbanized area – at the furthest edge of the trade area of downtown. As cities have expanded outwards since

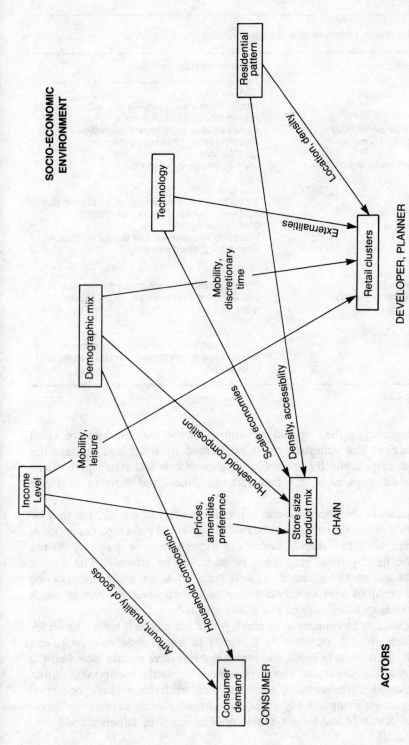

**SOCIO-ECONOMIC ENVIRONMENT**

Residential pattern

Location, density

Technology

Externalities

Mobility, discretionary time

Retail clusters

**DEVELOPER, PLANNER**

Demographic mix

Scale economies

Density, accessibility

Household composition

Income Level

Mobility, leisure

Prices, amenities, preference

Store size product mix

**CHAIN**

Household composition

Consumer demand

Amount, quality of goods

**CONSUMER**

**ACTORS**

**Figure 8.1** The changing retail environment

*Source:* The authors

**Table 8.1** Retail change within the metropolis

| Sources of change | Response of retail structure |
| --- | --- |
| *Residential pattern* | |
| Growth | Almost entirely suburban – favors suburban malls. Accelerates all forms of change |
| Declining household size | Favors smaller, more convenient facilities |
| Neighborhood transition | Alters the form of inner city decline or specialization |
| Downtown social segmentation | specialization in older strips |
| *Income* | |
| Increase | Throughout metropolitan region, increasing retail space everywhere. Favors specialization, downtown shopping. |
| Leisure | Weekend, recreation-linked shopping. Tourism. Favors specialized shopping |
| *Mobility* | |
| Increase | Permits specialization, increased store size |
| Type (e.g. car or transit) | Transit favors downtown, car favors suburban malls |
| *Technology* | |
| Automation | Increased scale of store, chain. Accelerates depreciation, favors new investment. Deskilling of labor force |

*Source:* The authors

their beginnings, their spatial structures mirror the sequence of retail technologies. The suburban tracts are served by malls and automobile-oriented strips while the inner-city neighborhoods still retain pedestrian-scale retail strips along the main arterial streets and early rapid-transit routes.

Increases in real income occur across the whole metropolis, but may be intensified in certain neighborhoods when one social class replaces another. For example, if the average household income rises or drops by 30 per cent, the nearby retail strip must immediately be affected. The mix of products and stores will change as well. Also, while the replacement of one lifestyle group by another may not alter the income level, the type of goods and services required may be drastically affected.

Accessibility has improved as much within the city as it has at the settlement scale. Rapid increases in the level of automobile ownership and massive investments in roads and transit systems have greatly increased the spatial range of stores and shopping centers within the metropolis. Within these overall improvements, powerful local differences have occurred, favoring stops along subway lines, for instance, or at expressway intersections. Some of the largest retail concentrations in America today are found near freeway interchanges that didn't exist twenty years ago. Consumers respond to the relatively greater mobility in the suburbs than in the central city. People who move easily around the periphery are frustrated by the traffic and parking problems of downtown. On the other hand, consumers who work downtown find it convenient to shop there.

How has the retail structure actually responded to these forces? Where has the growth of retail activity occurred? In what kinds of retail clusters? This chapter is concerned with these questions.

Table 8.2 and Figure 8.2 summarize the changes in retail structure in the Chicago metropolitan area over thirty-five years. Chicago has long been one of the great laboratories for the study of retail structure. Between 1954 and 1982 the six-county region increased in population by 33 per cent and income per capita by 19 per cent. As a result, the overall market grew by 59 per cent and would probably grown faster if 1982 had not been a recession year. Retail sales for the region as a whole kept pace with a

### Exhibit 8.1
### OVER-STORING?

Shopping centers are both cause of and response to the restructuring of the retail fabric. Over one-half of today's retail space has been built since 1960, with perhaps 40 per cent of the increment in the form of planned shopping centers (Graph A). The growth is a response both to the increased real income of consumers in the post-war period and to the spatial redistribution of housing within the metropolitan region. Many older retail buildings have been abandoned.

But the creation of new retail space has proceeded much more rapidly than the increase in retail sales, as Graph B indicates. In 1987 the floor area in shopping centers grew at twice the rate of growth in retail sales. The result has been a steady decline in the intensity of sales (sales per square foot) and thus in the average rents per square foot paid to shopping center developers. In 1983 there were already fifty square feet of retail space for each American.

Where will this end? Somehow most of the retail space is rented, although the share occupied by various services and professional offices increases. Strip malls compete for retail uses that traditionally located independently on an arterial street. Developers shave costs, and look for different kinds of tenants. Larger shopping goods malls are competing among themselves, trying to develop amenities or specializations that will give them an edge.           (cont.)

*Sources:* Shopping Center World (1988); *Directory of Shopping Centers in the US and Canada*, Communications Channels: Atlanta; The Energy Information Administration (1983) *Characteristics of Commercial Buildings*, Washington; Urban Land Institute (various years) *Dollars and Cents of Shopping Centers*, Washington

Exhibit 8.1 (*continued*)

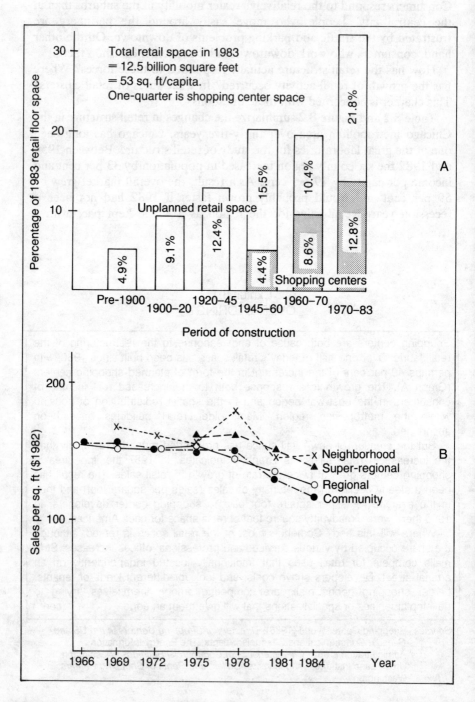

**Table 8.2** The change in retail structure: Chicago* (all values in 1982 dollars)

|  | 1954 | 1958 | 1963 | 1967 | 1972 | 1977 | 1982 |
|---|---|---|---|---|---|---|---|
| *Market size* | | | | | | | |
| Population (000s) | 5,457 | 5,816 | 6,466 | 6,774 | 7,161 | 6,950 | 7,238 |
| Income/capita ($) | 8,150 | 9,620 | 10,055 | 11,765 | 10,360 | 13,460 | 9,685 |
| Market income ($ millions) | 44,200 | 55,950 | 65,000 | 79,700 | 74,200 | 93,700 | 70,100 |
| Retail sales ($ millions) | 25,600 | 28,000 | 31,200 | 36,000 | 39,800 | 40,200 | 33,100 |
| Sales/store ($ thousands) | 468 | 509 | 635 | 740 | 748 | 851 | 702 |
| | | | | | | | |
| *Share of sales (%)* | | | | | | | |
| CBD (the Loop) | 10.0 | 8.3 | 6.8 | 6.6 | 5.0 | 3.7 | 3.4 |
| Rest of the city | 60.3 | 57.0 | 50.2 | 45.0 | 38.5 | 28.7 | 27.8 |
| MRCs | – | 8.0 (22)** | 7.3 (30) | 7.1 (28) | 6.4 (25) | 4.5 (18) | 3.1 (18) |
| Other | – | 49.0 | 42.9 | 37.9 | 32.1 | 24.2 | 24.7 |
| Rest of SMSA | 31.2 | 34.7 | 43.0 | 48.4 | 56.5 | 67.6 | 68.8 |
| MRCs | – | 2.2 | 10.3 | 12.0 | 14.1 | 10.4 | 10.6 |
| Planned | – | 2.0 (7) | 6.8 (27) | 8.4 (31) | 11.1 (43) | 8.1 (34) | 9.5 (31) |
| Unplanned | – | 0.2 (1) | 3.5 (16) | 3.6 (10) | 3.0 (14) | 2.3 (7) | 1.1 (3) |
| Other | – | 32.5 | 32.7 | 36.4 | 42.4 | 57.2 | 58.2 |
| | | | | | | | |
| *Growth in sales ($ millions)* | | | | | | | |
| CBD | | −245 | −198 | +237 | −390 | −486 | −369 |
| Rest of the city | | +531 | −359 | 578 | −891 | −3,775 | −2,337 |
| MRCs | | – | 22 | 298 | −38 | −722 | −278 |
| Other | | – | −381 | 280 | −853 | −3,053 | −2,059 |
| Rest of the SMSA | | +2,097 | +3,700 | +4,043 | +2,753 | +3,230 | −3,595 |
| MRCs | | – | 2,603 | 1,125 | 1,268 | −1,428 | −672 |
| Planned | | – | 1,562 | 911 | 1,377 | −1,173 | −77 |
| Unplanned | | – | 1,041 | 214 | −109 | −255 | −595 |
| Other | | – | 1,097 | 2,918 | 3,732 | 6,085 | −3,691 |

*Source:* Bureau of the Census (various years) *Census of Retail Trade*
*Notes:* *Includes Cook, Dupage, Kane, Lake, McHenry and Will counties. CBD, central business district; SMSA, standard metropolitan statistical area; MRC, major retail center.
**Numbers in parentheses indicate number of centers.

growth rate of 29 per cent, although 15 per cent of the stores disappeared.

This apparent stability masks a massive spatial reorganization of the Chicago market. The older part of the region, represented by downtown (the Loop) and the rest of the City of Chicago, essentially a pre-Second World War landscape, has declined markedly, losing 55 per cent and 40 per cent of 1954 retail sales in the downtown and city areas, respectively. Most of this decline was due to the redistribution of market income, especially after 1972. Meanwhile, retail sales in the suburbs, some of them at least middle-aged by now, continued to grow: 180 per cent for the inner suburbs in Cook County and over 200 per cent in the outer suburbs. As the

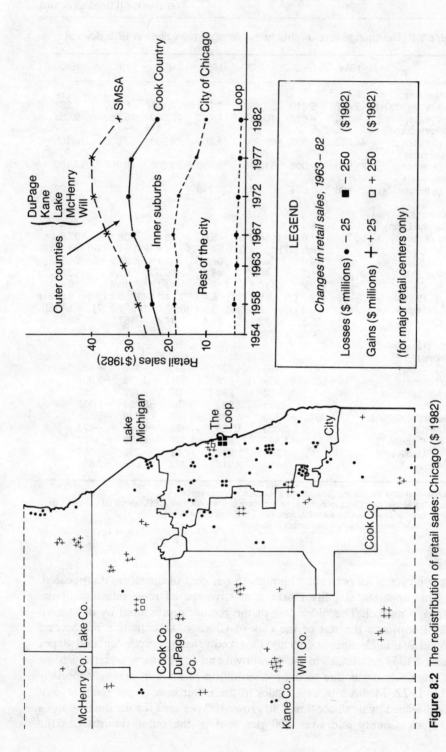

**Figure 8.2** The redistribution of retail sales: Chicago ($ 1982)

*Source:* Bureau of the Census (various years) *Census of Retail Trade*, Washington

suburban markets grow, the range of retail facilities that they can support improves and they attract more shoppers, even from the City.

The Table also summarizes data from the *Census of Retail Trade* about major retail centers, with the warning that these results partly reflect decisions to increase the number of centers included in 1958 and to decrease them in 1977. It appears that in both the City of Chicago and the suburbs, the major retail centers – especially the unplanned ones – are losing ground to the unstructured retail strips and free-standing stores. The retail structure, described in such detail by Berry (1963), is melting away. Half of the unplanned centers within the City no longer generate enough sales (about $20 million in 1982) to make the list. Sixty-third and Halsted, the largest center outside the Loop in 1963, is just another declining inner city strip.

While the suburban planned centers grew rapidly in the 1960s, they have since lost ground to the activities that lie outside the conventional clusters – either in smaller centers and strips, or in automobile-oriented strips. Between 1977 and 1982, however, the recession devastated all parts of the metropolitan area.

The map of change in retail sales in major retail centers since 1963 (Figure 8.2) confirms the pattern of decentralization. Massive losses in the downtown shopping area have been partially offset by the growth of the fashion district along Michigan Avenue, a mile to the north. Almost all the retail centers in the low-income areas on the south side have disappeared, including once thriving Black retail centers on 47th and 63rd streets. The most visible pockets of growth in the suburbs are the super-regional centers that surround the older city. With over 1 million square feet of shopping space and up to $200 sales per square foot, they quickly absorb any increase in market income.

The sections that follow examine four aspects of spatial adjustment in the retail structure. Decentralization diminishes the relative importance of downtown and inner city retail activity within the metropolitan area. Why do some downtowns survive? What kinds of roles remain for inner-city retailing areas? This process is partly due to rapid growth of planned centers and we will examine how they have evolved within the metropolis and how they compete with each other. At the same time, increasing retail activity takes place outside the planned centers, but even here the shift towards larger stores and retail chains has implications for corner stores, older shopping areas, and strip developments. Finally, we look at the effects of neighborhood change, such as the expansion of low-income areas, gentrification, or ethnic group shifts on traditional shopping streets.

## Decentralization

As the city grows it expands in space, generating competition between the retail activities concentrated at the very center of the city (downtown) and the growing markets at the periphery. New shopping facilities to serve these new markets truncate the trade areas of older retail clusters. Figure 7.1 described the spatial distribution of consumer demand in Atlanta in 1980. Atlanta, one of the fastest growing metropolitan areas in the country, has undergone rapid change over the last decade (Figure 8.3a), but as we saw in Chicago, even slow-growth communities have had to adjust.

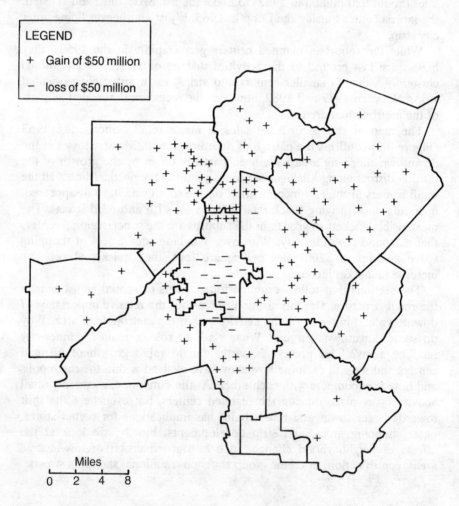

LEGEND

+ Gain of $50 million

− loss of $50 million

Miles
0  2  4  8

**Figure 8.3** Changing patterns of consumer demand and retail sales: Atlanta (a) Growth in income, 1970–80 ($ 1982)

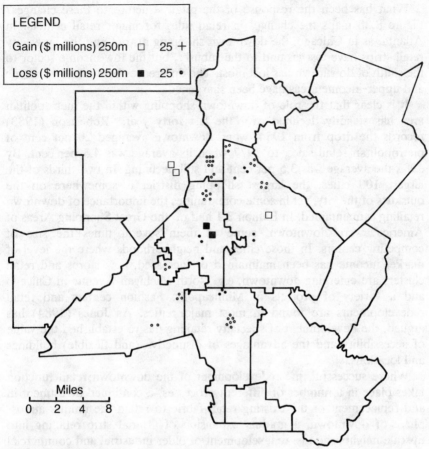

**Figure 8.3** (*continued*)
(b) Growth of major retail centers, 1972–82

*Source:* Bureau of the Census (various years) *Census of Retail Trade*, Washington

The most dramatic change in Atlanta is the continued redistribution of households and market income into new housing at the edge of the city, so that most growth occurs 10–15 miles from the city center. In addition, the growth in real income per household has benefited many neighborhoods just inside the ring of growth, while the decline of the central city has dramatically reduced the purchasing power in the core by more than $500 million! In Atlanta this income growth is much more pronounced to the north, in the high-income sector. Investments in expressways and rapid transit have reduced travel time at off-peak hours by half. As a result, every retail location now faces more competition from neighboring stores and plazas.

What has been the response of the retail structure to these changes? Figure 8.3b maps the changes in retail sales for major retail centers. In Atlanta, as in Chicago, the downtown shopping district and the inner-city retail strips have lost ground to the suburbs, but the low-income sector to the south of downtown has lost most. The differences between low-income and upper-income areas have been sharpened.

It is clear that the role of downtown shopping within the metropolitan area has steadily declined over the last forty years. Robertson (1983) records the drop from 1954, when downtown averaged 20 per cent of metropolitan retail sales, to 1977 when its average was 4.3 per cent. By 1982 the average was 3.5 per cent and still declining. In two-thirds of the largest 100 cities, the largest shopping district is somewhere on the outskirts of the city, yet in some communities the importance of downtown retailing is maintained. In Exhibit 3.1 half of 'the Great Shopping Areas of America' were downtown, some of them several times the size of competing centers. In those cities and neighborhoods where the level of market income has been maintained or increased, new stores and retail clusters are emerging downtown, e.g. North Michigan Avenue in Chicago and a variety of projects in Minneapolis. Fashion centers and retail redevelopments are found in most major cities. As Jones (1984) has argued, the development of specialty retailing has re-established the value of accessibility and the advantages of distinctive (and flexible) buildings and locations.

Where successful, the redevelopment of the downtown retail function takes place in a number of different processes; a continued investment in and replacement of the existing retail fabric to retain the unique atmosphere of downtown, a gradual expansion of arterial strip retailing into upscale neighborhoods, redevelopment of older industrial and commercial sites for specialized retail purposes, and the construction of new, high-rise office and apartment buildings. The result is an expansion of retail structure in several directions (and at several elevations) simultaneously, as suggested in the study of Chicago (Exhibit 8.2).

If it is to survive, downtown must evolve in function and in location. The relocation may not be dramatic – perhaps only a few blocks – and often simply reflects the addition of different downtown activities, but it is necessary to replace the inevitable losses to freeways, to office buildings, or to parking lots. Almost every downtown has an internal structure that features a growing edge and a declining edge, and a historical sequence of buildings and activities that records the events of the past.

Still, in the majority of American cities downtown retailing has been pretty well written off by the private sector. Much of the retail infrastructure, the distinctive buildings, the small business and the variety of retail activities, have disappeared. Only substantial infusions of public funds for land, parking, and financial backing will lure retail development

## Exhibit 8.2
## CHICAGO: THE LOOP AND BEYOND

For years the Loop in Chicago has been one of the great retail concentrations in America. It is not spatially dispersed like downtown Los Angeles, nor mixed in with other land uses like New York. The Loop is based on an intense concentration of access to a large and prosperous market. Enclosed by the elevated transit track, which is itself bounded by the lakefront land uses and the Chicago River, it is also served by underground transit and commuter lines. Offices for the financial district and government are concentrated in the west of the Loop, and continue to expand.

The retail activity is located to the east. In the 1950s six great department stores were located along State Street, on one block after another. In 1948 the Loop generated $6 out of every $1,000 retail sales in the country, one-eighth of all sales in Chicagoland. However, 40 years later both Chicago and the Loop have declined in significance: the $6 has dropped to $1, and the 12 per cent to 3. Of the six great department stores, only Marshall Field and Carson Pirie Scott remain.

What happened? To the usual list of suburban growth, freeway construction, shopping plazas, and inner-city decline, we can add the dramatic reduction of purchasing power in the immediate trade area south and west of downtown, as

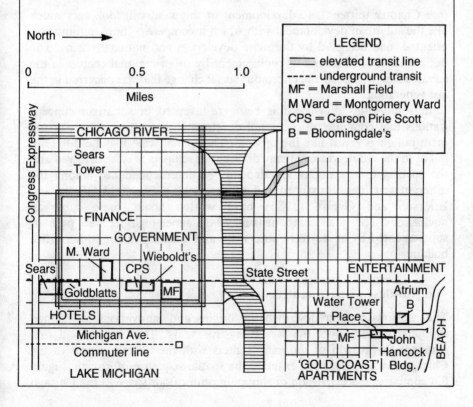

Exhibit 8.2 (*continued*)

shown in Figure 8.2. At the same time, gentrification and expensive condominiums flourish on the north side of the city. Upscale retailers have detached themselves from the mass markets of the Loop and created a flashy new retailing environment on North Michigan Avenue. It is only a mile or so away but the atmosphere is worlds apart: different customers (different access patterns), different stores (Neiman-Marcus, Saks), and dramatic success. In the next *Census of Retail Trade* it will overtake the Loop. Michigan Avenue has become the greatest fashion retail location between Fifth Avenue and Rodeo Drive, anchored by Water Tower Place (Marshall Field) and The Atrium (with Bloomingdale's). The malls are designed both to exclude unwanted customers and attract the well-to-do.

In this sense the Loop survives at a different spatial scale. The new facilities – like the former version – have the capacity to attract shoppers from communities all over the mid-west, looking for the goods and excitement that they can't get at home.

(see Chapter thirteen). Redevelopment of this kind will look very much like the suburban development with which it competes – new, automobile-oriented, and designed by the same developers and national chains. The decline of downtown and its replacement by super-regional centers in the suburbs simply reflects the enormous social change that has occurred in the last generation.

In some cities downtown is being re-invented in suburban concentrations that combine offices, retail developments, freeway access, apartment buildings – just like the original. The spatial scale may be different, but as in the old downtown many different developers may be involved and the success of the nucleation depends on interdependence among the different activities. Hartshorn and Muller (1986), Baerwald (1978), and Erickson and Gentry (1985) have written about these suburban nucleations. The retail component may be a super-regional mall, perhaps supplemented by an adjacent strip mall, and ancillary malls, within office buildings.

## The growth of planned centers

The previous chapter described the origins and innovations in planned shopping centers over the last thirty-five years. This section will first compare the growth of shopping centers with the overall growth of the Chicago market, and then examine the spatial sequence of growth. Figure 8.4 compares the expansion of shopping center floor space in the Chicago

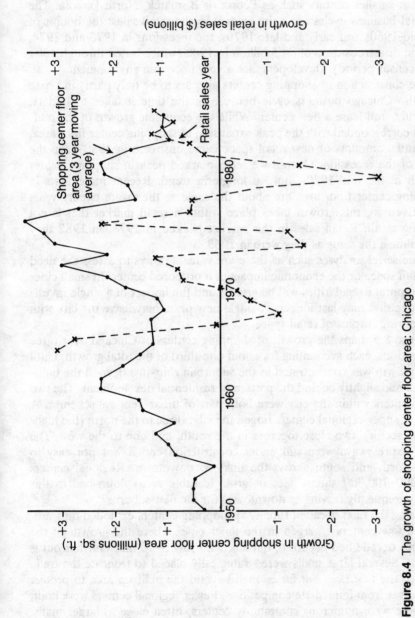

**Figure 8.4** The growth of shopping center floor area: Chicago

*Sources:* Bureau of the Census (monthly) Current Business Reports Monthly, *Retail Trade, Sales and Inventories*, National Research Bureau (annual) *Directory of Shopping Centers in the United States and Canada*

metropolitan area to the growth of retail sales. Note that both growth series are quite irregular, even after the shopping center data have been smoothed by the use of a 3-year moving average. The changes in retail sales appear to be especially volatile, considering that Chicago is a large and supposedly stable, urban economy. Imagine the fluctuations that must occur in smaller centers such as Peoria or Bismarck, North Dakota. The national business cycles are quite evident in the retail sales: the booms of the mid-1960s and early and late 1970s, the recessions in 1973 and 1974, and the disastrous drop of $4.5 billion in 1980 (which lasted through 1981 – the census period). Developers face a very uncertain environment.

The construction of shopping centers appears to be only partly in phase with the Chicago business cycle because of the time it takes to initiate, construct, and lease a new center. While the economic growth of the mid-1970s corresponded with the peak expansion of shopping center floor area, substantial amounts of new retail space came onstream in 1980–1, in the heart of the recession. Overall we see a marked peak in shopping center growth in the mid-1970s, but no longterm trend. Recent increments in shopping center floor area are about the same as they were twenty years ago. Even so, this growth takes place within a retail market that is not growing at all. Retail sales in this market peaked in 1978; in 1982 they were almost the same as they were in 1963.

Time series analyses such as these are valuable ways to assess the need for retail space or the economic impact of a proposed center. In small cities the temporal irregularities will be greater and the impact of a single investment decision may last longer. A single new plaza may leave the city with an enduring surplus of retail space.

Figure 8.5 maps the growth of shopping centers in Chicago over three time periods, each accounting for about one-third of the total growth. Until 1965 growth was concentrated in the suburban ring, just beyond the built-up area and slightly behind the pattern of residential development. The two small centers within the city were both part of urban renewal schemes. A series of super-regional centers ringed the city: three to the north (the high-income sector), two close together in the south, and one to the west. The major expressways were still under construction and it was not easy to travel north and south across the links to downtown. Regional centers (300,000–700,000 square feet of gross leasable area) flourished in this period, frequently serving as downtowns for the new suburbs.

During the next decade (1965–75) shopping centers exploded outward. Only a few centers emerged in the inner cities where the growth of the previous decade had occurred, but a second ring 5–10 miles further out is evident. Several large malls were strategically placed to truncate the trade areas of the first ring, but far enough beyond the built-up area to protect themselves from immediate competition. Fewer regional centers were built, but there were numerous community centers, often close to larger malls.

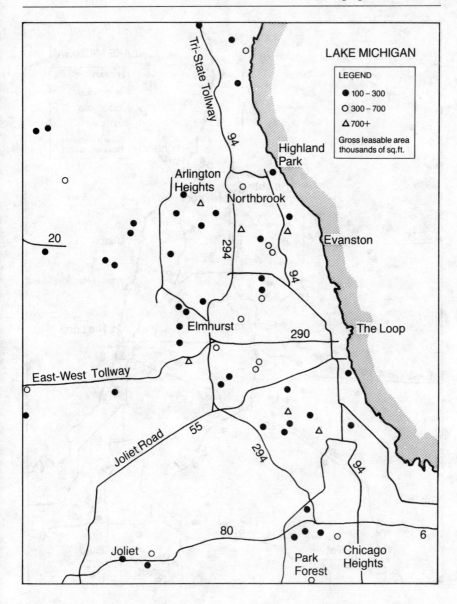

**Figure 8.5** The spread of planned centers: Chicago
(a) To 1965

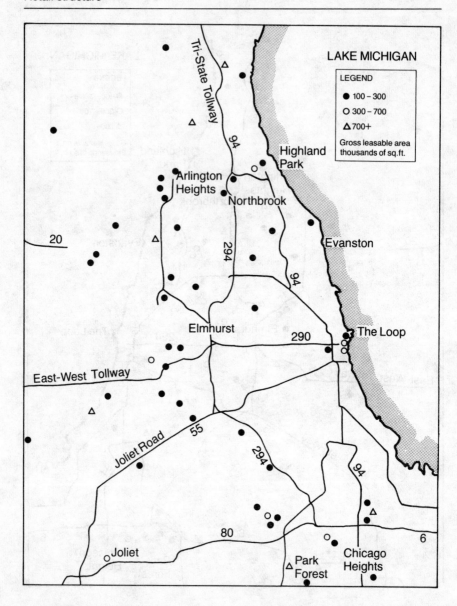

**Figure 8.5** (*continued*)
(b) 1966–75

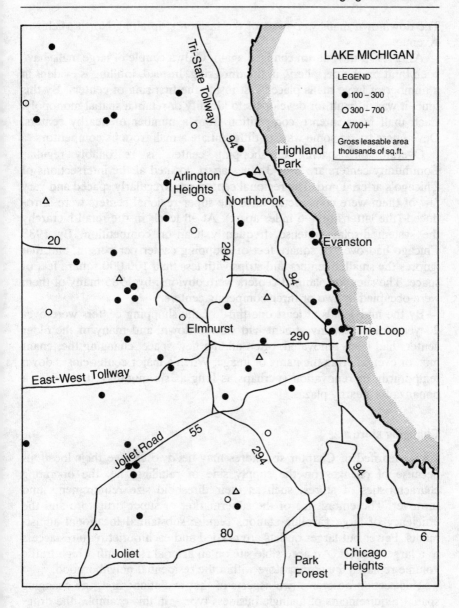

**Figure 8.5** (*continued*)
(c) 1976–85

*Source:* The authors, based on National Research Bureau (1989) *Directory of Shopping Centers in the United States and Canada*

The downtown malls were part of the fashion strip along North Michigan Avenue.

After 1975 the pattern changed again. Only a couple of large malls have been built on the periphery, in the third ring. Instead, infilling is evident in a number of large malls placed just inside the first ring of centers. By this time, it was difficult for developers to identify or retain a spatial monopoly. Each mall faces intense competition from a number of nearby centers. Developers try, in some way, to differentiate a mall from its competitors.

Overall, the spacing of shopping centers is reasonably regular. Community centers are 2 or 3 miles apart, located at the intersections of Chicago's arterial grid. The regional centers are irregularly spaced and very few of them were constructed once the super-regional centers were introduced (the latter are 4–6 miles apart). At all levels in the retail hierarchy the system displays intense, frequently head-on competition. By 1985 Chicago had over 10 square feet of shopping center per person, and that ignores the smaller centers and strips with less than 100,000 square feet of space. The sites for planned centers were obvious: by 1985 many of them were occupied by two or three competing centers.

By the mid-1980s at least one-third of the shopping centers were over 20 years old. New investment had slowed down, and many of the older centers had been renovated, often adding new space, changing the tenant mix, or even altering the name or image. When a major center closes down temporarily or renovation (perhaps as long as six months), it provides a bonanza for nearby plazas.

## Changing store size

As we learned in Chapter six, stores may need to change their locations because of changes on the supply side of retailing; i.e. the operating characteristics of stores, such as their threshold size requirements and turnover. The emergence of the supermarket or super drugstore and the efficiency of large gasoline stations require substantial locational adjustments. Fewer but larger outlets are needed and each outlet requires access to a larger market. An accessible site on an arterial road with a high traffic volume replaces the corner store within the residential neighborhood.

This section describes two aspects of that evolution: first, the changing spatial requirements of a single business type – in this example, the drugstore, and second, the evolving locational strategies of a number of retail chains that operate within major cities.

Before we look at the maps of change, however, it is worthwhile pondering the pressures that affect decisions about store size and, therefore, location. Simmons (1964) showed that the average store size for most business types has been increasing steadily since the 1930s, or even earlier. The initial impetus to increase store size derived from the very nature of the independent retail enterprise. As real income levels increased overall, the merchant also demanded a higher rate of return, hence more sales, and this could be accompanied by modest investments in technology, such as cash registers and self-service, when accompanied by greater customer mobility. These forces have continued to operate in many retail sectors. Scale economies in supermarkets (Holdren, 1960) and in gas stations (Claus and Hardwick, 1972) are well-documented. The prerequisities include (1) customer willingness to travel, (2) a production function that permits labor saving or deskilling, and (3) inexpensive real estate. The K mart junior department store exemplifies the result of these processes. The large shopping center also favored the larger store. By assembling large number of customers and minimizing the amount of internal competition, it defined a cost curve that forced other stores, even independents, to respond.

What are the limits to this trend? While the average size for certain business types may continue to increase as smaller stores are forced out of business, retailers are beginning to recognize some upper limits to store size. In Chapter seven we noted the consumer's reaction against conventional shopping centers (larger stores) in favor of more specialized strips and ancillary malls (smaller stores), in part a reflection of changes in the nature of households. Also within the plazas themselves the evidence (Table 8.3) suggests that average store floor area is declining for most business types in larger centers (see also Urban Land Institute, 1984). In a large plaza, a store's rent is usually linked directly or indirectly to its floor area. As a result there is a continual pressure to increase sales/floor area by intensifying inventory, increasing the turnover of merchandise, and reducing the storage area.

For the retail system as a whole (see Figure 8.6), the effect of changing store size is much less important than the spatial redistribution of consumer demand. In the Baltimore region (population 2.3 million in 1980; growth rate 5.3 per cent from 1970 to 1980), the number of stores has grown by 26 per cent overall, with the number of large stores (more than twenty-five employees) increasing by 41 per cent. However, this change is largely due to the shift of growth towards suburban areas where large stores are twice as likely, on average.

The regional map shows consistent growth in the suburbs with concentrations of new stores at planned centers. Within the central city hundreds of stores have disappeared in older neighborhoods but this decline is partially offset by downtown redevelopment. In the city itself the number of stores, both large and small, is almost unchanged. Still, there are some interesting variations in the types of business. While the massive decline in the number of drugstores displays the same spatial pattern as retail stores overall, the growth of liquor stores shows an inverse pattern, expanding rapidly in the inner city.

For some business activities, particularly those not confined to plazas,

**Table 8.3** Store size in planned centers (floor area)

| Store name | Bramalea built 1976 (sq. ft) | Promenade built 1986 (sq. ft) | Floor area 1986/1976 |
|---|---|---|---|
| Fairweather | 8,180 | 3,620 | 0.44 |
| Dalmys | 3,920 | 2,960 | 0.76 |
| Lipton's | 3,480 | 2,510 | 0.72 |
| Town and Country | 2,680 | 2,290 | 0.85 |
| Shirley K | 1,100 | 780 | 0.72 |
| Thriftys | 1,920 | 2,250 | 1.17 |
| Jack Frazer | 4,050 | 3,490 | 0.86 |
| Kinney Shoes | 3,090 | 2,030 | 0.66 |
| Belinda | 1,160 | 630 | 0.54 |
| Mappins Jewellers | 3,730 | 1,010 | 0.27 |
| Key Man | 300 | 390 | 1.29 |
| Camera | 2,420 | 1,070 | 0.44 |
| Collacutt | 1,310 | 1,490 | 1.14 |
| Willson Stationery | 2,330 | 2,220 | 0.95 |
| Bowring | 1,230 | 1,790 | 1.46 |
| St Clair Paint | 1,750 | 1,580 | 0.90 |
| Lighting Unlimited | 1,940 | 1,630 | 0.84 |
| Drugstore | 13,250 | 7,070 | 0.53 |
| Peoples Jewellers | 2,490 | 1,110 | 0.45 |
| Radio Shack | 1,560 | 1,170 | 0.75 |
| Tip Top Tailors | 3,290 | 3,990 | 1.21 |
| Average | – | – | 0.80 |

*Source:* The authors
*Note:* This table compares the floor area of stores assigned to major retail chains in two different super-regional plazas in the Toronto region; one of them opened in 1976, and the other ten years later.

the trend toward larger store size continues. The drugstore example shown in Figure 8.6 and Exhibit 8.3 describes the spatial implications of the transition from small, independent neighborhood stores to large chain branches. Between 1972 and 1982 drugstore outlets and sales stayed roughly constant but the share of sales by the chain stores increased from 33 to 53 per cent. Drugstore sales should increase in the future because they sell income-elastic goods to a target market (the aged) that is also growing.

Individual retail chains make their own choices amid these pressures from both the demand and supply sides. Figure 8.7 shows how three department store chains have chosen to expand in Atlanta. K mart we all know: it came to Atlanta in the mid-1960s, locating seven stores in a conventional suburban ring pattern, with a single central location on the north side. Note that even a 'discount' department store prefers the wealthier side of town. Only five of the twenty-three present stores are located on the southern half of the map. The next three stores (1969–73) simply fill out the suburban ring, but the third wave of thirteen stores is

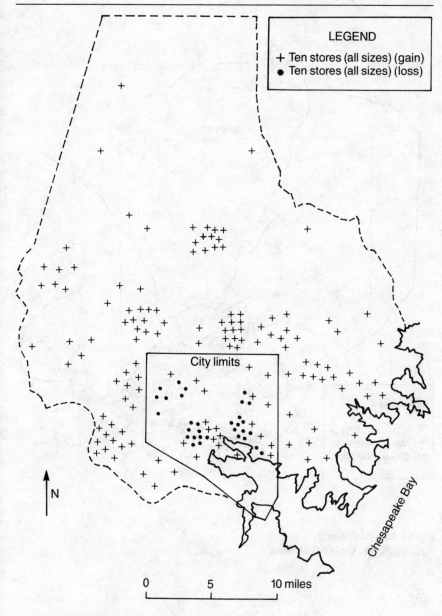

**Figure 8.6** Changes in store location: Baltimore (1970–83)
(a) All retail stores, Baltimore Co.

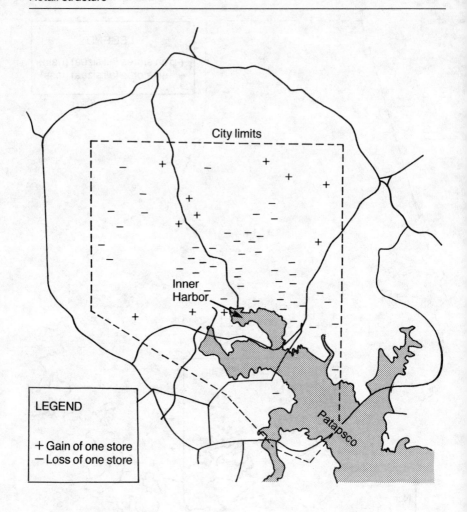

**Figure 8.6** (*continued*)
(b) Drugstores, City of Baltimore

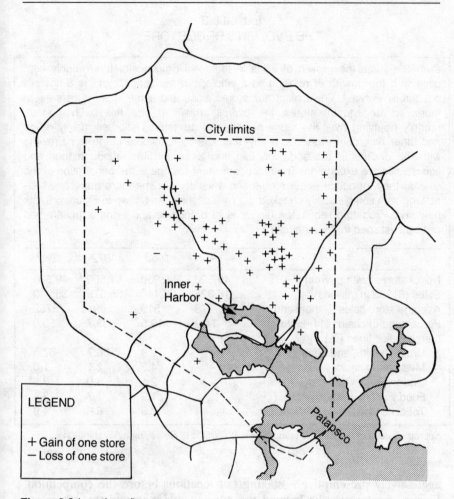

City limits

Inner +
Harbor

Patapsco

LEGEND

+ Gain of one store
− Loss of one store

**Figure 8.6** (*continued*)
(c) Liquor stores, City of Baltimore

| | No. of stores, 1970 | | No. of stores, 1983 | | Change | |
| | Small | Large | Small | Large | Small(%) | Large (%) |
|---|---|---|---|---|---|---|
| City | 3,145 | 373 | 3,033 | 368 | −112(−3.6) | −5(−1.3) |
| Rest of region | 2,126 | 374 | 3,527 | 684 | +1,401(65.8) | 310(82.8) |
| Total | 5,271 | 747 | 6,560 | 1,052 | 1,289(24.5) | 305(40.8) |

(d) For the region

*Source:* S.P. Shao Jr (1987) 'An analysis of retail firms in the Baltimore region, 1970–83', Mayor's Advisory Commission on Small Business, Baltimore

## Exhibit 8.3
## THE EVOLVING DRUGSTORE

Over the years the growth of sales in the retail drug sector has roughly kept pace with the growth of retailing as a whole, but the concept of the drugstore has subtly evolved. While giant drugstores exist, and some chain outlets seem more like department stores, the overall growth in size has been modest, roughly doubling over the study period, and drugstores still sell mainly drugs and other bathroom products. If anything, the merchandise range is narrowing with the decline of the soda fountain and tobacco sales, although food and liquor sales are expanding. The most consistent change is the penetration of the chains: they introduce larger stores and a variety of dime store merchandise – as long as it can be easily checked out by a cashier. As shown in Figure 8.6, the new style drugstore requires a higher level of income and income growth than can be sustained in the inner city.

|  | 1954 | 1963 | 1972 | 1982 |
| --- | --- | --- | --- | --- |
| No. of stores (with payroll) | 49,500 | 50,950 | 51,500 | 49,500 |
| Sales ($1982 in millions) | 18,325 | 26,440 | 35,575 | 36,240 |
| Average store sales ($ thousands) | 373 | 519 | 691 | 732 |
| Percentage of chains (11 + stores) | 14.9 | 19.5 | 33.7 | 53.0 |
| Merchandise lines (%) |  |  |  |  |
| Drugs, health, and beauty | – | 71.9 | 66.7 | 67.5 |
| Meals and snacks | – | 4.3 | 2.1 | 1.0 |
| Liquor | – | 2.1 | 3.0 | 3.3 |
| Food | – | 1.9 | 1.7 | 3.4 |
| Tobacco | – | 8.8 | 6.6 | 4.9 |

*Source:* Bureau of the Census (various years) *Census of Retail Trade*, Washington

aggressively pre-emptive – staking out locations before the competition. Five of these stores lie beyond the edge of our map and the others are placed beyond the edge of the built-up area. The most recent stores fill out this second location strategy.

The other department stores are the local representatives of two national chains: Rich's was part of Federated Department Stores, now part of the Campeau Corporation, and Macy's (formerly Davison) represents the New York firm. Both began as downtown stores and moved to the suburbs early. Rich's first stores followed the suburban growth to the north and east, and then slowly expanded outward, quadrant by quadrant. The pattern appears to be quite regular in space; one can predict that the next store will be to the south. These department stores are the anchor tenants for the regional malls and they work closely with developers to identify new sites. In Atlanta the two chains end up in the same malls – they share eight locations – as if they want to exclude any new chains from entering the

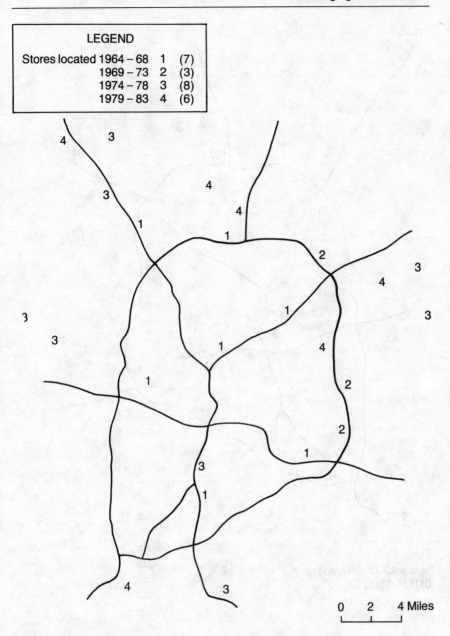

**Figure 8.7** Evolving location strategies of retail chains
(a) K mart in Atlanta

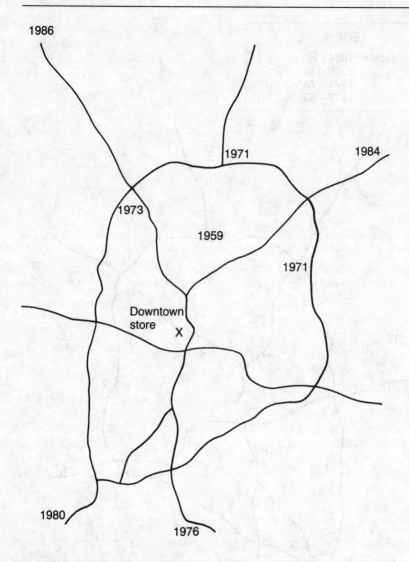

**Figure 8.7** (*continued*)
(b) R.H. Macy Co.

market. Rich's, however, has some independent locations that must be among the poorer sites in the urban area.

The metropolitan region poses a particularly complex challenge for retail chains. Each location provides access to a different set of customers

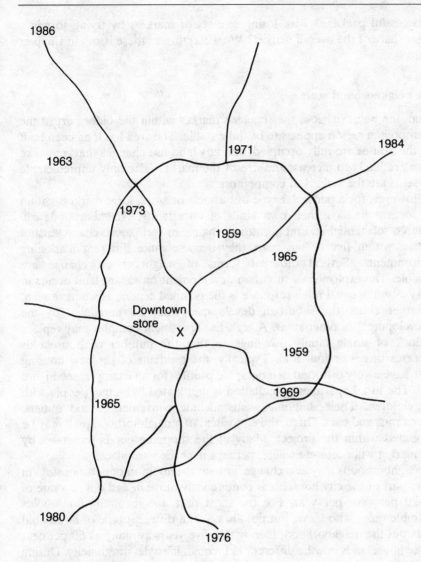

**Figure 8.7** (*continued*)
(c) Rich's department stores

*Source:* The authors

and a distinct pattern of competition. The logic of expanding a chain with a
fixed product mix and store image may appear to be quite straightforward,
but at some point the limits to opportunities in the market (and the actions
of competing chains) necessitate difficult decisions. Stop growing? Change

271

a successful package? Risk losing one set of markets by trying to win a larger share of the overall market? We will return to these issues in Chapter twelve.

## The neighborhood scale

From one point of view, the retailer's market within the older part of the metropolitan region appears to be quite stable. The area has long been built up, the houses are fully occupied, and any land use changes that may take place are likely to increase the size of the market. The only unpredictable elements are the actions of competitors.

However, for a particular type of business or store, local markets within the metropolis have their own kinds of uncertainty. Neighborhoods can undergo substantial and rapid rates of change in their social characteristics so that within five or ten years they become quite different marketing environments. Several different forms of neighborhood change are possible. The explosion of suburban development on vacant land occurs in every city: the usual retail response is the planned center, as we have seen. In larger cities, the suburban development may be paralleled by the redevelopment of older areas. A high-rise apartment complex may replace a block of single family dwellings so that the number of households increases three- or four-fold. Typically, the residents of the new housing units have a very distorted demographic profile (for an example, see Figure 2.9). The usual apartment population is dominated by young people with few children. Their shopping wants include convenience food outlets, restaurants, and bars. Often, the equivalent of a neighborhood mall may be integrated within the project. Many of the shopping goods purchases by this market will occur elsewhere, perhaps near the workplace.

Neighborhoods may also change without the addition of new housing. In every part of the city households continuously move in and out at a rate of 15–20 per cent per year. For the most part, the incoming households resemble those who leave, but not always. If a different type of household seeks out the neighborhood, then within five years as many as 60 per cent of the households may be different in income, lifestyle, or ethnicity. During the 1950s and 1960s many neighborhoods in major cities shifted from White to Black or Hispanic. More recently, Asian or South American communities may have moved in. At the same time, traditional working-class neighborhoods may have been renovated or 'gentrified' by middle-class professionals. Exhibit 8.4 examines the impact of social change in Chicago.

The retail structure must adjust to these changes. Does the average household income increase or decline? Do the new families spend more or less of their money locally? Do they look for different products or shopping amenities? Can the merchant adjust to this new clientele, or is there no choice but to give way to someone who knows the styles, the culture, and the language? Fortunately, the usual rate of turnover for retail stores is at least as rapid as it is for households.

In many retail strips the transformations appear to be almost miraculous. Store after store changes hands within a short time and the retail strip becomes the focus for a new lifestyle, in some cases attracting customers from all over the city. The process of change is complex: many merchants are new, seeking out the particular market that has been defined, but some

## Exhibit 8.4
## THE IMPACT OF SOCIAL CHANGE: CHICAGO

Forty years ago, 63rd and Halsted was the largest retail center in Chicago outside the Loop. It was located about 8 miles from downtown, at a point where the elevated transit line connected with a network of bus and trolley routes, in the center of mile after mile of blue-collar and middle-class neighborhoods. A block-long Sears store was the main attraction but there were also Wieboldt's and Goldblatt department stores, a movie theater, and hundreds of smaller stores. In 1958 retail sales amounted to $250 million (in 1982 dollars), more than any of the new regional plazas that were springing up in the suburbs.

However, in the 1960s the retail activity began to decline and in the 1970s it collapsed. Blacks replaced Whites in the immediate neighborhood in the 1960s and household incomes declined. A recent market analysis suggests that while 45,000 households still live in the trade area, the average household income is less than $10,000. Forty per cent of the households earn less than $7,500 and 45 per cent of the population is twenty-five years old or less.

It is difficult to maintain a retail structure when there is so little money to spend. Sears moved out in the mid-1970s; Goldblatt's went broke. Of the 100 stores that remain, the only chains are Walgreen's, Jewel Foods, and Payless Shoes. People who have cars shop at Evergreen Plaza, a successful Black mall 6 miles away. The 63rd and Halsted center survives in an empty shell of abandoned stores and vacant lots. The pedestrian concourse that came with an urban renewal scheme two decades ago looks shabby and inappropriate. Declining income leads to fewer stores and fewer customers – a reversal of the growth cycle that sparked North Michigan Avenue.

Even so, relative to other retail areas on the south side of Chicago, 63rd and Halsted is a kind of success. It still has 100 stores, many of them locally owned, and sells $50 million dollars' worth of merchandise. It has the infrastructure: all it needs is customers with money.

*Source:* City of Chicago Planning Department (1987) *Englewood Concourse Revitalization Strategy*, Report prepared by Applied Real Estate Analysis. Brian J.L. Berry and R.J. Tenant (1963) *Chicago Commercial Reference Handbook*, University of Chicago, Department of Geography, Research paper No. 86

## Exhibit 8.4 (*continued*)

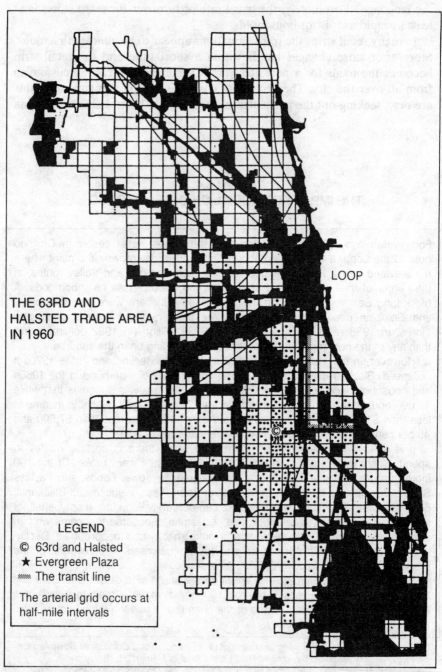

LOOP

THE 63RD AND
HALSTED TRADE AREA
IN 1960

LEGEND

© 63rd and Halsted
★ Evergreen Plaza
▨ The transit line

The arterial grid occurs at
half-mile intervals

*Note:* Areas in black are non-residential land users. Dots represent consumer residences in 1960.

of the retailers who were there before try to adapt as well. Others – perhaps independents nearing retirement age – make no attempt to cope with the transition. Their store continues to serve the remnants of the earlier neighborhood. Sometimes a collective decision accelerates the rate of change: the city or a local business improvement association decides to emphasize the direction of specialization by putting up distinctive signs and advertising to attract the target market. Exhibit 8.5 looks at the rate of retail change in Scottsdale, Arizona.

Some neighborhoods near the center of the city have undergone repeated changes, recycling, if you like. The stores – particularly the older buildings – reveal a record of different social classes and ethnic groups stretching back a century or more. How long does a given market last? How flexible must a retailer be? How soon should an investment in buildings and fixtures be recouped?

The evolution of retailing at the settlement scale demonstrates some long-term regularities that permit retailers to make some assumptions about the future (though not without uncertainty, as we shall see). The transitions within the metropolitan area are uncertain and their implications for retailing are unpredictable. The urban retailer survives in a

### Exhibit 8.5
### THE RATE OF RETAIL CHANGE: SCOTTSDALE, ARIZONA

As retail structure becomes more specialized and less amenable to the mass marketing techniques of retail chains, so the rate of turnover and potential instability increases. The Fifth Avenue shops in Scottsdale have developed as a successful upscale retail area, serving both local and tourist markets and emphasizing native crafts and jewelry. Very few chains have located here.

The area is vulnerable, however, because of the rapid turnover in stores – even though the retail structure has remained constant. Ninety per cent of the stores have been recruited in the last five years; it seems likely that three-quarters of them will be gone in another five years. Will the same kinds of shops replace them? Will there be vacancies? Or will the chains take over? The charm of retail areas such as this is often transient.

| Retail activity | 1983 | 1988 | No. of survivors | No. of entrants | % change |
|---|---|---|---|---|---|
| Specialty shops | 22 | 37 | 2 | 35 | 95.0 |
| Jewelry stores | 8 | 7 | 2 | 5 | 71.5 |
| Galleries/antiques | 7 | 9 | 0 | 9 | 100.0 |
| Restaurants | 5 | 8 | 2 | 6 | 75.0 |
| Total | 42 | 61 | 6 | 55 | 90.2 |

Source: Scottsdale Visitor's Guide, 1983 and 1988

Exhibit 8.5 (*continued*)

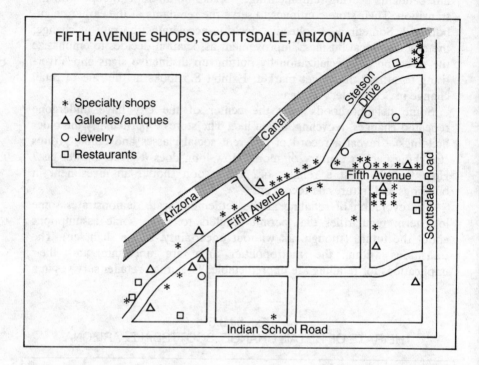

FIFTH AVENUE SHOPS, SCOTTSDALE, ARIZONA

* Specialty shops
△ Galleries/antiques
O Jewelry
□ Restaurants

highly competitive and erratic environment. The chapter that follows addresses this uncertainty and the strategies available to cope with it.

## Further reading

Baerwald, T.J. (1978) 'The emergence of a new downtown', *Geographical Review* 68, 3: 308–18.

Baerwald, T.J. (1989) 'Changing sales patterns in major American metropolises, 1963–1982', *Urban Geography* 10, 4: 355–74.

Claus, R.J. and Hardwick, W.G. (1972) *The Mobile Consumer: Auto-Oriented Retailing and Site Selection*, Toronto: Collier-Macmillan.

Dent, B.D. (1985) 'Atlanta and the regional shopping mail: the absence of public policy', in J.A. Dawson and J.D. Lord (eds) *Shopping Center Development and Prospects*, London: Croom Helm.

Erickson, R.A. and Gentry, M. (1985) 'Suburban Nucleations', *Geographical Review* 75, 1: 19–31.

Hartshorn, T.A. and Muller, P.O. (1989) 'Suburban downtowns and the transformation of metropolitan Atlanta's business landscape', *Urban Geography* 10, 4: 375–95.

Holdren, B.R. (1960) *The Structure of a Retail Market*, Englewood Cliffs, New Jersey: Prentice-Hall.

Jones, K.G. (1984) *Specialty Retailing in the Inner City*, monograph no. 12, Toronto: York University, Department of Geography.

Lord, J.D. (1985) 'The malling of the American landscape', in J.A. Dawson, and J.D. Lord (eds) *Shopping Centre Development: Policies and Prospects*. London: Croom Helm.

McKeever, J.R., May, E., Ress, W., and Salmon, W.J. (1985) *Shopping Center Development Handbook*, 2nd edn, Washington: Urban Land Institute.

Simmons, J.W. (1964) *The Changing Pattern of Retail Location*, research paper no. 92, Chicago: University of Chicago, Department of Geography.

Robertson, K.A. (1983) 'Downtown retail activity in large American cities', *Geographical Review* 73, 3: 314–23.

Urban Land Institute (1984) 'Shopping center development,' in *Development Review and Outlook, 1984–85*, Washington: 10–21.

# Location analysis

The four chapters in this part of the text approach the geography of marketing from a very specific point of view; that of the retail chain, one of the major protagonists in determining the spatial structure of retail facilities. Not only do these chains dominate the retail sector (and many personal and financial services as well), they stimulate almost all of the research in store location. The data for these studies are based on their operations and the location problems are couched in terms of their concerns. How effective is this location? Where should the next outlet go? Are we ready to expand into a different region of the country?

The material in Part three is not designed to transform the reader into a professional location analyst. However, just as the fan's enjoyment of a baseball game is heightened by an understanding of the choices available to the managers and the reasons for their decisions, our understanding of the retail landscape is improved as we study the kinds of decisions made by professional marketers: retail entrepreneurs, chain managers, and planning consultants.

Determining appropriate locations for a retail chain (or any system of multilocational facilities, such as high schools or playgrounds) is far more complex than dealing with a single outlet. The latter needs only to be (roughly) centered on the defined target market; in fact most independent stores are really not even 'located' in this sense. Once founded, they survive, adapt, or go out of business without much conscious consideration of the location problem.

Consider, in contrast, the location problem posed by the retail chain. Given an existing system of outlets, where should the next one be located? Each new facility may affect the level of sales at earlier locations. Thus, each of the earlier facilities restricts the choice of potential sites for the new branch. Decisions about new outlets, then, must be taken within a broader context – a marketing strategy – which involves answering a number of questions.

The first series of questions relates to the size and number of branches. Chain A's market share within the community, i.e. the proportion of all hardware sales sold by hardware chain A, determines total sales. The average level of sales allocated to each outlet then determines the number of outlets, the size of trade area, and the distance apart. But what happens if the market share is increased? Are new outlets added between the others? Or are existing outlets expanded? Must the whole system of branches be reorganized in space?

The second series of questions relates to the product mix at each store. Are the outlets identical in size, layout, and range of goods? Or are they permitted to vary from one neighborhood to the next, or even to serve different kinds of households in each neighborhood? Identical outlets ('cookie-cutter stores') emphasize spatial monopoly – keeping the branches separated in space so that they don't compete with each other. On the other hand, outlets that differ from one another operate like shopping goods facilities and need to be located nearer to the center of the market as a whole. For example, several different kinds of shoe stores within a megachain such as Kinney can be found in the same shopping plaza.

The third set of questions refers to competitors: Is their market share larger, or smaller? Where are they located? Should they be avoided or confronted directly? Can a chain benefit from the traffic that its competitors generate?

The recognition of this complexity has generated a growing market for location analysts, as indicated in Chapter one. Location analysts, in turn, continue to develop and refine new procedures to answer the questions posed above. The four chapters that follow discuss some of the current issues and techniques within the retail industry. Chapter nine elaborates upon a fundamental aspect of the chain's location decisions: they must be made with only partial knowledge. The marketplace includes some fundamental uncertainties about the economy, about the actual location of urban growth, and about the actions of competitors. Several responses to this uncertainty are identified, such as projections, data systems, and simulations. Chapters ten and eleven grapple with specific location problems. The former discusses the techniques for estimating the volume of sales at a specific site, based on the chain's experience at other locations. The latter looks at procedures particularly concerned with the size, extent, and market potential of spatial trade areas.

Chapter twelve discusses location strategy within a series of larger contexts. The location requirements emerge from the chain's overall marketing strategy: target markets, planned rate of growth, and attitude to competition. This strategy will be shaped in turn by the corporate environment of the firm. Is it growing? Is it generating profits?

It should become evident that the regularities that we observe in the overall retail landscape are the result of quite different strategies on the part of individual chains. A town of specified size and income will have a predictable array of goods and services in stores of predictable size and product mix, but this regularity is an aggregate of diverse stores run by a relatively small number of retail chains that focus on different target markets or niches.

Some retail chains will have passed up such a market entirely; it is too small, too large, or too competitive. Other chains are concerned with only a small portion of the market: the rich, the poor, the Italians. Some chains emphasize size and diversity, others stress their specialized selection and service. Hardly any retail chains approximate the overall average for their sector. Their decisions about location or size of operation do not reflect some overall optimal solution. Each chain tries to identify a special niche within the retail sector as a whole. As a result it competes directly with a very small number of other chains.

Yet the overall result of decisions by these highly specialized individual chains is a retail landscape that is relatively uniform from one place to another. Any missing dimension of a market constitutes an empty niche that attracts an appropriate solution, either a new outlet or service by an existing chain, or perhaps a new chain. It can be further argued that providing retail facilities by means of a number of specialized chains increases overall consumer satisfaction and the level of retail activity. To the extent that shopping is a social phenomenon linked to the self-esteem and prestige of individuals, the existence of different sources of the same goods is important. It contributes to one of the major rationales for consumption, i.e. the desire of individual consumers to set themselves apart from the rest.

# Chapter nine

# Making marketing decisions

**The long-term forecasts of economic activity are essentially the averages of past patterns.**

**Most great entrepreneurs had the good fortune to be in the right place at the right time.**

**The year-to-year variation in the sale of furniture is over twice as large as the variation in the sale of food.**

**A retail chain should expect to relocate 2–3 per cent of its outlets each year simply to adjust to the spatial restructuring of the market.**

Nothing better exemplifies the difference between the small independent retailer and the giant retail megachain than the decision-making process. Single-store entrepreneurs bow to location decisions made by forces beyond their control. If the income level in their market area dwindles, stores go out of business; when a competitor enters the market they may have to sell out. For the most part, retail operations of this kind locate by means of a kind of natural selection; those that are slightly more efficient or are fortunate enough to begin in the right place at the right time survive. Seeds planted in stony ground perish.

The retail chain, in contrast, attempts to ensure its own survival by adapting to changing conditions: choosing new locations in growth areas and relinquishing those that are no longer suitable, developing new product lines, or altering the scale of operations. The retail chain makes its own location decisions based on its appraisal of the future.

As the rest of this chapter argues, all marketing decisions are made in the face of uncertainty – uncertainty about the future patterns of market growth, about consumer preferences, about the action of competitors, and about the nature of product innovations. Independent retailers must accept this uncertainty and have limited ways to deal with it: they can, for example, reduce their own wage or borrow from the bank. Retail chains, however, can attack uncertainty and increase the odds of survival by improving their sources of information, preparing to modify their activities, and dispersing their resources. The chapters that follow examine specific techniques of marketing analysis that lead to better informed decisions: the evaluation of a particular site for a retail activity, the delimitation and measurement of market area, and the systematic evaluation of marketing options within the corporate and competitive context of the firm. First, however, we must confront the basic uncertainties within the retailing environment. The sections that follow discuss the problem of uncertainty and introduce four ways of dealing with it: monitoring the firm's own operations under various conditions, forecasting changes in the market, simulating the possible actions of competitors, and, finally, accepting uncertainty as part of the business and making decisions that take it into account.

## Uncertainty

According to the economic theory presented in Chapter three, the location decisions of retailers should be quite straightforward. They identify the map of demand at some future point in time (the target date), apply what they know about the market response to the product or the facility, convert the scale of operation into costs, identify the level of profitability, and translate this information into a go/no-go decision. In practice, however, this algorithm is bedeviled by uncertainty in at least four aspects of the problem. First, the economic environment affects the overall growth in consumer spending as well as interest rates and rates of inflation to which retailers are sensitive. Second, the location of growth of consumer demand within a spatial market is not easily predictable, either at the settlement scale or within the metropolitan region. Third, technological change, such as new organizational and accounting procedures or changes in the type of retail outlets or product innovations, modify the cost structure. Fourth, the actions of competitors can be simply unpredictable or downright hostile – the difference in uncertainty between playing solitaire and playing bridge.

Changes in the national economic environment are throughly discussed in the business sections of most newspapers and should be sufficiently familiar to the reader to illustrate the general problem of uncertainty.

First, all major economic indicators show considerable variation from month to month, quarter to quarter, year to year, and decade to decade. While seasonal fluctuations may be reasonably regular, the variations over longer time intervals are not, as Figure 9.1 indicates. Each one of these six economic indicators has undergone substantial year to year changes, culminating in the drastic decline in 1982 when the gross national product dropped by 2.5 per cent.

What do these variations mean to the retailer? The growth of the gross national product is closely linked to the overall level of income, and thus to consumer expenditure. Consumer spending in most major cities will follow the ups and downs of the gross national product. As a result, the sales of established retailers in a fixed market may vary by plus or minus 5 per cent over a year, and because of fixed operating costs profit levels will fluctuate much more widely – from 10 to 20 per cent per year (see Figure 9.2). Profits lag behind sales growth and are particularly sensitive to changes in the rate of growth of sales. An increase in sales growth of 2 per cent (in constant dollars) may translate into a profit growth of 10 per cent.

For entrepreneurs who are opening a new business, the timing of economic growth is crucial. Existing retailers have powerful advantages in a stagnant or declining market when no one makes a profit. Most new businesses aim at the growth component of a market; without any increase in consumer spending during the vital first year of operation a business may die still-born. A sudden jump in interest rates (as in 1981) may be even

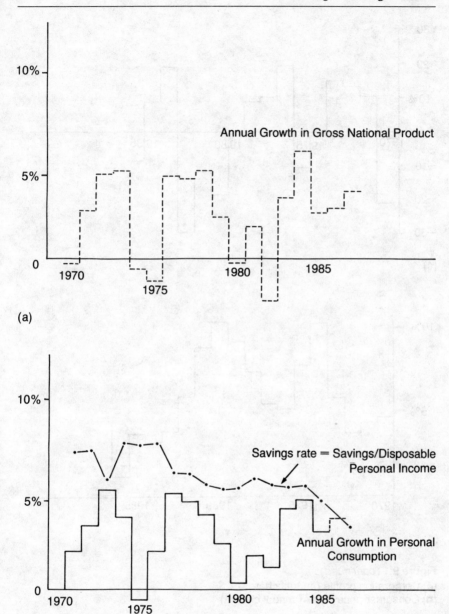

**Figure 9.1** Fluctuations in economic growth
(a) Growth in gross national product (%)
(b) Growth in personal consumption

*Source:* Bureau of the Census (various years) *Statistical Abstracts of the United States*, Washington

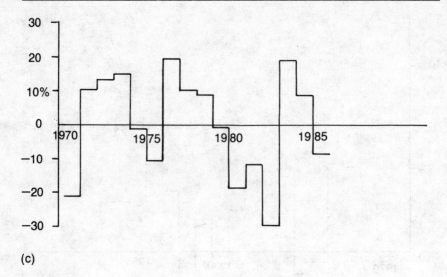

(c)

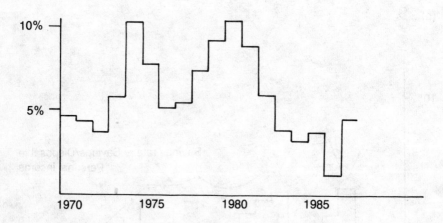

(d)

**Figure 9.1** (*continued*)
(c) Corporation profits (annual charge)
(d) Consumer price index (annual charge)

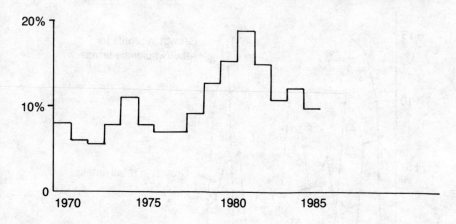

(e)

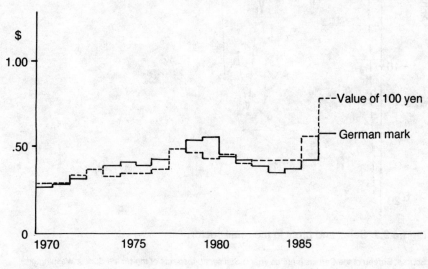

(f)

**Figure 9.1** (*continued*)
(e) Interest rates (banker's prime rate)
(f) US dollar in terms of Japanese yen and German marks

289

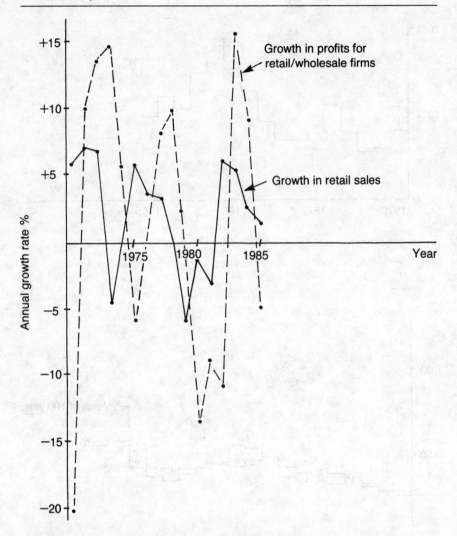

**Figure 9.2** Sales and profit in the retail sector

*Source:* Bureau of the Census (various years) *Statistical Abstracts of the United States*, Washington

more traumatic for the new retailer, since the costs of carrying inventory may increase by 20 or 30 per cent within a year. High rates of inflation act like a wild card for retailers because inflation usually varies considerably among different goods. If price increases are particularly high in out-of-store items such as shelter, energy, or transport, the result is a reduction in consumer expenditures in all stores. Inflation in food prices may lead to buyer resistance or to a shift towards discount products, as in the wave of 'no-frills' packages in the late 1970s. In the same unpredictable fashion, changes in the value of the dollar relative to the yen may differentially affect retailers who sell imported lines of goods, like Japanese cars or electronics. (Exhibit 9.1 illustrates the uncertainty of market share in the automobile industry.)

While economic conditions are variable and of great importance to retailers, this kind of uncertainty is not particularly responsive to analysis. A number of private and public agencies carry out elaborate economic modelling (see Appendix B), but most forecasts are limited to a time horizon of less than three years (the rest of the business cycle). Beyond that point most studies simply fall back on a prediction based on the average outcome of the recent past. Econometric models cannot reproduce the variability that exists in the real world.

None the less, even short-term projections are useful to retail chains that are ordering inventory and leasing stores for the following season. Many retailers subscribe to economic analyses for the interpretations of possible outcomes. How sensitive are retail sales to interest rates? If people pay less for housing will they spend the money they save on cars?

While the aggregate data in Figures 9.1 and 9.2 suggest the variability of growth at the national scale, Table 9.1 indicates that sectoral and local variations may be far greater. Furniture, for example, is a kind of fair-weather purchase that is easily postponed in periods of economic decline or high interest rates. The year-to-year variation in growth rate (standard deviation) is three times greater than the variation in food sales, the most stable kind of expenditure. Spatially, the American market as a whole (standard deviation, 3.4) is more stable than its smaller components, e.g. California (standard deviation, 3.9) or San Francisco (4.6). Larger markets average out variations in different locations and sectors. One advantage of national chains is their ability to minimize this kind of uncertainty.

Perhaps the most convincing evidence of uncertainty in the retail environment is the high rate of failure in the marketplace (Table 9.2). Think of the retail strip near your home and recall the variety of different stores that have come and gone at that location. Retailers go broke – up to 50 per cent of new retailers disappear in the first year. They may be forced to sell or merge, or else they adapt to the retail environment by relocating or altering their product mix. Altogether they turn over at a rate of about 15–20 per cent per year; in five years almost half of them will have disappeared. Hence the vacant stores, renovations, and 'under new management' signs that are such a familiar part of the retail environment. However, Table 9.2 also reveals that the chances of survival are much greater for larger firms that can respond to the changes in the retail environment.

The first year of a store's operation is the most hazardous, since all the uncertainties about market size and response are introduced at that time.

## Exhibit 9.1
## THE UNCERTAINTY OF MARKET SHARE

Automobile dealers face a particularly virulent form of uncertainty. Since they sell an especially cyclical product, sales rise and fall disproportionately with the growth of the economy. At the same time they must suffer any changes in the market share of their product brand name. If Ford, Chrysler, or General Motors has a bad (Edsel!) year, a surge in dealer bankruptcies results. Conversely, a hot new product (Mustang!) can make dealers wealthy. The hero of John Updike's *Rabbit Rich* inherits a small used car lot that picked up a Toyota dealership in the 1960s.

The graph below tracks the growth of new car sales in the US. Note that there has been no overall increase in cars sold, although there have been considerable cyclical fluctuations (and truck and four wheel drive vehicle sales have increased). Over the study period each of the 'Big Three' automobile firms lost market share to the Japanese. Honda, Nissan, and Toyota have surged from 4 per cent to 19 per cent of the US market. Ford and Chrysler have each lost 6 per cent. However, from one year to the next the fortunes of each firm vary considerably. In 1978 Ford had a great year, General Motors a bad one. By 1980 Chrysler was really hurting. Chevrolet, one of the most stable brands, has varied from 1.2 to 2.5 million cars sold per year.

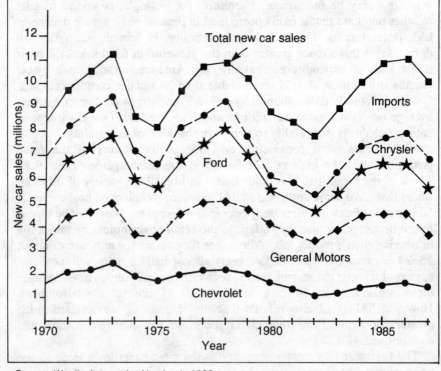

*Source: Ward's Automotive Yearbook, 1988*

**Table 9.1** Uncertainty in retail activity: variation in demand, 1970–86

| | United States | | | | San |
| | All retail sectors | Furniture | Food | California | Francisco |
|---|---|---|---|---|---|
| Average growth rate* (%) | 2.0 | 3.4 | 0.9 | 2.3 | 1.4 |
| Standard deviation (%) | 3.4 | 6.4 | 2.2 | 3.9 | 4.6 |

Source: Bureau of the Census (monthly) 'Monthly retail trade', *Current Business Reports*, Washington
Note: *Sales in constant dollars.

**Table 9.2** Uncertainty in retail activity: effect on United States retail and wholesale establishments, 1969–76

| Establishment size (no. of employees) | Probability of closing between 1969 and 1976* |
|---|---|
| 1–20 | 0.50 |
| 21–50 | 0.34 |
| 51–100 | 0.32 |
| 101–500 | 0.29 |
| 501+ | 0.27 |

Source: Data from Dun and Bradstreet (annual) *Market Profile Analysis*, analyzed by D. Birch (1987) *Job Creation in America*, New York, The Free Press
Note: *Total no. of establishments in 1969 = 1,108,000.

New businesses are almost inevitably under-capitalized because they have no track record to justify a loan. The accumulated experience and access to capital of the retail chain reduces this level of risk. Chains, on the other hand, are vulnerable to internal reorganization or takeover, which may require massive restructuring.

One of the most provocative early papers on retailing (Alchian, 1950) argued that the retail structure was not the product of a rational scientific adjustment to changes in demand, but the result of a selection process carried out by a random economic environment. The successful entrepreneur, one can argue, is simply lucky: he or she is the fortunate one who happened to be in a retail sector that expanded rapidly or in a town that grew. Much of the research in marketing simply tries to improve the odds of success slightly, first, by increasing the awareness of the kinds of uncertainty that are faced, and second, by building in some strategies that take uncertainty into account.

The remainder of this chapter looks at procedures that can alter the probabilities of success or failure. Independents face the greatest uncertainties and generate most of the closings. The retail chain is able to balance out the variations in the growth rate of various markets and product lines.

## Monitoring

Certain kinds of variability defy analysis in an open economy. The stock-market can be effectively analyzed as a random process, very much like a horse race or a lottery. Still, there are ways of reducing some kinds of uncertainty. In order of complexity they are monitoring, forecasting, and simulation. Monitoring means keeping detailed records of past and current operations, or 'counting'. Forecasting attempts to extend the patterns of the past into the future, incorporating whatever trends can be found within the data. Simulation develops models of the present that can be applied to study specific alternative situations in the future. For instance, what happens to the Kroger Company if another major supermarket chain pulls out of a market? Each approach has its uses for different problems. In the sections to follow we apply forecasting techniques to the problem of changing spatial patterns of demand, and simulation techniques to anticipate the actions of competitors.

Monitoring, in the sense of keeping up-to-date records on performance over time, is something that every retail establishment now does to some extent, thanks to the tax man. On an annual basis, at least, sales, costs, inventories, and profits must be summarized. However, it is possible to do a great deal more. In order to make monitoring a useful analytical tool, the retailer must gather sufficient information to be able to make some connections between cause and effect. It is not sufficient to note that Saturday afternoon sales have been increasing unless you can sort out the relative contributions of additional sales personnel, advertising specials, or mall-wide promotions.

Table 9.3 shows the kind of regular report submitted by a chain outlet to its head office. It includes data on sales, inventory, special promotions, and selling prices, and it is supplemented by the additional information implied in the orders for new merchandise and the return of goods that didn't sell, as well as data on employment and store operating expenses. The head office is interested, first, in the performance of this outlet relative to expectations (as will be discussed in the following chapter), but it is also interested in its peculiarities: how the performance changes over time and how this store differs in the mix of sales when compared to other outlets.

More and more often these days, such information is gathered and transmitted by computers. Point-of-sale monitoring applies cash register information to inventory control and ordering, but it can also be diverted to provide useful information for locational decision making. All the information on sales by product group or item is available: as well as the timing

**Table 9.3** The monthly report from an outlet of a major chain to its head office

| Data | Source | Derived calculations |
| --- | --- | --- |
| Sales* | Cash registers | Turnover rate, |
| Inventory cost* | Shipments, by type of good | Gross margin, Sales/sq. ft |
| Customer count | Cash registers | Sales/customer |
| Customer count | Turnstile | |
| Employment | Payroll | |
| Rent/utilities | Billings | Gross return on sales |
| Promotion costs | Billings | |
| | | Year-to-date totals |
| | | Year-to-year comparisons |
| | | Comparisons with similar stores |

*Note:* *For regular merchandise, categorized by product category, and for promotional goods.

of sales – the computer even identifies the sales clerk. Special software packages help retailers to sort out the data in order to answer the appropriate questions. Consider the implications for employee performance. Supermarket cashiers are supposed to handle twenty-one items per minute: the computer-linked cash register automatically keeps a stop watch on every cashier in the store.

Each chain has its own set of questions to apply to the data, but the chances are that they include many of the following: Is the overall product mix of sales at each outlet shifting? How well are new products selling? What is the response to our promotions, advertisements? How well is this outlet performing, relative to last year, last month? Relative to other locations, other chains? Are the personnel performing satisfactorily? Is the outlet overstaffed? Understaffed? In order to answer these questions the monitoring procedure may require additional data inputs – on specials, promotions, or sales for the mall as a whole (if available). Also, if marketing researchers are to identify the response to possible innovations they may also want to set up experiments, perhaps at a limited number of outlets. 'Let's try out this new line of merchandise, cut down on the number of sweaters and promote sweatsuits.' 'What if we re-arrange the store or double the number of part-time employees on Saturday afternoon?' There is really only one way to answer these questions, and that is by eternally tinkering and observing the sales response.

The chain's continuing retail problem is how to maximize sales and profits on the space it has leased, but with 200 outlets and $75 million per year in sales at risk it cannot move too quickly in any one direction. Instead, careful experimentation and incremental change are required. In the future, as malls become more specialized in order to serve distinctive target markets and the chains try to fine-tune their offerings to suit their clientele, the need for this kind of analysis will grow.

In addition to monitoring the progress of each outlet over time, the chain needs to evaluate the strengths and weaknesses of each outlet within the network. A database is needed to enable management to make useful comparisons from one outlet to another. While each chain may have slightly different data requirements (we will probe some of the relationships between the task and the information required in the next two chapters), the general outlines for an information system for a retail chain are shown in Table 9.4. Data on outlet performance must be analyzed in the context of the peculiarities of the facilities, the location, and the competitive environment.

Successful performance monitoring often requires external data for comparison also. The Bureau of the Census and various industry publications (see Appendix B) help retailers to evaluate their performance relative to competitors (market share), relative to the growth of the local market (from income and population growth data), or relative to the retail sector as a whole.

In order to refine and develop a market strategy the chain may also have to monitor the performance of competitors. While retailers cannot get the kind of detailed data on their competitors that is available for their own firm, a successful internal monitoring program will suggest key measures of performance and possible substitute indicators. Two or three products may be the key to identifying a shift in the competitor's product mix. Changes in number and size of outlets indicate shifts in market share. What does their corporate financial performance imply?

Monitoring provides a means for identifying problems before they become disasters. For the most part, though, it works best for short-term adjustments to the operating side of the retail relationship. In order to devise longer-term strategies and to investigate shifts in the demand side, we must turn to forecasting.

### Forecasting market growth

Forecasting procedures attempt to extrapolate past trends in marketing variables into the future. They begin with the assumption that the same kind of conditions will apply in the coming year as in the past. Whether this assumption is appropriate depends very much on the variables under consideration. Some relationships, like the proportion of disposable income that is spent in retail stores, change very gradually and regularly. Others, such as the number of tractors purchased per year, change drastically.

It is distressing for location analysts to have to admit how variable the location of economic growth is, and how helpless we are to forecast it. None the less, we must live with this uncertainty. Consider, for example,

**Table 9.4** Compiling a data base

*Categories of data for a strategic planning base*

| | | | |
|---|---|---|---|
| *Facility data* | | *Trade area characteristics* | |
| Gross area (sq. ft) | ____ | Size, shape | ____ |
| Total selling space (sq. ft) | ____ | | |
| Departments | ____ | Area population | ____ |
| Selling space/linear footage | | Population characteristics | |
| by department | ____ | (age, sex, income etc.) | ____ |
| Number of checkouts | ____ | Expenditure potential | ____ |
| Lease information | ____ | | |
| Age of store | ____ | Market penetration | ____ |
| Date of last remodel | ____ | Market share | ____ |
| | | Drawing power | ____ |
| *Performance information* | | | |
| Average weekly sales | | Access patterns | ____ |
| (by month since opening) | ____ | Travel barriers | ____ |
| Sales per sq. ft | | | |
| Total store | ____ | *Competitive environment* | |
| Selling area | ____ | Operators | ____ |
| Weekly sales by department | ____ | Locations | ____ |
| Sales per sq.ft/linear ft | | | |
| by department | ____ | For each store: | |
| Number of employees | ____ | Age of store | ____ |
| Sales per employee | ____ | Years since last remodel | ____ |
| Profit/loss by month and year | | Gross area (sq. ft) | ____ |
| Total store | ____ | Selling space (sq. ft) | ____ |
| By department | ____ | Departments present | ____ |
| Overall composite rating | | Estimated weekly sales | ____ |
| (each store) | ____ | Sales per sq. ft. | ____ |
| | | Number of checkouts/registers | ____ |
| *Site characteristics* | | Number of employees | ____ |
| Location type (free-standing, | | Selling space/linear footage | |
| shopping center) | ____ | (by department) | ____ |
| Shopping center size and type | ____ | Estimated departmental sales | ____ |
| Position in center | ____ | Site characteristics (parking, | |
| Year center built | ____ | co-tenants, visibility etc.) | ____ |
| Other anchor tenants | ____ | Overall composite rating | |
| Parking spaces total | | (each store) | ____ |
| within vicinity of retail unit | ____ | | |
| Ingress/egress to site | ____ | | |
| Visibility of store | ____ | | |
| Highway type | ____ | | |
| Signage | ____ | | |

*Source:* J. Ritchey (1984) 'Developing a strategic planning data base', in R.L. Davies and D.S. Rogers (eds) *Store Location and Store Assessment Research*, New York, John Wiley & Sons

Exhibit 9.2. These forecasts about the population of states in 1985 were based on data from 1960 and 1965. Twenty years later it is apparent that the forecasts are considerably in error. Only one-third of them lie within the projection band. These sizable errors occurred in forecasts well within the operating life of major shopping centers.

## Exhibit 9.2
## HOW WRONG CAN YOU BE?

In 1967 the Bureau of the Census, armed with their best information on population trends and demographic patterns, compiled a series of population projections for the year 1985. The projections combined two sets of assumptions: low and high fertility, and low and high levels of interstate migration. The difference between the highest and lowest of these four combinations ranged from 10 to 12 per cent for most of the states – as shown in the table. The diagram below the table displays the overall error level of the projections. The projection band of 10 per cent is identified (seventeen states fell within that range), and the degree of error in either direction is displayed for the remaining states. In general, the projections tend to be too high, underestimating the decline in birth rates (see the US box). Most of the 'rust belt' states are over-predicted: New York is out by 17 per cent, i.e. 1 per cent per year. Conversely, the 'sun belt' states are under-predicted. The major curiosity is California. On the basis of its dramatic earlier growth it was projected to grow even faster than it did. Projections in space, like projections over time, are unable to replicate the variation that actually takes place.

| | | | Projected, 1985 | | | High–Low | Outside |
| State | Observed 1960 | Estimated 1965 | Low | High | 1985 value | difference (%) | band error |
|---|---|---|---|---|---|---|---|
| VT | 390 | 404 | 465 | 513 | 535 | 10.3 | + 4.3 |
| CT | 2,535 | 2,830 | 3,713 | 4,109 | 3,174 | 10.7 | −14.5 |
| NY | 16,782 | 18,106 | 21,416 | 23,583 | 17,783 | 10.1 | −17.0 |
| IL | 10,081 | 10,641 | 12,667 | 13,942 | 11,535 | 10.0 | − 8.9 |
| KS | 2,179 | 2,248 | 2,414 | 2,705 | 2,450 | 12.1 | − |
| NC | 4,556 | 4,935 | 5,801 | 6,497 | 6,255 | 12.0 | − |
| FL | 4,952 | 5,796 | 9,012 | 10,535 | 11,366 | 16.9 | + 7.9 |
| TX | 9,580 | 10,591 | 13,392 | 14,869 | 16,370 | 11.0 | +10.0 |
| ID | 667 | 693 | 817 | 901 | 1,005 | 10.3 | +11.5 |
| CA | 15,717 | 18,403 | 27,937 | 31,704 | 26,365 | 13.5 | − 5.6 |

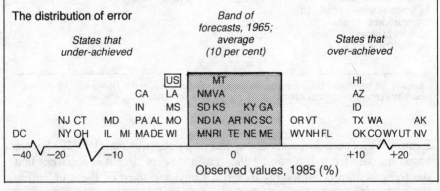

**The distribution of error**

States that under-achieved — Band of forecasts, 1965; average (10 per cent) — States that over-achieved

Observed values, 1985 (%)

*Source:* Bureau of the Census (1967) 'Revised projections of the populations of the states, 1970 to 1985', *Current Population Reports*, Series P-25, no. 375

Within the city the difficulties are even greater. Figure 9.3 shows the population shifts in Atlanta during the 1970s. While the population of the area shown on the map grew by 300,000, the older residential areas south of downtown lost over 75,000 people. However, just where or when these changes will occur is not always easy to anticipate. A final example (Figure 9.4) shows another aspect of the problem. Much of the population growth observed in subnational markets is due to net migration, i.e. the difference between the numbers of in-migrants and out-migrants. The overall rate of migration is consistently high: one in five Americans moves each year. However, the pattern of net inflow is frustratingly changeable, as the graphs suggest. The shaded portion between the in-migrants and out-migrants represents the population gain to the state. Unshaded areas represent population losses. Look at Oregon: riding high in the 1970s, attracting migrants from everywhere, then losing migrants in the 1980s when the recession begins. New Mexico, in contrast, continues to gain in

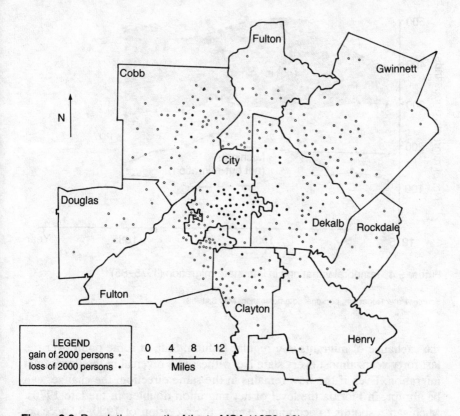

**Figure 9.3** Population growth: Atlanta MSA (1970–80)

*Source:* Bureau of the Census (1980) *Census of Population,* Washington

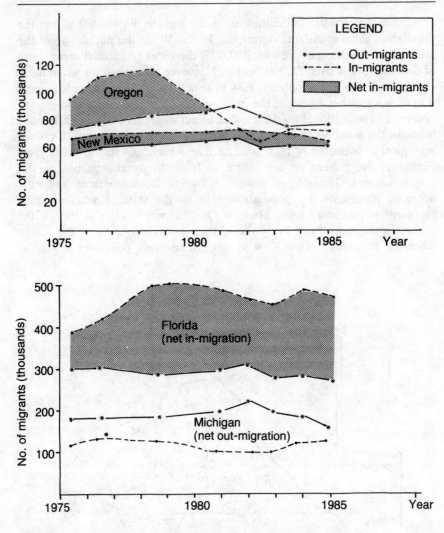

**Figure 9.4** Temporal variations in interstate migration (1975–85)

*Source:* Peter Rogerson, personal communication, May 5, 1988

the exchange of migrants in a regular fashion. Still, at some point over the last forty years almost every state has witnessed a reversal in the flow of net migration. Even if the flow remains in the same direction, the changes can be abrupt. In Florida the level of net migration doubled in the late 1970s. Michigan responds to economic events: the recession of 1980–82 accelerated the out-migration and reduced in-migration, causing a loss of 200,000 extra residents over three years.

The art and science of forecasting uses a variety of techniques to peer into the future (Figure 9.5), each of them applicable in different contexts. Extrapolation is the most familiar procedure. Using only one variable, such as population, the analyst fits a line to the observed values from the past, geometrically or by means of a regression equation. The line is projected into the future to generate the required forecast. The line need not be straight: a variety of nonlinear models can be used.

The Ratio Method relates the variable of interest (in this case the population of Ohio) to a larger unit (the United States) which may have a well-known trajectory. The ratio itself is extrapolated into the future and, in combination with the projected national population, gives the required result. This has a happy result for large chains in that the sum of all local forecasts can be made equal to the forecast for the country as a whole. Neither extrapolation nor ratio techniques have much value for suburban markets or frontier communities where growth occurs in a rapid burst of five or ten years and then stops. (Such a dramatic and short-lived transformation has been called the 'butterfly' effect.)

The Indirect technique also deals with two variables, but both measures apply to the same spatial unit. For example, in Chapter five we observed that retail sales could be related to market income. Clearly then, if we are able to project market income we can apply our equation to obtain a projected value for retail sales, and ultimately an estimate of the number of stores and floor area. This approach is particularly useful for marketers who often have access to a number of basic relationships between such measures as trade area population, sales per square foot, and profitability. These relationships may be obtained longitudinally by observations of the same location over time, or cross-sectionally, by observing different places at one point in time.

Disaggregation is useful when the population or market is composed of several subgroups or segments that behave differently. For example, various age-groups within the population may grow at quite different rates and in different spatial patterns. The procedure simply breaks down the target variable into its components, projects each one separately, and then recombines them at the end. For example, the 'cohort' model projects each age-group in turn, using assumptions about rates of birth and death. Retailers focusing on various submarkets within a population find this approach useful.

The Normative procedure is frequently used to project suburban trade areas or developments in resource towns where growth occurs up until some maximum or optimal point is reached (like water filling a glass). For the suburb, the 'norm' may be decided by the planning staff who apply standard restrictions on residential density, the amount of public facilities, roads, and shopping space in order to determine the servicing requirements. Thus, 200 acres of suburban development may include 800 houses,

*Extrapolation*
Uses a geometric model to extend a single time series into the future. The model may be nonlinear.

*Application*
A single large complex market, in which one is concerned with the whole population rather than some subgroup: nation, metropolitan area, province. Not appropriate for suburbs or frontier situations, where growth occurs in a short burst (the 'butterfly' problem).

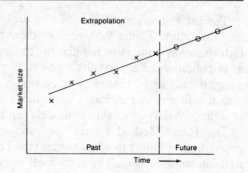

*Ratio*
The market size of a local area is calculated as some proportion of the size of a larger (and better known) spatial unit.

*Application*
Systems of markets (good for chains) in which individual forecasts must be compatible with the national market forecast. Not appropriate where individual units grow at different rates or for different reasons.

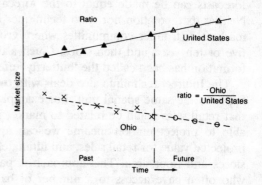

$$\text{ratio} = \frac{\text{Ohio}}{\text{United States}}$$

*Indirect*
The size of a certain aspect of the market, such as sales of particular products, is linked to other more predictable aspects of the market – such as number of people or households.
Permits chains of relationships
A→B→C, etc.

*Application*
For specialized kinds of markets – age or lifestyle groups, or for linking other requirements (capital investment, employment) to sales forecasts.

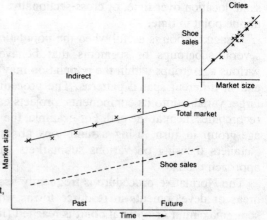

**Figure 9.5** The techniques of forecasting

*Source:* The authors

*Disaggregation*
The market is subdivided into various components (such as age groups) which are each projected independently, and then aggregated to give a value for a total.

*Application*
For markets in which there may be considerable growth variation within the various sectors or components – particularly when the selected sectors are target markets themselves.

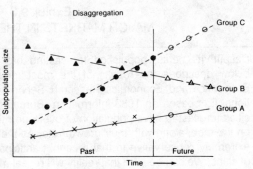

*Normative*
The final size of the market is determined externally by policy, in order to satisfy environmental or servicing constraints (i.e. the planner determines market size).

*Application*
Residential developments in a suburb, in which the planned density is a significant constraint on the ultimate market size. Or the development of a mining town to serve a mine of specified size. The difficult part is deciding on the *timing*.

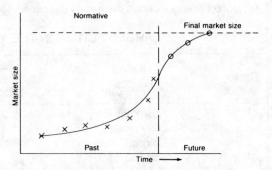

2 miles of road, one school, one church, three stores, and a half-acre play-ground. The size of a frontier mining community depends on the corporate decision about the scale of the mill or mine: 2,000 jobs at the mine will generate 5,000 jobs altogether, a population of 18,000, and a $150 million market. The trick in this procedure lies in determining the timing. Will the norm be reached in three years or in ten? Or never?

Exhibit 9.3 illustrates the use of forecasting in predicting the populations of large cities in the year 2035. Exhibit 9.4 shows the difficulties inherent in forecasting population size when various external factors can affect it unpredictably.

Forecasting helps the marketer to address the crucial issue of market size in the future, but because the procedures are so closely linked to past trends it is difficult to develop a strategy that can introduce an innovation or begin with a different assumption. How will an aging population affect retail location? To answer these questions we must turn to the technique of simulation.

## Exhibit 9.3
## MAJOR MARKETS IN THE YEAR 2035

Despite its perils, population forecasting has a certain fascination. The map below describes the results of the most recent OBERS (Office of Business Economics and Economics Research Service) exercise in long-range projections. It is based on 1983 information (Bureau of Economic Analysis, 1985). All cities forecast to have population of over one million in the year 2035 are shown on the map, along with their growth rate. As the table suggests this projection is extremely conservative in that it cannot anticipate much re-ordering in the rank of cities. We can be sure that reality will reveal more dramatic changes than this.

Nonetheless, the map suggests that the US market will be more widely dispersed by 2035. Many of the major centers in the north-east will barely grow at all, while cities in the west and south will continue to expand rapidly. The projection simply extends the trends described earlier in Exhibit 6.2.

## LARGEST CITIES IN THE YEAR 2035

| Rank in 2035 | City | Population in 2035 (thousands) | Present Rank |
|---|---|---|---|
| 1 | New York | 20,992 | 1 |
| 2 | Los Angeles | 17,064 | 2 |
| 3 | Chicago | 8,794 | 3 |
| 4 | San Francisco | 7,803 | 4 |
| 5 | Philadelphia | 6,474 | 5 |
| 6 | Houston | 5,687 | 8 |
| 7 | Boston | 4,990 | 7 |
| 8 | Dallas | 4,786 | 10 |
| 9 | Washington | 4,582 | 9 |
| 10 | Detroit | 4,524 | 6 |
| 11 | Miami | 4,116 | 11 |
| 12 | Atlanta | 3,820 | 14 |
| 13 | Phoenix | 3,591 | 22 |
| 14 | Seattle | 3,328 | 18 |
| 15 | Minneapolis | 3,197 | 17 |
| 16 | San Diego | 3,174 | 19 |
| 17 | Tampa | 3,106 | 20 |
| 18 | Denver | 3,030 | 21 |
| 19 | St Louis | 2,738 | 13 |
| 20 | Cleveland | 2,678 | 12 |
| 21 | Baltimore | 2,572 | 16 |
| 22 | Pittsburgh | 2,417 | 15 |
| 23 | Portland | 1,922 | 26 |
| 24 | Sacramento | 1,915 | 30 |
| 25 | Cincinnati | 1,860 | 23 |

*Source:* Bureau of Economic Analysis (1985) *1985 OBERS Regional Projections*

Exhibit 9.3 (*continued*)

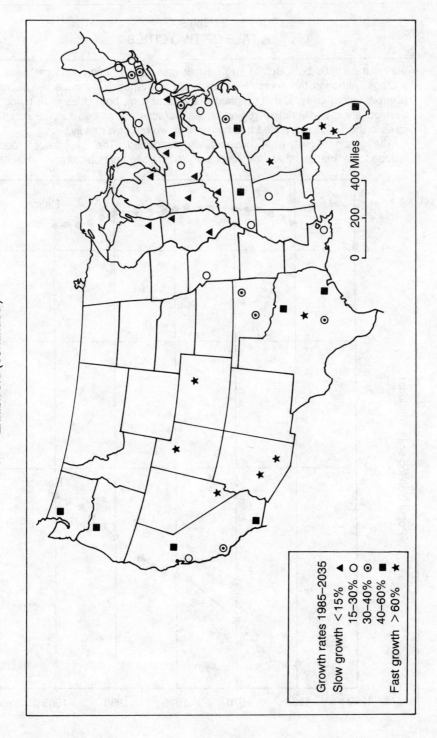

Growth rates 1985–2035
Slow growth <15% ◀
15–30% ○
30–40% ◉
40–60% ■
Fast growth >60% ★

0   200   400 Miles

## Exhibit 9.4
## A TALE OF TWO CITIES

During the 1950s both Detroit and Denver grew more rapidly than the national average. Although the economy of each city was specialized in certain sectors (Detroit, automobiles; Denver, agriculture and mining), both cities were trying to develop a more diversified regional role. Forecasts prepared for the nation's cities in the 1960s suggested that both places would grow rapidly.

The graph shows what has actually happened. The over-valued dollar reduced the market share of American automobile manufacturers, while the

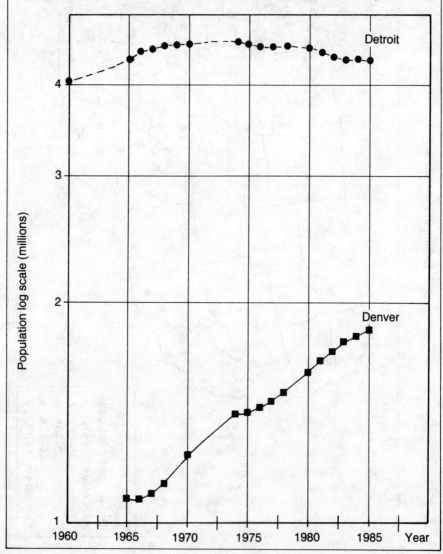

price of oil and gas increased fivefold during the early 1970s. As a result, Detroit's population reached a peak in 1975 and has lost 200,000 people since then. Denver, in contrast, accelerated its growth rate to 3 per cent per year, beyond the level of any previous estimates, until the crash in oil prices occurred in the early 1980s. However, Denver still continues to grow, aided by the explosion in recreation activity. Detroit was almost five times bigger than Denver in 1960, but is now only two and a half times as big.

*Source:* Bureau of the Census (various years) 'Population estimates and projections', *Current Population Reports*, Series P-25

## Simulating the actions of a competitor

One of the major sources of uncertainty for a retailer operating within a specific market is the action of competitors. The competitor alters the retailer's market (or market growth) by modifying market share:

Sales of store A = market size × market share$_A$.  (eqn 9.1)

If the competitor's market share expands more rapidly than the market itself our retailer loses just as surely as if the country had plunged into a depression. Alternatively, if the competition is vulnerable to attack then our retailer can behave as if the market were growing rapidly. This is why retailers dislike competition. Not only does the presence of a second firm increase the degree of uncertainty in a given situation; but also, as a competitor the second firm is acutely sensitive to and responsive to the decisions made by the first. Each locational choice becomes part of a chess game in which the opponent may demolish what looked like a great move. Just as chess is rather more complex than parcheesi, dealing with a determined competitor is more challenging than simply forecasting demand.

For example, developer A decides to enter a small city that is still largely served by its aging downtown area. Analysis suggests that the market is ripe for a shopping center. Should it be located near downtown or on the highway to the east side of town? The former may cost more in terms of land assembly and political negotiation but it has the virtue of pulling in customers from trade areas both to the east and west of town. Just as the project is about to open developer B initiates a center just east of the city limits. Either the two centers fight like cat and dog until the market expands sufficiently to support them both, or else one is forced to close.

In Chapter twelve we will discuss some of the competitive strategies used by retailers, but here we will introduce the technique of simulation as a way to evaluate various competitive situations. The process of simulation depends on three inputs: some forecasts of what is likely to occur in the future (preferably in a mathematical form), a set of relationships among important retail variables (such as sales, floor area, consumer income, and so forth; see Exhibit 5.2), and a set of questions about the future. These questions may concern any dimension of retail decisions which can be modelled: we shall focus on a locational issue.

What would happen to the sales of firm A, located at site X, if competitor B located a store at site Z? The location analyst proceeds to trace through the implications of such a decision as it might affect sales in various branches of firm A, and ultimately lead to lay-offs or declining profit. Perhaps the analyst would proceed further, to work out the results of either closing down one of A's locations, or anticipating B's move by opening up a competing site first. A simulation, then, requires a series of relationships, appropriately calibrated, that together make up a model.

Exhibit 9.5 shows the widely used Huff model, here applied to the impact of a new retail facility on existing shopping centers. This model is simply an elaboration of the gravity model introduced in Chapter four. It recognizes that the customer's choice of store or shopping center depends on (1) attractiveness (or size) and (2) accessibility (distance) relative to other shopping alternatives. The data are easily obtained and the program can be set up on a microcomputer so that it can be quickly replicated to answer a variety of 'what if' questions. The model first estimates the spatial distribution of store purchases, which are calculated as a function of household income. Note that this relationship can be calibrated precisely to generate all store purchases, just non-automotive purchases, or purchases of shoes, if needs be. The equation simply generalizes the information given in Table 2.2 and Figure 2.8.

The allocation of a neighborhood's purchases to a specific shopping facility depends on the distance decay effect discussed in Chapters two and four. In a wide variety of situations the aspect of human behavior consisting of the probability of making a trip from place i to place j has been shown to be positively related to the size, complexity, or number of opportunities at place j ($S_j$), and inversely related to the distance between i and j ($d_{ij}$). Migrations, telephone calls, mail flows, air travel, and all sorts of other interactions follow this relationship. For shopping trips the distance effect may be interpreted as an effective increase in the price of the product due to travel costs, and the size of the shopping facility might be interpreted as the number of different products available – the range of choice. In practice, a variety of indicators may be used: number of stores, floor area, sales, or number of different types of stores. Thus:

$$\text{Sales}_{ij} = K \times S_j / d_{ij}{}^b. \qquad \text{(eqn 9.2)}$$

$\text{Sales}_{ij}$ predicts the sales by customers living in area i at the stores of shopping center j, where $S_j$ is a measure of store attraction, $d_{ij}$ is a measure of distance (or time or cost), and K and b are constants that must be determined empirically. The value of b, the distance exponent, is quickly established for a given retail chain or type of store by plotting market

### Exhibit 9.5
### IMPACT ANALYSIS: THE HUFF MODEL

*Goal*
To examine the impact of a new shopping center on a system of existing centers within an urban area.

*Inputs*
Number of households and average household income by neighborhood (census tract), from Bureau of the Census, *Census of Population*. Floor area and location of shopping centers within the urban area from National Research Bureau (annual), *Directory of Shopping Centers in the United States and Canada*. See also Bureau of the Census, *Census of Retail Trade*, 'Major retail centers', for shopping center size expressed in sales.

*Procedures*
(1) Estimate percentage of household income spent in shopping centers as a function of household income, using data from the Bureau of Labor Statistics, *Consumer Expenditure Surveys*. This share will vary with the level of income. For example:

retail sales $= \$4,054 + 0.289$ (average income) $- 0.62 \times 10^6$ (income)$^2$
where income is measured in 1982 dollars.

(2) Calculate shopping center sales by census tract:

Sales in tract$_i$ = number of households$_i$
$\times$ average shopping center purchases$_i$ (from item 1).

(3) Allocate sales from tract$_i$ to various shopping centers using the Huff model:

Proportion of sales$_i$ purchased at shopping center$_j$ =
proportion$_{ij} = (FA_j/d_{ij}^b) / \sum_{j=1}^{m} (FA_j/d_{ij}^b)$

where $FA_j$ is the floor area of the jth shopping center, $d_{ij}$ is the distance between tract$_i$ and center$_j$, b is a parameter that can be used to vary the slope of the spatial demand curve, and m is the number of shopping centers in the market. b usually has a value somewhere between $-1$ and $-2$; let's use $-1.5$.

(4) We can calculate the total sales occurring at center j as:

$\sum_{i=1}^{n}$ sales$_i \times$ proportion$_{ij}$ (from item 3);

where n is the number of census tracts in the market.

(cont.)

Exhibit 9.5 (*continued*)

(5) Run the model with and without the proposed new shopping center and map the changes in the sales expected at each competing center.

(6) Extend the model to calculate sales per square foot at each center (dividing item 5 by the floor area of the center). What kinds of stores could survive in that kind of environment?

penetration (the proportion of households which shop at the store) against distance for each census tract and evaluating the slope, or by using a regression model. Once calibrated, the model can be applied to new locations; b usually has values between $-0.5$ and $-2.5$, and is larger (that is, the slope of the spatial demand is steeper) for convenience goods, and smaller (shallower) for shopping goods (as was shown in Figure 2.4). Exhibit 9.6 illustrates the use of the Huff model for a store in the center of a city.

Huff (1963) incorporated the effect of competition into the model by comparing the estimated sales from neighborhood i at facility j with estimated sales for all other potential destinations.

$$P_{ij} = (S_j/d_{ij}^{\,b})/\Sigma_j(S_j/d_{ij}^{\,b}) \qquad \text{(eqn 9.3)}$$

$P_{ij}$ is the proportion of sales from a neighborhood that goes to a particular shopping center, j, in the context of all competing facilities. The origins and elaborations of the model are discussed at length in Ghosh and McLafferty (1987).

The denominator sums over all the potential destinations for the consumer. (This assumption may not be completely accurate for households at the edge of the study area.) The model argues that the customers visit a number of different stores, with the probability of a visit depending on the size and distance of the facility. The probability of shopping at store j, when multiplied by the sales potential of ($SP_i$) tract i, projects the sales from tract i at store j. Summing over all census tracts i gives the equation:

$$\Sigma_j (SP_i \times P_{ij}) = \text{sales}_j. \qquad \text{(eqn 9.4)}$$

The analyst can use this equation to project total sales at store j (given the existing configuration of competing stores). The spatial structure of competition is central to the model.

The model is used to test different alternatives by feeding in different input data. A new center? A change in the spatial distribution of households? Higher incomes? Increased mobility (leading to a reduced value for b)? The incoming developer can use the model to evaluate the potential sales at several alternative sites. Which one is best? Figure 9.6

## Exhibit 9.6
## THE HUFF MODEL IN THE CENTRAL CITY

A large apartment complex with eighteen buildings is served by three super-markets, all nearby (store C is off the map). Since most customers walk to the store, the value of the distance parameter b is high (about 3.0). The numbers and contours on the map show the market share of shopping center A as predicted by the Huff model. Given the number of apartments in each block and the estimated grocery expenditures per household, a sales forecast is quickly established for store A.

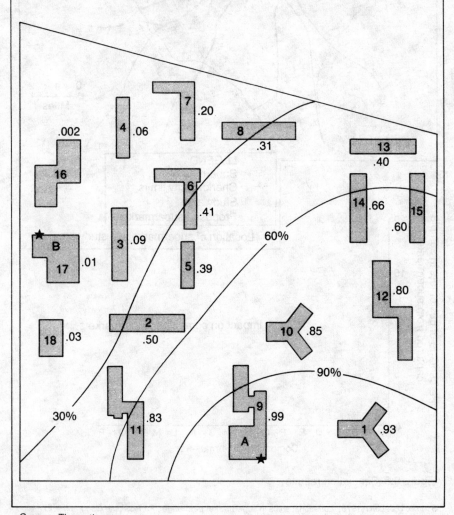

*Source:* The authors

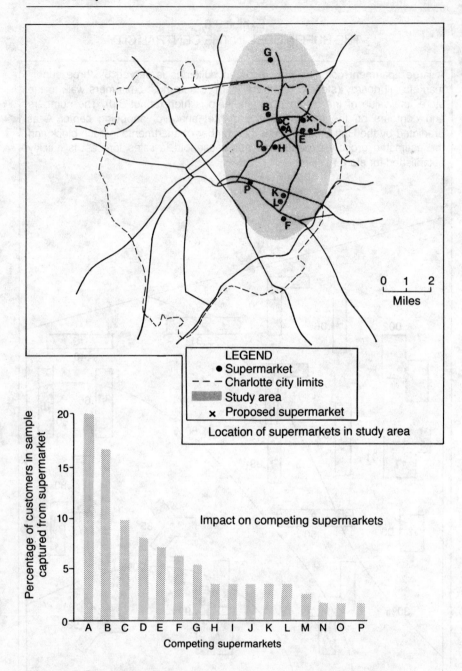

LEGEND
● Supermarket
-- Charlotte city limits
▓ Study area
× Proposed supermarket

Location of supermarkets in study area

Impact on competing supermarkets

**Figure 9.6** Simulation results

*Source:* D.J. Lord (1975) 'Locational shifts in supermarket patronage', *Professional Geographer* 27: 310–14. Reproduced by permission of The Association of American Geographers

comes from a paper by Lord (1975) who used a similar model to examine the spatial pattern of effects of a new supermarket in a small American city.

Existing retailers and shopping center managers can predict the effect of a new development proposal on their own sales, and whether overall income increases or local population growth will compensate. Should they attack the proposal on planning grounds? Should they try to compete by developing a specialized retailing niche?

Municipal planning staff are concerned with the overall balance between retail facilities and demand, and may attempt to manage the rate of development of new facilities. They build simulation models to see whether consumers will benefit from the competition, or whether the new facility will simply create problems in existing centers. What will the new center do to the downtown area? A study by the Edmonton Department of Planning and Building (1986) suggested that the West Edmonton Mall had diverted between 28 and 38 per cent of sales away from downtown Edmonton.

Over the past two decades, gravity models of this type have become widely accepted by major retailers, shopping center developers, consultants, and planners as a means to simulate market penetration for all new retail developments and their impact on existing outlets. Many of these gravity-based retail impact models have been described in the retailing literature or are available for a fee from consultants. Some are tailored for specific users; for example, SCOPE (Supervalu) and MODEL (Scrivner Inc.) are designed for supermarkets, RETLAW (Dayton-Hudson) for department stores, SCOPE (Decision Science) and FORESITE (Systems, Science, and Software) for planners.

## Decision-making under uncertainty

Monitoring, forecasting, and simulation are ways of reducing the uncertainty faced by a retail chain, but they cannot completely thwart the fickle finger of fate. The monitoring process looks back rather than forward, focusing on the uncertainties of last week or last month. Forecasting peers into the gloom ahead but makes no pretence of great accuracy. Its central assumption, that most things will stay the same, is its major weakness. At best, forecasters can identify the things that are most likely to change. While simulation can investigate a variety of alternative futures and identify those most likely to be troublesome, it lays out far too many possibilities for most decision makers. One can depict an extraordinary range of future scenarios.

How do retailers make decisions under such conditions? How do they balance the chance of success against the risk of failure? How do they insure themselves against catastrophic declines in a local market? Each retail chain has its own answers to these questions, answers rooted in its own corporate environment and experience. However, three general approaches to uncertainty help to differentiate the operations of today's retail megachains from the independent retailer of the past.

The first principle appears in every small business manual. Maintain sufficient resources – in capital, credit, guarantees, or whatever – to carry the business through the start-up period as well as the recessions and local slumps that will surely come. The larger firm with a solid, established base and credit rating has obvious advantages here. The multilocational chain can simply cut its losses and move elsewhere if the new outlet doesn't work out. Uncertainty, it seems, favors large and sophisticated retail firms.

The second principle – spread the risk – also favors the larger chain. Risk (uncertainty) justifies higher rates of return on investment. (Retailing ranks high on both measures.) Extensive research into the management of investment portfolios suggests that investments should include a mixture of low-risk 'interest rate' activities and high-risk 'capital gains'. A retail chain can achieve this mix by locating in a variety of regional markets, since most regions of the country and most communities grow independently of one another. The greatest variability in growth rates, and hence the highest risk of gain and loss, occurs in smaller places, in agricultural or energy-based regions, and in new suburban plazas where the competitive structure is not yet clear. Low-risk, low-return locations are found in older cities and older suburban plazas where markets are stable in size and share. The megachain may also balance its portfolio by diversifying its range of business types. Computer software or high fashion are less predictable, but potentially more profitable, than groceries or work boots. In general, the more special-ized the retail niche, the greater the uncertainty in the market; but some sectors and locations are much more stable than others.

In addition to maintaining substantial reserves and a diversified distri-bution network, the retail chain needs to incorporate a sense of uncertainty into every aspect of its marketing strategy. Flexibility must be one of the criteria for every decision. Is this marketing strategy adaptable to changes in the target market? Can we alter the product mix and image? How many locations would have to be dropped or diverted into another chain? Is this location vulnerable to competition? Should we sell off all our inner-city locations before the rest of the industry catches up with the changes in the market? In short, location decisions are based not on today's retail environ-ment but on expected changes in the market and in the production function. A volatile retail environment favors chains that have the flexibil-ity to handle a wide range of growth scenarios: chains that can adapt to different target markets, remain profitable across a wide range of sales volumes, and adjust their format or profit mix to different locations. This latter capacity is particularly important as chains move beyond the expansion phase and begin to rationalize and consolidate existing locations. Most department store chains, for example, do not contemplate much further expansion into new locations. Instead, they are trying to fine-tune operations at their existing outlets in order to maximize sales. A chain becomes many different stores in different locations: it can be upscale, downscale, a fashion store, or a mass merchandiser as the local market demands.

Given what we know about the rate of change in both the demand and supply side of retailing, we can argue that even without expansion a retail chain should expect to replace or relocate 2–3 per cent of its outlets each year. We know that in twenty-five years the retail structure within an urban area will be largely reorganized, and that at the settlement scale many of the largest markets will have been shoved aside by more rapidly growing cities.

Ghosh and McLafferty (1987) suggest more formal solutions to decision-making under uncertainty. Scenarios of alternative future events lay out explicit models of all eventualities. They permit the chain to choose the robust strategy, i.e. one that performs best for all alternatives. In another approach, the best solution commits the fewest resources now, and/or in the most generally acceptable fashion, leaving the rest of the decisions until more information is available (options planning). For example, a retail chain may select three outlets that are necessary to every possible network configuration and hold off on the rest until the merger is completed, until the economic data improve, or whatever. Game theory makes assumptions about the rational actions of competitors in order to minimize the impact of their decisions. If the competitor behaves sensibly, it should be possible to derive a best response.

While the difficulties of predicting future change and the large investments at risk encourage more sophisticated locational analysis, they also limit the usefulness of such research. No one really knows whether the market will grow or not: the location analyst can only restrict the range of possible outcomes and update the forecasts as soon as possible. As we will see in the chapter that follows, many marketing decisions are based on minimal information ahead of time, but maximum attention and evaluation after the fact. Trial and error!

Chapters ten and eleven will introduce some of the techniques used in location analysis to identify and evaluate specific locations. Site selection studies compare the merits and demerits of different store locations in a variety of contexts: evaluating existing outlets, choosing among potential new locations, and simulating results under future conditions. Studies of trade areas are concerned with the spatial pattern of market penetration of a single store outlet. Such models may also be used to investigate the effect of new facilities on existing centers.

**Further reading**

Alchian, A.A. (1950) 'Uncertainty, evolution and economic theory', *Journal of Political Economy* 58: 211–21.

Beaumont, J.R. (1989) 'Toward an integrated information system for retail management', *Environment and Planning, A* 21, 2: 299–309.

Edmonton Department of Planning and Building (1986) 'The retail impact model: operation and results',

Epstein, B.J. and Schjeldahl, D.D. (1984) 'Supermarket innovation and retail market equilibrium', *GeoJournal* 9, 2: 155–62.

Finn, A. (1987) 'Characterizing the attractiveness of retail markets', *Journal of Retailing* 63, 2: 129–62.

Georgoff, D.M. and Murdick, R.G. (1986) 'Manager's guide to forecasting', *Harvard Business Review*, Jan./Feb.: 110–20.

Ghosh, A.J. and McLafferty, S. (1987) *Location Strategies for Retail Chains* Chapter 7, 'Location strategies in uncertain environments', Lexington, Massachusetts: D.C. Heath & Co.

Goodchild, M.F. (1989) 'Geographical information systems and Market Research', *Paper and Proceedings of Applied Geography Conferences*, 12: 1–8.

Huff, D.L. (1963) 'A probabalistic analysis of shopping center trade areas', *Land Economics* 39: 81–90.

Lord, J.D. (1975) 'Locational shifts in supermarket patronage', *Professional Geographer* 27: 310–14.

Ritchey, J. (1984) 'Developing a strategic planning data base', in R.L. Davies and D.S. Rogers (eds). *Store Location and Store Assessment Research*, New York: John Wiley & Sons.

Wrigley, N. (1988) 'Retail restructuring and retail analysis', in N. Wrigley (ed) *Store Choice, Store Location and Market Analysis*, London: Routledge.

# Chapter ten

# Site selection

**Retailers have only two assets – their inventories and their locations.**

**The site selection procedure used by a retail chain should reflect the chain's stage in the life-cycle.**

**As retail clusters become more specialized, the site selection process for the retail chain must become more precise. Each different market niche requires a distinct location model.**

Now that we, as retail analysts, have developed skills in evaluating information, forecasting, and modelling, how do we apply these techniques to the location problem? The site selection process evaluates the particular set of measures that are most important for the retail chain in question. Some chains are primarily concerned with demand conditions, such as market size or lifestyle. Others look to the supply-side conditions, rent, traffic, or a location within a regional shopping center. Still others avoid certain competitors or seek out compatible retail chains. Some chains are expanding rapidly; others are trying to rationalize their networks by eliminating marginal outlets. The goal of this chapter is to show how these locational requirements are developed and applied.

The site selection process clearly differentiates the retail chain from the independent. For most independent stores, location is fixed: the business evolves to suit the site. A survey of specialty retailers in Toronto showed that less than 2 per cent had engaged in any location research. The site looks good, there is a vacant store with an acceptable rent in an area in which the retailer feels comfortable, or the retailer has faith that the real estate agent will find the best site. For retail chains site selection is a continuing process – the outcome of a marketing strategy. The firm may decide to (1) select a new location, thus expanding an existing service network, (2) expand an established outlet, (3) renew an existing lease, (4) relocate an existing outlet, (5) remerchandise at a given location to appeal to a different target market, or (6) close an outlet. Larger corporations, sometimes with non-retail backgrounds, are now acquiring retail chains and their existing networks of outlets. McGrory's buys T,G & Y stores, Pepsico buys Kentucky Fried Chicken, Barnes and Noble buys B. Dalton Booksellers. Part of the assets include facility locations. Often the outcome of such a take-over is a systematic re-evaluation of each store to see how each one fits into a modified marketing strategy. (Exhibit 10.1 describes the divestment of Dominion Stores.)

Retail chains may use a variety of site selection techniques, ranging from a reliance on 'gut-feeling' to statistical forecasting models. In most cases store location research is undertaken in the real estate or marketing departments. Often, the degree of sophistication in location decisions reflects the growth and history of the firm. In the early years, a 'pick any site' philosophy dominates. Quick-fix solutions are sought, using simple ratios

## Exhibit 10.1
## THE DIVESTMENT OF DOMINION STORES

In Toronto, Dominion Stores have been one of the two leading supermarket chains over the last twenty years, as this map indicates. However, Dominion's outlets were smaller, older, and, it appears, less profitable than those of other supermarket chains. The corporate parent – the Argus conglomerate – decided to wind it down rather than invest more money.

Getting rid of stores requires as much site evaluation as opening new ones, but the performance data are better. Dominion proceeded, first, to replace non-plaza outlets with 'independent' Mr Grocer outlets, tied to Dominion's wholesale subsidiaries (which it later sold to another supermarket chain), and second, to negotiate sales of other outlets to the A & P supermarket chain. A & P has retained the Dominion name, still potent in Toronto, for the stores they took over.

A & P was faced with a different site evaluation problem: given its preexisting network of outlets (presumably successful), which Dominion stores did it wish to acquire in order to complete its system? The choice was complicated by the knowledge that the stores it did not purchase would probably remain in business as competitors. What kind of evaluation procedure can place a price on putting a competitor out of business? A & P decided to avoid the central city outlets (too small) and to focus on the older suburbs where A & P itself was not well positioned.

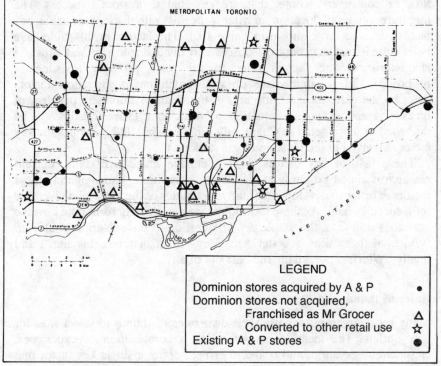

METROPOLITAN TORONTO

LEGEND

| | |
|---|---|
| Dominion stores acquired by A & P | • |
| Dominion stores not acquired, | |
| Franchised as Mr Grocer | △ |
| Converted to other retail use | ☆ |
| Existing A & P stores | ● |

*Source:* The authors

that allow the company's real estate analyst to compare potential sites. In this expansionary period the company generally experiments with site selection methods, but its ability to formulate a sound procedure is constrained, both by the lack of historical sales data and by the limited number of existing locations. After five or ten years the retail chain may reassess its corporate position; lease expirations also underline the need to understand which factors make a site good or bad. During this period of rationalization the chain will encourage experimentation with new store location methods.

More recently, a number of retailers have developed a third level of locational competence. In this phase, geographically referenced real estate information systems and computer-based census data are used to evaluate and forecast sales performance.

This chapter reviews various approaches that the location analyst can take to retail site selection. The discussion will proceed from the simple to the complex, presenting six distinct approaches to retail site evaluation: rules of thumb, descriptive inventories, site rankings, ratios, regression models, and location-allocation procedures.

Each of these approaches begins with the notion of the key factors, the idea that the chain can identify a small number of variables, such as traffic flow or consumer income, that are essential to a store's success. The literature on retail location inevitably begins with lists of possible key factors, such as those shown in Table 10.1. The factors in this table have been culled from a variety of sources and divided into site and situation characteristics. Site factors refer to the store property (existing or proposed) and its immediate physical environment. Situation factors describe the surrounding trade area – the demand side. The problem of measuring and evaluating situation or trade area characteristics will be discussed in more detail in Chapter eleven. (Exhibit 10.2 describes the key factors involved in the location of gas stations.)

These lists of key factors do not change much over time: current research is aimed primarily at identifying, combining, and weighting these factors in order to develop quantitative estimates of the value of a given site for a specific chain. As these techniques are described in turn, note how the questions shift from the simple yes/no question 'Is this site appropriate?' to 'Which of these sites is better?' to 'How much better is this site?', and finally, 'Which is potentially the best site of all?'

## Rules of thumb

Many retail organizations use their own rules of thumb to select sites for new outlets. The location analyst, using a combination of experience, empirical observation, and trial-and-error, isolates a single key factor that appears to be directly related to sales performance, and thus store success

**Table 10.1** Site selection: key factors

*Situation*
1. *The spatial extent of the market*
   No. of households or population as a function of distance. (From census material, airphotos, planning studies, Zip code information.)
   Where is the outer limit (range)?
   Are there natural barriers?

2. *Temporal change*
   What changes in the market are forecast over the next ten years?
   How accurate is the forecast?

3. *Household characteristics*
   What is the household income? (From census or housing data.)
   Is it likely to change?
   Age?
   Lifestyle?
   Female participation rate?

4. *Competition*
   How many competitors in this market?
   How far away?

5. Existing market penetration by other outlets in the chain, as indicated by credit cards, or sales slips.

*Site*
6. *The site constraints*
   Lot size/shape
   Zoning/planning restrictions
   Building Condition/sales area
   Cost/lease
   Services

7. *Local access patterns*
   Traffic volume, speed
   Curbs, cuts, grades
   Transit stops
   Pedestrian flow

8. *Parking*
   How much?
   How far?
   Shared?

9. *Visibility*
   Sign potential – restrictions?
   Sign clutter?

10. *Nearby attractions*
    Complementary stores
    Other generative land uses

*Source:* The authors

## Exhibit 10.2
## KEY FACTORS FOR GAS STATIONS

The analysis of key factors for gas stations has become a fine art (Claus and Hardwick, 1972). As table (a) below suggests, different kinds of stations have different location strategies, and therefore different key factors. Independents depend on the attractiveness of a single site. Chains locate new outlets relative to existing outlets and rely on images created by national advertising. Variants in each case occur for highway (single stop) and neighborhood (repeat) locations. The success of the highway independent depends on a huge sign saying 'cheap gas'. Your neighborhood Texaco dealer relies on the number of Texaco cardholders within six blocks.

### (a) Key factors in the gas station model

| | Single stop (through traffic) | Repeat (local market) |
|---|---|---|
| | Site variables | Trade area variables |
| Independent | Visibility, access | Trade area income composition (price sensitivity) |
| Chain | Signage, location of other chain outlets | Brand loyalty, number of credit card holders, competitors |

*Source:* The authors

Just as Eskimos are reputed to have 300 words to describe snow, gas station analysts have dozens of measures of accessibility.

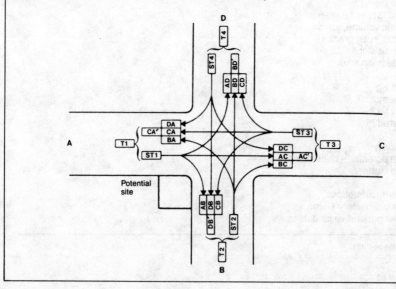

Table (b) indicates twelve different kinds of highway traffic that can pass a corner gas station, each one with a different probability of stopping at the site as shown.

### (b) Approximate rates of retail customers drawn from different traffic lanes on a city street*

| Rank order of traffic lanes relative to potential customer rate | Traffic lane | Site No. 1 customer rate |
|:---:|:---:|:---:|
| 1 | AB | 0.0333 |
| 2 | BA | 0.0148 |
| 3 | AD | 0.0065 |
| 4 | CB | 0.0052 |
| 5 | BC | 0.0047 |
| 6 | DA | 0.0042 |
| 7 | DB | 0.0042 |
| 8 | AC | 0.0031 |
| 9 | DC | 0.0026 |
| 10 | CD | 0.0018 |
| 11 | BD | 0.0017 |
| 12 | CA | 0.0014 |

*Source:* R.J. Claus and W.G. Hardwick (1972) *The Mobile Consumer*, Toronto: Collier Macmillan. Reproduced by permission of the publisher
*Note:* * Proportion of cars/lane that stop.

(see Table 10.2). Once this untested relationship becomes accepted as a reliable indicator, it is adopted as the major locational criterion, and used to screen potential locations. Some retail chains are expanding so rapidly that they have time for only the most rudimentary investigations. The Wal-Mart department store chain opens over 100 new stores per year – that's two per week.

Rules of thumb procedures cost very little for analysis and permit rapid decisions. They are appropriate for firms that are primarily concerned with increasing market share, confident of their ability to weed out unsuccessful locations later, or for firms (e.g. discount gas stations) which are relatively insensitive to location. They are also characteristic of chains whose target market is not clearly fixed and who wish to maintain the flexibility to modify their operation and therefore the type of site selected in the future. Even so, rules of thumb procedures are overly simplified and subjective. No attempt is made to understand or articulate the complex relationships that determine store performance or the peculiarities of local conditions, such as the competitive structure.

**Table 10.2** Rules of thumb

| Characteristic | Operating rule | Type of chain |
|---|---|---|
| Trade area size | At least 2,000 households | Convenience store |
| | 5,000 households within 2 miles | Fast-food outlet |
| | 16,000 car registrations within 2 miles | Specialized auto service center |
| | 10,000 households within 15 minutes drive | Branch bank |
| Site | Free-standing site on access road to regional shopping center | Toy store |
| | Rents for less than $5 per sq. ft | Discount store |
| | Within 7 minutes walk of downtown office blocks | Downtown restaurant |
| Competition | At least 3 miles from competing outlet | Catalogue store |

*Source:* The authors

## Descriptive inventories

In the expansionary phase a retail chain has relatively little information on outlet performance under various conditions. All outlets are recent and still under evaluation. Location selection may still be carried out by the original entrepreneur who lacks special training in location analysis. Later, site selection may be re-assigned to real estate people, and still later to marketing experts with a special interest in spatial analysis. As data improve, the firm gains experience in the market, personnel responsibilities shift, and site selection becomes increasingly sophisticated.

The descriptive inventory is a good way for such firms to begin to analyse the location problem. In this approach a list of key factors is developed, identifying the most relevant locational criteria for a particular chain, and used as a framework to evaluate and select potential retail locations. Much of the early literature in retail location was based on these lists or inventories.

Relevant key factors vary from chain to chain. For example, Table 10.3 presents some of the factors important to service station chains. Because gasoline purchasers want to buy gas along their travel routes, these activities are particularly sensitive to site considerations, although, as we will show in Chapter twelve, there are several different service station marketing strategies, each using a different set of key factors.

The descriptive inventory can be thought of as a preliminary stage to more quantitative evaluation methods. The chain tries to articulate the relationship between sales and location characteristics but makes no attempt to examine precise relationships. The checklist approach is useful in assessing single sites but has limited value as a general locational model.

## Exhibit 10.3
## HOW FAST CAN A RETAIL CHAIN GROW?

Wal-Mart, a chain of discount department stores, began with one store in Rogers, Arkansas in 1962. Since then they have expanded in small centers throughout the South and West, managing to double their sales every two years by moving into markets that older chains were abandoning (see Figure 6.8). By 1987 they had moved into third place in department store sales, behind Sears Roebuck and K mart. Since they operate in small centers that are not growing much faster than the nation as a whole, they must be diverting sales from other retailers.

| Year | Sales ($ millions) | No. of stores |
|------|--------------------|---------------|
| 1967 | 13 | 24 |
| 1968 | 22 | 27 |
| 1969 | 31 | 32 |
| 1970 | 45 | 38 |
| 1971 | 79 | 51 |
| 1972 | 126 | 64 |
| 1973 | 169 | 78 |
| 1974 | 238 | 104 |
| 1975 | 343 | 125 |
| 1976 | 482 | 153 |
| 1977 | 683 | 195 |
| 1978 | 906 | 229 |
| 1979 | 1,263 | 276 |
| 1980 | 1,648 | 330 |
| 1981 | 2,450 | 491 |
| 1982 | 3,384 | 551 |
| 1983 | 4,677 | 642 |
| 1984 | 6,414 | 745 |
| 1985 | 8,451 | 859 |
| 1986 | 11,909 | 980 |
| 1987 | 16,600 | 1,000 + |
| 1988 | 20,650 | |

Source: The authors

## Ranking

Site ranking instruments provide a simple means to quantify the merits of retail locations. Site ranking schemes were developed by real estate analysts who needed quick comparisons of different sites on the basis of pre-selected criteria. These procedures are particularly common in the assessment of gasoline, fast-food, and convenience food outlets.

**Table 10.3** Key factors in the gas station model

*Trade area variables (situation)*
Predominant land use type
Type of housing
Household density
Household income
Automobiles per capita
Growth characteristics
Number of competitors in area
Sales volume of competitors
Credit representation in area (i.e. number and type of cards)
Number of our credit cards held

*Site variables*
Type of traffic artery
Traffic volume
Average speed
Traffic origin (local, tourist, etc.)
Traffic purpose (work, shop, leisure)
Intersection characteristics
Site visibility (curve? hill?)
Site grade (level? barriers?)
Site size, frontage
Site layout
Operating constraints – hours, services, etc.

*Source:* Adapted from R.J. Claus and W.G. Hardwick (1972) *The Mobile Consumer: Auto-Oriented Retailing and Site Selection*, Toronto, Collier-Macmillan

While ranking provides a rapid comparison of alternative sites, in its simplest form it does not distinguish the importance of various criteria. It's like choosing a mate: does a shared liking for Chinese food compensate for differences in wealth, intelligence, good looks, and ethnic background? Some of these factors are much more important to people than others. Over time, most ranking systems have been modified by weighting each factor.

Table 10.4 shows a site rating schedule adopted by a bank. It is based on seven key factors: the first three describe the trade area and the last four the development in which the site is located. A value from 0 to 10 is assigned to each factor. The analyst goes out and looks at the property and assesses each factor, placing the property in one of three to five categories. (Note that for item B, family income, a middle-income neighborhood gets the highest mark.) The property's score on the factor is the assessed value multiplied by the development multiplier: a measure of the expected timing of the project. A standardized score for the site is obtained by summing over the seven scores. The highest-ranking sites are then considered for acquisition.

Different business types and different chains will have different ranking

**Table 10.4** A site ranking scheme for a bank

Region: _____

|  | Ranking | Score |
|---|---|---|
| Location: _____ |  |  |
| _____ |  |  |
| _____ |  |  |

| | Weights | Ratings | Devel. P | D | Multipliers* EX | EX+D | Total weight |
|---|---|---|---|---|---|---|---|
| **A Growth trends** | | | | | | | |
| ____ Rapid growth | 10 | | | | | | |
| ____ Growing | 6–8 | | | | | | |
| ____ Stable | 5 | | 0.7 | 1.4 | 1.4 | 1.75 | |
| ____ Declining | 0 | | | | | | |
| **B Family income levels** | | | | | | | |
| ____ Over $50,000 | 5 | | | | | | |
| ____ $36,00–50,000 | 6–7 | | | | | | |
| ____ $24,000–36,000 | 8–10 | | 0.7 | 1.4 | 1.4 | 1.75 | |
| ____ $12,000–24,000 | 2–4 | | | | | | |
| ____ Under $12,000 | 0 | | | | | | |
| **C Competition** | | | | | | | |
| ____ None established | 10 | | | | | | |
| ____ Established but poorly located | 8 | | | | | | |
| ____ Long established | 6 | | | | | | |
| ____ Well located and long established | 4 | | 0.7 | 1.4 | 1.4 | 1.75 | |
| ____ Planned and well located | 2 | | | | | | |
| **D Residential development** | | | | | | | |
| ____ High density, multi-family | 7–10 | | | | | | |
| ____ Medium density, single and multifamily | 4–6 | | 0.7 | 1.4 | 1.4 | 1.75 | |
| ____ Low density, single family | 1–3 | | | | | | |
| **E Commercial development** | | | | | | | |
| ____ Major concentration (greater than 600,000 sq. ft) | 7–10 | | | | | | |
| ____ Medium concentration (400,000–600,000 sq. ft) | 4–6 | | | | | | |
| ____ Minor concentration, scattered, unimportant (100,000–399,999 sq. ft) | 1–4 | | 0.7 | 1.4 | 1.4 | 1.75 | |
| ____ Next to no concentration | 0 | | | | | | |

327

**Table 10.4** (*continued*)

| | Weights | Ratings | Devel. P | D | Multipliers* EX | EX+D | Total weight |
|---|---|---|---|---|---|---|---|
| **F** *Industrial development* | | | | | | | |
| ____ Major concentration (more than 640 acres) | 6–10 | | | | | | |
| ____ Medium concentration (= 640 acres) | 5 | | | | | | |
| ____ Minor concentration, scattered, unimportant (less than 640 acres) | 1–4 | | 0.7 | 1.4 | 1.4 | 1.75 | |
| ____ Next to no concentration (__ acres) | 0 | | | | | | |
| **G** *Office/financial development* | | | | | | | |
| ____ Major downtown core | 6–10 | | | | | | |
| ____ Medium concentration auxiliary core | 5 | | | | | | |
| ____ Minor concentration, scattered, unimportant | 1–4 | | 0.7 | 1.4 | 1.4 | 1.75 | |
| ____ Negligible development | 0 | | | | | | |

*Development multipliers
| P, | planned | = 0.70 | Total score |
| D, | developing | = 1.40 | |
| EX, | existing | = 1.40 | |
| EX + D, | new development of existing | = 1.75 | Scored by: _____ |
| | | | Date: _____ |

*Source:* The authors

schemes. A gas station, for instance, weights factors such as traffic flow and access to site more highly than trade area characteristics.

While the site ranking approach permits the analyst to compare alternative locations, the ranking schedule itself is not evaluated. Are these factors really significant indicators of performance? Too often the variables are chosen intuitively with little regard for overlap or double counting. Only rarely do the analysts test the strength of the relationship between sales performance and site rank. These ranking schemes are usually developed for specific marketing environments (e.g. sites in urban areas, the west coast market, or central city locations) and cannot be readily transferred to other regions.

**Ratio methods**

The weakness in both the descriptive inventory and site ranking approaches is the lack of a demonstrable association between key factors and measures of store performance. Ratio methods tackle this problem directly by developing a variety of indicators to describe outlet performance. They are called ratio methods because they usually control for the size of the market by means of a denominator.

Ratio methods are usually applied to markets (i.e. trade areas) rather than specific sites, and are based on aggregate data, often gathered by official statistical agencies. At the settlement scale, for example, a chain might be interested in indices of market saturation, as shown in Table 10.5. These figures were calculated for drug stores using data from the *Census of Retailing*. The data can be supplemented by sales information from the chain's own outlets as well. The ratios indicate the degree of penetration (or competition) across the cities of the region. The ratios for these cities are similar, suggesting a well-adjusted retail structure. Larger cities (e.g. Boston, Hartford) have larger stores – but what about Bangor? Sales per capita largely reflect income variations, although New London is low and Providence is high. Where would you put your next store? Which of these indicators is most useful in identifying a potential market?

This approach may be useful for chains that serve mass markets since they can attract a fixed share of any trade area, but it may be inappropriate for chains that focus on a particular segment of the market, such as high-income neighborhoods or college students.

In applying ratio methods to individual sites, company records or field work are used to generate measurements of performance such as sales/employee, sales/checkout, sales/capita, sales/square foot, turnover (sales/inventory), or sales/front foot. Such indicators quickly evaluate existing or potential store locations. Some chains calculate ratios of their sales to those of other firms in order to determine whether a particular location looks promising. For example, chain X, a record store, may know through past experience that in a comparable retail setting (e.g. a regional shopping plaza) they make 1.5 times the annual sales of chain Y, a women's fashion store. By sharing information with chain Y, the analyst can obtain a rough estimate of the likely sales level of a proposed store.

Since ratio methods describe the comparative performance of an existing store or market rather than the potential of an undeveloped 'green field' site, they are often used to supplement other site selection procedures. The emphasis on the variety of measurements of store performance permits the chain to evaluate various key factors, as shown in Figure 10.1. The graphs indicate that trade area population is not a useful predictor of retail sales in the central city (top), but that it has some validity for suburban locations (bottom).

## Regression models

Consider the location analyst who works for a large retail chain operating in a variety of marketing environments on a continuing basis. He or she

**Table 10.5** Performance indicators for New England cities

| Metropolitan statistical area | Population, 1984 | Growth rate 1970–84 | Income/capita, 1983 $ | No. of drug-stores | Drugstore sales ($ millions) | Sales/ store $ | Sales/ capita $ | Population/ store |
|---|---|---|---|---|---|---|---|---|
| Hartford, CT | 1,069,000 | 3.3 | 14,525 | 269 | 187.2 | 696,000 | 175 | 3,975 |
| New Haven | 770,000 | 3.4 | 13,175 | 169 | 104.4 | 618,000 | 136 | 4,560 |
| New London | 245,000 | 2.6 | 13,150 | 52 | 31.2 | 600,000 | 127 | 4,710 |
| Boston, MA | 3,695,000 | −0.4 | 14,300 | 863 | 622.4 | 721,000 | 168 | 4,280 |
| New Bedford | 478,000 | 7.7 | 10,825 | 125 | 66.5 | 532,000 | 139 | 3,820 |
| Pittsfield | 142,000 | −4.7 | 11,875 | 42 | 21.2 | 505,000 | 149 | 3,380 |
| Springfield | 584,000 | 0.2 | 11,400 | 166 | 84.6 | 510,000 | 145 | 3,520 |
| Worcester | 654,000 | 2.7 | 11,325 | 186 | 101.4 | 545,000 | 155 | 3,520 |
| Bangor, ME | 138,000 | 10.4 | 9,650 | 28 | 19.9 | 711,000 | 144 | 4,930 |
| Lewiston | 100,000 | 9.5 | 9,725 | 24 | 11.5 | 479,000 | 115 | 4,170 |
| Portland | 223,000 | 20.5 | 11,900 | 57 | 38.7 | 679,000 | 174 | 3,910 |
| Manchester, NH | 295,000 | 31.8 | 13,000 | 67 | 42.6 | 636,000 | 144 | 4,400 |
| Portsmouth | 300,000 | 43.3 | 12,350 | 64 | 43.5 | 680,000 | 145 | 4,690 |
| Providence, RI | 878,000 | 2.7 | 11,675 | 202 | 158.1 | 783,000 | 180 | 4,350 |
| Burlington, VT | 126,000 | 22.9 | 11,150 | 28 | 16.6 | 593,000 | 132 | 4,500 |

*Source:* Bureau of the Census (1986) *State and Metropolitan Area Data Book,* Washington

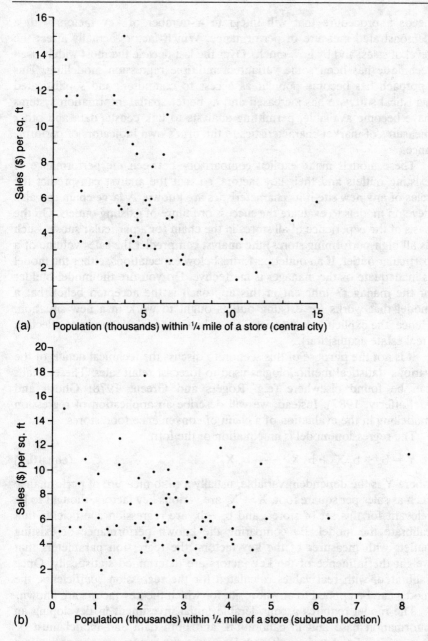

(a) Population (thousands) within ¼ mile of a store (central city)

(b) Population (thousands) within ¼ mile of a store (suburban location)

**Figure 10.1** Using performance ratios to evaluate a key factor

*Source:* K.G. Jones and D.R. Mock (1984) 'Evaluating retail trading performances', in R.L. Davies and D.S. Rogers (eds) *Store Location and Store Assessment Research*, Chichester: John Wiley and Sons

needs a procedure that will integrate a number of key factors with a demonstrated measure of performance. Which factors actually affect the level of sales, and by how much? Over the last decade the most widely used technique has been some variant of multiple regression modelling. This approach has become popular as access to computers and sophisticated statistical software has increased and as better spatial information systems have become available, permitting analysts to link census data and other measures of market characteristics to the firm's own indicators of performance.

These models make explicit comparisons between the performance of existing outlets and their key factors, so that the analyst can predict the sales of any new site if its characteristics are known. A large chain can also develop models to evaluate the success or failure of existing outlets. On the basis of the experience of all stores in the chain (or a particular subset, such as all high-performing stores) the analyst can predict the sales volume of a particular outlet. If an outlet performs below expectations, either the model is inadequate or the manager is ineffective. Do you fire the model-builder or the manager? Inherent in this approach is the accepted belief that a model that works for existing outlets ought to work in a new situation. Hence, the explicit link between site evaluation (analysis) and site selection (real estate acquisition).

It is not the purpose of this section to discuss the technical details of the various statistical methodologies used to forecast retail sales. These details can be found elsewhere (e.g. Rogers and Green, 1978; Ghosh and McLafferty, 1987). Instead, we will describe an application of regression modelling in the evaluation of a chain of convenience food stores.

The regression model is an equation of the form

$$Y = b_o + b_1 X_i + b_2 X_2 + \cdots b_k X_k \qquad \text{(eqn 10.1)}$$

where $Y$ is the dependent variable, usually a ratio measure of performance such as sales per square foot, $X_1 - X_k$ are various key factors, thought to be relevant for this set of stores, and $b_o - b_k$ are regression coefficients that calibrate the model. By comparing the known performance of existing outlets with measures of the key factors, the regression parameters that weight the influence of the key factors are determined statistically. Once calibrated, with real values calculated for the regression coefficients, the model can be applied to any new site for which the key factors are known.

The model requires a considerable initial investment in developing an information base and in calibration, and both data and model must be regularly updated and monitored. However, the results can be applied in a variety of ways: to evaluate the performance of existing sites as well as the potential for new ones, and to explore the possibilities of variants of the chain or the chain itself in new environments.

These statistical models are most successful in predicting performance levels of low-order convenience goods where consumer behavior is relatively simple. The model is also more accurate and reliable for chains large enough to support a series of models for particular kinds of outlets (according to size or product mix) or types of marketing environment (upscale, suburban, etc.). Applications of the model are restricted to sites within the same general environment: same region, same time frame, and same segment. A different setting requires a new calibration.

The chain of convenience stores to be studied here had reached a stage in its life-cycle where all aspects of its operation were under review. The real estate department was asked to develop a more rigorous site selection strategy because past procedures had resulted in a number of ineffective store locations. Re-evaluation was especially important because a number of leases on existing sites were expiring and the company had projected a major expansion of 500 new stores during the next five years.

The search for an improved decision-making procedure included three objectives:

(1) To construct a comprehensive data file on the characteristics of each existing store location.
(2) To isolate the key locational and business environment factors associated with successful outlets.
(3) To develop and assess a computerized site evaluation model that could predict the sales potential of prospective locations.

The *Census of Population* provided basic socio-economic characteristics for trade areas such as family size, average family income, and occupation. Postal walk information was used to develop a detailed record of area population and residential structure by city block. The retail chain itself provided numerous measures of site characteristics and store performance (Table 10.6).

The marketing literature recognizes that quite different business environments exist within major metropolitan regions, but prior to this study the company had failed to incorporate this basic geographical fact in its evaluation. Sites had been evaluated solely in relation to population thresholds and leasing arrangements. It was apparent that the site selection procedure could be improved by grouping sites according to similarities in retail environments. Five distinctive environments were identified: the central city, suburbs, old established strips, the urban fringe, and the non-metropolitan locations. The process of identifying these different environments is called segmenting the market, and it can be done on the basis of: (1) the firm's experience, (2) the geography, (3) the firm's administrative structure (e.g. the New England branches), or (4) statistical grouping (e.g. cluster analysis) to identify outlets or environments that are most alike.

To find out which of the many variables available were most relevant for each retailing environment, a series of cross-tabulations between individual

**Table 10.6** Site and situation variables for a convenience store site evaluation model

| Site variables | | Situation variables | |
|---|---|---|---|
| Variable description | No. | Variable description | No. |
| Building information | 15 | Neighborhood accessibility information | 13 |
| Site accessibility information | 6 | Traffic conditions | 13 |
| Parking facilities | 10 | Housing characteristics | 8 |
| Internal retail environment | | Competitive businesses | 7 |
| (from field survey) | 19 | Potential business generators | 4 |
| Internal retail environment | | Lease information | 1 |
| (head office records) | 13 | Trade potential | 20 |
| Total | 63 | Total | 66 |

Source: K.G. Jones and D.R. Mock (1984) 'Evaluating retail trading performance', in R.L. Davies and D.S. Rogers (eds) *Store Location and Store Assessment Research*, London, John Wiley & Sons, Ltd. Reproduced by permission of the publisher

key factors and sales performance was carried out (Table 10.7). The relevant variables were then put into a series of stepwise regression models, one for each retail environment (see Table 10.8). The statistical procedure identified the variables that were most effective in explaining variations in sales performance. The regression parameters indicate the linear relationship between weekly sales and each of the key factors retained in the model. The $R^2$ values indicate the proportion of store-to-store variance in weekly sales that can be explained by a particular combination of key factors.

The regression equations proved to be quite successful. The three models calibrated for the more stable, developed, urban environments yield the highest coefficients of determination ($R^2$), explaining 69 per cent, 85 per cent, and 95 per cent of the aggregate variation in weekly sales among stores. It is more difficult to predict store performance in the constantly changing urban fringe, and especially uncertain in the fast-growing towns surrounding the metropolitan area.

Let us take a closer look at the suburban model. The variation in weekly sales was best explained by three measures: the percentage of the neighborhood that had recently been developed, accessibility of the site by car, and (inversely) the number of competitors within three blocks. By applying the regression parameters from this equation to data for other suburban sites, the relative revenue-generating potential of each location can be determined. For example, each increase of 1 per cent in the share of new houses has an impact of $120. Each nearby competitor reduces sales by $656 per week.

While regression modeling is now widely used by retail chains to select and evaluate sites, it is by no means the perfect solution. First, it depends

**Table 10.7** Key factors associated with high weekly sales for each retail environment

*Central city*
1. Pedestrian access
2. Few competitors within one block
3. Schools and services are not an asset in the immediate area
4. Areas of dense population
5. Close to crosswalks
6. Close to subway

*Suburbs*
1. Plaza location
2. Divided street
3. Maximum number of curb cuts, good car access
4. Homeside location
5. Bus stop
6. Maximum number of parking spaces
7. Area with new development
8. Maximum vehicular traffic
9. Few competitors

*Old established strips*
1. Area with new development
2. Single-family dwellings within half mile
3. Mature family structure
4. Near schools and business generators
5. Not necessary to have parking on site
6. Not necessary to avoid competitors
7. Maximum vehicular traffic

*Urban fringe*
1. Free-standing structure
2. Area with new development
3. Access to two streets
4. Maximum population within $\frac{1}{4}$ mile
5. Near a major intersection
6. Sales indifferent to high concentration of apartments or single-family homes

*Non-metropolitan*
1. Free-standing structure or neighborhood plaza
2. Sidewalk, pedestrian traffic
3. Parking lot
4. On-street shopping
5. Near schools or service generators
6. Newly developing areas
7. Maximum single-family dwellings within $\frac{1}{2}$ mile

*Source:* K.G. Jones and D.R. Mock (1984) 'Evaluating retail trading performance', in R.L. Davies and D.S. Rogers (eds) *Store Location and Store Assessment Research*, London, John Wiley & Sons, Ltd
Reproduced by permission of the publisher

on access to large amounts of information, in particular the sales response at enough locations (thirty or more) to calibrate the model. Thus, it works better for convenience stores than for a highly specialized shopping goods chain. Second, it takes into account only those variables entered into the regression model. To introduce other key factors requires a recalibration of the whole model. Furthermore, the model itself may be unstable in the sense that the regression parameters change as other factors are added or deleted. This problem, known as multicollinearity, reflects the fact that the key factors are themselves related to each other. For instance, if the average value of a home is added to the model, the apparent importance of the family income factor may decline. Finally, as we have seen, the segmentation of outlets into different types may alter the model dramatically. What kind of segmentation is appropriate for such a model? To which segment does a potential site belong?

**Table 10.8** Stepwise regression models

*Central city sites**

$$Y = \$5,792 + 34.45X_1 - 32.33X_2 - 351.11X_3 + 176.29X_4$$

| where: | | | $R^2$ |
|---|---|---|---|
| | $Y$ | = weekly sales in dollars | |
| | $X_1$ | = percentage apartments within $\frac{1}{2}$ mile | 0.297 |
| | $X_2$ | = percentage customers who are pedestrians | 0.523 |
| | $X_3$ | = car accessibility | 0.658 |
| | $X_4$ | = number of competitors within three blocks | 0.693 |

*Suburban sites†*

$$Y = \$3,629 + 120.18X_1 - 656.32X_2 + 503.02X_3$$

| where: | | | $R^2$ |
|---|---|---|---|
| | $Y$ | = weekly sales in dollars | |
| | $X_1$ | = percentage newly developed neighborhood | 0.813 |
| | $X_2$ | = number of competitors within three blocks | 0.837 |
| | $X_3$ | = car accessibility | 0.849 |

*Old established strip sites†*

$$Y = \$2,994 - 120.92X_1 - 9.07X_2 + 8.27X_3$$

| where: | | | $R^2$ |
|---|---|---|---|
| | $Y$ | = weekly sales in dollars | |
| | $X_1$ | = percentage newly developed neighborhood | 0.862 |
| | $X_2$ | = percentage single-family dwellings within $\frac{1}{2}$ mile | 0.895 |
| | $X_3$ | = number of parking spaces | 0.953 |

*Urban fringe sites**

$$Y = \$1,555 + 100.14X_1 + 1.19X_2 + 455.59X_3 - 762.16X_4$$

| where: | | | $R^2$ |
|---|---|---|---|
| | $Y$ | = weekly sales in dollars | |
| | $X_1$ | = percentage newly developed neighborhood | 0.319 |
| | $X_2$ | = population within $\frac{1}{4}$ mile | 0.478 |
| | $X_3$ | = condition of road | 0.582 |
| | $X_4$ | = number of competitors within three blocks | 0.646 |

*Non-metropolitan sites*

$$Y = \$2,756 + 35.51X_1 - 33.85X_2 + 137.48X_3 + 15.63X_4 - 6.16X_5$$

| where: | | | $R^2$ |
|---|---|---|---|
| | $Y$ | = weekly sales in dollars | |
| | $X_1$ | = pedestrian count | 0.091 |
| | $X_2$ | = percentage customers who are pedestrians | 0.182 |
| | $X_3$ | = number of sales generators in area | 0.302 |
| | $X_4$ | = percentage of single-family dwellings within $\frac{1}{2}$ mile | 0.354 |
| | $X_5$ | = number of parking spaces | 0.397 |

*Source:* K.G. Jones and D.R. Mock (1984) 'Evaluating retail trading performance', in R.L. Davies and D.S. Rogers (eds) *Store Location and Store Assessment Research*, London, John Wiley & Sons, Ltd. Reproduced by permission of the publisher
*Notes:* *Equation significant at $p = 0.05$. †Equation significant at $p = 0.01$.

The sales predictions from regression modelling, combined with site-specific data on leasing cost, services, labor, and other related expenditures, assist the analyst to select profitable locations. As a result of the study in our example, the chain evaluated new sites by combining the subjective assessment of experienced real estate professionals with the objective application of the appropriate sales potential model. The company's new policies on identifying, evaluating, and procuring new sites were presented in a real estate handbook made possible by the improved database. The analysis of the data bank destroyed misconceptions about convenience stores and identified a number of stores that were performing below expectation. In addition, the survey techniques refined during the study allowed the company to update the data file on each store, and thereby monitor the changing retail environment in which it operates.

## Location-allocation

Most site selection problems faced by retailers are incremental in that they consider only a limited number of possible location alternatives within the larger network of facilities. For instance, the addition of a new chain outlet on the north-west edge of a city affects only two or three neighboring outlets of the same chain. Such problems are readily handled by one of the site selection methods described above.

However, on occasion the introduction of a new marketing strategy requires the evaluation of the entire network of facilities, asking the question 'How do all these outlets work together?' or even 'How could we build a better network of outlets, starting from scratch?' Such a problem crystallizes when one chain takes over the outlets of another and has to decide which sites to keep and which ones to sell (as in the Dominion Store merger described in Exhibit 10.1). It also emerges when a fundamental change is introduced into the technology of the supply side – such as an increase in the average size of service stations or supermarkets, or the recent introduction of automated teller machines to the banking sector. When the whole network of facilities is evaluated simultaneously, the analyst can turn to location-allocation techniques. Ghosh and McLafferty (1987) provide a useful overview.

These techniques can be tailored to a wide variety of specific problems, but fundamentally they are designed to allocate a given spatial distribution of demand to a specified number of outlets (see Figure 10.2). Much of the research on this topic has been done in the public sector, where planners must designate service areas for fixed facilities such as schools or fire stations in the most efficient fashion. Which neighborhood should be served by which fire station? However, the procedure is also appropriate for choosing the best set of locations for schools or supermarkets to serve a given market. The solution can be further modified to fit many variants of

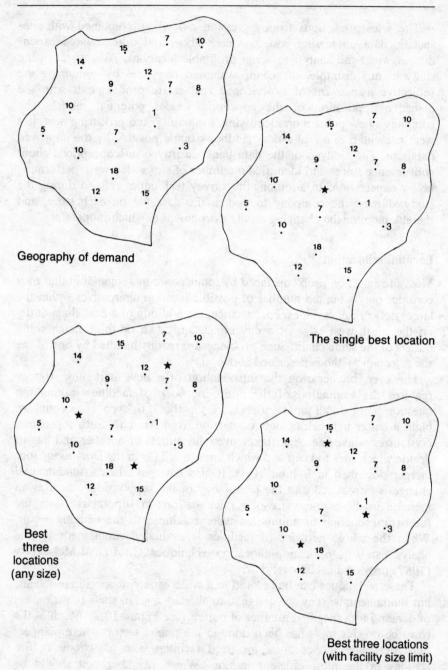

**Figure 10.2** Location–allocation procedures

*Source:* The authors

the location problem. For example, certain pre-existing sites may be included, a competitor's outlets can be avoided, or an upper or lower level may be set on the size of a facility (thus the trade area served at each outlet).

The analysis begins with a geography of demand in which submarkets are assigned to point locations. The problem is to locate a specified number of outlets to best serve this overall market. Without getting into the details, a computer program very rapidly evaluates all possible combinations of outlet locations with respect to all the submarkets (the point locations) and chooses the most efficient alternative. The criterion for efficiency usually minimizes some function of the total distance travelled (or time or cost), but again, many variations are possible. By making certain assumptions about consumer behavior, the programmer may be able to maximize consumption. Or, by considering the costs of operating at different sites or at different scales, it may be possible to use profitability as the efficiency criterion.

While the location-allocation procedures have not been widely used by retail chains, they have considerable potential for a variety of retail location problems, once the usual site selection and evaluation questions are rephrased. 'Which outlet is least efficiently located?' 'What would happen to adjacent outlets if outlet X were closed?' 'If we cut back the number of outlets in this market to six, which ones should we retain?' The techniques are undoubtedly more useful for convenience activities where the assumptions about consumer behavior are relatively simple. Only experimentation will tell whether sufficient regularities exist in consumer behavior towards shopping goods to justify such models.

Location-allocation techniques are very powerful weapons in the hands of the experienced analyst, who can use them to simulate a variety of future scenarios. The emphasis is on long-term marketing strategies rather than short-term decisions about opening or closing a given location. It is possible to consider the structure of the competition as well as the outlets of the chain under study. Because location-allocation models are best suited to planning five, ten, or fifteen years down the road, they should be tied to information on target markets, market share, and investment costs. (Exhibit 10.4 describes the use of the location-allocation procedure in the evaluation of sites for a gas station.)

Six different approaches to the retail site selection problem have been presented in this chapter. Each procedure is still widely used and is particularly appropriate for certain situations and certain kinds of retail chains. Table 10.9 provides an overview of the strengths and weaknesses of each. One important consideration is the cost and time available for the selection process. Firms that are growing rapidly, and/or changing their marketing strategies, will not find procedures that necessitate detailed inventories or elaborate models to be cost-effective.

## Exhibit 10.4
## LOCATION ALLOCATION AND GAS STATION SITE EVALUATION

The merger of two chains of gas stations in a small city required an evaluation of each station (there were thirty-one in all) within the context of the full set of outlets. Which sites could be sold and which ones could be combined or expanded? This problem could be analysed on a site-by-site basis, using a multiple regression model, but the location-allocation approach is more appropriate because it adjusts all outlets in the system simultaneously.

First, the thirty-one existing gas stations were considered as potential sites. It was decided that only twenty outlets would be retained, including four of the newest and highest-volume locations. The selection process was reduced to choosing sixteen out of twenty-seven sites. Second, the potential demand for gasoline was measured in two ways:
(1) The residential population in each of 600 census enumeration areas across the city.
(2) The traffic flow (number of cars × length of link) in each of 560 road links.
Each of these measures was offset by a distance decay effect. Thus,

$$\text{demand}_j = A \sum_i \text{Population}_i/(1 - a\,d_{ij}) + B \sum_k \text{Traffic}_k/(1 - a\,d_{kj})$$

where A and B are weights that can be modified to favor either trade area demand or traffic flow demand. (The parameter a does not have to be calculated to derive a solution.) Many ways of formulating these relationships are possible. One alternative would be to insert the location of competitors in order to find locations that were relatively isolated from them.

Given the inputs, the problem is to choose twenty sites (including the four that were already specified) that collectively maximize gasoline sales. Not only does the location-allocation procedure carry this out (see the maps below), but it indicates the sales or market share at each site, and how the site might be even more effective if slightly relocated. The isolines indicate the decline in effectiveness from the optimum site (value = 100).

The analysis can be repeated using different distance decay parameters and different weights for A and B in the equation to reflect different marketing strategies. An emphasis on trade area demand (high value for A) favors central locations (map (a)), and an emphasis on traffic flow generates more dispersed sites (map (b)). Suburban households drive more and buy more gas. Nonetheless fifteen of the twenty sites are the same.

*Source:* M.F. Goodchild and V.T. Noronha (1987) 'Location allocation and impulsive shopping: the case of gasoline retailing, in A. Ghosh and G. Rushton (eds) *Spatial Analysis and Location Allocation Models*, New York: Van Nostrand and Reinhold

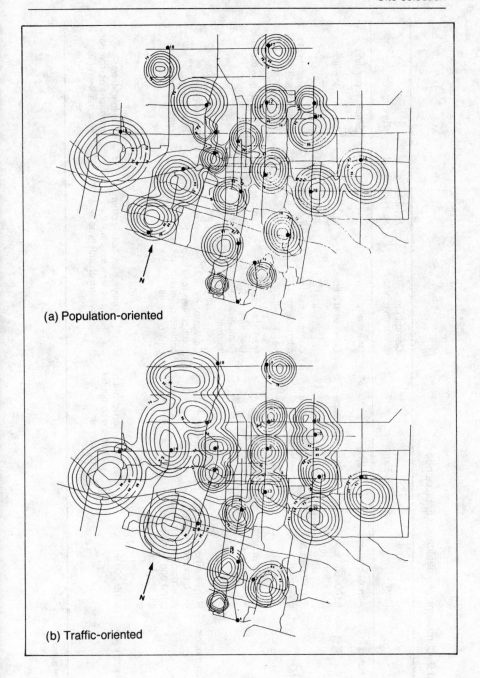

(a) Population-oriented

(b) Traffic-oriented

**Table 10.9** Comparing site evaluation approaches

| | Cost | Expertise | Comparing alternative sites? | Evaluating sales potential | Type of firm |
|---|---|---|---|---|---|
| Rules of thumb | Almost costless | None | One site at a time | No | Small, expanding |
| Descriptive inventories | $100–500/site for data collection | Only experience | One site at a time | No | Growing: location sensitive |
| Ranking | $100–500/site for data collection | Only to identify the weights | Compares several alternatives | Indirectly | Chains beginning to evaluate site and performance |
| Ratios | Inexpensive, unless field work required | Only modest | Market areas rather than sites. Comparisons provide 'norms' | Directly | Entering new markets |
| Regression models | Requires historical data as chain performance plus model maintenance. $100,000 + for major studies for national chain. | Location analyst required | Calibrated by comparisons (can also contrast different retail environments) | Yes, explicitly | Large chains, monitoring performance |
| Location-allocation | $100,000 + | Experienced location analyst and computer programmer | Analyses impact on other sites. How to adjust the system of outlets as a whole | | The long-term: megachains, mergers, new marketing strategies |

*Source:* The authors

Sophisticated models are not always possible either. Chains that have highly specialized target markets, or that include outlets varying widely from one location to the next, will find it difficult to build a good model. Chains that have few outlets or a brief historical record are simply not in a position to evaluate the strengths and weaknesses of their locations.

However, large chains dealing in several markets have a competitive advantage because of their experience and their data about sales performance. They will build elaborate models in order to make more efficient decisions – decisions that not only affect the choice of site but also help them to negotiate leases with plaza developers or to refine the marketing mix. The size and complexity of the site evaluation model is simply another kind of business decision. The best model is the one that is cost-effective for a particular chain and the problems it faces.

## Further reading

Achabel, D., Gorr, W.L. and Mahajan, V. (1982) 'MULTILOC: a multiple store location model', *Journal of Retailing*, 58, 2: 5–25.

Claus, R.J. and Hardwick, W.G. (1972) *The Mobile Consumer: Auto-Oriented Retailing and Site Selection*, Toronto: Collier-Macmillan.

Davies, R.L. and Rogers, D.S. (eds) (1984) *Store Location and Store Assessment Research*, New York: John Wiley & Sons.

Ghosh, A. and McLafferty, S. (1987) *Location Strategies for Retail and Service Firms*, Chapter 6, 'Developing retail outlet models', Lexington, Massachusetts: D.C. Heath.

Goodchild, M.F. and Noronha, V.T. (1987) 'Location allocation and impulsive shopping: the case of gasoline retailing', in A. Ghosh and G. Rushton (eds) *Spatial Analysis and Location Allocation Models*, New York: Van Nostrand and Reinhold.

Green, H.L., Applebaum, W., and Dupree, H. (1978) 'When are store locations good? The case of the National Tea Company in Detroit', *Professional Geographer*, 30, 2: 162–7.

Hise, R.T., Kelly, J.P., Gable, M. and McDonald, J.B. (1983) 'Factors affecting the performance of individual chain store units: an empirical analysis', *Journal of Retailing*, 59, 1: 1–18.

Jones, K.G. and Mock, D.R. (1984) 'Evaluating retail trading performance', in R.L. Davies and D.S. Rogers (eds) *Store Location and Store Assessment Research*, New York: John Wiley & Sons.

Mercurio, J. (1984) 'Store location strategies', in R.L. Davies and D.S. Rogers (eds) *Store Location and Store Assessment Research*, New York: John Wiley & Sons.

Penny, N.J. and Broom, D. (1988) 'The Tesco approach to store location', in N. Wrigley (ed) (1988) *Store Choice, Store Location and Market Analysis*, London: Routledge.

Rogers, D.S. and Green, H.L. (1978) 'A new perspective on forecasting food sales: applying statistical models and techniques in the analog approach', *Geographical Review*, 69: 449–58.

# Chapter eleven

# Trade area analysis

**About 30 per cent of a supermarket's sales come from within 1 mile of the store.**

**If you know your customers you can identify your trade area. If you know your trade area you can identify your customers.**

**A retail chain's main asset is the set of locations that it leases. Its success depends on its ability to extract sales from these locations.**

Trade area analysis and site evaluation are complementary procedures: the former specifically focuses on the demand side, on situation factors; while the latter combines the demand side with the many operating requirements of the retail chain. Generative activities like supermarkets and shopping centers are concerned with the size and characteristics of trade areas. Gas stations and other suscipient activities focus on site evaluation. Trade area analysis permits large chains to make better use of their existing facilities; it becomes increasingly important to many retailers as competition increases, operating costs rise, and the growth of population and real income stabilizes. A detailed knowledge of the customers is essential to the processes of rationalization or 'productivity enhancement' (achieving more sales per square foot) currently so popular in the industry.

A variety of techniques have been used to delimit trade areas, ranging from simple customer dot maps to sophisticated spatial modeling. This chapter will introduce three different concepts of the trade area: spatial monopoly, market penetration, and dispersed markets (see Figure 11.1). Each approach will be discussed in detail and the chapter will finish by outlining procedures for estimating trade area populations.

As you may have guessed, location analysts are somewhat schizoid in their treatment of trade areas. On the one hand, it is often analytically simple to link a retail facility directly to the trade area which it is near (or at least nearer than some alternative facility). Thus, it can be assumed that Downtown Chicago (the Loop) serves the Chicago metropolitan area and the analyst can associate the characteristics of the Chicago market with the characteristics of retailing in the Loop. This is the concept of spatial monopoly, which is often a convenient approach to begin the discussion of how big or how rich a trade area is required to support the facility. On the other hand, it is well known that many customers to a store or shopping center come from an extensive territory on a regular basis, often bypassing similar facilities. Woodfield Mall also serves Metropolitan Chicago, but the proportion of customers who prefer Woodfield Mall to the Loop varies regularly over space, with a distinct pattern of market penetration for each center. In addition, there are some stores whose trade area (or target market) is highly specialized or selective and may be widely and irregularly dispersed across the city. The three concepts of trade area analysis presented in this chapter are each useful in particular research

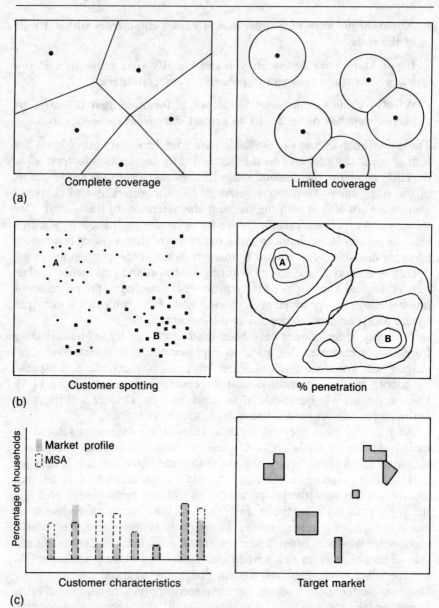

**Figure 11.1** Approaches to trade area analysis
(a) Spatial monopoly
(b) Market penetration
(c) Dispersed market

*Source:* The authors
*Note:* MSA, metropolitan statistical area.

contexts and for particular types of retail firms. The characteristics and applications of each approach are outlined in Table 11.1 and will be elaborated in the sections that follow. Throughout this chapter our discussion of trade areas is restricted to the metropolitan scale.

## Spatial monopoly

It is often convenient to treat trade areas as if they were entirely assigned to a single facility or center – assuming implicitly that 100 per cent of the

**Table 11.1** Approaches to trade area analysis

| | Spatial Monopoly | Market Penetration | Dispersed Markets |
|---|---|---|---|
| Trade area form | Residential area Exclusively assigned to one facility – all areas assigned? – unserved areas identified? | Spatial variation in the proportion of households served by a facility Overlapping trade areas | Only neighborhoods with specified characteristics are assigned to trade area – discontinuous |
| Spatial definition | Thiessen Polygon Driving time (isochrone) Primary trade area | Customer spotting Distance decay models Primary–Secondary classification | Census tract analysis PRIZM-type markets Analogy with facilities serving same market Behavioral studies |
| Application | Convenience goods Facilities within a chain Standard shopping centers Analyses at the settlement scale | Shopping goods Specialized shopping centers Competing chains with strong, hard image | Extremely specialized goods Facilities catering to distinctive income, ethnic, or demographic group |
| Context | Site selection Market composition | Evaluation and re-orientation | New store location, promotion |
| Example | State liquor stores Post offices | Department stores, supermarkets | Upscale furniture store |
| Related procedures | Market profile 'Vacuum' method Trade area forecasting | Market-share models – regression – Huff model – Analog | Centrality studies |

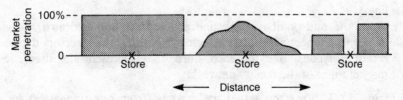

*Source:* The authors

households in all neighborhoods deal with the center. For example, if a small town has a single drug store, all the characteristics of that town – its size, income, and demographics – may be linked with the sales of that outlet. Within a metropolitan area, where significant social variations exist among neighborhoods, we can identify the effect of these differences by analyzing the sales and product mix of each local drug store as a direct reflection of the characteristics of the nearby residents, even though we recognize that some of these customers will spread their spending among half a dozen drugstores, some of which are located in quite different parts of the city.

Such analyses are appropriate when we are discussing the qualitative (what kinds of people?) rather than the quantitative (how many sales?) aspects of the market. Implicitly, these studies discount the market size and ignore the less-than-perfect penetration rate, in order to permit simple spatial analyses that assume evenly distributed households and sales. Perhaps the best examples of this approach are the early rules of thumb for supermarket locations that used the five- and ten-minute isochrones. The store's trade area was assumed to extend within a ten minute driving range and to include all those households within the isochrone. Such studies are still used for shopping centers, particularly at the neighborhood and community scale, where it is accepted that trade areas are largely distance-defined. More sophisticated location studies would modify these patterns to take into account the penetration rates of competitors.

The spatial monopoly approach can be applied to more complex systems of facilities by means of Thiessen polygons, a geometric procedure for delimiting theoretical trade areas for a network of similar (including competing) activities in space. The approach assumes that each retail unit sells an undifferentiated product and that consumers will use the closest facility. Space is assumed to be homogenous, thus permitting equal access in all directions: no physical or psychological barriers exist. The technique is most appropriate to studies of chain outlets that are basically identical (e.g. automated teller machines).

To construct a set of Thiessen polygons (see Figure 11.2):

(1) Lines are drawn joining a given store to each adjacent store in the chain.
(2) Each of these inter-store lines is bisected to obtain the mid-point of the line.
(3) From the mid-point of each line a boundary line is drawn at right angles to connect with other bisectors. Together the bisectors define a set of polygons, one for each store, that represent the theoretical market areas of the facility network.

Figure 11.3 shows the actual trade areas (from questionnaires) for a series of Brewers' retail outlets in Ottawa, Canada, compared with the

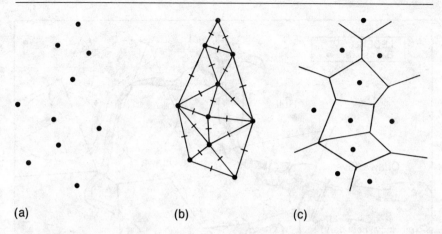

(a)                              (b)                              (c)

**Figure 11.2** Stages in the construction of Thiessen polygons

*Source:* K.G. Jones and D.R. Mock (1984) 'Evaluating retail trading performance', in R.L. Davies and D.S. Rogers (eds) *Store Location and Store Assessment Research*, Chichester: John Wiley and Sons. Reproduced by permission of the publisher

theoretical trade areas that were constructed using this technique. (Brewer's retail outlets sell only beer and have a monopoly on beer sales in the province. They are the poor man's equivalent of a state liquor store.)

The Thiessen polygons can be used as a descriptive and predictive device. By examining the market areas one can observe the degree of coverage, identify areas of under-representation as obvious 'gaps in the map', and thus spot potential new sites. As a predictive tool, the Thiessen technique can be used to select locations that maximize distance from sister stores or competing activities. In Figure 11.4 the edges of each market area represent a set of points that are equidistant from two super-regional malls, while the vertices of the polygons are equidistant from at least three of them. Super-regional malls are the centers larger than 700,000 square feet in Figure 8.5. Prior to 1965 the large malls located in various suburban sectors, effectively truncating the markets served by the Loop and older inner-city shopping areas (not shown). In the prosperous northern sector, however, three nearby centers also bound each other's trade areas. The truncation pattern continued during the 1965–75 period, as a second ring of centers bound the outer limits of the trade areas of the first ring.

After 1975 a new pattern emerges. Three new centers are located along the boundaries of the earlier polygons, while four more centers at the periphery continue the truncation process. It is evident that trade areas are both spatial and temporal phenomena!

When applied to outlets for a single retail chain, the Thiessen polygons describe the chain's location strategy and provide a tool for visualizing the

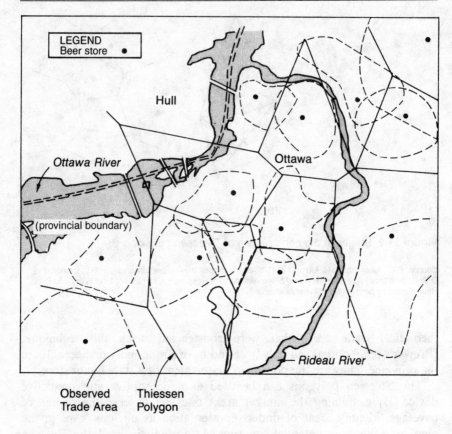

**Figure 11.3** Trade area for beer stores, Ottawa

*Source:* The authors

impact of potential changes in strategy. As ideal market areas, the polygons can also be used to assemble and/or collect demographic and customer information, and they are inexpensive. In half an hour, the location analyst has obtained a reasonable approximation of real trade areas.

Once the trade area is delimited in space, the analyst can examine the composition of the market by means of a market profile, as shown in Figure 11.5. By treating the trade area as a unit, one can use census information to generate a breakdown of the number of households in various income groups, demographic categories, ethnic and racial origins, or lifestyle combinations. To get a better sense of the peculiarities of the market under study, it may be useful to compare the trade area data with data for a larger market, such as the state or metropolitan area. The customer profile may then be compared to actual survey data collected from customers. Does the

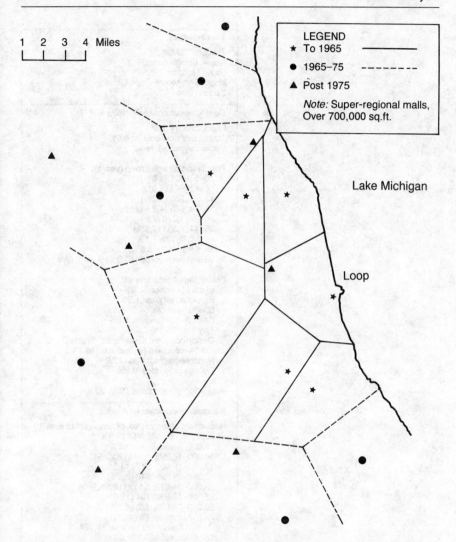

**Figure 11.4** Thiessen polygons for super-regional malls: Chicago

*Source:* The authors

customer profile fit the profile of the adjacent market area? Should the store's product mix be adjusted to suit the trade area? Should the store relocate?

Thanks to the computer, market research firms have developed the capacity to disaggregate census data obtained for census tracts, municipalities, and counties into Post Office Zip code areas, or any other small spatial

351

**Vital statistics**

Zip code: 33936
Name: Lehigh Acres
State: Florida
Metro: Fort Myers–Cape Coral
County: Lee

**Demographic characteristics**

Population: 14,122
Total no. of households: 6,615
Median age: 60.1 years

**Population by age group (years):**
   0–5  : 501 (3.5%)
   6–11: 673 (4.8%)
   12–17: 733 (5.2%)
   18–24: 675 (4.8%)
   25–34: 1,076 (7.6%)
   35–44: 1,034 (7.3%)
   45–54: 1,005 (7.1%)
   55–64: 2,659 (18.8%)
   65 and over: 5,766 (40.8%)

**Percentage breakouts of**
   Black population: 2.0%
   Black households: 1.8%
   Spanish population: 1.6%
   Spanish households: 1.2%
   Families: 75.3%
   Owner-occupied households: 81.3%
   Renter-occupied households: 18.7%
   Noncollege graduates: 70.9%
   College graduates: 8.6%

Population growth since 1980: 23.9%

**Socioeconomic characteristics**

**Household income: (No. of households with $;)**
   Less than $5,000: 458 (6.9%)
   5,000–9,999: 913 (13.8%)
   10,000–14,999: 1,345 (20.3%)
   15,000–19,999: 947 (14.3%)
   20,000–24,999: 648 (9.8%)
   25,000–34,999: 1,112 (16.8%)
   35,000–49,999: 794 (12.0%)
   50,000–74,999: 320 (4.8%)
   75,000 or more: 78 (1.2%)
   Median household income: 18,124
   Total income: 163,102,000

Employment (1984): 2,118 (15.0%)

**Retail sales characteristics**

Total retail sales: $40,312,000
Buying Power Index (BPI): 0.0049

**Retail store counts (1984):**
   Supermarkets: 4
   Department stores: 1
   Apparel: 6
   Eating and drinking places: 10
   Furniture, home furnishing, appliance stores: 2
   Automobile dealers: 4
   Gasoline service stations: 3
   Building material dealers: 2
   Drugstores: 2

**Figure 11.5** A market profile: Lehigh Acres, Florida

*Source: Sales and Marketing Management*

units. If the retailer can map the store's trade area (or is satisfied with a Thiessen polygon or even a set of distance bands), the consultant can quickly provide a market profile. For example, a retail chain could develop Thiessen polygons for every major shopping center in a metropolitan area and draw up market profiles to compare alternative locations. Which shopping centers have access to the largest markets, the wealthiest markets, or the markets with the highest proportion of young professionals? Which shopping centers best fit the known customer profile of the chain?

The vacuum approach is a specialized type of retail analysis that treats the trade area as a spatial monopoly. The goal is to find out if and when sufficient market opportunity will exist in a given area to accommodate additional retail capacity. This additional retail space can then be translated into either a new retail location or an expansion of an existing facility.

The method has been used extensively, both by major retailers (e.g. department store chains) and by consulting firms, in order to explore the possibility of future entry into selected market areas. It can be regarded as an elementary form of feasibility analysis, based on aggregate census information plus data on accepted industry norms (such as average sales/square foot). In addition, the analysis may incorporate surveys that measure consumer behavior.

The case study (Table 11.2) explores the potential for a supermarket in

**Table 11.2** The vacuum approach: food store, medium-sized city[a]

|  | 1985 | 1990 | 1995 | 2000 |
|---|---|---|---|---|
| *Primary Market* | | | | |
| Market potential ($ thousands) | 45,877 | 52,270 | 59,601 | 68,599 |
| Market performance ($ thousands) | 95% | 95% | 95% | 95% |
| Sales potential ($ thousands) | 43,583 | 49,657 | 56,621 | 65,169 |
| *Secondary Market* | | | | |
| Market potential ($ thousands) | 28,918 | 33,917 | 39,994 | 45,955 |
| Market performance ($ thousands) | 35% | 33% | 31% | 29% |
| Sales potential ($ thousands) | 10,121 | 11,219 | 12,398 | 13,327 |
| Total sales potential ($ thousands) | 53,704 | 60,876 | 69,019 | 78,496 |
| Less existing facilities[b] ($ thousands) | 53,704 | 56,389 | 59,208 | 62,168 |
| Market opportunity ($ thousands) | 0 | 4,487 | 9,811 | 16,328 |
| New sales per sq. ft criteria ($) | 275 | 300 | 325 | 350 |
| Additional floor space requirements (sq. ft) |  | 14,957 | 30,188 | 46,651 |

*Source:* The authors
*Notes:* [a]About 50,000 people in 1985. [b]Allow 5 per cent increase in sales per square foot every 5-year period commencing 1985.

a city of population 50,000. In this case, a two-level trade area is defined with the primary trade area including the first 60 per cent of the customers and the secondary trade area the next 25 per cent. The trade areas are delimited by any one of a variety of procedures: telephone surveys, street interviews, licence plate searches, or point-of-sale questionnaires (these procedures will be elaborated on in the next section). Once the trade area is established, the market potential for both the primary and secondary trade areas can be calculated using census materials. So many households, with so much income, generate the market potential. Each of these markets can be projected into the future, using the techniques described in Chapter nine, and the expenditure on food is estimated with the help of the expenditure surveys discussed in Chapter two. Present or future sales potential is estimated by weighting the market potential by the percentage of expenditures that are captured by the local shopping facilities. For this city, a sample study estimated that 95 and 35 per cent of the food dollars from the primary and secondary trade areas, respectively, would be spent within the city limits – here referred to as the market performance.

In the next stage of the analysis the sales potential is compared to the existing (1985) retail facilities by means of an inventory of the total square footage of food retailing in the community. It is assumed that the facilities are adequate for the present level of demand and can handle an additional 5 per cent increase in sales every five years. In 1990, existing food retailers could satisfy a market size of $56,000,000 but the town is projected to have a retail food sales potential of $60,000,000: a residual vacuum of $4,487,000 in food sales will be available. If new food retailers perform at the industry average – $300 per square foot in 1990 – an additional 15,000 square feet of food retailing space is required. The retailer then must decide whether this projected vacuum is sufficiently large to risk entry into the market.

As we saw in the last chapter, many site selection models treat trade areas as spatial monopolies. The location of each existing or proposed outlet site defines a trade area – a Thiessen polygon, perhaps, or simply the region defined by a 2-mile boundary or some other arbitrary rule. The characteristics of these trade areas, when compared to store performance, provide a valuable input to the site selection model by giving the chain a sense of the limits on potential sales at the site. No manager can be expected to extract more sales than the trade area will generate and it is clear that the sales potentials of different locations vary widely.

## Market penetration

The spatial monopoly approach to trade areas is frequently used in selecting sites for new stores and for modeling the evolution of a system of chain locations. A market penetration approach, on the other hand, is more relevant to a single operating retail outlet that wishes to increase its sales, either by extending its trade area in space or by attracting a greater proportion of households within the existing trade area. The procedures to be discussed in this section focus on the proportion of customers within a given neighborhood who deal with the store or shopping center, i.e. the outlet's market penetration.

These analyses require two kinds of data: first, a list of customers that can be allocated to residential areas, and second, for the same set of spatial units, reference information on the total number of potential households or customers. In some instances the actual level of retail sales per neighborhood and potential sales are substituted, respectively. Data on customers and/or sales are obtained by sampling sales slips, conducting in-store raffles, or interviewing customers at the store. In the latter case customers are asked for their address or Zip code and information concerning their demographics, shopping behavior and attitudes, and travel patterns. The method of mapping these customers as points (see Figure 11.6a) is called 'customer spotting' (Applebaum, 1968). In itself, the resulting map tells us a great deal about how far customers will travel to this facility and (if other information is plotted) the effects of competing retail facilities, non-residential land uses, and travel barriers. For example, the irregular distribution of customers on this map reflects non-residential land uses and open space. (See also Exhibit 8.4.) A customer-spotting program permits management to assess the performance and impact of a new store, to diagnose a problem store, or to examine the effect on a store of a major change in its marketing environment – such as a new competitor.

The customer-spotting map is more useful if it is adjusted to take into consideration the variation in household density across the metropolitan region. Data on the number of households are available for census tracts at ten-year intervals (*Census of Population*), and are estimated for Zip code areas on an annual basis by market research firms (e.g. Figure 11.5). This information may be further updated by the local planning agency. The number of households provides the denominator that converts a map of customer locations into a map of market penetration (Figure 11.6b).

Customer spotting leads easily into the delimitation of the primary trade area and the evaluation of penetration rates within it. The area around the store is divided into a series of geographical zones. For supermarkets Applebaum suggested that the most effective system is $\frac{1}{4}$-mile grids, but for shopping goods, census tracts or even Zip codes may be more appropriate. The grid system is placed over the customer-spotting map and the number of customers in each grid cell is counted. Dividing this number by the total number of households in the grid cell generates a map of market penetration.

In a variant of this procedure, the analyst estimates the sales per grid cell in the following manner: total store sales = \$500,000 (for example); the

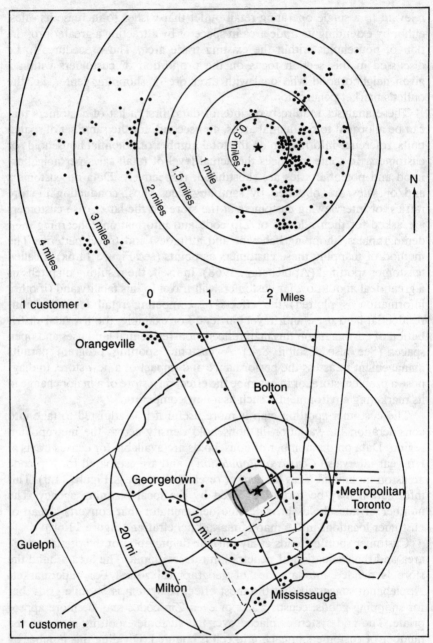

*Note:* Upper diagram represents enlargement of shaded area in lower map.

**Figure 11.6** Customer spotting, market penetration and primary trade areas for a regional shopping center
(a) Customer spotting

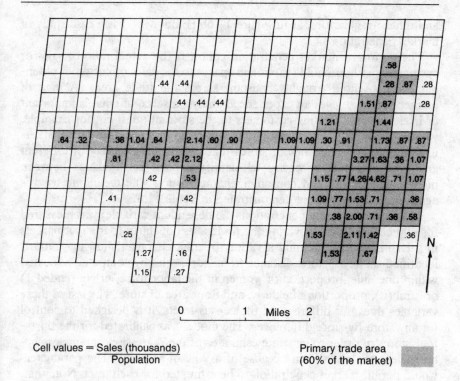

Cell values = Sales (thousands) / Population

Primary trade area
(60% of the market)

**Figure 11.6** (*continued*)
(b) Primary trade area

*Source:* K.G. Jones and D.R. Mock (1984) 'Evaluating retail trading performance', in R.L. Davies and D.S. Rogers (eds) *Store Location and Store Assessment Research*, Chichester: John Wiley and Sons. Reproduced by permission of the publisher

share of sales from grid cell i is equal to number of customers$_i$/total customers in sample. Thus, sales in cell i = \$500,000 × customers$_i$/total customers.

From this value it is possible to estimate the sales per household in each cell. Sales per household is another way of describing the variation in market penetration across the trade area. Usually the market penetration is highest near the store and declines irregularly with distance. Some analysts generalize this pattern into two zones: the primary and secondary trade areas. The primary trade area is obtained by ranking the grid cells according to penetration rate and then aggregating them until 60 per cent of the customers are included. These high-penetration cells make up the primary trade area. The secondary trade area includes the next 25 per cent of customers. Needless to say, the boundary lines for these trade areas are not precise and can be smoothed and adjusted to reflect topography, land use,

357

and other irregularities, as in Figure 11.6b (Exhibit 11.1 is a case study of market penetration.)

The notion of market penetration contrasts the actual ratio of sales or customers per household (varying in space) to the sales or customer potential per household (roughly constant across the trade area). A map of market potential gives an experienced analyst a sense of what is important or irrelevant in attracting customers to the store in question; for example, what is the impact of competition? However, in order to develop a marketing strategy for a network of stores that operate in a variety of different environments, it is necessary to identify explicit relationships between market penetration and consumer characteristics. The technique used is again multiple regression, demonstrated in Table 11.3.

In this study, market penetration (the dependent variable) was measured for 400 census tracts, covering the trade areas of thirty-four supermarkets in a chain. After examining a variety of tract characteristics, the authors identified six key factors: distance from store, sales by competitors located within one mile, proportion of women in the labor force, urban (coded 1) or rural (0), proportion of elderly, and floor area of store. The last of these variables does not differentiate the census tracts, it is designed to control for any store-by-store differences. The model was calibrated for the thirty-four stores in order to generate estimates of the regression parameters $b_0$–$b_6$. (These are not shown because of a vow of secrecy!) The parameters would permit market penetration to be estimated for each tract. Note that, whereas the site selection models use store sales as observations and

## Exhibit 11.1
### A CASE STUDY OF MARKET PENETRATION

A Toronto men's tailor had two stores, one at either end of the city. Arguing that tailoring is a highly specialized service, with a high degree of consumer loyalty, the tailor decided to close the east end store. He hoped that his east end customers would seek out the west end shop.

The tailor's customer records permit an evaluation of the move by means of customer spotting. The first map (a) shows the primary and secondary trade areas of the east end store before the decision to close. The second map (b) displays a measure of customer loyalty – the proportion of east end customers who shifted their patronage to the west end store. Their loyalty appears to be overwhelmed by a strong distance decay effect. Less than one-third of them made the change. The third map (c) describes the pattern of market penetration for the west end store after the move. The tailor is now reconsidering his decision.

*Source:* K.G. Jones and D.R. Mock (1984) 'Evaluating retail trading performance', in R.L. Davies and D.S. Rogers (eds) *Store Location and Store Assessment Research*, Chichester: John Wiley and Sons.
Reproduced by permission of the publisher

Exhibit 11.1 (*continued*)

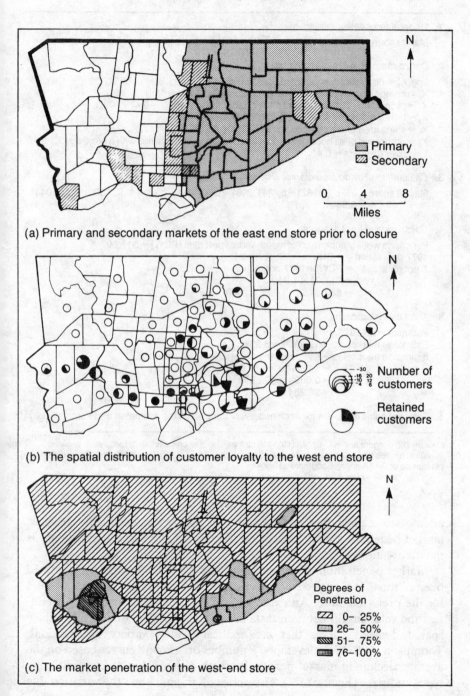

(a) Primary and secondary markets of the east end store prior to closure

(b) The spatial distribution of customer loyalty to the west end store

(c) The market penetration of the west-end store

**Table 11.3** A regression model of market penetration

1. *General forecasting model:*

    Market share $= b_0 - b_1(\log_e X_1) - b_2(X_2) - b_3(X_3) - b_4(X_4) + b_5(X_5) + b_6(X_6)$.

2. *Data example:*

    $\log_e X_1 =$ distance from center of tract to the site $= \log_e(1.3) = 0.26$;
    $X_2 =$ competitor sales within 1 mile of tract $= \$341,000$;
    $X_3 =$ proportion of females aged 14 + in labor force in 1970 $= 0.479$;
    $X_4 =$ urban $= 1$; surburban $= 0$;
    $X_5 =$ sales area of the planned store $= 22,000$ sq. ft;
    $X_6 =$ proportion of all households that are husband–wife families with a head aged
    over 65 years $= 0.41$.

3. *Calculation of trade area market share:*

    Market share $= a - b_1(0.262) - b_2(341,000) - b_3(0.479) - b_4(0) + b_5(22,000) + b_6(0.041)$
    $= 6.99\%$.

4. *Calculation of tract potential:*

    Per capita weekly supermarket merchandise potential (PCW) $= \$17.09$
    1977 population $= 1,912$,
    Tract potential $=$ PCW $\times$ 1977 population
    $= \$17.09 \times 1,912$
    $= \$32,676$.

5. *Tract sales forecast:*

    Potential $= \$32,676$,
    Estimated market share (step 3) $= 6.99\%$,
    Estimated tract sales $=$ estimated market share/100 $\times$ potential
    $= 6.99/100 \times \$32,676$
    $= 0.0699 \times \$32,676$
    $= \$2,284$.

6. Total the sales forecasts for each and every tract within the estimated trade area.

*Source:* D.S. Rogers and H.L. Green (1979) 'A new perspective on forecasting food sales: applying statistical models and techniques in the analog approach', *Geographical Review* 69: 457. Reproduced by permission of the American Geographical Society

attempt to explain them with trade area data as independent variables, market penetration models focus on the sales of trade area components as the observations.

Market penetration, when multiplied by market potential and summed over all tracts in a projected trade area, provides a precise estimate of sales for the projected store. An extensive literature on retail 'analogs' generalizes the relationship between distance and market penetration to produce spatial demand curves that are applicable in a variety of situations. Thompson (1982) has developed a number of 'normal' curves based on the average decline in market penetration with distance for stores of differing types and sizes (Figure 11.7). This series of graphs shows the variation due

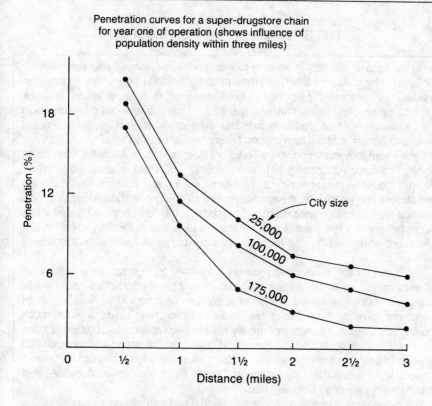

Penetration curves for a super-drugstore chain
for year one of operation (shows influence of
population density within three miles)

Figure 11.7 The analog approach: market penetration and distance

Source: J.S. Thompson (1982) Site Selection, New York: Lebhar-Friedman Books. Reproduced by permission of the publisher

to population size of the city – from 25,000 to 175,000 people. For a particular new site an experienced analyst may further adjust the curve upwards or downwards to compensate for the effect of competition.

Exhibit 11.2 describes the use of the spatial interaction model in determining the relative importance of various store characteristics for attracting customers.

## Dispersed markets

As individual retailers, chains, and even shopping centers try to sharpen the specialization of product mix to suit a specific consumer lifestyle, the spatial structure of their trade area and the pattern of market penetration becomes more and more irregular. Customers are found in a wide variety of locations and concentrations. At the extreme, a small store specializing

## Exhibit 11.2
## THE SPATIAL INTERACTION MODEL

Retail analysts would like to be able to incorporate the various characteristics of each particular outlet in a chain into their models of market penetration. If they can evaluate the customer's response to such things as an in-store bakery, a snack bar, or a better parking lot, they can make better decisions about investments in store improvements or product mix. In the terminology of retail consultants, what is the 'hot button' that will turn around the performance of a store?

One means of exploring these relationships is to use a spatial interaction model. The basic relationship between customer and store is assumed to follow the Huff model as presented in Chapter nine: customer trips from neighborhood i to store j are related to the attractiveness of the store (positively), and the distance from the store (negatively). The model combines both the site selection model (where are the sales?) and the market penetration model (where do the customers come from?), so it requires considerably more data than either one of them.

The value of the model depends on the ability to incorporate a number of different measures of store attractiveness. In the spatial interaction model actual data about customer flow patterns to a number of stores (i.e. the number of customers traveling from i to j) are obtained from credit cards or some such source, and used to estimate statistically the relative importance of different store characteristics in attracting customers. If there are nineteen stores and 200 neighborhoods (census tracts) in the city, what variations among the stores account for the observed patronage patterns? Floor area differences? Age of store? Parking spaces? Opening hours?

The development of regression methods that use nominal data (measures like Black, manager, apartment, instead of per cent Black, per cent white-collar, etc.) permits analysts to use the wealth of data available for individual consumers, as opposed to census tracts. The consumer's decision to use one center rather than another will depend jointly on the characteristics of the individuals and the characteristics of the centers.

Research of this type identifies the central issues in developing a marketing strategy, but the statistical procedures push against the very margins of statistical reliability (see the discussion in Ghosh and McLafferty, 1987; Chapter five). Each store has a unique location within the city, and relative to its competitors, so that it is difficult to sort out the additional effect of its mix of services. The solution may require the addition of information for different time periods to permit 'before and after' comparisons of innovations. Given information about sales per store over time for a network of outlets (or even customer flows over time), a chain should be able to evaluate the impact of some external event, such as the opening of a competing store.

in Dungeons and Dragons paraphernalia may attract a certain type of intense teenager from all over the metropolitan region. Other stores find themselves specializing in one or two lines of furniture, a narrow selection of books, or serving an ethnic group that is widely scattered – Finns, Australians, Filipinos.

How can such a market be targeted in order to reach new customers and expand sales? The distance decay relationship is weak, the customers are widely dispersed in space, yet such a specialized activity must attract distinctive types of households. Surely the level of market penetration varies sufficiently to make some districts more promising than others? This problem is also faced by firms that are entering a market for the first time: how can they identify the most promising market areas?

The process of targeting markets begins with the customer profile of the store: age, income, ethnicity, lifestyle. What does the product (e.g. European ski equipment), the retailer's previous experience (in other cities or similar kinds of chains), or behavioral research tell us?

Given the target customer profile, the analyst goes back to the file of census tract of Zip code information used in developing a market profile and asks which locations have the greatest concentration of people with the desired characteristics. Different firms or individuals define their priorities for social environments – be they jewel thieves, ethnic food stores, or aggressive singles. The example in Figure 11.8 describes how a direct mail firm could identify potential customers in Albuquerque. The target is older Hispanic households with above average income – for a travel promotion. Using a Zip code data compilation by CACI, Inc., we look at the distribution of values on three variables over seventy-four Zip codes. The variables are the percentage of Hispanics in 1980, median household income in $1984 dollars, and median age in 1984. The distributions suggest an initial cutoff point at 30 per cent, $20,000, and 28 years, respectively. The maps show the distribution of Zip codes that qualify on each variable, including about half the codes in each case. However, only three of the seventy-four Zip codes share all high values on all three indicators. By manipulating the cutoff points for each variable, we can designate as many 'target' Zip codes as we desire.

Marketing research companies have developed procedures for identifying the spatial distribution of these target markets at the local level. One widely used form of analysis is shown in Table 11.4. The PRIZM approach (developed by the Claritas Corporation) sorts out all the 35,000 postal Zip code areas across the United States on the basis of a large number of census measures (city size, age, income, education, ethnicity, family structure, etc.). The aim is to identify clusters of Zip code areas that have similar characteristics (and give them catchy identifiers) and then to evaluate the clusters in terms of marketing behavior. Which clusters read *Time* magazine? Watch educational TV? Give to charities? Vote

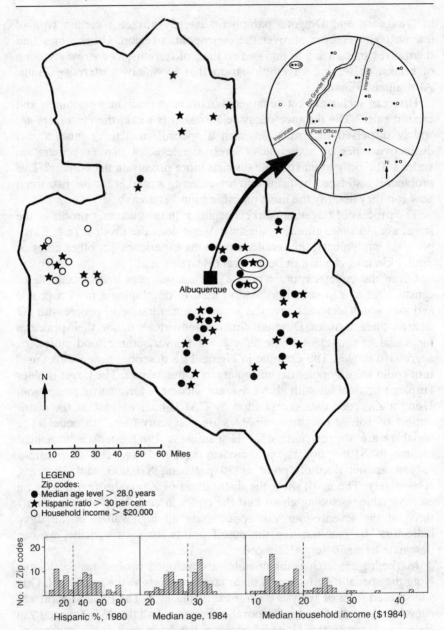

**Figure 11.8** Target marketing: Albuquerque

*Source:* CACI, Inc. (annual) *The 1984 Sourcebook for Demographics and Power for Every Zip Code in the USA*

**Table 11.4** Lifestyles from census data

| Exemplar Zip clusters | | Selected demographic variables | | | | | | Indices of audience concentration for selected national magazines | | | | | | Consumption patterns | | | | | |
|---|---|---|---|---|---|---|---|---|---|---|---|---|---|---|---|---|---|---|---|
| | | Socio-economic | | Occupations | | Ethnicity | | General interest | | Male interest | | Female interest | | | | | | Automobiles (1) | |
| Cluster number | Nicknames | $50K + income | 4 + Years college | Percent-age prof. managers | Percent-age farm labor | Percent-age pop. Black | Percent-age foreign stock | Readers Digest | Time | Playboy | Field & Stream | Cosmo-politan | Ladies Home Journal | CB radios | Outdoor power tool | Total personal loans | Total compacts | European luxury |
| 1 | God's Country | 138 | 164 | 134 | 117 | 5 | 85 | 125 | 130 | 122 | 136 | 104 | 110 | 167 | 213 | 117 | 105 | 176 |
| 3 | Old Melting Pot | 78 | 66 | 83 | 8 | 125 | 284 | 72 | 93 | 88 | 34 | 121 | 77 | 32 | 1 | 40 | 74 | 54 |
| 11 | Dixie-Style Tenements | 33 | 64 | 66 | 50 | 415 | 79 | 68 | 80 | 67 | 70 | 71 | 81 | 24 | 10 | 72 | 54 | 19 |
| 23 | Bunker's Neighbors | 113 | 107 | 109 | 17 | 60 | 161 | 94 | 134 | 125 | 85 | 128 | 105 | 54 | 18 | 85 | 108 | 147 |
| 28 | Blue Blood Estates | 920 | 406 | 244 | 17 | 9 | 150 | 95 | 278 | 87 | 46 | 108 | 108 | 69 | 35 | 90 | 138 | 813 |
| 29 | Coalburg and Corntown | 50 | 64 | 79 | 117 | 23 | 58 | 114 | 82 | 62 | 176 | 108 | 85 | 147 | 277 | 119 | 106 | 55 |
| 37 | Bohemian Mix | 114 | 191 | 140 | 8 | 316 | 176 | 69 | 172 | 232 | 21 | 106 | 74 | 7 | 3 | 45 | 29 | 156 |
| 38 | Share Croppers | 26 | 36 | 59 | 442 | 169 | 22 | 106 | 44 | 50 | 143 | 56 | 119 | 110 | 181 | 72 | 50 | 12 |

*Source:* Claritas Corporation (1980). Reproduced by permission

*Note:* US average = 100

Republican? Listen to country music? Buy Volvos? Use credit cards? CACI, another market research firm, bases its clusters on a smaller spatial unit – the 260,000 census enumeration districts across the country – but the applications are the same.

As the market research firm adds clients and customer lists, the clusters gain meaning, and the firm's ability to fine-tune the projection of consumer behavior improves. Consultants are quick to apply the experience of one firm to the problems of the next – another version of the analog approach. A distinctive store or chain bears some relation to another store for which a spatial pattern or model has been previously developed. 'Dungeons and Dragons' customers may be compared to a mix of *Mad Magazine* subscribers and the customer list of an adult games store. Any neighborhood that gives money to the Heart Fund is likely to donate to the Arthritis Foundation and will be deluged with mailed requests from every medical charity in the country. A firm can spend thousands of dollars developing a target market analysis tailored to a particular enterprise, or adapt a more general model and spend the money saved on more advertising flyers or media time. (Exhibit 11.3 examines the methods used to tailor a product to a specific market.)

An important application of lifestyle groups to marketing strategy occurs in the use of the media. Marketing consultants build up a file of relationships between market characteristics, customer locations, and the media (see Table 11.4 again). A Mercedes dealer who wants to reach the 'blue-blood estates' cluster will advertise in *Time* rather than the *Reader's Digest*. If Chain C or product F has the highest penetration in blue-collar Black districts and newspaper J has a similar penetration pattern, the marketing strategy is simple: advertise in newspaper J.

Lifestyle groups can thus be treated as distinctive types of consumers. In one approach, the analyst creates a profile of lifestyle groups within a given region or trade area, moving easily from location to customer mix. Conversely, given a consumer profile in terms of lifestyle groups – perhaps from another store or even another part of the country – the analyst can quickly target the most appropriate locations locally, or debate the pros and cons of redefining the store's customer profile. (Exhibit 11.4 describes the use of Zip codes and census tracts in market research, i.e. to identify areas containing certain lifestyle groups.)

It may well be that the use of spatial aggregations of consumers for market analysis will be outdated within a few years by the explosion in data systems. Market research firms are rapidly compiling and categorizing lists of all households in the country (at least all those that are serious consumers). Start with a telephone directory, add credit card information or automobile registrations, throw in assorted mailing lists from publications and charitable organizations and they will know who you are, how old you are, how old your car is, and what you drive. The chances are that there

## Exhibit 11.3
## TAILORING THE PRODUCT TO THE MARKET

The importance of the techniques of trade area analysis seems likely to increase as national manufacturers, as well as retail chains, explore ways of differentiating products to fit various market segments. For each product – be it automobiles, frozen dinners, or lingerie – what are the significant patterns of variation in sales? Are the taste patterns regional; should they use more spices in the south-west? Or ethnic; which group responds to chrome? Or are preferences class- or age-linked; what kind of Americans like the taste or color of avocado? Concerns like these reflect the intensification of competition among major companies. They have turned their attention to the market niches occupied by smaller regional firms. This strategy is made possible by new technologies that permit shorter production runs, more precise inventory management, and the detailed monitoring of consumer buying patterns.

The manufacturer can target a market segment in at least three ways: the best developed procedure – one that seems likely to accelerate in the future – is to disaggregate and decentralize advertising campaigns by taking advantage of local media and interest group television channels to focus on the qualities of the product that appeal to different market segments. The average household in North America now has access to thirty different television channels. Who watches what? You can sell an Oldsmobile to a truck-driver or a school-teacher, but you may want to use a different sales pitch. Each member of the household now relates to different communications media and sources. Several different television channels or radio stations may be turned on simultaneously.

Both retail chains and manufacturers are developing greater expertise in inventory monitoring to adapt product mix to regional market segments. What colors do Hispanics or Asian Americans wear? What size ranges? Styles? What's the appropriate mix of men's shirts for a store outlet in Kansas City? Is it the same mix that you shipped to Boston six months earlier?

The major re-orientation toward market segmentation is taking place in product design. Campbell's Soup and other food manufacturers are trying to expand the market for their products by exploring the preferences of consumers who reject the bland 'American' taste of mass consumption. How many variations of tomato soup are profitable, given the battle for supermarket shelf space? With basil? Chili? Oregano? Soy Sauce?

Thousand and thousands of products are involved, and all the techniques of studying consumer behavior will be needed: studies of product preference, the monitoring of consumer purchases, and the spatial analysis of market segments. It is the latter that is significant for spatial analyists, since the market for their expertise is extended enormously.

## Exhibit 11.4
## ZIP CODES AND CENSUS TRACTS

Over the last century the Bureau of the Census has developed a complete set of spatial units for description and analysis: for example, the metropolitan statistical area describes the functioning city, the census tract identifies a neighborhood, and the enumeration area or block provides the basis for aggregating spatial units of any size or shape.

While these spatial units have been rigorously defined and are quite satisfactory for academic research, market researchers found that Zip code areas, as introduced by the US Postal Service, were more useful. All sorts of data files containing addresses of customers or competitors were already coded into Zip addresses; mailings to different target groups could be specified by Zip codes, and customers who were approached in 'spotting' studies would more readily reveal their Zip code than their actual address.

A substantial market developed for census data re-organized into Zip areas, and/or extended using other public or private data sets that include Zip addresses – such as automobile registrations, income tax returns, business directories. It is now possible to obtain a wide spectrum of information and forecasts for each Zip code area, and, as shown in the PRIZM example (Table 11.4), these units have also become the building blocks for sophisticated multivariate analyses.

**Fort Myers area census tracts**

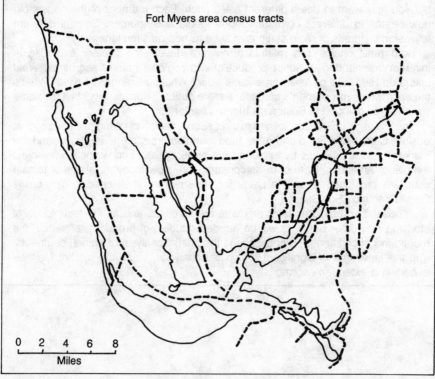

0　2　4　6　8
Miles

However, the Zip codes are imperfect spatial units. They were designed to be functional administrative units for the postal service. Their size and shape reflect the amount of mail delivered in each area and the layout of delivery routes. In large cities they describe business geography with small Zips for downtown offices. In small cities, like Fort Myers, Zip codes approach equal area units while census tracts contain equal populations. Zip codes are large, averaging 10,000 persons, two and a half times the average population of a tract, and too large for many trade area studies. Their numbers and their boundaries evolve over time in patterns that are not always consistent, nor well recorded.

However, they are improving. The Bureau of the Census now provides aggregations of census data to Zip codes, plus information about the boundaries. The familiar five-digit Zip codes are being extended to include another four digits (Zip + 4), providing units that are as small as a single block front or apartment building. As this process is completed, any such address can be instantly translated into a variety of census contexts. The market analyst assigns to the consumer all the characteristics of the neighborhood in which the person lives: if you live at 64 Bellwood Avenue you are assumed to be a White, blue-collar homeowner, and your presence at such and such a shopping mall or on a certain mailing list is so interpreted. The more precise the Zip address, the more homogeneous the resident population, and the more accurate this labeling process becomes.

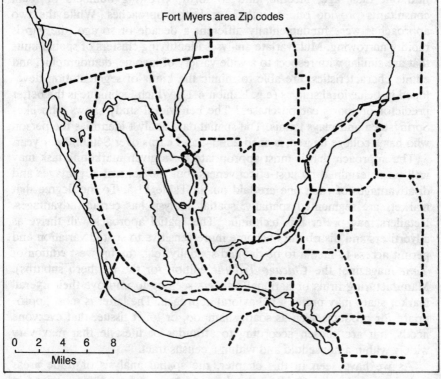

Fort Myers area Zip codes

0 2 4 6 8
Miles

*Source:* The authors

will be an automobile or insurance salesman knocking on your door just about the time you are ready to buy.

Widely dispersed markets are characterized by very shallow distance decay curves, so that store location is not particularly important. Activities serving such markets are likely to be oriented less to the spatial distribution of their customers than to the overall accessibility patterns of the city. 'Dungeons and Dragons' fans use public transit or bicycles, Club Med customers have sports cars.

The study of dispersed markets has also benefited from development of statistical models and computer-based data sets. Regression models of market penetration for trade areas are readily applied to dispersed markets. Only the distance variables are omitted. It is also possible to calculate various measures of centrality relative to the dispersed market, using spatial statistics. Just as in location-allocation techniques (discussed in Chapter ten), retailers may wish to identify the single most central location relative to this set of customers in terms of distance or travel time.

Analyses that use the household's neighborhood as a means of identifying household characteristics and target markets may be contrasted to a variety of behavioral techniques that survey customers directly, in order to find out their age, income, and so forth. Growing numbers of retail consultants provide one or other, or both approaches. While the two approaches were fundamentally different a decade or so ago, the gap is rapidly narrowing. Multivariate analyses identifying clusters of spatial units that are similar with respect to a wide variety of income, demographic, and ethnic characteristics, are able to mimic the kinds of segmentation developed in behavioral studies (e.g. Exhibit 4.1). Which technique is the better predictor of sports car purchases? The behavioral study shows who likes Springsteen and plays tennis. The spatial data analyst identifies the person who has a college degree, is aged 25–34, and earns over $40,000 per year.

The approach that is most appropriate for a given marketing task may well be determined by cost-effectiveness, but the general advantages and disadvantages of each one are laid out in Table 11.5. To the degree that markets are segmented spatially, spatial analysis has certain advantages. Retailers may prefer this technique. The spatial approach will thrive as advertisers and distributors become more sensitive to spatial variation and permit access to media to be defined spatially (e.g. the far west edition of *Time* magazine; the *Chicago Tribune* edition for the northern suburbs). Manufacturing firms or national retailers seeking to improve their overall market share may prefer a behavioral approach. The latter is most appropriate for products such as soap, shampoo, or toilet tissue, that everyone needs, but are chosen according to attitudes or lifestyle that may vary widely within a household and within a census tract.

As we have seen in this chapter, the spatial analysis of trade areas includes a wide variety of approaches and techniques, as summarized in

Exhibit 11.5
PRIORITIES IN LOCATION RESEARCH

---

Tesco, a major British supermarket chain, employs twenty-five people to choose and evaluate potential store locations. They are concerned with the entire process of gathering and analyzing information about store performance and locations. These are their priorities for the analysis group:

(1) *Accuracy*: Estimates must lie within 10 per cent of outlet sales figures over the first three years of operation.
(2) *Timeliness*: Data for any given site to be provided within five working days.
(3) *Volume*: The group must be able to handle 300 evaluations per year.
(4) *Intuitively Sound*: The models must have an internal logic that is acceptable to management. They reject models that they can't understand.
(5) *Monitoring*: The system must provide evaluation and feedback about earlier estimates and decisions.
(6) *Flexibility*: The models must have the capacity to evaluate several alternative store formats – stores of different sizes, plus strategic options such as additions, closures, etc.

---

*Source:* N.J. Penny and D. Broom (1988) 'The Tesco approach to store location',
in N. Wrigley (ed.) *Store Choice, Store Location and Market Analysis*, London: Routledge

Table 11.6. The costs and the kinds of product generated also cover a wide range. Each procedure is appropriate for a certain kind of retail chain, at a certain stage in its life-cycle, and with a certain kind of marketing problem.

### Estimating trade area population

Once the spatial extent of the trade area is measured, the analyst's attention shifts towards the determination of market potential – i.e. buying power – both now and in the future. The key variable in linking the trade area to the actual level of sales is the number and income level of households within the market area. To project the level of sales into the future, then, requires a projection of the number and type of households. In this section we apply the ideas about forecasting, raised in Chapter nine, to a particular issue, i.e. the prediction of trade area sales five to ten years on.

Most forecasts begin with a time series of information on population levels at earlier points in time. These data indicate (1) the present population, (2) the trend or pattern of change over time, and (3) the degree of variability in this trend caused by difficulties of measurement or unexpected events. The three main sources of population information at the trade area level are compared in Table 11.7.

**Table 11.5** Spatial analysis or behavioral analysis?

|  | Spatial | Behavioral |
|---|---|---|
| Technique | Customer list → market penetration → customer characteristics → target locations | Telephone book or customer list → sample interviews → customer characteristics |
| Cost | Approximately $100,000 + for a national model | Approximately $10,000 for 1,000 interviews |
| Common | Information on income, demographics, ethnicity of customers as input to marketing strategy. Permits identification of appropriate media | |
| Advantages | Explicit spatial input → location decisions → spatial target markets → store investment decisions | Wide open attitudinal data → product image, simulation of alternatives → competitor profiles |
| Disadvantages | Limited to census variables. No attitudinal or lifestyle measures (though the Zip-code clusters approach → a lifestyle alternative) | Requires additional spatial analysis to locate markets or plan distribution strategy |
| Who uses? | Retail chains concerned with location decisions | Manufacturers or retailers serving national markets, using national media |

*Source:* The authors

**Table 11.6** Comparing trade area studies

| Technique | Cost ($) | Expertise | Product | Type of chain |
|---|---|---|---|---|
| *Spatial monopoly* | | | | |
| Fixed radius, Thiessen polygons | 1,000 | Minimal | Market size, profile | Convenience stores |
| Vacuum method | 30,000 | Experienced | Forecasts market opportunity | Supermarkets, department stores, large outlets |
| *Market penetration* | | | | |
| Customer spotting | 10,000 | Experienced | Primary, secondary trade areas | Supermarkets, plazas, and other large outlets |
| 'Normal' curves | 5,000 | Experienced | Market penetration by distance | Supermarkets, plazas and other large outlets, especially 'standard' retailers |
| Regression models | 100,000 | Experienced location analyst | Penetration by distance: household characteristics | Multiple outlet chains with 'cookie-cutter' stores |
| *Dispersed market* | | | | |
| Developing a customer profile | 10,000 | Experienced | Penetration rates by household characteristics | Specialized retailers |
| Identifying a target market | 10,000 | Experienced | Map of potential customers | Specialized retailers |

*Source:* The authors

**Table 11.7** Sources of data for trade area forecasts

| | Spatial units | Data-gathering agency | Frequency | Length of time series | Variables |
|---|---|---|---|---|---|
| Census | (1) City blocks: up to 500 people<br>(2) Census tracts: up to 10,000 people | Bureau of the Census | 10 years; 1980, 1990, etc. | From 1910 | Population, household composition, ethnicity, income |
| Postal<br>Zip code | Zip code area: variable in size, up to 60,000 people | Market research firms | Annual estimates and forecasts | Since the 1970s | Population, income |
| Local government | Governmental units, planning areas, possibly other units | Local planning departments | Annual, from real estate tax records or ground survey | Will vary widely | Demographics, housing, property values |

*Source:* The authors

The Bureau of the Census has subdivided the built-up areas of most American metropolitan areas into census tracts of 5,000–8,000 people (2,000–4,000 households). Population and household totals are published on this scale every ten years, along with data on income, age structure, and ethnicity. Where necessary (especially in smaller centers), the same information is available in special tabulations for groups of city blocks (about 500 persons). Census tracts are oriented to residential populations and usually mark out recognizable neighborhoods.

The Zip code areas (see Exhibit 11.4), because of the activities of market analysis firms, provide more up-to-date information on the number and income level of households, although they may be awkward units for spatial analysis because they are large (up to 5,000 households) and designed for mail delivery. As a result they are often too small in the center of the city where business mail is heavy, and too large in residential areas. Also, the postal service frequently changes the boundaries. None the less, a number of private data-providing firms provide annual estimates and forecasts of population and income at this spatial scale, using data compiled from other governmental agencies – federal (income tax), state (auto registrations), and municipal (tax rolls, school enrolment). At a price they can also provide estimates for other, smaller spatial units within a Zip code area.

A third possible source of information is the local municipality or planning agency, which may obtain annual estimates of population from the tax assessment process, or from building permits and school records. While the data are less precise than the Census, they may be much more up-to-date. Not all municipalities provide this information and, because of changes in the definitions of spatial units, there is no guarantee that a time series can be assembled.

Obviously the researcher must make some trade-offs between accuracy and consistency (Bureau of the Census), cost (a market analysis firm), and up-to-date estimates based on local conditions (planning agencies). If the trade area is growing rapidly the analyst may emphasize recent estimates of size over older measures of household characteristics. In a more stable neighborhood, the longer time trend provided by the census may be useful. If a number of alternative markets are under consideration, it may prove worthwhile to purchase data from one or more market research firms.

No matter what data set is used, the spatial units must be adjusted to the trade area boundary by referring to planning maps that show land use and built-up areas, or by carrying out field work. (How many blocks in this census tract are excluded from the trade area?) The map in Figure 11.9 indicates the three essential components: the trade area boundary, which is assumed to be fixed over time, the pattern of non-residential land uses that are unlikely to be converted into housing, and the set of spatial units (census tracts or Zip codes) that cover the trade area.

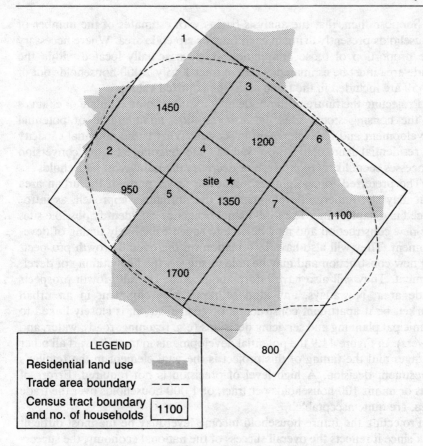

| Tracts | 1980 households | (Adjusted) | Estimated change 1980–1990 | 1990 households (projected) |
|---|---|---|---|---|
| 1 | 1,450 | 1,000 | −50 | 950 |
| 2 | 950 | 600 | +100 | 700 |
| 3 | 1,200 | 1,200 | +300 | 1,500 |
| 4 | 1,350 | 1,350 | +150 | 1,500 |
| 5 | 1,700 | 1,700 | −100 | 1,600 |
| 6 | 1,100 | 1,000 | +400 | 1,400 |
| 7 | 800 | 750 | +2,250 | 3,000 |
| Trade area | 8,550 | 7,600 | +3,050 | 10,650 |

**Figure 11.9** Estimating trade area population

*Source:* The authors

Suppose then, that the analysis begins with estimates of the number of households presently living in each tract or zip code area. Where necessary the proportion of those households which is actually located within the trade area must be estimated. Thus, in tract 1 only 1,000 households out of 1,450 are included in the trade area (the adjusted value).

Projecting the future of the trade area requires some estimate of changes in the housing stock. This, in turn, requires an appraisal of potential development and redevelopment processes. What is the potential capacity of residential land that is now vacant? Do ongoing housing conversion processes seem likely to increase or decrease the number of households?

The preferred forecasting technique for those parts of the urban area that may still undergo development is the normative approach, as introduced in Chapter nine. The local planning agency can identify possible sites for new construction and may be able to suggest the likely timing of development. They will also have information on the overall growth prospects for new construction and may be able to suggest the likely timing of development. They will also have information on the overall growth prospects trade area. Nowadays, any kind of rapid redevelopment in an urban market, be it apartment construction or gentrification, is closely linked to municipal planning and servicing decisions (e.g. rezoning, roads, water, and sewers). In Figure 11.9 the potential developments in tract 7 dwarf all other changes and the timing of this project is the vital element in the retailer's investment decision. A high level of precision is not required. Errors of plus or minus 100 households per tract, or 1,000 households over the trade area, are quite acceptable.

Projecting the future household income level may be the most difficult task since it reflects the overall success of the national economy, the success of the local economy relative to all other urban areas (see Table 2.1), and any shifts within the local community. Sometimes, a decline in local property values (hence income level of residents) is due to the construction of large amounts of competing housing elsewhere.

Still, most neighborhoods do not change their social status very quickly. The ten year census provides an estimate of average income per household, and the ratio of average income in a particular tract to the metropolitan area average is reasonably stable over time. Annual estimates of metropolitan area income are published by the National Revenue Service (about two years later). One can also rely on the close relationship between housing prices or rental levels and income. Households tend to buy property with three or four times their annual income. A $200,000 home suggests an income of $50,000; $400 apartments are rented to people earning $1,500 per month or $18,000 per year. The local real estate agent can be more precise. The stability in income levels is based on the relative inflexibility of the existing housing stock: large houses are found in well-to-do areas while poorer neighborhoods have walk-up apartments. Income levels are most likely to change when the housing stock changes significantly.

## Further reading

Applebaum, W. (1968) *A Guide to Store Location Research*, Reading, Massachusetts: Addison-Wesley.

Epstein, B.J. (1984) 'Market appraisals', in R.L. Davies and D.S. Rogers (eds) *Store Location and Assessment Research*, New York: John Wiley & Sons.

Flowerdew, R. and Goldstein, W. (1989) 'Geodemographics in practice: developments in North America', *Environment and Planning, A,* 21, 5, 605–17.

Fotheringham, A.S. (1988) 'Market share analysis techniques: a review and illustration of current US practice', in N. Wrigley (ed) *Store Choice, Store Location and Market Analysis*, London: Routledge.

Ghosh, A. and McLafferty, S. (1987) *Location Strategies for Retail and Service Firms*, Chapter 5, 'Spatial-interaction models', Lexington, Massachusetts: D.C. Heath.

Haggblom, D. (1985) 'Directory of micro computer products for demographic analysis', *American Demographics* 7, 3: 28–35; plus subsequent surveys in this journal.

Jones, K.G. and Mock, D.R. (1984) 'Evaluating retail trading performance', in R.L. Davies and D.S. Rogers (eds) *Store Location and Store Assessment Research*, New York: John Wiley & Sons.

Houston, F.S. and Stanton, J. (1984) 'Evaluating retail trade areas for convenience stores', *Journal of Retailing* 60: 124–36.

Lord, J.D. and Lynds, C.D. (1984) 'Market area planning strategy: an example of interstate banking markets in USA', *Geojournal* 9, 2: 145–54.

Roca, R.A. (ed) (1980) *Market Research for Shopping Centers*, New York: International Council of Shopping Centers.

Rogers, D.S. and Green, H. (1978) 'A new perspective in forecasting store sales: applying statistical models in the analog approach', *Geographical Review* 69, 4: 449–58.

Thompson, J.S. (1982) *Site Selection*, New York: Lebhar-Friedman.

Weinstein, A. (1987) *Market Segmentation*, Chicago: Prohus.

Weisbrod, G.E., Parcells, R.J. and Kern, C. (1984) 'A disaggregate model for predicting shopping area market attraction', *Journal of Retailing* 60, 1: 65–83.

Weiss, M.J. (1988) *The Clustering of America: a Vivid Portrait of the Nation's 40 Neighborhood Types – from the Urban Gold Coast to Hardscrabble*, New York: Harper and Row.

Chapter twelve

# Choosing a location strategy

**The number of retail outlets required to serve a market equals market size × market share/size of outlet.**

**If it weren't for the presence of competitors, retail location would be a simple and logical process. A single equation would suffice.**

**A chain's share of the market largely determines its strategic options.**

The previous three chapters have described various techniques used in retail location studies: the tactical approach to location issues. In this chapter we shift from the narrow viewpoint of the location analyst to the wider perspective of management. Managers need a larger framework, a strategy or plan of attack, to determine the priorities and parameters for location decisions. The retail chain, for example, must make decisions about store size, product mix, standardization of outlets, advertising themes, and rates of return and growth before it can specify its site requirements. This interdependent mixture of criteria is known as a strategy. Explicitly or implicitly, each retail chain has a marketing strategy which should be apparent in the operations of its stores and in its choice of locations. This strategy is subject to continual re-evaluation. Changes in strategy, both gradual and abrupt, are usually evident in the pattern of branch closures and new openings.

Every marketing strategy leaves a spatial imprint. Exhibit 12.1 describes the evolving location patterns of three national supermarket chains in Louisville. Each chain pursues a strategy of opening new outlets and closing old ones: the differences lie in the rate of change and the kind of new sites that are selected. In this example the sudden withdrawal of A & P seems to have affected the location strategies of each of the two survivors.

A large retail chain has a considerable investment in its existing marketing strategy and cannot rapidly change to a new format. Large sums of money are committed to the current network of sites and leases, but they are only appropriate for a certain store size and market share. To increase store size, given a constant market share, means that fewer outlets are required, but at more accessible locations. There is also inertia in consumer behavior. The chain has spent millions of dollars advertising so that customers knew where the stores are and what to expect in terms of product mix, quality, and price. This accumulated experience and information is not readily altered.

None the less, modifications in marketing strategy – some sudden, some gradual – are very much part of the corporate game, and many location analysts are employed in the continuing appraisal of past strategies and adjustments to the future. In some retail sectors a sudden burst of change occurs as all the major chains simultaneously realize that store technology has changed. It happened in the food industry in the 1950s and to gasoline stations in the 1960s; it is currently happening in consumer banking. The dramatic growth of banking activity as the use of bank accounts diffuses through the population is almost complete, and the parallel expansion of credit-card transactions has reduced branch bank activity. Deregulation has

## Exhibit 12.1
## LOCATION STRATEGIES: SUPERMARKETS IN LOUISVILLE

Location choices and other aspects of business strategy are interdependent, as revealed in this example. Louisville is a good-sized metropolitan area (population about one million), growing at a moderate rate (5.4 per cent, 1970–80) and expanding continuously into surrounding suburban areas. The study begins in 1950 with two national chains: A & P (seventeen stores) and Kroger (twenty-seven stores). Both chains moved to the suburbs with their clientele. They were joined by a third chain, Winn Dixie, in the early 1960s when that chain purchased seven stores from a local firm. Winn Dixie, too, expanded outward rapidly. As new outlets opened, other smaller, older outlets were closed. The average length of occupancy was twenty years for Korger and twenty-six years for A & P. In the early 1980s A & P withdrew from Louisville.

Why did A & P leave? Why did Winn Dixie enter? These decisions undoubtedly reflect aspects of business strategy unrelated to events in the local market. Until the departure of A & P the three firms appeared to expand in much the same manner, but since that event Kroger and Winn Dixie have moved in opposite directions: the former selects more peripheral sites for larger stores, the latter retains older locations and looks for infill sites in the older suburbs.

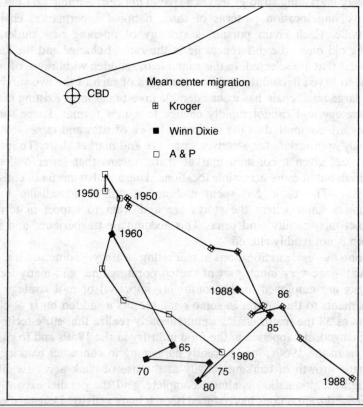

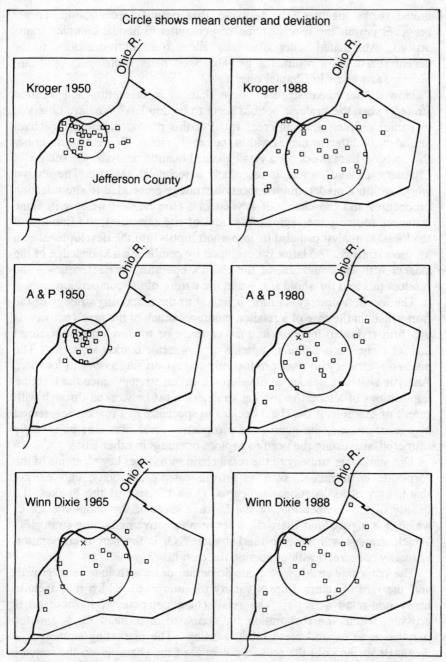

Source: A.W. Dakan (1988) 'Evolution of a trade area: predicting new sites with a space-
time perspective', *Papers and Proceedings of Applied Geography Conferences*
11: 1–9
Note: X = Central business district, Louisville.

linked banks together into networks that permit specialization. Larger branches permit the specialization of personnel to handle complex transactions. Automated teller machines allow routine transactions to be decentralized. As a result, the neighborhood bank is changing or disappearing, as we saw in Chapter one.

How do we make sense of these changes in marketing and location strategy when the strategic options seem to be limitless? We have observed in earlier chapters that different retail chains pursue different objectives and identify different niches within the retail system. Figure 12.1 describes the decision framework for a retail chain. Location analysis, the subject of Chapters ten and eleven, is essentially a technical exercise. The analyst works within a predetermined location strategy embedded in site selection procedures and the choice of key factors. However, as we saw in some instances (notably the regression model of site selection), the findings of the location analyst can also be important inputs into the development of a location strategy. The latter is developed by combining a knowledge of the market with an evaluation of the chain's operating characteristics – the product mix and threshold size – and the nature of the competition.

The location strategy, in turn, is linked to the marketing strategy of the firm which, in the case of a retailer, embraces much of the firm's activity. Is this firm trying to increase its market share or to develop a specialized market niche? Is is pursuing upscale or downscale market segments? The marketing strategy involves product mix and advertising as well as location. Analytic skills are needed to develop a location strategy since the location implications of alternative market strategies must be worked through with care. For example, if the chain decides to specialize in a market segmented by age or income, the number of prospective local sites may be severely restricted, suggesting the need to explore openings in other cities.

The marketing strategy of the retail chain introduces key elements of the corporate environment, such as growth rate, profitability, and market share, as well as locational concerns. Does the size of the market, the quality of the competition, or the balance sheet of the conglomerate of which it is a part limit the chain's set of alternative marketing strategies? Which strategy will increase market share? Or is the parent corporation primarily concerned with increasing the cash flow?

The corporate strategy of a conglomerate deals with long-term growth and the rate of return from a variety of enterprises, which may include many non-retail activities. The retail chain competes with these other activities within the corporation for access to investment funds and for permission to expand or to retain earnings. The marketing strategy is a means of spelling out the growth potential of the chain: given the state of the retail sector and the chain's position in the market, what is the likelihood of growth? At the same time, those retail chains that are independent of conglomerates are sensitive to the threat of take-over – if profitability

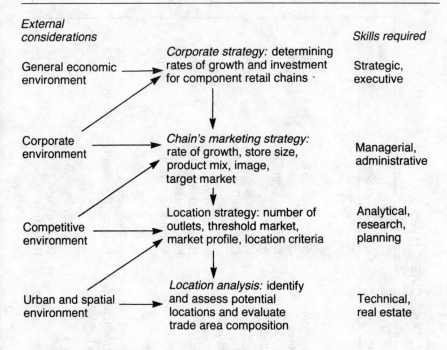

**Figure 12.1** Decision structures in the corporate environment

*Source:* The authors

falters or the firm misjudges investment opportunities. Exhibit 12.2 lists the major retail take-overs between 1985 and 1986.

We must emphasize the creative two-way interchange that exists between each pair of levels in the decision framework. Each kind of strategy is shaped by the information, requirements, and constraints of the levels of strategy above and below it in the diagram. For retail chains, the relationship between location strategy and marketing strategy is particularly close. The chain's most important assets are its locations (i.e. leases) and thus the sets of customers to which it has access. The diagram in Figure 12.2 shows the variety of strategic decisions and the difficulty of trying to lock them into any logical sequence. Each choice affects many other possible choices, and does so in all directions.

We begin with a discussion of marketing strategy. Each marketing strategy leads to a different set of location requirements, as exemplified by the major gasoline retailing chains. A strategy may be modified to anticipate a competitor's move or to retaliate. The final two sections of this chapter examine the corporate environment of the retail chain itself. The major elements of this increasingly important determinant of retail activity

## Exhibit 12.2
## STORE WARS: MAJOR RETAIL TAKE-OVERS (1985–6)

| | What's sold (no. of stores) | Buyer | Seller | Price ($millions) |
|---|---|---|---|---|
| Building materials | Home improvement chain (108) | Wicke's Co. | W.C. Grace | n.a. |
| General | J. Byron's chain | Amcena (Netherlands) | Jack Eckerd | n.a. |
| | G.C. Murphy variety stores | Aime's Dept Stores | — | n.a. |
| | Boston Store Division (8) | Bergner and Co. | Federated Dept Stores | 80 |
| | Department stores (12) | Dillard Dept Stores | R.H. Macy | n.a. |
| | Discount chain (35) | Heck's Inc. | Maloney Enterprises | n.a. |
| | Gold Circle discount stores | Kimco Division | Federated Dept Stores | n.a. |
| | R.H. Macy | Management group | — | 3,500 |
| | Household Merchandising | Management group | Household International | 700 |
| | T, G & Y Stores (743) | McCrory Corp. | Household International | 2,000 |
| | Almy Stores (25) | Stop and Shop | Federal Street Inv. | n.a. |
| | Jefferson Ward Stores (18) | Stop and Shop | Montgomery Ward | n.a. |
| | Wieboldt Department Stores | WSI Acquisitions | — | n.a. |
| | Gaylord's National | Zayre Corp. | — | n.a. |
| | Gimbel's Stores (9) | Allied Stores | BAT Industries | 150 |
| | Department Stores (23) | Amcena Corp. (Netherlands) | Howland-Steinbach Hochschild | n.a. |
| | Allied Stores | Campeau Corp. (Canada) | — | 3,400 |
| | Pamida, Inc. (164) | Citicorp | — | 170 |
| | B. Altman and Co. (8) | Conti Investments | — | n.a. |
| | Gemco Discount Stores (12) | Dayton-Hudson | Lucky Stores | 440 |
| | Department Stores (12) | Dillard Dept Stores | R.H. Macy | n.a. |

| Category | Company | Buyer | Parent | Value |
|---|---|---|---|---|
| | Joseph Horne Division | Management group | May Co. | n.a. |
| | Associated Dry Goods | May Co. | — | 2,500 |
| | John Wanamaker Stores | Taubman Inv. | Carter Hawley Hale | 183 |
| | Heck's Inc. (discount chain) | Investment group | — | 145 |
| | Parts of seven shopping centers | Unidentified | R.H. Macy | 472 |
| Food | Safeway Stores Inc. (2,300) | Kravis Kohlberg Roberts | — | 4,200 |
| | Piggly Wiggly Southern (87) | Management group | — | 520 |
| Automotive | Northeastern States Distribution | Cumberland Farms | Chevron | n.a. |
| | Getty Oil Distribution (550) | Power Test Corp. | Texaco | 95 |
| | Arco stations (400) | Shell Oil Co. | Atlantic Richfield | n.a. |
| | Auto parts stores (77) | Southland | Lucky Stores | n.a. |
| | Checker Auto Parts (378) | Northern Pacific | Lucky Stores | 155 |
| Apparel | Lerner Stores (800) | The Limited, Inc. | Rapid-American | 260 |
| | Scoa Industries (Shoes) | Management group | — | 637 |
| | Women's World Shops | Amcena (Netherlands) | Wicke's Co. | n.a. |
| Furniture | Levitz Furniture Corp. | LFC Holdings | — | 300 |
| | Color Tile Inc. (60) | General Felt Ind. | — | 293 |
| Eating and drinking | Jack-in-the-Box (800) | Management group | Ralston-Purina | 500 |
| | Diversifoods, Inc. | Pillsbury | — | n.a. |
| | Restaurant Division (690) | Management group | W.R. Grace | 537 |
| | Kentucky Fried Chicken Corp. | Pepsico | RJR Nabisco | 840 |
| | Ponderosa Inc. | Management group | — | 235 |

Exhibit 12.2 (*continued*)

| | What's sold (no. of stores) | Buyer | Seller | Price ($millions) |
|---|---|---|---|---|
| Other retail | Pay Less Drug Stores, NW | K mart | — | 487 |
| | Hook Drugs, Inc. | Kroger | — | 161 |
| | Jack Eckerd (Drug Stores) | Management group | — | 1,200 |
| | American Home Video Corp. (207) | Tandy Corp. | Jack Eckerd | n.a. |
| | Morrow's Confectionary (250) | Tenneco | | n.a. |
| | Revco Drug Stores | Management group | — | 1,250 |
| | B. Dalton Bookseller (796) | Barnes and Noble | Dayton Hudson | n.a. |
| | Gray Drug Stores (358) | Management group | Sherwin-Williams | n.a. |
| | Adams Drug Company (400) | Compact Video Inc. | Revlon Group | 95 |
| | Drug Stores (662) | Hook-Super X | Kroger | n.a. |
| | Super X Drug Stores (115) | Rite Aid Corp. | Kroger | n.a. |
| | Gray (81) and Drug Fair (22) | Rite Aid Corp. | Sherwin-Williams | n.a. |

*Source:* Cambridge Corporation (annual) *Yearbook on Corporate Mergers, Joint Ventures and Acquisitions*, Boston
*Note:* n.a., not available.

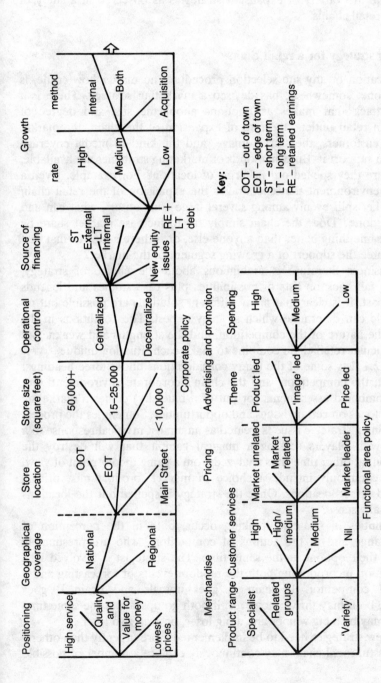

**Figure 12.2** A policy decision tree

*Source:* D. Knee and D. Walters (1985) *Strategy in Retailing: Theory and Application*, Oxford: Philip Alan

*Note:* There is no necessary order or sequence to these decisions, but there is a high degree of interdependence. One option may affect several other choices.

**Key:**

OOT – out of town
EOT – edge of town
ST – short term
LT – long term
RE – retained earnings

are the set of other firms with which the retail chain is grouped in the corporation and their respective market positions and profitability. Finally, we examine the variety of expansion strategies as observed in a study of Canadian retail chains.

## Marketing strategy for a retail chain

The implication of any site selection procedure, no matter how crude, is that someone, somewhere, has devised a marketing strategy. There is a plan of attack that makes assumptions about the size and degree of variation in retail outlets, the rate of expansion of the chain, the market profile of customers, the store's image, and the kind of media coverage required to support it. But what kinds of marketing strategies are available, and how are they spelled out in terms of location? For example, given a corporate environment that encourages the expansion of the retail chain and a market split evenly among several large competitors, what can and should be done? Does the chain simply try to increase market share by doing the same thing better than anyone else, or is there a new format that will guarantee the support of a growing segment of the market?

The business literature is ambiguous about the choice of strategy, tending to fall back on lists of possibilities plus case studies and legends from the past. It is clear that many different solutions are possible but no simple logic can determine which strategy is best. The conditions in the industry, the nature of the competition, and the strengths and weaknesses of the particular retail chain combine to make each situation unique.

Table 12.1 lists some of the many considerations under three headings: the market, the competition, and the chain's corporate environment. Out of these combined assessments (or out of a blue sky) comes a marketing strategy, a focus on certain issues and opportunities. Sometimes the process of identifying a strategic issue is treated as an almost mystical response to a situation, with players seeking a magical gambit that will destroy the competition; at other times it is analyzed from a game theory point of view. Strategies commonly include a choice of market, product mix, pricing policy, and target locations. Once the strategy is spelled out the locations begin to make sense.

Uncertainties in strategic thinking occur, both in the perception of market change and in the actions of competitors, who are presumably rethinking their options at the same time. The strategist is involved in a game situation incorporating both the random events of forecasting and a malevolent competitor. If chain A goes upscale and chain B goes downscale, both may thrive; however, if both go upscale at the same time the result may be a big winner and a big loser, or even two losers.

Some new strategies need to be implemented more urgently than others. The successful retail chain may continuously explore a number of possible

**Table 12.1** Strategic considerations in marketing strategy (each of these issues is considered in the present and as projected in the future).

*Market conditions*
Long-term growth rate: demographics, income, product penetration.
Market composition: has the target market shifted to older/younger households?
    Lower-income households?
Product innovation: has the mix of goods sold evolved?
Marketing innovations: scale of store, level of service, advertising procedures, personnel
    requirements, the economics of supply.
Government regulations: taxes, product restrictions.

*Competition*
Have major new players entered the market? Have others left?
How important are barriers to entry or change such as (1) economies of scale, (2) brand
    loyalty, (3) capital requirements, (4) leasing arrangements, or (5) distribution facilities?
Is price competition frequent?
What strategies do competitors pursue? Are they aggressive? Efficient? Likely to retaliate?
    Vulnerable?

*The corporate environment*
What are the chain's current strengths – market share, efficiency, recognition, location?
    Should these strengths be accentuated or diversified?
What are its weaknesses? Can they be overcome or ignored?
Does the corporate environment stress growth or profitability?

*Source:* The authors

strategies by modifying existing outlets or trying out new locations. Change across the chain as a whole may be gradual and evolutionary, with an emphasis on reducing risk. A retail chain that is in trouble, however, or one that suddenly realizes that it has been left behind in the market, may have to undertake a high-risk crash program in an attempt to turn around. Sometimes the direction of the necessary strategic change is clearly evident: for instance, when a firm has to catch up with an innovation that is sweeping the industry. However, sometimes a gamble on the unknown is the only alternative to surrender. New management may be brought in, a number of stores sold off or closed down, or a merger with another chain attempted. The goal is to restructure the chain in accordance with the revised strategy as soon as possible.

Figure 12.3 suggests how the major general merchandise chains have dealt with two dimensions of marketing strategy: the degree of market segmentation and the type of growth strategy. Many other dimensions of marketing strategy could be treated similarly. Segmentation in this context refers to the level of variation that exists within the retail firm. At one extreme there is the chain that sells a limited product range, in the same kind of outlet, in the same kind of location – exemplified by K mart which sells to the same mass market in the same format everywhere, and seeks out community shopping centers in metropolitan areas. At the other extreme is the megachain that develops a variety of different types of outlets or chains and may even extend across a variety of different retail sectors – hardware, convenience stores, and drugstores. Dayton-Hudson, for example, began as a department store, merged with other regional department stores, and has now expanded into several specialty formats – discounter (Target) and electronics (Lechmere).

The second dimension on the graph (Figure 12.3) differentiates between firms that grow by creating and locating additional outlets (Wal-Mart), and firms that grow by acquiring existing chains (Allied/Federated). Because acquisition necessitates a major financial outlay, strong corporate support is necessary.

Dozens of other dimensions of marketing strategy could be discussed, if we had the space. They are not always made explicit, certainly not to the

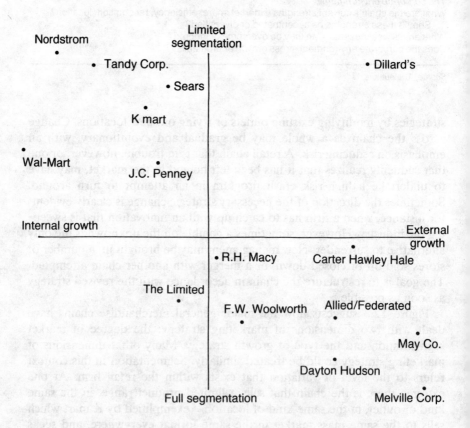

**Figure 12.3** Growth strategies of selected general merchandisers

390

| General merchandiser | Chain format | General merchandiser | Chain format |
|---|---|---|---|
| Campeau Corp. *Toronto* | Allied Stores Corp.   Bon Marche (41)   Jordan Marsh (28)   Maas Brothers/Jordan Marsh (39)   Stern's (24) Federated Department Stores Inc.   Abraham & Straus (14)   Bloomingdale's (17)   Burdines (29)   Goldsmith's (6)   Rich's (20)   Lazarus (43) Ralphs Grocery Co./Giant (129) | Melville Corp. *Harrison, New York* | Accessory Lady (50) Berman's (203) Chess King (563) CVS (745) Fan Club/Open Country (99) Freddy's (18) Kay-Bee (710) Linens 'n Things (141) Marshalls (300) Meldisco leased depts. (2,131) Prints Plus (72) This End Up (217) Thom McAn (944) Wilson's (243) |
| Carson Pirie Scott & Co. *Chicago* | Arcadia Shops Inc. (22) Carson Pirie Scott (36) County Seat Stores (371) | Montgomery Ward & Co. *Chicago* | Montgomery Ward (323) Montgomery Ward (liquidation stores) (23) |
| Carter Hawley Hale Store Inc. *Los Angeles* | The Broadway-So. Calif. (43) The Broadway-Southwest (11) Emporium Capwell (22) Thalhimers (24) Weinstock's (12) | Nordstrom Inc. *Seattle* | Nordstrom (42) Nordstrom Rack (10) Place Two (6) |
| Dayton Hudson Corp. *Minneapolis* | Dayton's (17) Hudson (20) Lechmere (27) Mervyn's (213) Target (341) | J.C. Penney Co. Inc. *Dallas* | J.C. Penney (1,378) Thrift Drug (407) |
| Dillard Department Stores Inc. *Little Rock, Arkansas* | Dillard's (146) Higbee Department Stores (12) (Owned jointly with The Edward J. DeBartolo Corp.) | Sears, Roebuck & Co. *Chicago* | Eye Care Centers of America/EyeMasters (79) McKids (3) NTW (59) Pinstripes, Petites Inc. (27) RoadHandler CarCare Center (1) Sears (824) Sears Business Systems Center (59) Sears Catalog Outlet Stores (112) Sears Catalog Stores (611) Sears Home Store (1) Sears Paint and Hardware (99) Sears Sleep Shops (3) Tire America (70) Western Auto Supply Co. (296) |
| K mart Corp. *Troy, Michigan* | Bargain Harold's (150) Brentanos (26) Builders Square (118) Jupiter (3) K mart (2,223) Kresge (85) Makro (4) Office Square (1) Payless Drug Stores (254) Reader's Market (203) Walden Books (1,168) | Wal-Mart *Bentonville, Arkansas* | dot Discount Drug (13) Hypermart USA (3) Sam's Wholesale Club (100) Wal-Mart (1,230) |
| The Limited Inc. *Columbus, Ohio* | Abercrombie & Fitch (25) Express (404) Henri Bendel (1) Lane Bryant (677) Lerner (773) The Lerner Woman (398) The Limited (749) Victoria's Secret (308) | F. W. Woolworth Co. *New York* | Activeworld (10) Afterthoughts (197) Anderson-Little (126) Ashbrooks (3) Athletic X-Press (188) Canary Island (6) Carimar (3) Champs/Robby's (100) Cotton Supply Co. (2) Face Fantasies (3) Foot Locker (1,017) Frame Scene (12) Fredelle (91) Frugal Frank's (22) Fun & Fashion (3) Herald Square Party Shop (5) Kids Foot Locker (3) Kids Mart (336) |
| R.H. Macy & Co. *New York* | Aeropostale (8) Bullocks Wilshire (7) Bullock's (24) Charter Club (3) Fantasies of Morgan Taylor (3) Macy's (91) I. Magnin (25) | | Kinney (1,815) Lady Foot Locker (328) Lewis (10) Little Folk Shop (15) Live Wire (6) Mini Shops (20) Northern Reflections (11) |
| The May Department Stores Co. *St Louis* | L.S. Ayres & Co. (14) Caldor (119) Famous-Barr(17) Filene's (18) Foley's (16) G. Fox (10) Goldwaters (9) Hahne's (9) Hecht's (23) Kaufmann's (14) Lord & Taylor (49) May Co., Calif. (35) May Co., Cleveland (9) May D&F (13) Meier & Frank (8) O'Neil's (8) Robinson's (24) Sibley's (11) Venture Stores (74) Volume Shoe Corp./ Payless ShoeSource (2,545) | | Raglans (31) Randy River (66) Richman (173) Robinson's (74) Rubin (11) The Rx Place (12) Sportelle (84) Susie's (249) Williams the Shoemen (159) Woolco (120) Woolworth-U.S.A. (1,140) Woolworth (223) Woolworth Express (4) Woolworth-Canada (169) |

**Figure 12.3** (*continued*)

*Source:* The authors, compiled with the assistance of Kenard Smith, The May Co.

## Exhibit 12.3
## MARKET SEGMENTATION

From the retailer's point of view, the kinds of market segments described in Chapter two as income, demographics, or lifestyle, have meaning only as they are translated into differences in purchasing patterns. The entrepreneur may be less interested in the demographic structure of a market than its strategic segments – defined in terms of buyer behavior. For example, the market could be subdivided on the basis of consumer objectives: is the car to be used for recreation, for commuting, or for deliveries? Or, one could subdivide the market according to its accessibility, not only in spatial terms but also in its openness to advertising or commitment to a competitor's store. How reachable, if you like, is customer X? A matrix of strategic segments, according to both customer objectives and accessibility, provides the basis for developing a more complex marketing strategy.

This comprehensive list of possible market segments – locational, demographic, and behavioral – shows the possibilities for strategies focused on market groups. Not all segments are available to every firm: the geography is restricted by the chain's scale of operation, and the product mix may prevent access to certain household types.

A dominant firm trying to improve market share may find that segmented markets require a whole range of strategies and formats in order to exploit the market fully.

| Variables | Typical breakdowns |
|---|---|
| *Geographic* | |
| Region | Pacific, mountain, west north central, west south central, east north central, east south central, south Atlantic, middle Atlantic, New England |
| County size | Rural, urban center, metropolitan |
| City or SMSA size | Under 5,000, 5,000–19,999, 20,000–49,999, 50,000–99,999, 100,000–249,999, 250,000–499,999, 500,000–999,999, 1,000,000–3,999,999, 4,000,000 or over |
| Density | Urban, suburban, rural |
| Climate | Northern, southern |
| *Demographic* | |
| Age (years) | Under 6, 6–11, 12–19, 20–34, 35–49, 50–64, 65 + |
| Sex | Male, female |
| Family size | 1–2, 3–4, 5 + |
| Family life cycle | Young, single; young, married, no children; young, married, youngest child under 6; young, married, youngest child 6 or over, older, married, with children; older, married, no children under 18; older, single; other |
| Income | Under $3,000, $3,000–$5,000, $5,000–$7,000, $7,000–$10,000, $10,000–$15,000, $15,000–$25,000, $25,000 and over |

| Occupation | Professional and technical; managers, officials and proprietors; clerical, sales; craftsmen, foremen; operatives; farmers; retired; students; housewives; unemployed |
|---|---|
| Education | Grade school or less; some high school; graduated high school; some college; graduated college |
| Religion | Catholic, Protestant, Jewish, other |
| Race | White, Black, oriental |
| Nationality | American, British, French, German, Scandinavian, Italian, Latin American, Middle Eastern, Japanese |
| Social class | Lower-lower, upper-lower, lower-middle, upper-middle, lower-upper, upper-upper |
| *Psychographic* | |
| Lifestyle | Straights, swingers, longhairs |
| Personality | Compulsive, gregarious, authoritarian, ambitious |
| *Behavioristic* | |
| Purchase occasion | Regular occasion, special occasion |
| Benefits sought | Economy, convenience, prestige |
| User status | Nonuser, ex-user, potential user, first-time user, regular user |
| Usage rate | Light user, medium user, heavy user |
| Loyalty status | None, medium, strong, absolute |
| Readiness stage | Unaware, aware, informed, interested, desirous, intending to buy |
| Marketing-factor sensitivity | Quality, price, service, advertising, sales promotion |

*Source:* P. Kottler (1980) *Marketing Management*, 4 edn, Englewood Cliffs, New Jersey: Prentice-Hall.

public. They have to be inferred from a study of a chain's behavior, particularly its location decisions. Exhibit 12.4 considers consumer behavior and how it affects marketing strategy, particularly with reference to consumer loyalty to brands or to stores.

## Location implications

Each marketing strategy includes locational priorities – more outlets, different kinds of sites, or different target markets. Sometimes the locations are central to the strategy; even when they appear to be peripheral, the evolution of the network of outlets provides a visible guide to a chain's changing marketing strategy. In this section, gasoline retailers are used to demonstrate a highly visible link between the overall marketing strategy and the location selection.

Gasoline retailing has steadily increased its share of all retail sales. It includes a number of well financed major players. The large integrated oil

Exhibit 12.4
## CONSUMER BEHAVIOR AND MARKETING STRATEGY

One of the most intensely researched aspects of consumer behavior concerns the likelihood of buying a given brand within a product group. The approach focuses on the statistical distribution of chance variations around the average purchasing pattern – in the same way that characteristics of the normal curve are used in statistics. The research has been extended to many other aspects of customer behavior, including the choice of store. The theory, supported by many empirical studies, suggests that:

(1) Given an average frequency of purchase (items per year per household), the probability of a given household purchasing any specified number of the items in a given time period can be estimated. For example, it is quite unlikely that the Smith family will buy exactly nine cans of baked beans at any one time; much more likely that they will buy two.

(2) Given the market share of various brands in a product category, the probability of a given household buying any one brand can be estimated in the same fashion. Households try out different brands, in proportion to their availability.

(3) Given the market share of the various retail chains that sell this product, the joint probability of a given household buying a given brand at a given chain outlet can be estimated: will the Smiths buy two cans of Heinz baked beans at a Safeway outlet within the next two weeks?

(4) If it is possible to specify an integrated spatial market so that the market share of each outlet is known, the likelihood that our given household will shop at each of the various outlets within the market can be estimated.

While these results may not seem startling, they have significant implications for the way that we treat competition among retailers. First, it is clear that brand, chain, or store loyalty is largely a myth. Panel studies show that each household purchases a variety of brand names from a variety of retail chains (see the table below). The variety of purchases roughly reflects the distribution of options, i.e. the allocation of market share, in terms of brands and/or chains. Second, it is apparent that while chains must face the fact that 'their' customers actually buy more from the competition (two-thirds of purchases of instant coffee, for instance), chains can also depend on exposure to a steady stream of customers who typically shop elsewhere. While only 300,000 households buy instant coffee at A & P in any one week, by the end of a year 5.5 million different households will have done so.

For groceries, at least, there is little evidence of segmentation, either. Supermarkets compete with all other kinds of food stores, not only with the ones that superficially resemble them most. As the table suggests (the duplication index), each chain picks up sales from the others at a rate roughly proportional to its market share. No supermarket chain is able to overcome this 'Duplication of Purchase Law', although there are two additional qualifications: first, the overlapping locations of certain chains intensifies competition between them; second, households that purchase a product more often are slightly more likely to choose the chain with the largest market share (perhaps because of greater price sensitivity).

The strategic choices for a retail chain, then, must revolve around market share (its proportion of the total sales in a given market), and the costs and benefits of increasing it. Can a chain expand the opportunities for shoppers to create the illusion of higher market share? Why should a chain attempt to improve customer loyalty in the face of an apparent iron law of consumer behavior? In some cases it makes sense strategically to expand the product group or retail sector into related sectors rather than to compete against other chains in the same sector. Or, if the small independent stores hurt supermarket sales as much as the perceived competing chain, attack them because they are more vulnerable.

In short, competition is more widely diffused than simple military or game-theory strategic analogies imply, and customer loyalty is very difficult to maintain.

## DUPLICATION OF INSTANT COFFEE PURCHASES IN US GROCERY CHAINS (48 WEEKS)

| | | | | Percentage who also bought at: | | | | |
| --- | --- | --- | --- | --- | --- | --- | --- | --- |
| | UC | Co-op | Misc. | Kroger | A & P | Safe-way | Winn Dixie | Lucky |
| Unnamed chains | – | 19 | 13 | 9 | 7 | 7 | 5 | 4 |
| Co-ops | 70 | – | 15 | 11 | 6 | 6 | 4 | 4 |
| Miscellaneous | 42 | 13 | – | 6 | 5 | 6 | 3 | 2 |
| Kroger | 73 | 23 | 14 | – | 5 | 6 | 5 | 4 |
| A & P | 65 | 14 | 14 | 5 | – | 5 | 8 | 2 |
| Safeway | 64 | 15 | 16 | 6 | 5 | – | 1 | 9 |
| Winn Dixie | 69 | 16 | 11 | 9 | 13 | 1 | – | 2 |
| Lucky | 60 | 16 | 7 | 7 | 4 | 16 | 2 | – |
| Average duplication | 63 | 16 | 13 | 7 | 7 | 7 | 4 | 4 |
| Market share % | 49 | 13 | 8 | 6 | 6 | 6 | 4 | 3 |
| Market share (× 1.3) | 63 | 17 | 10 | 8 | 7 | 7 | 5 | 4 |

Source: M.D. Uncles and A.S.C. Ehrenberg in N. Wrigley (ed.) (1988) Store Choice, Store Location and Market Analysis, London: Routledge
Note: The duplication index, in this case equal to 1.3, is the constant by which market share is multiplied in order to obtain the average duplication.

companies use their downstream retail outlets both to guarantee their refineries access to markets and to create visibility and consumer loyalty. Sometimes the retail outlets are profit centers within the larger corporations, sometimes not, but all the major companies play the retailing game. Table 12.2 shows a number of possible strategies for service stations.

The profitability of a gas station is directly linked to the amount of gas pumped. Most stations have considerable excess sales capacity – they could

**Table 12.2** Marketing strategies for service stations

| Strategy | Locational implications |
|---|---|
| *Market share*<br>Maintains or augments market share to obtain scale economies and maximize return from advertising<br>Stresses brand loyalty. | Balanced/dispersed to catch all market segments. Size and location of outlets depend on market share; a network approach. |
| *Price cutting*<br>Discount gas, self-serve, may require separate brand name for major oil companies. | Low-cost sites, young, male customers, blue-collar area. Each site must succeed on its own. |
| *Saturation*<br>Emphasizes availability, no advertising, impulse buying. | Low cost, widespread over all possible locations. |
| *Segmentation*<br>Targets only selected submarkets – by income, age, lifestyle, travel patterns, e.g. credit card holders. | Clustered around target group and their routes. |
| *Comprehensive development*<br>Oriented to spatial monopoly – a neighborhood; plays down brand loyalty. | Avoid competition, central to target community. |
| *Cross-merchandising*<br>Linked with other services: shopping plaza, restaurant, variety store; or expanded automobile services – tires, carwash, mechanic, etc. | Must serve dual purpose. Different site requirements to suit both activities. |

*Source:* Claus and Hardwick (1972) *The Mobile Consumer: Auto-Oriented Retailing and Site Selection*, Toronto: Collier–Macmillan.

handle many more cars per day on the same lot, even with the same personnel. Bigger, high-volume stations require lower markups to break even. The strategic problem is how to generate gallonage, and location is an important component of the marketing strategy.

A company's market share is its proportion of all sales in a retail sector within a market. Market share is of particular interest in the section that follows. Chains that are dominant, i.e. those that have the largest share of the market, operate differently from those ranked second or third, and even more differently from those that account for less than 10 per cent of the market. The business literature often assumes that market share is synonymous with profitability because of scale economies and the ability to control the nature of competition within the market. Table 12.3 suggests that there is some basis for this assumption in retailing. The larger firms are more profitable in almost every respect, i.e. they show higher profits relative to assets or net worth or sales. The only exception is the very

**Table 12.3** Size and profitability in retailing (retail and wholesale firms: 1984)

| | All firms | Size of firm (annual sales, $ millions) | | | | | | |
| --- | --- | --- | --- | --- | --- | --- | --- | --- |
| | | <0.5 | 0.5–1.0 | 1.0–2.5 | 2.5–5.0 | 5.0–10 | 10–50 | 50 + |
| No. of returns | 896,500 | 535,100 | 136,000 | 119,000 | 50,400 | 28,400 | 24,000 | 3,500 |
| Assets ($ billions) | 899.0 | 50.8 | 36.6 | 65.3 | 57.5 | 60.2 | 141.1 | 487.4 |
| Net worth ($ billions) | 283.3 | 10.6 | 12.6 | 23.6 | 21.5 | 20.6 | 47.9 | 152.7 |
| Sales ($ billions) | 2,307.6 | 92.4 | 98.2 | 190.7 | 179.6 | 202.1 | 476.9 | 1067.6 |
| Net income ($ billions) | 42.011 | −0.972 | 1.037 | 3.300 | 3.197 | 3.435 | 9.059 | 22.955 |
| Income/assets (%) | 4.67 | −1.91 | 2.83 | 5.06 | 5.55 | 5.70 | 6.42 | 4.71 |
| Income/net worth (%) | 14.83 | −9.17 | 8.22 | 14.01 | 14.90 | 16.70 | 18.92 | 15.03 |
| Income/sales (%) | 1.82 | −1.05 | 1.06 | 1.73 | 1.78 | 1.71 | 1.90 | 2.15 |
| Sales/assets (%) | 2.57 | 1.82 | 2.68 | 2.92 | 2.75 | 3.36 | 3.38 | 2.19 |
| Sales/net worth (%) | 8.15 | 8.72 | 7.78 | 8.09 | 8.37 | 9.82 | 9.96 | 6.99 |

*Source:* United States Department of the Treasury, Internal Revenue Service (1987) 'Statistics of Income – 1984: Corporation Income Tax Returns,' Washington, DC

largest category (over $50 million in sales). This group includes both super-markets and department stores which are currently among the less profit-able retail sectors.

The largest oil companies compete for market share, attempting to keep sales in each market within a certain range – 20–25 per cent of total sales, perhaps. High market share is profitable both at the station level and for the firm as a whole. It extracts the maximum return from advertising campaigns and administration. However, at some level of market share (30 per cent?) the outlets within the chain begin to compete with each other. Market share strategies stress advertising, brand names, and image (friend-liness, quality, cleanliness), and play down price competition. Each outlet's location is part of a larger network, with station size and spatial separation dependent on overall market share. New sites are chosen to fit into the network rather than on the basis of their intrinsic site advantages. The corporate flag must be kept flying throughout the market. However, market share is surprisingly volatile, as we saw in Exhibits 12.1 and 9.1 (on automobile sales).

Price-cutting is a strategy best suited to local chains and independent service stations. Major oil companies that play the price-cutting game often hide behind a subsidiary with a discount image. Occasionally, a major chain will recycle a site from the prestige brand name into a discount brand, even though the location requirements are fundamentally different. Discount stations with low levels of service (often self-service) appeal to blue-collar households and to young male drivers (gasoline is one product that poor people consume as much of as the rich). The sites are usually inexpensive, not competing with other land uses. The result is a well-defined geography of gasoline price that usually reflects the high- and low-income sectors of the city (see Figure 12.4). In Toronto, for instance, the blue-collar crescent, stretching from the north-west through downtown and out to the eastern part of the metropolitan region, includes all the least expensive outlets. High prices are observed near the core, to the far west and to the north. Prices can differ by as much as 25 per cent. Nodes of local competition and co-operation are also evident.

Saturation is an alternative technique used by local chains who develop large numbers of low-cost sites, emphasizing convenience and availability. Cheap sites reduce overheads and the high level of impulse buying, linked to trip patterns, captures market share. The location strategy tends to be opportunistic, picking up cheap sites whenever possible, and possibly selling them later for redevelopment.

Segmentation takes the opposite point of view, focusing on a particular market segment, such as travelers, businessmen, upscale, suburban, credit-card holders, etc. (see Exhibit 12.3). For gasoline vendors, behavioral segments are particularly important because each different type of travel pattern suggests a different location priority. Whatever the segment, one

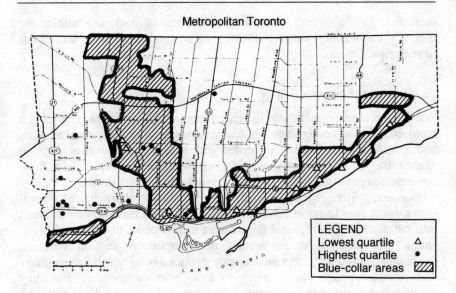

Figure 12.4 Gasoline prices in Toronto

*Source:* The authors

expects a very structured spatial pattern of outlets, centered on home, workplace, or major travel routes.

Comprehensive developments are service stations integrated within a residential community. In order to serve its spatial monopoly the chain plays down the brand name and plays up service. Such stations are oriented to the land use and transportation design of the residential area – near the neighborhood shopping plaza or at the entry point to the subdivision from the major arterial street.

Cross-merchandising links the service station with other retail or service activities, either automotive (mechanic, carwash, tires) or otherwise (snack bar, gift shop). Perhaps the fastest-growing kind of gas station is the one in front of the convenience store outlet on an arterial street. The location of the facility must satisfy the market and site requirements of both activities. This may lead to an awkward site plan and create traffic access problems. It has also made convenience store chains into significant competitors in gasoline retailing and led some oil companies (such as ARCO) to open convenience stores – major strategic decisions in both cases.

The service station chain, like most other retailers, can compete in a variety of ways. The decision may depend on the national marketing strategy, or on an obvious local opportunity. Perhaps the most important point to make is that no matter what strategy is pursued, each retail outlet must fit into the overall network. The success of each one affects the others. It is not good enough to locate each unit independently on the basis of site criteria alone.

## Fending off the competition

The section above emphasized the importance of market share in shaping a retail chain's marketing strategy. Chains with a monopoly, such as state liquor stores, need only be concerned with weighing the level of demand against the costs of supply in order to maximize profits. These firms compete against other forms of consumption and against saving.

Dominant firms, which have the largest market share in their retail sector, must guard against competition from smaller firms and new entrants into the market. The regional department store worries about the national chain. The national chain worries about specialty fashion retailers. Dominants, since they depend on scale economies to control the market and generate profits, have much to lose from competitors, but they are also in a position to determine the nature of the competition: will it be in terms of price or quality or access? How do they discourage other chains from entering the market?

Oligopolists compete with two or three similar firms within a market, each conscious of possible changes in marketing strategy by the others. All stand to lose from a new entrant. All stand to gain if one of the others goes broke. Sometimes the best strategy is simply to wait for one of the others to fail.

Underdog firms, usually independents or small chains, operate within a retail environment shaped by the largest firms in their retail sector, which determine the standards for price, product mix, and service. The underdog firm responds by identifying a niche: a location, a product, or a market segment that is not well served by the dominant. Jones (1984) explores the variety of niches that have developed among women's fashion outlets in Toronto. He compared each store or chain with respect to thirty-six variables, measuring different aspects of the product or market, and used these measures to group the stores that were most alike. The most frequent specializations focus on income and age of target customer on the demand side, and on the source of merchandise on the supply side.

Is there perfect competition in retailing? Are there any retail markets that are so crowded with independents and small chains that no single retailer can affect the competitive situation? It is difficult to think of an example, given the degree of specialization and the spatial dispersion of markets. At any rate, such firms would be so restricted by the pressures of the marketplace that there could be little room for a marketing strategy. Costs, rents, and a desperate scramble for enough trade to stay in business would overwhelm them.

Let us consider the options of monopolists, dominants, and oligopolists in turn. Monopolists, of course, face no competition at all, at least for sales of their particular goods. Their only concern is consumer indifference to their product, represented by a sloping demand curve. State liquor stores are the obvious retail example, but many other public- and private-sector activities, such as recreational or medical facilities, operate similarly; the only bowling alley or dentist in town, for example.

The monopolist's central concern is how much to sell (see Figure 3.2). At what point along the demand curve should consumption occur? Sales may be restricted, either by raising the price or reducing the number of outlets. Locating more liquor stores in small towns or neighborhood plazas will increase overall sales, but will also increase average costs.

The monopolist operates most effectively if the market can be segmented in order to impose differential price structures. Why not price liquor differently in one place from another? Demand curves and cost curves are different in each place. Wealthy people will pay more, especially for better goods and better shopping environments: increase the price at upscale shopping plazas and given them a better wine selection. If small-town stores operate at an inefficient scale, charge the customers enough to cover the costs. Effective segmentation, however, requires social sanction and works best for products that are not easily transported from one place to another. Concert halls and baseball games segment the audience by charging variable prices. Rich and poor pay differing amounts to see the same performance. Airlines segment their markets by means of service and ticket availability. Banks are beginning to provide extra services for depositors with big accounts.

Dominant firms must protect their market share because they depend on economies of scale for their profits. Lowering prices is one way to discourage new entrants into a market, but is ultimately self-defeating. A number of locational strategies may be substituted (see ReVelle, 1986). Tietz (1968) outlined one aspect of the theory: by extending Hotelling's model of the ice cream vendors (Exhibit 2.1) to more complex forms of spatial competition, he demonstrated that the dominant firm can translate a superiority in store numbers into an even greater superiority in sales, if outlets are located so as to truncate the competitor's trade area. For example, a three-to-one advantage in number of stores should lead to a five-to-one advantage in sales, assuming the stores are appropriately located.

Pre-emption (West, 1981) is another way in which major retail chains and shopping center developers use their capital resources to prevent new entrants into the market. As the suburbs extend across the landscape the developer identifies the possible sites for retail development, long before the residential area is actually built. (In Chapter seven we called this catalytic development.) By the time the houses are built and the residents move in, the shopping facilities are already in place, sometimes a year or more ahead of time. The capital costs of anticipating the market by tying up the site ahead of time are borne by the developer and the retailers (and ultimately the consumers). In western Canada in the early 1970s, the dominant super-market chain, Safeway, used its market position to gain entry into almost every major shopping center development, thus pre-empting any initiatives by its competitors.

West and Von Hohenbalken (1984) also describe the technique of predation as practiced by this same supermarket chain in Calgary. If a competing supermarket opened up, the dominant chain made a point of opening nearby, bearing the loss if necessary, until the competitor withdrew. These aggressive location tactics resulted in a steady decline in the number of competing outlets during a period of rapid growth in the Calgary market. Any supermarket chain that wished to enter western Canada in a big way had to be prepared to make a very considerable financial investment over a long period. Finally, Safeway was charged with violating federal trade restrictions; since then its share of the Alberta market has dropped from 80 per cent to less than 40 per cent.

Market share is a major determinant of chain strategy. Dominant firms can: (1) stay on the offensive by attempting to control the pace and direc-tion of innovation, (2) maintain share by emphasizing brand names, developing new locations, and reducing prices to make entry and growth by competitors difficult, or (3) compete aggressively, including the use of retaliatory pricing and predatory location. Underdogs, in contrast, often seek out: (1) the vacant niche – a small market isolated by location or market segment from competition by larger chains, (2) a specialist role for certain product lines or customer segments, or (3) a quality image.

Oligopoly is the more usual condition in American retailing. Each retail sector in each market is served by three or four competitors of varying size. Each competitor scrambles for minor fluctuations in market share by negotiating a lease in the new mall, cutting prices, or initiating a major advertising campaign. Any major changes in market share are unlikely: such changes would require a complete restructuring of outlets. Mergers are more frequent means of altering market share.

Sometimes a firm's marketing strategy will aim directly at a competitor, sensing a corporate vulnerability and the possibility of a permanent shift in market share. More often the permanence of the competition is accepted and the major firms develop specialized niches and images that avoid direct confrontation. The best analogies to oligopolistic competition are those of international politics: border skirmishes, ritual indignation, and the occasional all-out war.

Now that planned shopping centers have come to dominate the location opportunities for retail chains, the territorial aspects of these battles are fought out in the leasing negotiations with developers. Major tenants, such as department stores, have negotiated alliances with major shopping center developers in order to guarantee access to markets. More specialized retail chains, in such lines as clothing or shoes, want to be represented in every regional mall. Developers know this. In the long run they too prefer retail oligopoly to dominance by a single chain.

## The corporate environment

Perhaps the most neglected element in the analysis of a retail chain's location decision making is an awareness of the corporate environment in which it is embedded. The corporate environment includes the set of other firms within the corporation, their relative growth and profitability, and thus the level of achievement of the corporation as a whole. It also includes the size, profitability, and position within the market of the chain itself. What other activities are part of Atomic Enterprises besides furniture retailing? How prominent is the retail operation within their network of companies? Is this retail chain dominant or largely irrelevant among the furniture retailers in the region? Is profitability growing or declining? Is it debt-laden or debt-free? Has it over-expanded? Absorbed several mergers? Should it try to continue to grow, or should it rationalize its holdings?

Consider, for example, the corporate environment of some of the major department store chains. Each one operates within a different context; many of them have undergone substantial changes within the last five years. The fortunes of Allied and Federated Department Stores are discussed in Exhibit 12.5. Sears Roebuck is America's largest retailer (see Table 3.5), and one of the most centralized and homogeneous in its operations. In recent years, however, Sears has also become a major financial firm with its own credit operations, plus All-State (insurance), Coldwell Banker (real estate), Dean Witter Reynolds (stockbroker), and Harbridge House (management consulting).

Montgomery Ward, until recently, was a subsidiary of the Mobil Corporation, along with the petroleum exploration, refining, and marketing divisions, and the Container Corporation of America. It, too, has developed a strong financial group, but it has also been trying to develop a number of specialty chains in building supplies, auto accessories, electronics, and jewellery. The recent management buyout may modify this strategy.

J.C. Penney, like Sears, is a highly centralized and standardized retail organization. The many vertical linkages in real estate, finance, and wholesaling all reinforce the central retail function. K mart, in contrast, has diversified horizontally by acquiring other retail chains such as Walden Books and Payless Drugstores, while selling off the original parent, the Kresge dime-store chain (Figure 12.5). Dayton-Hudson is a strong regional

## Exhibit 12.5
## CAMPEAU: ACQUISITION AND DIVESTMENT

When the Canadian shopping center developer Robert Campeau bought Allied Stores in December 1986, his bankers imposed a condition: that he sell sixteen of the twenty-two retail divisions within two years. This was acceptable with Campeau, who is alleged to be more interested in real estate than retailing.

| Before (Allied Stores) | Headquarters | No. of stores | SIC | After |
|---|---|---|---|---|
| Bonwit Teller | NY | 13 | 5621 | Sold to Hooker Corp. |
| Brooks Brothers* | NY | 45 | 5611 | |
| Jordan Marsh* | Boston | 19 | 5311 | |
| Jordan Marsh* | Miami | 17 | 5311 | |
| Maas. Bros* | Tampa | 21 | 5311 | |
| Dey Brothers | Syracuse | 4 | 5311 | Sold to May Dept Stores |
| The Bon Marche* | Seattle | 40 | 5311 | |
| Donaldson's | Minneapolis | 15 | 5311 | Sold to Carson Pirie Scott |
| D.M. Read | CT | 6 | 5311 | Transferred to Jordan Marsh |
| Stern's* | NJ | 26 | 5311 | |
| Plymouth | NJ | 51 | 5621 | Sold to Tribeca Holdings |
| Pomeroy's | PA | 10 | 5311 | Sold to Bon Ton |
| Ann Taylor* | NY | 90 | 5621 | |
| Garfinckel's | DC | 10 | 5311 | Sold to Raleigh Stores |
| Joske | TX | 26 | 5331 | |
| Cain-Sloan | Nashville | 4 | 5311 | Sold to Dillard |
| Miller's | Knoxville | 12 | 5311 | Sold to Hess Dept Stores |
| Miller-Rhoads | Richmond | 17 | 5311 | Management buyout |
| Catharine | Memphis | 205 | 5621 | Management buyout |
| Jerry Leonard | Omaha | – | 5611 | Sold to King-Size |
| Herpolsheimer's | MI | 2 | 5311 | Sold to Federated |
| Block's | IN | 10 | 5311 | |
| Heers | MO | 2 | 5311 | Sold |
| Total | | 645 | | |

Source: The authors
Notes: *Retained initially. 1986 sales = $4,196 million. SIC, standard industrial classification.

At the end of 1987, as summarized above, Campeau claimed that he had given up 38 per cent of sales, 50 per cent of floor space, but only 13 per cent of profit. Meanwhile, all over the country department stores were changing hands, downsizing, remerchandising, and trying to adjust to dramatically different competitive conditions.

Then, in April 1988, Campeau repeated the process by purchasing Federated Department Stores for $8.8 billion, with the results shown below. In addition,

Brooks Brothers has been sold to the British chain of Marks and Spencer, and Ann Taylor to a buyout group organized by Merrill-Lynch.

By the end of 1988, after all these divestments, Campeau was left with nine department store chains, with annual sales of $6.5 billion and an enormous burden of debt. In September 1989 his creditors intervened and he lost most of his control of the enterprise. Bloomingdale's, the prize possession, was put up for sale. Within two years almost every traditional department store chain in the country has changed ownership and assumed a massive debt load.

| Before (Federated Dept Stores) | Headquarters | No. of stores | SIC | After |
|---|---|---|---|---|
| Main Street | Chicago | 27 | 5621 | Sold to Kohl's Dept Stores |
| Children's Place | Chicago | 202 | 5651 | Sold to TCP Acquisitions |
| Foley's | Houston | 38 | 5331 | May Co. |
| Filene's | Boston | 16 | 5331 | May Co. |
| Bullock's | L.A. | 29 | 5331 | R.H. Macy |
| I. Magnin | S.F. | 25 | 5331 | R.H. Macy |
| Gold Circle | OH | 76 | discount | Kimco Developments |
| Ralph's | L.A. | 127 | 5311 | |
| Abraham & Straus* | NY | 15 | 5331 | |
| Lazarus* | Cinn. | 32 | 5331 | |
| Rich's/Goldsmith's* | Atlanta | 20 | 5331 | |
| Bloomingdale's* | NY | 17 | 5331 | |
| Burdines* | Miami | 29 | 5331 | |
| Total | | 653 | | |

Source: The authors
Notes: *Retained initially. 1986 sales = $11.2 billion. SIC, standard industrial classification.

department store chain that has remained independent and expanded by adding other retail sectors: B. Dalton (books) – since resold, Target and Mervyn's (discount), and Lechmere (electronics).

While most American retailers have been able to remain independent of the most diversified corporate conglomerates, almost all of them participate in a variety of vertical linkages, as exemplified by the K mart example. Financial service subsidiaries provide consumer credit and wholly owned specialty firms purchase, manufacture, or wholesale certain product lines. Of growing importance is the link between the department store chains and shopping center developers. Campeau is a real estate firm with close financial ties with DeBartolo, the largest shopping center developer in the country. Sears controls Homart. Most department store chains have a property group that invests in malls and has close ties with real estate companies. As the major anchor tenants in these malls, the department stores may obtain a reward for the traffic they generate by acting as landlords for the rest of the stores.

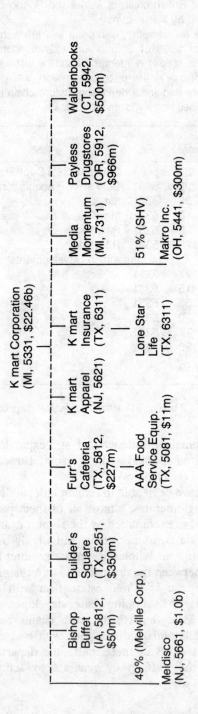

K mart Corporation
(MI, 5331, $22.46b)

| | | | | | |
|---|---|---|---|---|---|
| Bishop Buffet (IA, 5812, $50m) | Builder's Square (TX, 5251, $350m) | Furr's Cafeteria (TX, 5812, $227m) | K mart Apparel (NJ, 5621) | K mart Insurance (TX, 6311) | Media Momentum (MI, 7311) | Payless Drugstores (OR, 5912, $966m) | Waldenbooks (CT, 5942, $500m) |

49% (Melville Corp.)

Meldisco
(NJ, 5661, $1.0b)

AAA Food
Service Equip.
(TX, 5081, $11m)

Lone Star
Life
(TX, 6311)

51% (SHV)

Makro Inc.
(OH, 5441, $300m)

K mart Corporation
Headquarters: Troy, MI
SIC Sector: 5331 (mass market department store)
Annual sales (1986): $22.46 billion

**Figure 12.5** The corporate environment: K mart

*Source:* Compiled by the authors from Dun and Bradstreet (1988) *America's Corporate Families and International Affiliates,* 2 vols, Parsippany: New Jersey

The corporate strategy is concerned with the appropriate role for the retail chain within the corporation as a whole. Suppose that a corporation is in good shape financially and wishes to maintain a diversified portfolio of business activities. Which of the businesses that it controls should it encourage to grow? Which ones should be left to sit on a back burner? This decision has been the subject of a great deal of debate in the literature on corporate strategy over the last decade. The problem is elaborated in the well-known growth–share portfolio matrix shown in Figure 12.6, which describes the various divisions within a corporation (such as K mart) in

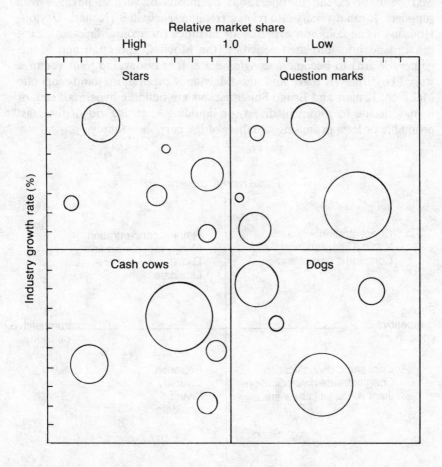

**Figure 12.6** The growth-share business portfolio matrix

*Source:* The authors
*Note:* Relative market share is defined by the ratio of one's own market share to the market share held by the largest rival firm. (Size of circle represents size of firm.)

terms of their market share and the growth rate of their sector. The four-way breakdown separates the 'stars' which generate both high profits and growth, from the profitable 'cash cows', the unfortunate 'dogs', and the continuing 'question marks'. The stars get full attention while the steady returns from cash cows can be applied to growth opportunities elsewhere. The dogs are to be disposed of.

In the broadest sense, the corporation can choose among a half a dozen or more strategies – as shown by the department store examples – but the choices are guided by its growth-share position (see Figure 12.7). It can concentrate on the growth of a single enterprise, as have Sears and Wal-Mart, and/or extend its operations by means of vertical linkages with suppliers. It can diversify into related (retailing) activities (K mart, Dayton-Hudson) using common expertise or facilities (horizontal linkages), or it can expand into unrelated activities (the Mobil Corporation and Montgomery Ward) to become a conglomerate. It may develop joint ventures with like firms (K mart and the Melville Corporation jointly operate Meldisco; K mart and Bruno Supermarkets are building hypermarkets), or it may decide to retrench, divest, or liquidate – getting rid of the least profitable or least promising members of the corporate family.

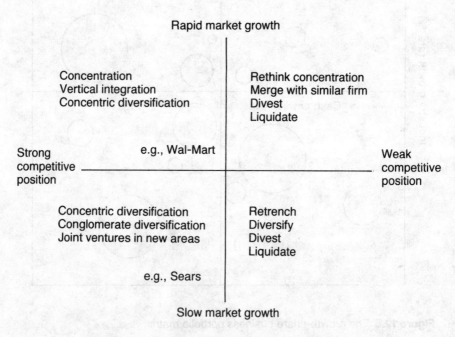

**Figure 12.7** Corporate strategy alternatives to fit a firm's circumstances

*Source:* The authors

These decisions are shaped by the circumstances of the corporation, especially the balance between its overall rate of expansion and the entrepreneurial energy and capital on hand. Slow growth, handsome cash flows, and vigorous middle-management personnel suggest the possibility for expansion. Heavy debts, recent take-overs, or money-losing subsidiaries discourage further growth. In recent years, corporate decisions have also been affected by take-overs, or the risk of take-overs. Profitable firms are taken over by corporate raiders or privatized by management and stockholder equity is replaced by junk bond debt at high interest rates. This change of control and debt load usually affects operations: the buyout of Safeway in 1986 resulted in a decline of one-third in sales and employment and a loss of half of the outlets, while profit levels were maintained.

When sales (market share) are plotted against recent growth values for the major department store chains (Figure 12.8), Sears and K mart emerge as strong rivals (note that only the sales from the department store division are considered here). Wal-Mart stands out for its exceptional rate of growth, just as J.C. Penney displays the slowest growth rate. The traditional 'downtown' department stores are clustered around the average growth rate for the retail sector. As we have already seen, two of them – Allied and Federated – have been swallowed up. The resultant Campeau chain is smaller than Federated, but larger than Allied: in the process, both The May Co. and R.H. Macy have grown as well.

A two-dimensional analysis such as this greatly oversimplifies the portfolio problem, which must also acknowledge such things as the 'fit' of the retail chain with the rest of the corporation, as well as management skills, scale economies, quality of competition, profit margins, and particular assets of the companies involved. Nonetheless, this picture of the corporate environment indicates some of the pressures that may lead a retail chain into otherwise unexpected decisions to expand or emerge, or even go out of business.

## The diversity of strategic choices

All the literature on business strategy emphasizes the variety of strategic solutions that are available, and the difficulty of deciding which one is appropriate. It is rather like growing up: your father gives you one kind of advice (go to college!), your mother another (find somebody nice and settle down), your buddy still another (let's party!). Each one may be right for some person at some point in time – or even for the same person. There is more than one right answer to the question 'What should you do?'.

Figure 12.9 makes this point for retail chains. It begins with the 694 chains that operated in Canada in 1979, chains varying in size, retail specialization, and spatial network, and observes the various choices that they made about expansion at the settlement scale. About 30 per cent of

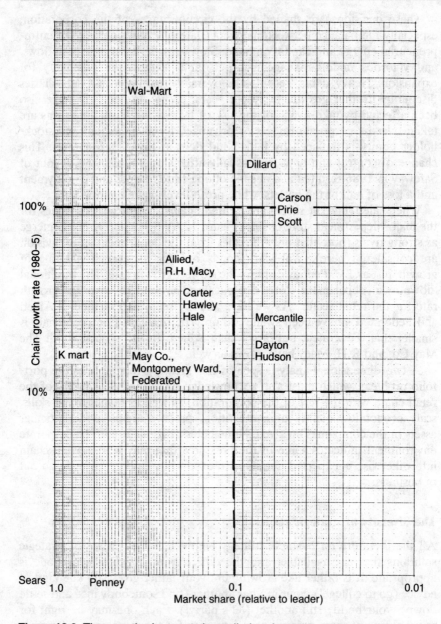

**Figure 12.8** The growth-share matrix applied to department stores

*Source:* The authors

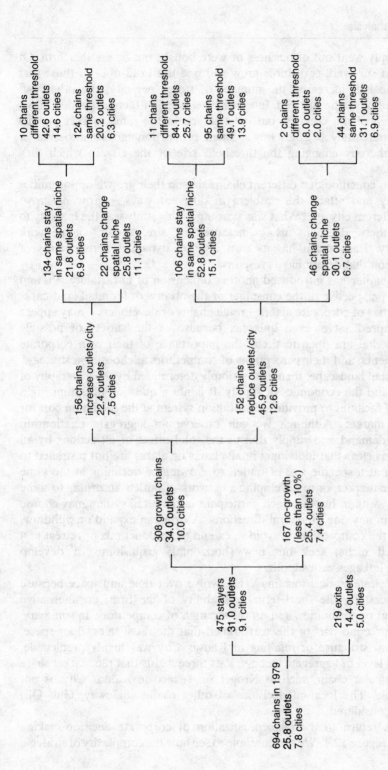

**Figure 12.9** Choices made by retail chains

*Source:* J. Simmons and B. Speck (1988) 'The spatial imprint of business strategy', *Discussion Paper no. 35*, University of Toronto, Department of Geography

them simply went out of business or were bought out by another firm. Of those that survived, two-thirds grew and one-third did not. Of those that grew, one half increased the number of stores per city; the other half sought out new cities instead. In either case, some of them expanded into a new region of the country, but most stayed in the same market (spatial niche) where they began. Only a small proportion moved into smaller centers, thereby changing the threshold size of the city in which they operated.

We can conclude that different chains size up their growth opportunities differently and attack the problem in different ways – grow/no-grow; same/different city, etc. What was startling in this study was the inability to explain these decisions using measures of size, sector, or network geography. Each chain has its own internal dynamics and patterns of competition that determine its response.

This chapter has introduced another dimension of uncertainty. Viewed from the perspective of the consumer or the observer of a retail landscape, the activities of corporate actors – retail chains or developers – may appear to be unpredictable, even quixotic, because of the variety of possible strategies that are open to them, the importance of their own corporate environments, and their perceptions of competitors in choosing a strategy.

The retail landscape, then, is not simply determined by the geography of demand and the economics of supply. It is not a question of optimizing a system of facilities to provide a distribution system at the minimum cost for a given market. Although we can observe an aggregate relationship between demand and supply due to the total effect of all actions by all actors, it is clear that individual retail chains or plazas are not restricted to operating at a specific size of outlet, to growing or declining at the same rate as the market, or to developing a network of outlets according to some simple algorithm. Instead, each participant in the retail system may choose to move in any one of several directions. A firm can expand or withdraw, confront the competition or avoid it, extend the product mix or retreat to a specialized niche, seek out new (horizontal) acquisitions or develop (vertical) linkages with suppliers.

These strategic decisions may also evolve over time and space because they depend on the short-term profitability of the firm, on alternative investment opportunities, and on the strength of competitors. In summary, while the second part of this text argued that the retail sales, floor space, and spatial structure of retailing in Kansas City was highly predictable, given the level of aggregate income, Part three insists that the market share of a particular chain, such as Kroger or Texaco in Kansas City, is not predictable. The location decisions of other chains (Safeway, Gulf Oil) must be considered.

Let us return to the conceptualization of corporate decision-making shown in Figure 12.1. We are now able to see how the complexity of strategic choices increases as we move upward on the graph from the lowest level. At each higher stage, the spatial scale becomes more extensive, the options become broader and fuzzier, and more and more managerial skills are required. Many different decisions at the lower level are nested within each upper level. For example, a lengthy sequence of site-by-site evaluations is part of the input to a single location strategy. The location strategy, in turn, is only one element of a marketing strategy that includes advertising, packaging, store design, and personnel policies. Also, the marketing strategy itself must fit within the financial strategy of the retail chain and its corporate parent. The point of a corporate strategy is to compare explicitly the different operating divisions.

Another form of complexity is the increasing spatial and sectoral scale of issues. At the bottom of the diagram the issues are quite specific, involving one site and one narrow sector. However, as we move upward, the spatial options expand to a network of sites, to alternative regions and market segments not yet evaluated, until we reach the corporate level where the vitality of the entire industry – indeed the national and international economy – becomes part of the concern.

## Further reading

Day, G. (1986) *Analysis for Strategic Marketing Decisions*, St Paul, Minnesota: West Publishing Co.

Epstein, B.J. and Schjeldahl, D.C. (1984) 'Supermarket innovation and retail market equilibrium', *GeoJournal* 9, 2: 155–62.

Ghosh, A. and McLafferty, S. (1987) *Location Strategies for Retail and Service Firms*, Lexington, Massachusetts: D.C. Heath and Co.

Knee, D. and Walters, D. (1985) *Strategy in Retailing: Theory and Application*, Oxford: Philip Alan.

Kotler, P. (1980) *Marketing Management* (4 edn), Englewood Cliffs, New Jersey: Prentice-Hall.

Johnson, G. (ed) (1987) *Business Strategy in Retailing*, Chichester: John Wiley & Sons.

Laulajainen, R. (1987) *Spatial Strategies in Retailing*, Dordrecht, Netherlands: D. Reidel.

Laulajainen, R. (1988) 'The spatial dimensions of an acquisition', *Economic Geography*, 64: 171–88.

Lord, J.D. and Wright, D.B. (1981) 'Competition and location strategy in branch banking: spatial avoidance or clustering', *Urban Geography* 2, 3: 189–200.

Lord, J.D., Moran, W., Parker, T., and Sparks, L. (1988) 'Retailing on three continents: the discount food store operations of Albert Gubay', *International Journal of Retailing* 3, 3: 3–54.

McDaniel, S.W. and Kolari, J.W. (1987) 'Marketing strategy implications of the Miles and Snow strategic typology', *Journal of Marketing* 51, 4: 19–30.

Mercurio, J. (1984) 'Store location strategies', in R.L. Davies and D.S. Rogers (eds) *Store Location and Store Assessment Research*, New York: John Wiley & Sons.

Ohmae, K. (1982) *The Mind of the Strategist: Business Planning for Competitive Advantage*, New York: Penguin Books.

ReVelle, C. (1986) 'The maximum capture or 'sphere of influence' location problem: hotelling revisited on a network', *Journal of Regional Science* 26, 2: 343–58.

Sparks, L. (1986) 'The changing structure of distribution in retail companies: an example from the grocery trade', *Transactions of the Institute of British Geographers* NS, 11: 147–54.

Simmons, J. and Speck, B. (1988) 'The spatial imprint of business strategy', *Discussion Paper No.35*, University of Toronto, Department of Geography.

Tietz, M.B. (1968) 'Location strategies for competitive systems', *Journal of Regional Science* 8: 135–42.

West, D.S. (1981) 'Testing for market presumption using sequential location data', *Bell Journal of Economics* 12: 129–43.

West, D.S. and Von Hohenbalken, B. (1984) 'Spatial predation in a Canadian retail oligopoly', *Journal of Regional Science* 24: 415–27.

# Part four

# The future

The final part of this book looks backward as well as forward, attempting to pull together the material from previous chapters into a coherent package, yet at the same time opening the discussion further to suggest some alternatives to the present retail environment.

A central theme in Part four is the close relationship between retail activity and the social system in which it is embedded. This theme was identified in Part one, but set aside in many of the intervening chapters where we focused on the direct interdependence of consumer and retailer.

Two aspects of the social environment will be discussed. Chapter thirteen describes some of the ways in which government affects retailing and specifically examines the planning function of local government. We argued earlier that the very existence of markets and retailing depends on the protection of the state. Without currency or legal systems to protect property and support contracts, without highways and marketplaces to deliver customers to the store, and without weights and measures and inspectors, the retail system that we know could not function. However, the benefits that society derives from more efficient consumption are partially offset by a variety of problems. Some people associate retailing with clutter, noise, visual pollution, or economic exploitation. Inevitably, the social system intervenes to correct these problems, regulating and investing in a variety of ways which together form the planning process.

It should be emphasized that these interventions by government are not new: in fact, they are almost universal throughout history and in many different countries. The very origin of cities derives from the need to set up controlled markets where people can trade freely, away from the anarchy of bandits and the feudal restrictions of kings and clergy. Planned, managed, and controlled markets are a necessary means of working out the complex relationship between consumption and society. The details of the market regulations and planning procedures reveal the priorities of the society: from attitudes to religion or liquor, to economic concentration and small business, to the relative importance of food or wine or the automobile.

From the location analyst's point of view we can see society, represented by government or the local planning agency, as another major actor in the retail system. The goals and procedures of this actor are laid out in legislation. Chapter thirteen introduces these activities as they affect retailers in a variety of issues: zoning, funding, and redeveloping. Government, it appears, is not always a protagonist in these debates. In many instances the conflicts pit one retailer, developer, or retail cluster against another. Sometimes it is difficult to identify the interests of the public in these debates.

In looking at the future of retailing, we must examine the trends of change in the social system, such as the rate of growth of different segments of society, the locations of residences, and the trends in lifestyle and behavior. This is the subject of discussion in Chapter fourteen where we try to match the changes in society with the changes in the supply side – the technological and organizational innovations that help to transform the distribution system. The list of topics that could be discussed here is almost endless: the media, transportation, planning policies, computers, new kinds of products. Inevitably, this chapter is broadly speculative, examining many changes that may never occur, but it also permits us to ponder the process of change itself, and how the ability to analyze retail environments can contribute to a wider understanding of the world in which we live.

# Chapter thirteen

# Planning and the retail environment

**The US government runs the seventh largest grocery chain in the country: its military commissaries sold $5.2 billion worth of goods in 1988.**

**Regulatory decisions that favor nationwide media and transportation systems also favor national brands and national retailers.**

**Almost every innovation in retailing – a new store, a new product, a new retail format – requires the approval of some public agency. In the process, almost every other aspect of the operation can be debated.**

**Planning agencies are more diverse and fragmented than development firms. There is always one local government willing to accept any proposal.**

As we emphasized in the first chapter, the values of society, as expressed in public policy, affect many different aspects of the retail environment. Dawson (1980), for example, has identified five different kinds of public intervention (Table 13.1). Location restrictions, derived from land use planning, are most closely related to the concerns of this chapter. Policies about pricing, business structure, efficiency, and consumer protection affect location only indirectly, although they may significantly modify the supply side of retailing. Dawson's table reinforces the argument that retail activity is firmly embedded within the needs and restrictions of the social system. Society's support of such institutions as private ownership, the enforcement of contracts, and law and order make retailing possible. In return for this support, limits are imposed on the retailer's freedom to deal with competitors and customers.

**Table 13.1** Types of government intervention

| Type | Level of government | Problems | Relevant policies |
|------|---------------------|----------|-------------------|
| Location regulation | Local | Incompatible land uses, competing retail activities | Land use planning |
| Pricing controls | State, federal | Merit, non-merit goods, local monopolies (services) | State liquor stores, gasoline prices, sales tax, subsidies, rent control |
| Business structure | State, federal | Maintain competition, increase local control, non-merit goods | Monopoly/competition, small business policy, co-ops, franchises, multinationals |
| Efficiency (controlled entry into the sector) | All three levels | Excess retail capacity, high turnover | Licenses, planning restrictions, corporate tax regulations |
| Consumer protection | All three levels | Consumer safety, ripoffs | Licenses, inspections, regulation |

*Source:* Adapted from J.A. Dawson (1980) 'Retail activity and public policy, in *Retail Geography*, London: Croom Helm

The policies that most directly shape retail location decisions are developed by local governments. As spelled out in the planning legislation of the various states, local councils and planning agencies have the right to regular land use, property subdivision, type and construction of buildings, and their density and spacing. In recent years they have also encouraged redevelopment of older retail areas by providing loans, parking facilities, and land assembly.

This legislation has emerged over time in order to deal with a variety of urban problems, many of which relate to retailers. In fact, a high proportion of all retail developments – a new store or shopping center, or even a new way of carrying on a business – may require planning approval. This chapter is primarily concerned with planning agencies as actors in the retail system. What aspects of retailing create planning problems? Why do we have planning legislation? What does it attempt to do? How do planning goals affect retailers and developers? Think of the planning process as creating an invisible environment of incentives and restrictions which become an important part of the location decision. Exhibit 13.1 examines the impact of interstate freeways on retail location decisions.

The sections that follow first introduce the general planning concern – that of spatial externalities – and then examine a series of planning issues that involve the retail sector. Land use conflicts between commercial land uses and their residential neighbors result from the spatial impact of noise and traffic. Partly because of the existence of this legislation, planners have also been drawn into the economic battles between competing shopping center developers.

Two issues in the older part of the city require local government to take more initiative (and to spend more money): first, the regulation and improvement of specialized retail strips that have emerged over the last decade, and second, the encouragement and management of redevelopment of aging commercial facilities downtown.

## Externalities

The rationale for extensive planning powers, planning agencies, and elaborate planning processes is the spatial externality. It can be defined as 'a cost or benefit to one activity (or location) as the result of the actions of another activity over which it has no control.'

Retailing provides many examples of externalities, some of which have already been discussed. For example, store A holds a giant sale. Neighboring stores B and C benefit from the increased traffic attracted to the sale since they sell different products, while store D down the block, which competes directly with A, sees its sales decline. Nearby residents reap the bargains but suffer from the traffic, the parking problems, and the noise. Store A's actions have affected three different neighbors in three different ways. Exhibit 13.2 examines the externalities generated by suburban shopping center – Perimeter Center in Atlanta.

Planners have always been concerned with reducing the immediate or short-term negative externalities of particular land uses, such as the noise and traffic from an all-night gas station located within a residential area. Land use regulation or zoning has a long history. In the period of rapid urban growth of the 1950s and 1960s, planners also became aware of the long-term negative impacts of growth that overloads roads, utilities, and schools. Thus, planners try to maximize positive externalities such as access

## Exhibit 13.1
## THE IMPACT OF THE INTERSTATE

The most important retail locations of the post-war period have been created by governments (almost accidentally) as the indirect effects of freeway construction. Not only did the explosion of highway building in the 1950s and 1960s improve the overall accessibility, shifting the location advantage toward the suburban malls, but it also designated a complete hierarchy of locations. Some kinds of intersections gave access to neighborhood markets, others to communities, and at freeway interchanges with major highways, regional shopping centers bloomed. A medium-sized city with a typical freeway network might give rise to perhaps twenty possible locations for major malls. Politics plays as great a role in suburban retail development as it does downtown.

Two recent papers suggest that the impact of interstate networks on retail activity can be specified quite precisely. Moon (1987) shows that retail structures around interchanges in non-metropolitan (hence non-zoned) areas depend on the morphology of the interchange and thus indirectly on the kind of road that intersects with the interstate. Double interchanges (with service roads) are most conducive to development; trumpet interchanges (often used for commuter suburbs) frustrate commercial developers; cloverleafs, diamonds, legs, and halfs rank in that order between the two extremes.

Norris (1987) is interested in the morphology of the retail development itself. On the I-75 (Detroit to Florida) the 354 exits have, on average, 7.3 commercial establishments, of which 37 per cent are gas stations, 24 per cent are restaurants and 14 per cent are hotels and motels. Gas stations and motels are usually found closest to the exit, with the major chains closer than the independents. Fast-food chains prefer the larger, more competitive exits, even if they have to settle for second-best sites.

The interstate network and its travelers have created a linear central place distribution with predictable retail clusters and predictable internal morphology – a product of decisions by highway engineers and state politicians to which the retail chains have responded.

*Sources:* H.A. Moon (1987) 'The relationship between interstate highway interchange design and nearby commercial development', *Proceedings of Applied Geography Conferences* 10: 112–18; D. Norris (1987) 'Interstate highway exit morphology: non-metropolitan exit commerce on I-75', *Professional Geographer* 39,1: 23–32

Exhibit 13.1 (*continued*)

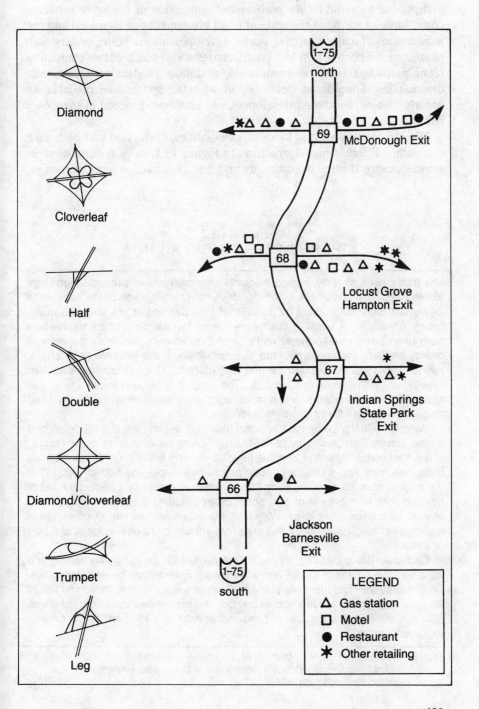

Diamond

Cloverleaf

Half

Double

Diamond/Cloverleaf

Trumpet

Leg

I-75 north

69 McDonough Exit

68 Locust Grove Hampton Exit

67 Indian Springs State Park Exit

66 Jackson Barnesville Exit

I-75 south

LEGEND

△ Gas station
□ Motel
● Restaurant
✱ Other retailing

to schools, to minimize negative, short-term externalities such as garbage dumps, and to avoid future problems of congestion or excessive servicing costs. More recently, as the scale of retail investment has increased and the implications of major shopping center developments are better understood, planners have been drawn into controversies about which of two competing retail projects should be encouraged, and how to deal with economic externalities. Should the development of retail space take place in an orderly fashion, or should developers, old and new, proceed at their own risk?

We can identify several kinds of externalities, both good and bad, each one with a different spatial structure. In Figure 13.1, store A benefits other stores because it attracts customers and has an attractive external design,

### Exhibit 13.2
### THE PERIMETER CENTER: ATLANTA

The traffic generated by a super-regional shopping center provides significant externalities to other stores or office activities. Over the years, the successful early malls were surrounded by a clutter of free-standing stores and strip malls, taking advantage of passing customers. Recently, the developers themselves have been trying to reap the advantages of the center by assembling groups of nearby activities that can profit from its accessibility. In the example shown here, the developer has surrounded the mall with office buildings to create a suburban 'downtown' with shopping amenities. The project is so successful that it has attracted other developers and new transportation investments, and now challenges downtown Atlanta as an office location.

Perimeter Center began as a regional mall (two department stores) developed by the Rouse Corporation in 1972. Nearby acreage was sold to major corporations for head offices, and to office developers. The Marriott Corporation built a hotel (see map) and a smaller upscale plaza (Park Place) was added – all part of the original plan. Then, in the early 1980s, a new expressway attracted a burst of development to the west of this development, adding three more hotels and several new office complexes. With over 20 million square feet of office space and many prestigious tenants, this area now attracts more new office space than downtown.

Each new office building reinforces the market for the shopping center, and enhances the attractiveness of earlier buildings. Externalities beget externalities. On the negative side, there are problems with sewage disposal, traffic and transit service, and aggressive attempts to buy out and rezone nearby residential areas. Can this suburban downtown expand indefinitely at a location where no one expected it to be?

Source: T.A. Hartshorn and P.O. Muller (1986) Suburban Business Centers: Employment Implications, final report for US Department of Commerce, Economic Development Administration

Exhibit 13.2 (continued)

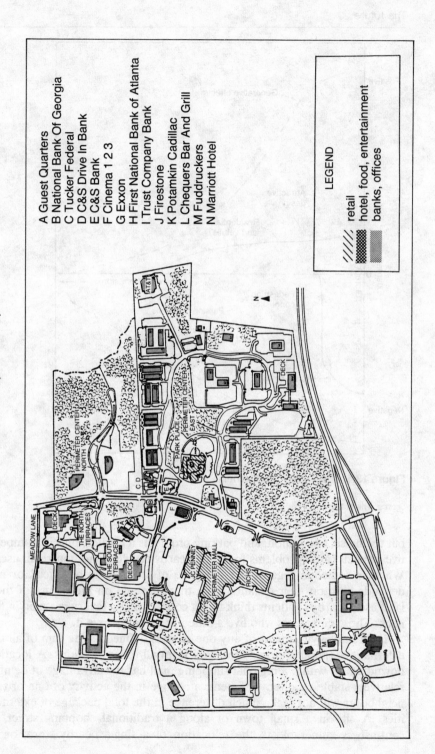

A Guest Quarters
B National Bank Of Georgia
C Tucker Federal
D C&S Drive In Bank
E C&S Bank
F Cinema 1 2 3
G Exxon
H First National Bank of Atlanta
I Trust Company Bank
J Firestone
K Potamkin Cadillac
L Chequers Bar And Grill
M Fuddruckers
N Marriott Hotel

LEGEND

/// retail
▦ hotel, food, entertainment
▨ banks, offices

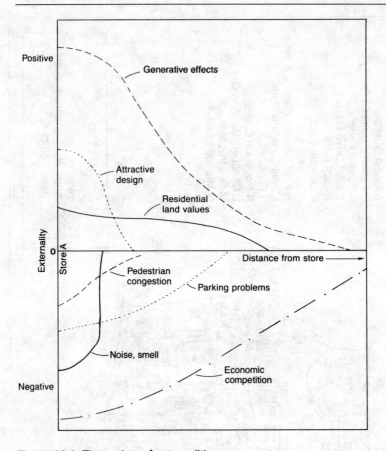

**Figure 13.1** The variety of externalities

*Source:* The authors

but the noise, congestion, and parking problems it creates, plus its competitive impact, cause problems for some nearby retailers and non-retail users. Whether someone regards the presence of store A as beneficial or not depends both on their distance from the store and on the nature of their land use. Nearby residents think that a country music tavern is a pain in the neck. Those customers who live a little further away love it.

The retail environment of any one store is defined as the sum of all the externalities (good and bad) received from all other locations. A location downtown or within a regional shopping mall has the advantage of being a relatively stable retail environment: a change in the activity of one or two neighbours will not make much difference in the total package of externalities. A site in a small town or along a traditional shopping street, in contrast, is vulnerable to the relocation of a single nearby store, or to invasions by a competitor. Recall that half the stores in an unplanned retail strip will change hands over five years. A stable retail environment is a major attraction of the planned shopping center for retailers. Most of the major externalities are controlled: traffic, parking, pedestrian flow, policing, tenant selection, and so forth.

Because of their concern with managing land use externalities, land use planners welcomed the innovation of the planned shopping center. Compared to the typical strip development, planned centers improve traffic control, eliminate parking problems, and reduce conflicts with residential uses. Also, because malls are designed for a fixed scale of operation, there are no further demands for roads or services. The planned mall is one of the keystones in a planned community. However, because planned shopping centers may add large amounts of retail space, planners have been drawn into acrimonious disputes about the allocation of urban markets among competing retail centers and shopping center developers. Should this new developer be permitted to locate near that existing mall? By helping to create and protect spatial monopolies, planners have encouraged disputes over the profits that result.

Over time, planners have come to take more direct responsibility for preserving and improving retail environments. Various initiatives have been taken to improve the retail strips within the city, from the viewpoint of both the merchant and the consumer. Everyone benefits from having a better place to shop. The concern with downtown development has a more practical motive. This is (or may have been) the most expensive real estate in the city and there is pressure to protect these investments as an important source of local tax revenues. Downtowns, too, are major factors in shaping the image of the city for visitors. They may suggest either vitality or decay.

While Americans harbor the illusion that governments play relatively little part in their lives, the reality is quite different, as the study of retail activity confirms. Tax considerations affect decisions to invest in new facilities, or to merge or divest. The geography of local government, real estate taxes, transportation investments and planning policies affect the location of investments. The great department stores depend on transit systems; the super-regional plazas seek out freeway interchanges. Politicians and planners control the level and pattern of retail competition by restricting the number of plaza sites and directing the flow of funds for redevelopment. The wealthier the neighborhood, the more restrictions on the retail presence.

Nonetheless, America may be less directly interventionist than other countries. Canada and Britain use land use controls more explicitly (and thereby invest less public money in redevelopment). European countries and Japan are more concerned with controls over retail operations: organization, pricing, size of store, opening hours, etc.

## Land use conflicts

Residential neighborhoods tend to be ambivalent about retail facilities. While homeowners appreciate the convenience and competition created by the presence of nearby stores, they tend to be less enthusiastic about stores that locate right next door. One of the major factors behind the complex land use regulations that have emerged in every major city has been the desire of residents to reject retail and service activities deemed undesirable. Originally residents were opposed to laundries and livery stables; later it was gas stations and fast-food outlets; more recently taverns, video arcades, and striptease bars. The history of these conflicts is embedded in the planning legislation that survives.

The system of land use regulation, as it has evolved over the years, has three major impacts on retail activities. First, planners have delineated locations judged to be suitable for retailing and areas to be kept as residential. This restricts the choice of sites for retail outlets. A desirable market in an upper-class suburb may leave no vacant sites for certain retail activities. Second, retail and service activities themselves have been sorted into groups according to their traffic requirements and externalities, to encourage clusters of retailers with similar nuisance levels. Third, the planning process permits the evaluation and modification of any significant change in the retail fabric. Intervention procedures, initially designed to prevent land use conflicts, now permit debate about economic conflicts as well as externalities.

The first response to the externality conflicts between residents and retailers was to separate the two land uses. This policy incorporated the conventional location logic of allocating retail activity to highly accessible sites and prevented the occasional off-beat occurrence of a family retail enterprise expanding within a residential street. The downtown area, major arterial streets, and all important intersections were zoned commercial (Figure 13.2). Retailers were encouraged to locate there, maximizing contact among retail activities and minimizing friction with residents.

Further problems emerged in the 1920s with the growth in use of the automobile and the development of the free-standing service station. Gas stations sought out isolated locations on major streets which were not yet developed commercially. They often stayed open late and on weekends and generated more noise and traffic than the corner grocery store. The automobile led to other kinds of arterial retailing, such as used car lots, bars, and motels. As a result, commercial zoning became more restrictive as planners began to sort out categories of retail and service activities that seemed to belong together, or that created similar externality problems (Table 13.2). Once commercial land uses were separated from the rest and classified into different clusters of activities, planners began to view metropolitan retail structure in the way it was presented in Chapter seven – as

428

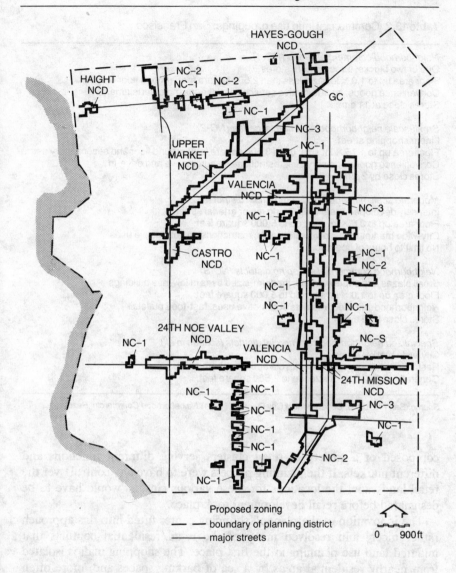

**Figure 13.2** The configuration of commercial zoning: San Francisco

*Source:* San Francisco, Department of City Planning (1984) *Neighborhood Commercial Rezoning*
*Note:* NC-1 NC-2 NC-3 NC-5 NCD = neighborhood commercial districts; GC = general commercial

**Table 13.2** Commercial land use groupings: San Francisco

*Neighborhood commercial center (NC-1)*
One or two blocks; three or more stores.
Floor area up to 1.0 × lot size; less than 2,500 square feet; ground floor only.
Convenience goods; no automotive services or drive-ins; no entertainment.
Stores close at 11 p.m.

*Small-scale neighborhood commercial center (NC-2)*
Linear shopping street
Floor area up to 1.75 × lot size; up to 3,500 square feet; ground floor and second story uses.
Convenience goods and services; restrictions on automotive and drive-in.
Stores close by 2 a.m.

*Moderate scale neighborhood commercial district (NC-3)*
Intensely developed linear strip, along major arterial street.
Floor area up to 3.6 × lot size; up to 5,000 square feet.
City-wide market areas; diversified uses; restrictions on automotive uses.
No limit to hours of operation

*Neighborhood commercial shopping districts (NC-S)*
Small plazas and supermarkets; medium-sized uses in low-rise buildings.
Floor area up to 1.0 × lot size; up to 5,000 square feet.
Neighborhood-oriented; restricts automotive uses, fast-food outlets.
Stores close by 2 a.m.

*Specialized neighborhood commercial districts (sixteen in all)*
City-wide market areas.
Restrictions tailored to functional role and neighborhood.
Generally up to 2.0 × lot size; up to 2,500 square feet.

*Source:* San Francisco, Department of City Planning (1984) *Neighborhood Commercial Rezoning*

composed of a variety of retail clusters serving different functions and different markets. If the planning process were to have any control over the retail landscape, the locations for these various clusters would have to be designated before retail development took place.

The innovation of the planned shopping center fitted into this approach rather nicely and resolved many of the retail/residential conflicts that initiated land use planning in the first place. The shopping mall is isolated from nearby residential areas by a sea of parking spaces and, more often than not, has been designed to fit within the layout of the entire community. Its size, traffic flow, tenant mix, and design are all appropriate for both the site and the market area, and the mall is sold to the public as a necessary community service.

However, the planned center did not solve all the externality problems. Successful malls attract traffic from a wide area, and other retail uses and strip malls attempt to locate on nearby access roads. Also, many stores and retail clusters continue to thrive outside the shopping malls. Some 60 per cent of urban stores are located along streets, arterial roads, or highways.

Debates between residents and retailers continue in these locations and there is concern about the size of large, free-standing stores, such as supermarkets and furniture retailers.

Furthermore, the fact that the shopping center is tailored to serve a finite residential market creates a new kind of planning problem. The planning agency designates potential sites for major shopping facilities on the basis of access to market, size of market, etc. – the kinds of criteria that we discussed in Part three. Each of these sites has a partial spatial monopoly over a given market (as indicated by a Thiessen polygon). The sales from that residential market will reward the shopping center developer, but which developer should get the rewards? To what degree will access to that market be protected from potential competitors? While the urban land market takes care of allocating retail sites as part of the development sequence, the protection of trade areas for shopping centers is very much part of the planning and political process. Planning agencies are placed in the position of defending or protecting the spatial monopoly of the developer, either by diverting other potential retail sites to non-commercial land uses, or by challenging the need for competing facilities. The shopping center is such a large and important economic element (or profit center, or competitor, depending on your point of view) that any new proposal is bound to generate controversy.

**Economic competition**

The use of political power to limit economic competition has ample precedent in America, in the early attempts to prevent catalogue sales or pedlars in small towns, or to exclude chain retailers from local markets. Still, the innovation of the large, planned shopping centers during the 1950s raised these conflicts to a new level. It became possible to create almost instantaneously a new retail facility as large as the existing downtown, or to locate another shopping mall across the street from an existing center, with dramatic implications for businesses committed to the original location. Politicians and planners were soon drawn into the conflicts and developed analytical procedures to try to cope with the problems.

The first set of issues threw independent retailers and downtown landowners into conflict with suburban shopping mall developers. Downtown retailers complained that the new malls, with their free parking, easy automobile access, and national retail chain outlets, took away their business. In larger, growing cities where there was rapid overall growth in retail sales, the retail system quickly adjusted. Downtown lost food stores and the mass marketing provided by Woolworths. Typically (but not always), the central area developed specialized retail roles. The early malls could not really challenge the variety and amenities of a successful downtown for specialty shopping. The smaller cities and towns were more vulnerable, however, and some developers have systematically exploited these markets with negatives effects on downtown retail activity and tax revenue. In these communities most of the shopping now occurs in the plaza on the edge of town, accessible only to those with cars, while downtown houses a collection of vacant and decaying store fronts, and serves the less mobile and the less affluent.

The politics of resolving these conflicts are made more complicated when downtown and the suburban malls are located in different municipalities. As a result of the mall the city loses tax revenue, while the neighboring county or suburb is delighted to receive the tax revenue from the shopping center, which requires a minimum number of services. Unless the state government intervenes there is no political mechanism to compel the city and the county to negotiate a solution. (Exhibit 13.3 examines the case of Minneapolis and the Mall of America.)

Within metropolitan regions, long and bitter disputes about the location of regional shopping malls have broken out between adjoining local governments. The regional mall serves a broad area, cutting across a number of different suburbs, and it generates large amounts of property tax. A 500,000 square foot regional center, generating $200 sales per square foot, produces $100 million in sales per year. If the real estate tax averages only 0.5 per cent of sales, revenue to the municipality amounts to $500,000 per year. In many parts of the country these economic conflicts are argued out as part of the land use planning process, and may eventually

Exhibit 13.3
## MINNEAPOLIS AND THE MALL OF AMERICA

The City of Minneapolis has invested considerable money over the years to maintain and improve its downtown retail function: for example, the Nicollet pedestrian Mall, the skywalk system (Exhibit 7.6) and a number of major private-sector retail redevelopments – over 3 million square feet of retail space in all. Imagine their reaction when the Triple-5 Corporation, of West Edmonton Mall fame, came to town with a proposal to build the biggest suburban shopping complex in the USA in a neighboring community.

When the Metropolitan Sports Facilities Commission built a covered stadium in downtown Minneapolis to replace the old stadium in the suburb of Bloomington, they recompensed Bloomington by giving them the site of the old stadium at a nominal price. Bloomington went looking for development prospects and attracted Triple-5, who offered to build a 4 million square foot shopping center, including seven department stores, plus water park, amusement part, ice rink, etc., and a convention center. The local council was attracted by the forecasts of 24,000 jobs and $650 million in real estate assessment ($29 million per year taxes) although subsidies from a variety of government levels account for about half of the $1 billion cost.

The City of Minneapolis was upset by the retail threat — such a project would absorb much of the future growth of retail sales in the region – and by the convention center, which would compete with their own convention center project. At the same time, since they had no direct control over Bloomington and were indirectly responsible for the provision of the site in the first place, they had to work cautiously. A series of reports by both the City and The Metropolitan Regional Council attacked some of the more obvious exaggerations in the Triple-5 proposal. (Triple-5, the only firm with experience in developing a center of this scale, refused to release sales data from the West Edmonton Mall.)

Eventually, these attacks on the credibility of the development led to difficulties in financing, and Triple-5 was forced to share the project with the better-known Melvin Simon & Associates (often financing approval is more difficult than planning approval). At present Triple-5 owns only 25 per cent and the project has been scaled down to 2.6 million square feet (retail), but it will still have a major impact on the downtown area.

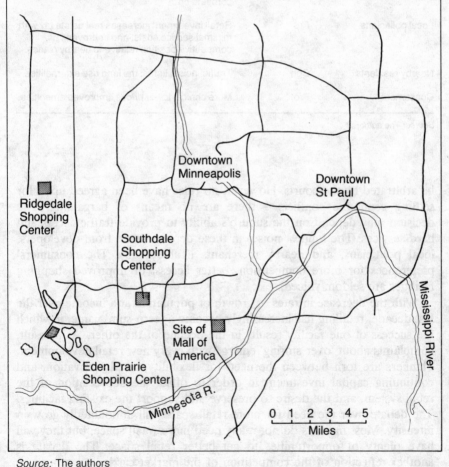

*Source:* The authors

**Table 13.3** Interest groups in the shopping center debate

| Actor | Attitude | Reasons |
|---|---|---|
| The developer who proposed the new mall | Pro | Perceived profit, due to market growth, market truncation, or a more innovative product. |
| The nearby mall | Con | Profit decline, for the same reasons cited above. |
| Downtown retail merchants | Con | Threatened by an overall surplus of facilities and shift in attractiveness away from central business district, plus introduction of national chains. |
| Planning staff | Mixed | Support planned centers as a retail form, but opposed to 'excessive' retail facilities and competition. |
| Local politicians | Pro | Retail investment increases real estate tax with minimal service costs, and improves competitive position relative to nearby places. |
| Nearby residents | Con | Traffic, noise, lights; the land use externalities. |
| Consumers | Pro | More choice, lower prices, improved amenities. |

*Source:* The authors

be arbitrated by the courts. However, no rules have been agreed upon for settling economic conflicts – there are no means of bargaining. The decision may depend on the suburb's ability to provide traffic access and hard services. The loudest noises in these debates come from developers, local politicians, and nearby merchants (Table 13.3). The consumers' preferences for more competition, better access, or improved shopping facilities are seldom voiced.

With the decrease in rates of growth of population and income over the last decade, retailing has increasingly become a 'zero-sum' game, in which the success of one facility results in the decline of the other. As a result, complaints about 'over-storing' emerge with every new retail development. Planners are torn between the need for flexibility, retail innovation, and continuing capital investment in order to offset the depreciation of the retail system, and the desire to preserve and support the existing facilities. The debate over the need for more retail space will undoubtedly grow in intensity. Most markets do not really need more retail space, but they will have plenty of opportunities to get better retail space. The debate is another reflection of the competition of the market carried on at a more aggregate level. At the same time, public agencies have begun to take more positive initiatives to bring about the kinds of retail structure they desire.

## Specialized shopping areas

While the residential neighbors of an inner-city retail cluster may be able to tolerate the problems caused by facilities that they themselves use, they strongly protest against stores that serve through traffic, or specialized stores that cater to customers from all over the city. Inner-city specialty retail clusters of this type generate far more controversy than corner grocery stores or snack bars.

Planning theory, derived from studies of the urban retail structure of the 1960s, still tends to think in terms of retail clusters that serve nearby neighborhoods. The reality, as shown in Chapter seven, has been the emergence of specialized retail groupings that serve portions of the entire metropolitan community. Consider a modest shopping street in an inner-city residential area. It served a working-class immigrant market, all within walking distance. As the population aged, they were replaced by middle-class professionals who liked the ambience of the housing and the shops, as well as the accessibility to downtown. One by one the houses were renovated, and soon after the old shops began to be replaced by upscale food shops, antique stores, and intimate little restaurants. After a couple of 'lifestyle' articles in the local newspaper, visitors from the suburbs began to come in to stroll around in the evening or on a weekend. As more stores flourish, the little shopping street that used to serve the neighborhood now serves thousands of people, living in all parts of the metropolitan region. They all show up to shop and eat on Saturday evening, with their cars. Greenwich Village, the near north side in Chicago, and Georgetown in Washington DC are long-standing examples of the problem. The residents of San Francisco's colorful neighborhoods are constantly at war with commercial interests. A recent protest in Haight-Ashbury between the survivors of the counter-culture and a super-drugstore chain resulted in a burnt-out store and the withdrawal of the chain. Exhibit 13.4 examines the planning restrictions imposed on a specialized retail area in San Francisco: Castro Street.

These patterns occur in various forms throughout the older parts of the city. Some areas are taken over by new immigrant groups, e.g. Hispanics or Asian communities, or by specialty functions, such as art and antique districts. Local residents are initially charmed by the shopping amenities that are generated, but are soon appalled by the accompanying noise and traffic that result, overwhelming the residential neighborhood and destroying the quiet ambience that originally attracted the residents. The small restaurants and coffee shops are transformed into bars that stay open later and later. Tourists are attracted by the colorful stores, busy streets, and

## Exhibit 13.4
## PLANNING A SPECIALIZED RETAIL AREA:
## SAN FRANCISCO'S CASTRO STREET

The San Francisco City Planning Department is trying to fine-tune planning restrictions to fit the varied types of functional specialization that are developing in older retail areas. Castro Street developed around an important transfer point on the cable-car system to serve an Irish-Catholic, working-class neighborhood. About 20 years ago it became an important commercial center for the gay community, attracting people from all over the San Francisco metropolitan area.

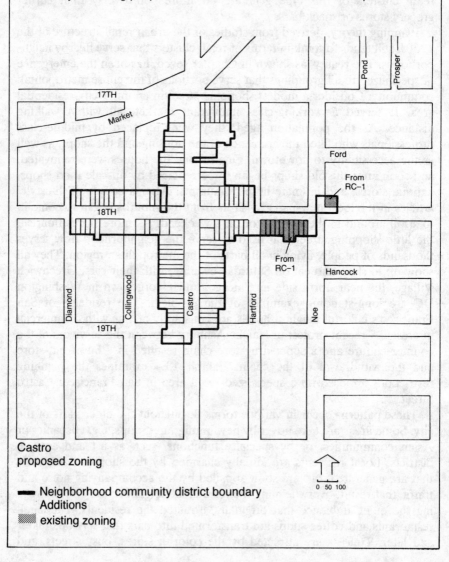

Castro
proposed zoning

— Neighborhood community district boundary
Additions
▨ existing zoning

> While a variety of convenience stores still serve the immediate neighborhood, by 1983 the specialized retail function had generated fifty-three bars and restaurants, intensifying traffic and parking congestion, and night-time noise. Residents protested. The new plan freezes the boundary of the district, restricts the height, lot size, and building size of new activities, prohibits new eating and drinking places, and restricts entertainment uses. Any further expansion will have to occur elsewhere.

*Source:* The authors

vibrant (i.e. noisy) nightlife. In part, the district functions like part of downtown, but without parking lots, public transit, or office buildings to isolate it from its neighbors. How do planners manage these externality problems without destroying the vitality of the retail development?

Many planners would like to turn back the clock by encouraging 'traditional' shopping streets, with small stores to serve local, pedestrian markets. They have not accepted the specialized shopping streets that are now so widespread. The problem seems intractable because of the traffic and the differential rates of expansion of the retail strip and the residential neighborhood. Even in San Francisco, where planners recognize the specialized neighborhoods, the expansion is discouraged. Perhaps there is no real solution; residents may have to adjust and decide for themselves whether to pay the price of living in the middle of all the amenities and costs of a particular lifestyle.

Still, a number of solutions present themselves, all costing money. Off-street parking in lots or garages is essential, plus improved transit facilities. Proper traffic and parking improvements in these areas may permit some form of pedestrian malls. Small investments in signs, benches, and landscaping can help to accentuate the special nature of the area.

Perhaps this land use conflict is more ephemeral than we realize. Specialized retail strips evolve and migrate, just like their clientele. Twenty years ago Haight-Ashbury in San Francisco threatened its conservative neighbors: now it in turn is threatened by the affluence of the residents who are moving into the area. People with money to spend both attract and welcome more stores. One specialization can replace another – from hippie to yuppie, from Italian to Hispanic, from punk to chic.

## Downtown improvement districts

Many older retail areas have difficulty attracting the number of shoppers and the level of investment required to preserve them as attractive and prosperous retail environments. The downtowns of smaller cities and some of the older retail strips of larger cities share the same problems. The rapid growth of planned shopping centers and changes in the character-istics of nearby residential areas leave such retail clusters vulnerable to various forms of blight or decline. If the same problem occurred in an aging shopping mall, the developer would renovate the facilities, upgrade the public space, change the image, and perhaps restructure the tenant mix. How can such renovations occur in an unplanned center?

For a long time no-one cared very much about this problem, but during the 1970s the energy crisis brought about a renewed concern for preserving and recycling older commercial areas. The Federal Government introduced Community Conservation Guidelines and Community Impact Analysis to prevent new developments from destroying the old. While the Reagan administration (1981–9) promptly rejected such programs, the concepts

### Exhibit 13.5
### PIKE PLACE MARKET: SEATTLE

A classic example of government involvement in the redevelopment of retail areas is the Pike Place Market in Seattle. The market originated in 1907 as an attempt by the municipal government to break a local wholesaler's monopoly over food distribution. The city sponsored an open-air, public market where local farmers sold their produce directly to the consumer. By the 1930s, the market had reached a peak with over 600 independent farmer-merchants selling on a daily basis. Two events led to its rapid decline. First, the internment of Japanese Americans in 1941 reduced the number of merchants by over 50 per cent, and second, the North American suburban shopping mall phenomenon reduced retail activity in the central city.

By the 1960s, Seattle's downtown business community, developers, and media supported an urban renewal plan that would have demolished the original market blocks. In response, a local citizens' action group mounted a 'Save the Market' campaign. As a result of the 1971 municipal election, the Pike Place Market was officially designated as an historic retail-commercial district and the 7-acre farmer's market was saved.

To co-ordinate the restoration and manage the project, the Preservation and Development Authority was chartered in 1973. This public, non-profit-making corporation manages 80 per cent of the property in the historic district and is responsible for leasing, parking lot management, promotion, advertising, main-tenance, and security.

By 1986 the Pike Place Market regularly comprised 225 commercial tenants, 100 farmers, and 230 artists and crafts people – all independents since no regional or national chains are permitted. The Authority estimates that the market attracts over 20,000 shoppers daily and generates a yearly gross revenue of $30.4 million, 75 per cent of which is food-related.

*Source:* The authors

Exhibit 13.5 (*continued*)

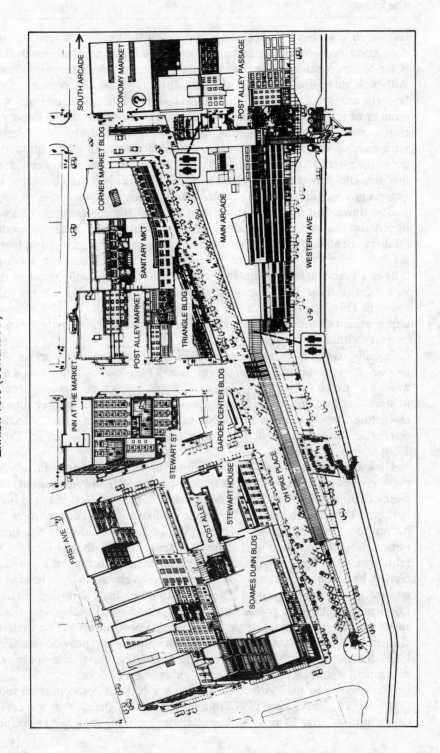

survive in a variety of approaches supported by local agencies. We can distinguish two levels of intervention: the downtown improvement district is funded by local merchants, using some form of special tax assessment. Although there are hundreds of these districts across the country, their budgets are small and the main impact is cosmetic. Nonetheless, in a number of instances these initiatives have led to more substantial improvements, such as street malls, that affect the flow of traffic and relative attractiveness of different retail sites. The second form of intervention, the downtown retail development, involves the construction of new retail facilities and may cost up to $100 million. The cost is shared between the various governments and the private sector participants.

The downtown improvement district requires the co-operation of local merchants. By working together, in phase and in the same direction, retailers are able to raise and spend money for improvements and to lobby for help from various levels of government. While the concept operates differently from state to state and from city to city, it usually requires the vote of the local businessmen and appropriate legislation by the city council. This legislation permits the merchants to set up a downtown improvement district with the power to levy a special property tax on each business within the designated area.

Initially, downtown improvement districts concentrate on 'bricks and mortar' improvements: planting trees, installing benches, improving sidewalks and parking, upgrading signs, and encouraging a common approach to store-front design. Once these improvements are in place, they turn to marketing surveys and promotional activities, replicating the collective activity of the planned shopping mall (see the typical budget in Table 13.4).

How effective are they? The amount of money that is spent directly by these groups is trivial, within the overall pattern of retail investment, but their expenditures are concentrated in areas and on projects that are both visible and very much needed: the public environments of private stores. In the more successful examples, the image of the retail district has been turned around from one of decline to a sense of growth and innovation (although, as in many retail success stories, the good fortune of a growing market has probably helped). Downtown improvement districts have also attracted investment by public agencies through their lobbying efforts. Local merchants get a good hearing from politicians. Local governments spend money on parking, or parks, or street improvements. The Federal Government or the state may have a parallel program to provide grants or loans for transportation improvements, upgrading the public space, or developing a cultural focal point, e.g. a gallery or a craft center.

The pedestrian mall is one of the most substantial outcomes of such organizations. Rubenstein (1978) identified 100 of them, with a median expenditure of over $1 million. The additional funding usually comes from

**Table 13.4** Downtown Improvement Districts: typical budget (1983)

| Main expenditures | Budget ($) |
|---|---|
| Administration | 9,810 |
| Street improvements (e.g. sidewalks, lighting, landscaping) | 4,920 |
| Street beautification and decoration (e.g. flowers, banners, flags, Christmas decorations) | 5,090 |
| Maintenance | 2,250 |
| Promotion/advertising | 15,030 |
| Special events | 3,640 |
| Parking/transit programs | 2,350 |
| Planning (studies, concept plan, consultant fees) | 1,350 |
| Other | 4,430 |
| Total budget | 48,870 |

*Source:* S. Fletcher (1985) 'A national overview of commercial area initiatives', Report for the Ontario Ministry of Municipal Affairs and Housing, Community Renewal Branch, Toronto

the Federal Government (before 1981) and local government agencies. Weisbrod and Pollakowski (1984) evaluate their impact as slowing the decline of downtown. In successful examples (e.g. Downtown Crossing in Boston; State Street Mall in Madison, Wisconsin) they attracted new activities – especially chain restaurants and apparel stores – and helped the rest of the central business district. However, some of them have not been effective (e.g. Lexington Mall in Baltimore). Success depends very much on the local context.

Perhaps the most important role of the downtown improvement district is to encourage independent retailers to work together and provide a countervailing political force to the economic power of the shopping center developer. Someone can speak for downtown or the older retail strips, but the downtown improvement districts speak for the business community, not for consumers or nearby residents: there is seldom any provision for their representation. As a result, a downtown improvement district may pursue solutions that exclude local residents, such as trying to move upscale, or encouraging specialized retail activities. A downtown improvement district may want to tear down housing to build parking garages, or to extend commercial zoning into residential areas. Security precautions may lead to conflict with residents. Downtown improvement districts may frustrate planning agencies attempting to improve traffic flow or to restrict the location of certain kinds of retail activity.

## Retail redevelopment

Land use planning procedures were originally designed to maintain the landscape the way it was rather than to create new structures. The implication was that retail clusters should maintain their form, their function, and their relationship to surrounding residential areas. As the previous sections have suggested, however, this goal sometimes flies in the face of other social and economic trends that transform the urban landscape. In every city, for example, the role of downtown has declined within the overall retail structure over the last two decades. Both the distribution of the market and the nature of the competition are fundamentally different. How should downtown adjust?

Changes in existing retail structure cannot be handled through the conventional land use planning process. They require initiatives in design, financing, and the provision of services that lie outside the provisions of planning legislation. Often, new agencies and initiatives are required in order to develop solutions to the changed relationships. Table 13.5 lists some of the major redevelopment projects that have occurred in the downtown areas across the country. Each one has required significant co-operation between the private sector and government; often two or more levels of government are involved. The Federal Government may provide funds (urban renewal, Urban Development Action Grants, transportation investments) or tax relief (*The Economic Recovery Tax Act*, provisions for rehabilitation). The local government may raise funds from bonds, give tax incentives, assemble land, provide infrastructure, award zoning bonuses, or transfer development rights.

Such complex projects take enormous effort and commitment by several different parties, often requiring up to a decade to come to fruition. Nonetheless, there are many examples across the country, many of them including substantial retail components. The major actors usually include the developer (often the Rouse Co.), who may or may not assemble the land, the major department stores, which control key sites and have a strong vested interest in redevelopment, and the local government agency, often a special-purpose public corporation set up for the purpose. The city provides the services and, in particular, the access to customers by road or transit. The negotiations among the participants are often difficult because their goals vary so widely and the financial commitments are sizeable. As Table 13.5 indicates, the various levels of government typically provide one-third of the cost, with little direct provision for return.

If successful, the redevelopment provides a new anchor for the whole downtown area and, paradoxically, involves many of those firms that built the suburban malls which threatened the central city in the first place. Not everyone benefits equally from these downtown redevelopments. Some major stores and most independent retailers are left out. A store's ability to take advantage of the transformed downtown depends on the micro-geography of the project: the layout of the new mall relative to other shopping streets, parking lots, and major office buildings. Some parts of downtown will become more central as a result: other parts more

**Table 13.5** Major downtown retail redevelopment projects

| City | State | Project | Date | Size (GLA) (thousands of square ft) | Cost ($ millions) | Anchors | Public funds |
|---|---|---|---|---|---|---|---|
| Fremont | CA | Fremont Hub | | | | | |
| Glendale | CA | Glendale Galleria | 1983 | | 75 | | |
| Hawthorne | CA | Hawthorne Plaza | 1977 | | | | |
| Long Beach | CA | Long Beach Plaza | 1982 | | | | |
| Oakland | CA | The Rotunda | | | | | |
| Pasadena | CA | Plaza Pasadena | 1980 | 585 | 110 | – | 50% |
| San Bernardino | CA | Central City Mall | 1972 | | | | |
| San Diego | CA | Horton Plaza | 1985 | | | | |
| San Francisco | CA | Pier 39 | 1978 | | | | |
| | CA | Embarcadero Center | 1982 | | 375 | | |
| San Jose | CA | The Pavilion | | | | | |
| Santa Monica | CA | Santa Monica Plaza | 1980 | | | | |
| Santa Rosa | CA | Santa Rosa Mall | 1982 | | | | |
| Sunnyvale | CA | Sunnyvale Town Center | | | | | |
| Bridgeport | CT | Crossroads Mall | | | | | |
| Stamford | CT | Stamford Town Center | | | | | |
| Washington | DC | Metro Center | | | | | |
| | | Georgetown Park | 1981 | | | | |
| | | Union Station | 1988 | | | | |
| Miami | FL | Omni International | 1977 | | | | |
| Chicago | IL | Illinois Center | 1982 | | | | |
| | | Water Tower Place | 1984 | | | | |
| | | Atrium | 1988 | | | | |
| Columbus | IN | Courthouse Center | 1973 | | | | |
| Baltimore | MD | Harborplace | 1980 | | | | |
| Detroit | MI | Renaissance Center | 1977 | | | | |
| Minneapolis | MN | St Anthony Main | 1978 | | | | |
| | | The Conservatory | 1986 | | | | |
| | | City Center | 1984 | | | | |
| | | BCE Center | 1988 | | | | |
| St Paul | MN | Town Square | 1980 | | | | |

**Table 13.5** (*continued*)

| City | State | Project | Date | Size (GLA) (thousands of square ft) | Cost ($ millions) | Anchors | Public funds |
|---|---|---|---|---|---|---|---|
| Kansas City | MO | Crown Center Shops | | | | | |
| St Louis | MO | St Louis Center | 1985 | – | 120 | Famous-Barr Stix et al. | $20 million |
| New York | NY | Union Station | 1985 | | | | |
| | | Trump Tower | 1983 | | | | |
| | | South St Seaport | 1983 | | | | |
| | | Herald Center | 1985 | | | | $22 million parking |
| Niagara Falls | NY | Rainbow Center | 1982 | 220,000 | 35 | – | |
| White Plains | NY | G. of White Plains | 1980 | | | | |
| Cleveland | OH | Tower City Center | | | | | |
| Columbus | OH | Columbus City Center | | | | | |
| Portland | OR | Pioneer Square | | | | | |
| Salem | OR | Nordstrom Mall | | | | | |
| Philadelphia | PA | G. at Market East | 1977 | 230,000 | 110 | Gimbels, Strawbridge & clothier | $40 million |
| San Antonio | TX | Galleria II | 1983 | | | | |
| Salt Lake City | UT | Rivercenter | | | | | |
| Bellevue | WA | Crossroads Center | | | | | |
| Seattle | WA | Bellevue Square | | | | | |
| | | Westlake Plaza | | | | | |
| | | Rainier Square | 1978 | | | | |
| | | Pike Place Market | | | | | |
| Green Bay | WI | Port Plaza Mall | 1977 | 850,000 | – | Boston Store, Penney, Prange | $40 million |
| Milwaukee | WI | The Grand Avenue | 1982 | – | 70 | Gimbels, | $35 million |
| Charleston | WV | Charleston Town Center | 1984 | 930,000 | 60+ | Sears, Penney Ward, Kaufman | 50% + $30 million loan |

Sources: J.T. Black et al. (1983) Downtown Retail Development: Conditions for Success and Project Profiles, Washington, Urban Land Institute; B.J. Frieden and L. Sagalyn (forthcoming) Behind the New Downtowns: Politics and Prospects, London, Croom Helm.
Note: GLA, gross leasable area.

peripheral. The developer of the project fights to minimize the external economic impacts: planners for the city want to increase these spillovers.

Figure 13.3 describes one of the most spectacular of these initiatives – the Galleria at Market East in Philadelphia. Although Philadelphia has always retained a lively downtown, supported by an important office complex and a long-standing mass transit system, the retail component has been threatened by the decline of an aging commercial area stretching east of City Hall toward the river, and a low-income residential area to the north. Market Street is the traditional shopping street, and at one time four department stores (Lit Brothers, Stern's, Strawbridge and Clothier, and Gimbel's) surrounded the intersection with Eighth Street. However, the office complex around City Hall, the John Wanamaker department store, and the high-income sector all pull the retail district westward. Lit Brothers went out of business, Stern's withdrew, and Gimbel's was reconsidering. One long block to the south of Market Street is the Chestnut Street transit mall (not a shopping mall), constructed in the 1970s with the help of several million dollars in federal funds.

The Galleria project required the co-operation of several participants. The City built a parking garage and skywalk, and renovated the transit station at a cost of $22 million. The Redevelopment Authority invested $18 million in the mall structure. Strawbridge and Clothier renovated its store at the east end of the project ($12 million); Gimbels crossed Market Street (and downsized) into a new building ($40 million). The Rouse project, The Gallery, only 200,000 square feet in size, links the two department stores. Its success led to a further expansion westward (Galleria II), incorporating a new J.C. Penney store, and to discussions for further westward extensions toward Wanamaker's.

The project solidifies the eastern anchor of downtown, linking the major retail nodes to the office complex further west. The parking garage, the new transit station and the skywalk linking the major shopping nodes insulate shoppers from the street, usually perceived as dirty, noisy, and dangerous. In the parallel pedestrian street that has emerged between Market and Filbert, access is controlled and security maintained for both shoppers and merchants. At the same time, the level of pedestrian traffic outside the mall has declined, affecting nearby merchants, especially those on the south side of Market Street. Redevelopment on that side is complicated by a number of public buildings. To some degree, then, the redevelopment potential of every retail site on the map has been affected by the transformation of customer traffic due to the Market East project. Every downtown redevelopment has this impact.

The Galleria has been a success for the developer, with over $40 million worth of sales per year. If it attracts other major developments it will have been a success for the public sector. The project has reshaped the opportunities for future developments because it is now necessary to be linked

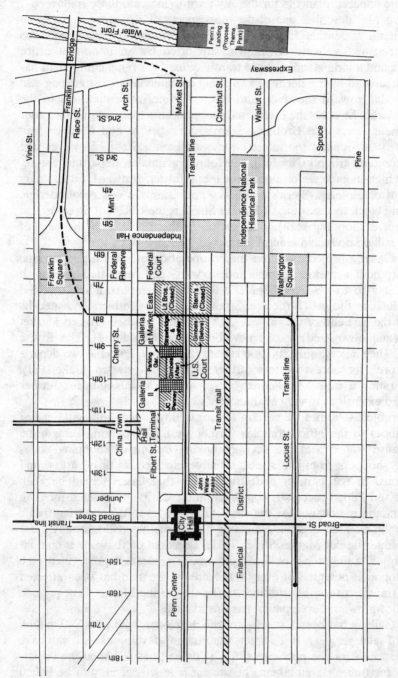

**Figure 13.3** Downtown Philadelphia: the Galleria at Market East

*Source:* The authors

into this off-street complex. Market Street may remain an important address for retailers, but they will increasingly face inward to the malls and atriums in the center of the block. The Rouse goal is to complete a link between the office and retail development around City Hall and the Independence Mall tourist complex eight blocks east.

This chapter has introduced the various retail conflicts dealt with by the political process: the regulation of land uses to control externalities, the analysis of economic impacts, and the encouragement of redevelopment. In each instance, society has a wider interest, which may be in conflict with the desires of individual entrepreneurs or consumers. The planning profession helps to define and represent the interests of society, but we should also note that planners often take a middle-class viewpoint. As well-educated professionals, they prefer retail environments that are clean, safe, diverse, and attractive in a sanitized way. They are less enthusiastic about inexpensive, unsanitary, grubby retail clusters that serve the poor or recent immigrant groups. They prefer the gentrified retail strips or shopping malls to the chaotic street markets that preceded them.

The public sector, then, tends to encourage the sameness that bedevils North American retailing. Planned centers are preferred over unplanned centers. Downtown improvement districts all impose the same solutions: interlocking brick sidewalks, sandblasted facades, and nineteenth century street lamps. The harborfront theme projects that have blossomed in so many cities have a remarkable sameness, as if their developers all read the same architectural magazines. They all serve the same upper-middle-class market with the same condominiums, marinas, exhibits, and expensive shops and restaurants. These places are the preserves of tourists and the well-to-do. To date, the most visible expressions of public influence on the retail environment have no room for the segments of the population that are poor, or not part of the predominant culture – the old, the young, the poor, the recent immigrants – all those who lack an effective political power base.

Does a social system need more diversity and innovation in the retail environment? We think so. How can we obtain it? Here are some suggestions. First, we need to readjust existing retail land use categories to recognize the nuances of the specialized retail clusters that are emerging. Each different type of retail cluster may need distinctive legislation and assistance. Ethnic retail strips may need public investment in parking and amenities. Fashion streets may simply need permission to be creative. Second, new forms of retail stores and retail clusters must be recognized if the retail environment is going to respond to social change. Should there be publicly supported, low-cost retail space available to new independent retailers? A kind of flea market or street market?

Third, we need to extend the variety of retailing forms oriented towards the lower end of the income scale. Planning assistance and public investment should be channelled to low-income retail strips, perhaps in the form of public washrooms instead of parking lots, with better policing instead of new sidewalks; in any case, an effort is needed to make even bargain shopping an attractive experience. Can we insist that major food retailers or banks maintain inner-city outlets to serve older people? Fourth, the public sector must conduct market research that is aimed at the full spectrum of the population, not just those households that can vote with their dollars. Where do senior citizens shop? What amenities do they want? How can we assist those residents of ghetto areas who can't 'outshop' to surrounding centers? What rights should teenagers have in the modern shopping plaza? Or in the redeveloped downtown mall? Can our laws be sufficiently flexible to tolerate the food customs of new Americans from the Orient or Central America?

How does the public sector participate in the process of change that connects the retail structure of the past with the retail structure of the future? Do we collectively resist changes in the retail environment, or actively encourage them? Or do we try to shape them in some way?

## Further reading

Alexander, L.A. (ed.) (1980), *Strategies for Stopping Downtown Shopping Centers: A Guidebook for Minimizing Excessive Suburban Shopping Center Growth.* New York: Downtown Research and Development Center.

Alexander, L.A. (ed.) (1986) *Downtown Retail Revitalization: The New Entre-preneurial Strategy.* New York: Downtown Research and Development Center.

Alexander, L.A. (1986) *Downtown Improvement Districts*, New York: Downtown Research and Development Center.

Black, J.T., Howland, L., and Rogel, S.L. (1983) *Downtown Retail Development: Conditions for Success and Project Profiles*, Washington: Urban Land Institute.

Davies, R.L. (1984) *Retail and Commercial Planning*, London: Croom Helm.

Dawson, J.A. (1980) 'Retail activity and public policy', in J.A. Dawson (ed.) *Retail Geography*, London: Croom Helm.

Dawson, J.A. and Lord, J.D. (eds) (1985) *Shopping Centre Development; Policies and Prospects*, especially Chapter 5, 'Federal and State intervention in shopping centre development in the USA),' London: Croom Helm.

Frieden, B.J. and Sagalyn, L. (1990) *Downtown, Inc.: How America Builds Cities*, Cambridge, MA: The MIT Press.

Levin, M.S. (1975) *Measuring the Fiscal Impact of a Shopping Center on its Community*, New York: International Council of Shopping Centers.

National Trust for Historic Preservation (1982) *National Main Street Center: Training Program*, Washington.

Rubenstein, H.M. (1978) *Central City Malls*, New York: John Wiley & Sons.

San Francisco Department of City Planning (1984) *Neighborhood Commercial Rezoning Study*.

Schwartz, G.G. (1984) *Where's Main Street, USA?* Westport, Connecticut: ENO Foundation for Transportation.

# Chapter fourteen

# Looking to the future

**It is possible that by the year 2000, stores as we know them will have disappeared, to be replaced by videos and teleshopping. It is not likely.**

**Once customers were no longer constrained by the tyranny of distance, the retail structure underwent an explosion of new forms and specializations. Perhaps the next constraint to be removed is time.**

**Technological changes will have less effect on future retailing patterns than the continuing shifts in household composition and income.**

Where is the retail system going? What parts of it will grow? What activities will decline? If only we knew!

Certainly the retail structure will change. Retail activities continually evolve with changes in demand, in the social environment, in retailing technology, and in corporate organization. New products, new stores, new locations, new chains, and new corporate linkages are introduced daily. Those innovations that succeed provide the blueprint for the future. Those that fail are simply dead ends, footnotes in the evolution of the retail system.

This chapter does not attempt to make predictions. Instead we look for some of the underlying factors and indicators that will affect the direction of change (see Table 14.1). On the demand side we consider household growth, increased income, and consumer mobility, and we raise questions about consumer behavior. Will continuing changes in household compos- ition and lifestyle alter the relationships between income and the level and pattern of in-store purchases? Will the demand for personal services, such as travel, fitness, or kinky sex, replace retail purchases such as shoes or furs? Would people prefer to own material things or to be part of exciting events? To shop for furniture or to be pampered in an expensive restaur- ant?

On the supply side, such prosaic innovations as automated cash registers, inventory control and store security systems are likely to have more effect than the more publicized 'Star Wars' forms of computerized shopping. Worth special mention are the implications of changes in the roles of major participants in the retail system. How far can the integration among developers and retail chains proceed? As retailers gain more autonomy and more debt through buyouts, will the failure rate increase? Will the trend towards national and international integration – leading to the North American, or even the world market – affect consumers?

**Consumer demand**

The amount of retail activity in the future will be governed by the level of retail sales; which, in turn, will be determined by the number of house- holds, the average income per household, and the household's propensity to expend that income in stores instead of banks or travel agencies. As Fig. 14.1 suggests, the growth in population has been extremely regular, at least since the end of the baby boom in the 1960s. Most of those who will be active consumers in the year 2010 have already been born; there is not much room for surprise. The Bureau of the Census estimates that the annual rate of growth of households will decline from the present rate of 1.5 per cent to below 1.0 per cent in the year 2000. The growth rate in households combines the growth of the population (particularly young adults) and their propensity to live together and have children. The former increases the number of households; the latter reduces it. The growing share of older (and therefore smaller) households keeps the household growth rate higher than the population growth rate.

**Table 14.1** Factors in retail change

| Factors | Trend | Implications |
|---|---|---|
| *Demand side* | | |
| More households | Regular growth 1.5% per year | Continued spatial expansion of city |
| Smaller, older households | Approaching limit? Diverse: old, singles; temporary liasons | Shifts consumption; specialized retail environments? |
| Higher incomes/ household | slowing down, erratic | Intensifies competition |
| Women in labor force | Increases, as new entrants replace aging housewives | Convenience over economy. Shifts in expenditures? Shop near work? Fashion-oriented. |
| *Supply side* | | |
| Automation in stores | Pervasive | Favors larger chains; barriers to entry |
| Larger stores? | Trend is reversing (greater specialization) | Scale economies less important |
| Part-timers | Increasing rapidly | Longer opening hours. Retailing linked to workplace, recreation instead of home. |
| Fewer teenagers | Labor shortage | Self-service |
| Catalogues, computer links | Variable penetration | Certain sectors, locations, or households may find this attractive. |
| Smaller inventories | Variable penetration | Smaller floor area, closer links to distribution |
| *The actors* | | |
| Developers | Growth of new plazas declines | Specialized inner-city developments |
| Megachains | Continue to expand, also franchising | Multi-sector, international |
| Department stores | Declining share | Intensify links with developers. Kiosking. |
| Planners | Decline of suburban growth, refocus on inner city | Upgrade retail environments: amenities, tourists |

*Source:* The authors

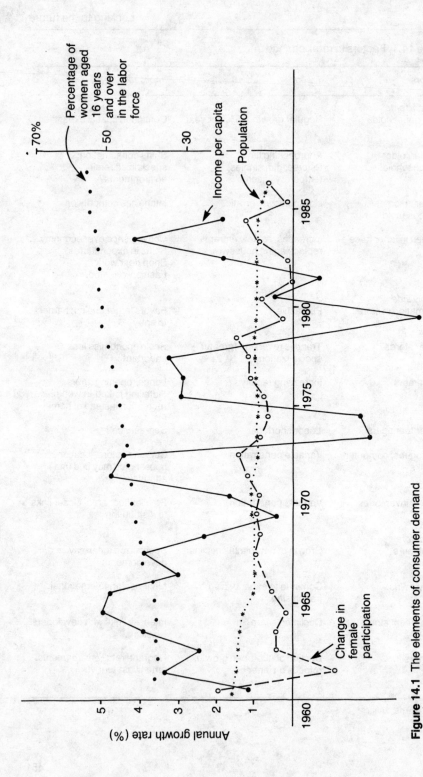

**Figure 14.1** The elements of consumer demand

*Source:* Bureau of the Census (various years) *Statistical Abstracts of the United States*

Changes in the age composition of households are also quite predictable: by the year 2000 the number of households under 25 years of age will decline by 10 per cent, the number aged over 65 will increase by 25 per cent, but the number aged 45–54 years will increase by 65 per cent (Sternlieb and Hughes, 1988). The proportion of Black households will grow from 12 to 13 per cent; the proportion of Hispanics from 7 to 9 per cent. All these changes will have disproportionate impacts on different retail sectors and locations.

The level of household income is more difficult to predict. As we emphasized in Chapter six, the increase in income per capita has been one of the great engines of growth in retail activity over the last century. The future, however, is less certain. The growth rate in income per capita has fluctuated wildly over the past decade, and no one can be sure that it will ever return to earlier levels of growth. As household size decreases, zero growth in per capita income means an actual decline in the real income per household, and an intensification of competition in the retail sector. Retailers also worry about a polarization of household incomes between rich and poor. Squeezed between the boutiques and the discount stores, traditional retailers who target middle-class customers aren't sure which way to go.

Some extensive forecasting exercises by a group of Federal Government agencies (Bureau of Economic Analysis, see Appendix B) make more optimistic assumptions (i.e. that the future will be like the past). They forecast a population of 268 million in the year 2000, and a Gross National Product of $5.6 trillion (in 1982 dollars), Personal income and retail sales should be more than 50 per cent greater than in 1982. Income per capita should rise by one-third.

The ratio of retail sales to personal income has declined steadily over the years. In part, this decline occurs because higher-income households spend proportionately less in stores, and because spending on health and in the public sector (hence taxes) has increased. Consumption is also inversely related to real interest rates (hence levels of savings). All things considered, the ratio seems likely to continue to decline.

The third major element, personal mobility, seems unlikely to have much further impact on the retail system. Among active adult consumers, access to the automobile is close to saturation. The great majority of people have one. Travel times may continue to decline and travel costs may change, but only the marginal retail locations will be affected.

Major changes may occur in consumer behavior, however, altering both the amount and the type of retail sales. Retailers are looking anxiously at the growth of non-store attractions for the consumer's dollar. Households have become smaller, with fewer children and more women working outside the home. There will be more older households and more one- and two-person households. Will these households divert their spending to housing, to travel, or to eating out? Or will they simply save their money?

The proportion of women working will approach the saturation level of 70 per cent in the next decade, but the implications for household behavior are not yet fully clear. In the past, women have dominated consumer decisions that were primarily household choices – about food, furniture, and children – and they devoted a considerable amount of time to the shopping process. Now women have access to more money but less time. Will they avoid certain kinds of routine shopping and apply their limited time and energy to selected items? Perhaps the time is right for a semi-automated convenience goods delivery system (the robot milkman?) Or will the middle-class concept of shopping as recreation become pervasive? The rapid growth in the number of women executives has already stimulated the fashion sectors.

To some degree, household income has become a function of demographics rather than occupation or social class (see Table 4.3). Within the spectrum of American households, those with two wage-earners are generally well off; those with none are not. Retired households and single parents are poor. Two low-skill jobs generate a reasonable household income; two professional jobs mean affluence.

## Changes in the production function

Will the store of tomorrow look much different from the store of today? Some of the trends have been mentioned earlier in the book: the automation of cash registers and inventory controls may well continue to reduce the inventory level and number of staff. The average floor area of stores has begun to decline. Part-time workers will continue to replace full-time employees. Improvements in information systems encourage the 'deskilling' of staff in branch outlets, as inventory and staffing decisions are centralized (see Exhibit 14.1 and Bluestone *et al.* 1981).

Retail organizations now talk as much about 'downsizing' as they do about expansion. Managers are urged to focus on the essentials of the business and to eliminate the rest. 'Does that retail chain contribute to our profits?' 'If not, let it go.' 'Don't carry unprofitable lines.' 'Sell off the outlets with low turnover.' 'Cut back on head office personnel.' Such moves not only increase profitability: they may also improve the store's image by targeting clientele and product line more precisely. The department store gives way to the fashion store.

The trend in store size is complex. As average household size declines, the scale of shopping (purchases per trip) has declined and a preference for more varied, specialized shopping environments has increased. Supermarkets are losing market share to fruit and vegetable stores, bakeries, and delis: at the same time 'superstores' and hypermarkets are booming. Department stores are giving way to clothing chains of various kinds, but

## Exhibit 14.1
## THE COMPUTER NETWORK OF A MAJOR RETAIL CHAIN

Sears Canada has developed a highly centralized operating system that replicates its US operations. The core of the system is a computer network, in which the central computer at the Toronto headquarters is linked to four regional processors, each in turn connected to point-of-sale and office terminals in individual stores. The Canadian head office also exchanges financial data with the head office in Chicago.

Sears Canada uses this system in order to centralize three types of decisions: the administration of personnel and financial activities, store operations involving day-to-day transactions with suppliers, and merchandising, including inventory control, pricing, and advertising. The system gives each store access to centralized information about such things as available inventory and credit card authorization. At the same time the head office is able to monitor almost every aspect of each store's operation.

The full implication for retailers of these information flows is not yet clear. Better information should lead to substantial savings in the purchasing, storage, and delivery of inventory, as it has in the provision of credit. Those chains that aim at a precise market segment and stock a narrow product mix may also make substantial savings by standardizing marketing procedures – essentially deskilling the personnel in the local store. Store layout, advertising, and ordering will all be predetermined. Store management decisions will be limited to personnel evaluation and selection. However, those stores that wish to fine-tune their activities to follow a changing market may need decentralized managerial skills if they are to translate a particular inventory mix into sales. To reach a sophisticated market segment requires continued and experienced attention to purchasing, advertising, and in-store promotion.

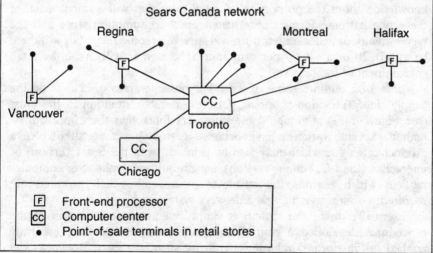

Sears Canada network

| | | |
|---|---|---|
| F | Front-end processor | |
| CC | Computer center | |
| • | Point-of-sale terminals in retail stores | |

*Source:* M. Hepworth (1987) *The Geography of the Information Economy*, unpublished Ph.D. dissertation, Geography Department, University of Toronto. Reproduced by permission of the author

some of them have responded by 'kiosking' – creating in-store boutiques for designer products. The smaller household is less concerned with price and more interested in quality and convenience. Economies of scale at the level of the store may be less important than the range of choice provided.

Paradoxically, then, as stores compete to automate and reduce costs, the customers may demand a higher level of service with better qualified personnel. Retailing is being pushed towards two extremes: a high-volume, low-mark-up, efficient, 'no frills' supermarket across the street from a specialized, hands-on, gourmet delicatessen, with imported foods served up by an avuncular butcher. Food retailers are aware that part of their competition comes from the fast-food industry which, despite its efficiency, is still an expensive way to sell ground meat. For the price of two quarter-pounders you can buy a nice piece of sirloin steak, if you are willing to grill it yourself. Will the microwave oven have as great an impact on the food sector as the refrigerator did 50 years ago?

Consumer demand is moving away from mass consumption, in which one person – typically the mother – purchased for all members of the household. The mass consumer is primarily concerned with getting the shopping done as quickly and efficiently as possible, favoring the one-stop solution: supermarkets, department stores, and suburban plazas that carry goods for the whole family. In contrast, many of today's households are made up of adults who purchase for themselves – their own clothes, records, and fast-foods. These consumers are choosier and more likely to seek out stores that specialize in the kind of goods they want. They enjoy shopping and comparing, and take pleasure in the selection process.

The great uncertainty in the retail industry stems from our lack of knowledge about the proportion of retail sales that will occur in each of these two extreme forms: the efficient mass consumption store and the high-amenity designer outlet. Both will survive in some form, but will there be an 80/20 or a 40/60 per cent split? The answer will shape the retail environment of tomorrow.

Table 14.2 outlines some of the other possible areas of change on the supply side. Television shopping gets considerable attention in the press (see Figure 14.2), although some observers think that the effect will be limited. Several varieties have been suggested, but they all involve a product catalogue which may also be printed (as in the Sears version) or interactive (the J.C. Penney version), a push-button telephone or computer modem which permits the customer to indicate which products are required, a charge system, and a delivery system.

Essentially, then, the system is simply an automated version of the procedures developed a century ago for catalogue sales and currently applied to in-store purchasing by firms such as Sears Roebuck and Montgomery Ward. The process is functional, but not very pleasurable, and is attractive mainly to those who dislike shopping or are unable to get

**Table 14.2** Areas of innovation

| Innovation | Implication |
| --- | --- |
| *Consumer contact* | |
| Vending machines | Greater variety of product: increased market share |
| Catalogue shopping | More upscale, specialized (L.L. Bean, Neiman-Marcus) |
| Telephone and cable shopping | Stay-at-homes |
| Home delivery | Fast-foods, convenience goods, staples |
| Sunday shopping/extended hours | Breaks down barrier between shopping, leisure; the 'theme' mall |
| Computerized sales information | In large stores and for complex items: cars, appliances, restaurants? |
| Video promotions | Fashion goods, restaurants |
| Coupon dispensers | Triggered by point-of-sale information |
| *Inventory control* | |
| Bar code scanning | No pricing, faster checkout, inventory monitoring |
| Point-of-sale monitoring | Records inventory, consumer behavior |
| Computer linkages | Centralizes inventory, personnel decisions |
| 'Just-in-time' restocking | Reduced storage, inventory, investment in goods |
| Anti-shoplifting devices | Fewer clerks required on floor; increased self-service |
| *Finance* | |
| Credit cards | Extended throughout population |
| Debit cards (electronic funds transfer) | Point-of-sale payment from customer's account |
| Smart cards | Microchips store data on consumer characteristics, behavior |
| 'Frequent Buyer' rewards | For regular, high-volume customers |
| Affinity cards | More segmentation in prices and merchandise |
| *Retail structure* | |
| Retail strips/small plazas | Growth of services, decline of department stores and traditional supermarkets |
| Hypermarkets: large 'combination' or 'warehouse' stores | Challenge plazas; confuse land use planners; intensify competition |
| Off-price retailers | Affect specialized retailers |
| Boutiques within department stores | |
| Auto service centers | Extend chain, franchise activities |

*Source:* The authors

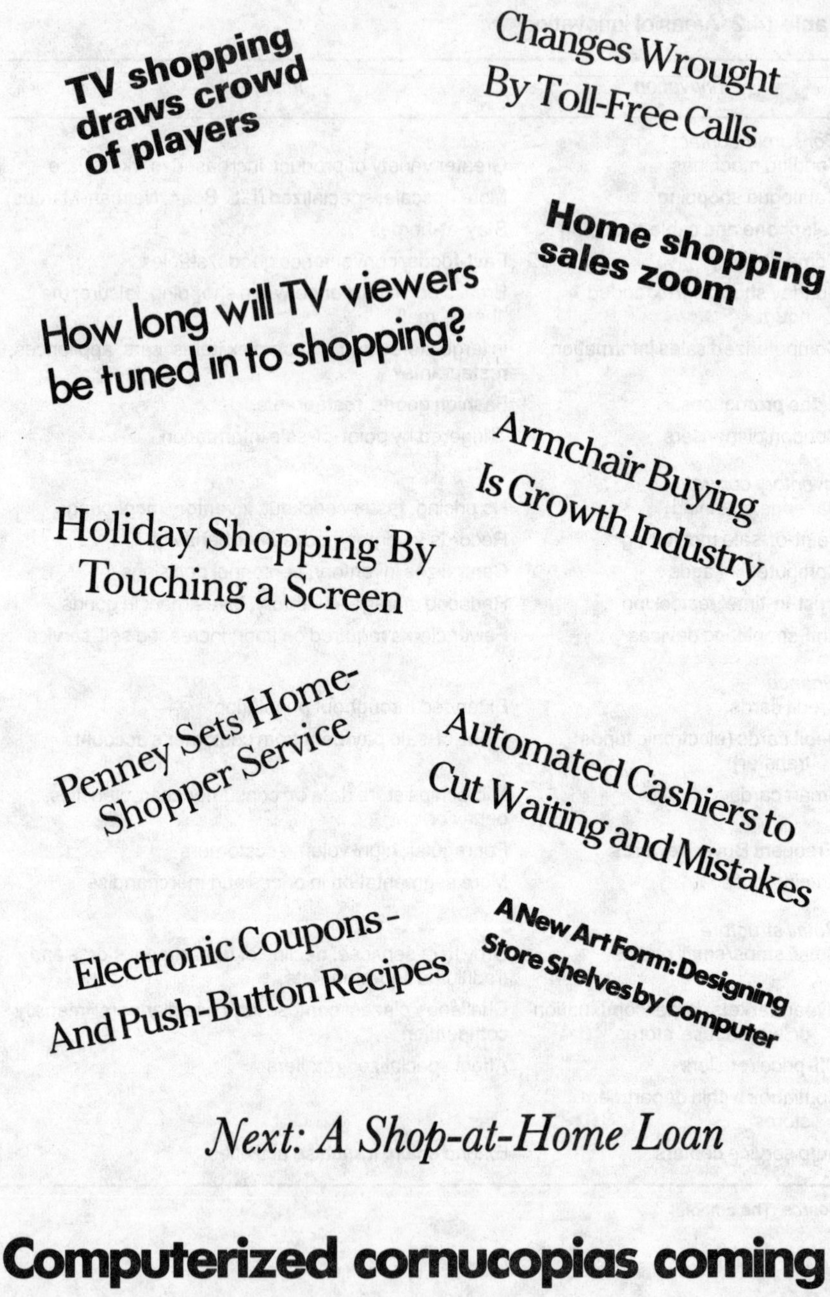

**TV shopping draws crowd of players**

Changes Wrought By Toll-Free Calls

**Home shopping sales zoom**

How long will TV viewers be tuned in to shopping?

Armchair Buying Is Growth Industry

Holiday Shopping By Touching a Screen

Penney Sets Home-Shopper Service

Automated Cashiers to Cut Waiting and Mistakes

Electronic Coupons - And Push-Button Recipes

A New Art Form: Designing Store Shelves by Computer

*Next: A Shop-at-Home Loan*

**Computerized cornucopias coming**

**Figure 14.2** The 'Star Wars' approach to retailing

*Source:* The authors

out. It leaves little room for examining products or serendipitous purchasing. No uncertainty, ambiguity, or exploration is permitted. Personnel savings in the store may be partially offset by the costs of delivery. The direction taken by these innovations may depend on whether they are dominated by retailers like Sears or communication firms such as cable television companies, or by entirely new firms. Retailers will sell the familiar products to familiar customers; telephone or cable companies may explore a variety of non-retail activities (escort services?) as well.

The pattern of penetration of such activities will be similar to catalogue shopping. Immobile households – the elderly, families with young children, and rural residents, will find it most useful. Brand names, appliances, and standardized purchases such as cleaning materials, will be most vulnerable. Sweaters, lettuce, and paperback books are still likely to be bought in the old-fashioned way.

The catalogue business itself has undergone a rejuvenation recently. The widespread diffusion of charge cards and private parcel delivery service removed a major source of irritation for both consumers and retailers, and the increased interest in upscale shopping has provided a market. Any resident of a small town in Iowa can order from Tiffany's, L.L. Bean, or Neiman-Marcus. Is this, too, the wave of the future? Mail order companies that you can trust because you buy the brand name rather than the product. Part of the growth in this sector reflects the demetropolitanization of America. The most rapid population growth has occurred in smaller centers inaccessible to the major metropolitan shopping areas. The aging of the American population helps too – over 10 per cent of all prescription drugs are now sold by mail.

Inventory control is one of the important areas of innovation in store operations. Savings in costs and time, and the improved service and range of goods that stores can provide as a result, have extended these procedures into every facet of retailing – from the largest department stores to the tiniest boutiques. Stores are able to target their stock precisely to whatever their customers need, with a minimum of excess inventory on which to pay interest or storage charges.

Until recently, these innovations benefited the larger retail chains because of the sizable investments in computer hardware and software required. Some chains have invested millions in this technology, but 'turnkey' packages are now becoming available for small independent retailers in various sectors. Will the microcomputer bring the efficiencies of inventory control within the reach of every independent store? Or will the larger chains maintain significant cost advantages? We suspect that the entire retail system will become more efficient, but it is difficult to say which components of the retail environment will benefit most.

Some analysts talk about 'economies of scope', referring to the opportunities that such technological changes provide for applications to new products. Sears Roebuck, for example, is anxious to extend the use of its information and outlet network to financial services. Travel agencies could sell insurance using the same kinds of facilities that make airline reservations. Point-of-sale data and inventory control change the relationship between retailer and manufacturer.

Financing customer purchases permits similar transformations. For a while in the 1960s, the major department stores attracted customers and built close ties with them because of their charge cards. Since then, the spread of bank credit cards has allowed every retailer to participate in the credit system. Major retailers are trying to develop new ways to use the credit card to strengthen the ties between store and customers – perhaps by giving bonuses to frequent buyers. In a sense these are simply variations on the old 'green stamps' idea.

Out of these imponderables of consumer demand and behavior, shifts in store size and type of store, and in-store technology, will emerge a different set of stores and location requirements. Many of these trends have been discussed in earlier chapters.

The retail structure – i.e. the spatial pattern of retail clusters – reflects the changing mix of stores as well as the shifts in consumer behavior. An interesting example of this relationship is the battle that pits traditional department stores and supermarkets against smaller chains and specialty outlets. Without the big stores to act as anchors and draw customer traffic, the pressure to build super-regional shopping centers has declined. The grocery superstore and the super-drugstore tend to be free-standing. As a result, the fastest growing retail clusters are now the small strip plazas, inner-city specialty strips, and downtown ancillary malls, all of which have no anchor tenants and cater to the smaller, specialized (even independent) retail outlets, as well as the expanding service sector.

Shopping oriented to the workplace and weekend or evening 'recreational' shopping seems certain to grow. Again, the driving force is a more individual pattern of consumption, in which consumers buy for themselves rather than other members of the household. Buying things for yourself is fun; buying things for other people is hard work!

However, for those households that still wish to buy in bulk and seek out bargains, other new kinds of outlets are also emerging. Huge free-standing hypermarkets sell groceries, drugs, and department store merchandise. Price-conscious stores like Wal-Mart and Target Stores are thriving. Off-price retailers and outlet centers sell brand-name merchandise at a discount. If the bargains are big enough, even mass merchandising can be fun.

### The actors

We have recorded the long-term expansion of the role of planned shopping centers and large retail chains within the retail system as a whole. How much further can these trends go? Are there new aspects to this relationship? Are new actors likely to participate? Table 14.3 indicates some of the more interesting possibilities for change in this direction.

Perhaps the key question concerns the prospect for increased concentration of control in the retail sector. While the largest retail chains and the major shopping center developers appear to have an overwhelming advantage at present because of their market power, their control over the most important shopping locations, and the barriers to entry imposed by the costs of large-scale automation, these advantages may prove to be illusory.

Retailing patterns continue to evolve. National and international chains are pushing into every market, intensifying competition throughout the spatial system. Independent stores are giving way to franchise operations. Access to new products, new procedures, and new means of financing makes for an unstable competitive environment. Corporate take-overs and

**Table 14.3** The actors

| Retail chains | Implications |
|---|---|
| **Retail Chains** | |
| International | Rapid diffusion of new products, procedures; intense competition |
| Franchises | Independents, too, develop uniform operations |
| Management buyouts | More debt; pressure for profitability |
| Vertical integration | Close links with suppliers, developers |
| Barriers to entry | Automation, control of key locations |
| Expansion into 'independent' sectors | Automobile, personal, repair services |
| Retailers push store brands; manufacturers open stores | Power struggle may change store/brand images |
| **Developers** | |
| Corporate linkages to finance and retail chains | Access to office, residential developments |
| Smaller, design-oriented firms | Greatest growth in smaller specialized units. Central city redevelopment |
| **Planners** | |
| Recreational shopping environments | Downtown? or Suburban? |
| Redevelopment rather than growth | Greater public input |
| **Government** | |
| Deregulation | Increased national and international competition; blurring of the lines between business types |

*Source:* The authors

management buyouts increase the debt loan and impose pressures for a continuing flow of profits. Increasingly, then, retail chains must operate within a narrow range of efficiency, profitability and growth.

At the same time, the barriers to entry for new retail chains may be declining. As suggested earlier, the innovations in computer technology for inventory control, accounting, and charge cards have diffused down to the level of the small retail chain. The variety of retail clusters means that a lease in a major regional shopping center may be less important than before for many specialty goods stores. Inner-city malls continue to grow in number, and specialized retail strips are expanding. In short, the pendulum could swing against the major actors in the retail system; the department stores and supermarkets.

The development industry is by far the most volatile of the major participants in the retail system. Developers build in accordance with the rate of growth of the retail market of the moment. They feed on trends and changes. Chapter eight traced some of the innovations in shopping center design and location. Currently, the industry is turning toward specialized facilities – particularly redevelopment projects – to create downtown or theme malls, and trying to renovate older plazas. Each change in the focus of the industry, however, opens the door to new entrants. Smaller retail strip malls attract local contractors. High-amenity fashion malls require special skills in design. Developers fight back by strengthening their corporate linkages to the firms that finance and anchor redevelopments and by exploiting the residential and office projects that create retail demand. The new Atrium Mall on Chicago's north side is closely integrated in every respect. The outlets in the mall are tied, floor by floor, into Bloomingdale's, and the Campeau Corporation, through Federated Department Stores, owns Bloomingdale's and is closely linked to the developer. We may see an intensification of the 'deal'; the package of design, location, anchors and finance that blows the competitors out of the water.

Planners are now more actively involved in designing retail environments as well. Inner-city redevelopment requires more complex political procedures for approval, permitting planners to impose their own requirements on the developer. Many downtown projects require substantial public investment.

One result of changes in the production side has been the ability of the megachain – with its specialized chain formats and relatively small outlets – to compete successfully against the department stores. The megachain has market power in purchasing and close operating control like a department store, but retains greater flexibility in adjusting to local market conditions. If the chain observes a decline in the income level of the trade area it can replace the upscale chain outlet A with a downscale outlet B.

However, there are other alternative solutions that work as well. The fastest-growing part of the retail system in the last few years has been the franchise sector. The franchised retailer, whether service station or fast-food outlet, applies the energy of the independent entrepreneur to a format and location determined by experts in marketing strategies and location analysis. In a franchise, scale economies of operation are preserved in purchasing, research, inventory control, and advertising. However, the attention given to day-to-day operations is decentralized, i.e. the treatment of personnel, knowledge of customers, and contacts with the community. Franchises have expanded particularly quickly in the food sector, beginning with the convenience store and more recently moving into supermarkets. Supermarket chains have discovered that much of their profitability is 'upstream' – from packaging and wholesaling. By turning over a store to a franchise owner they retain their profit but reduce their investment and avoid the hassles of personnel, administration, and union negotiations. Also, franchises have turned out to be more efficient in many cases, increasing sales by 20 per cent or more. From the point of view of the consumer, the result is almost the same: the outlet looks like every other member of the chain, has the same location requirements and standardized product mix, but the service may be better. Is there any reason why franchising couldn't work in the fashion sector?

## Watching the retail landscape

Whether or not you become actively involved in the retail industry, you can still enjoy the process of changing retail structure, both as a consumer and as a spectator. As we have argued in Chapters nine and twelve, adjustments to the retail environment as new outlets are opened or vacant stores emerge, are less and less random events and more and more the calculated response to changing demand, competition, and corporate environments.

Still, the retail landscape is full of failures – retail structures that have outlasted their popularity or projects that will never achieve success. Abandoned gasoline stations dot the landscape; major chains such as Korvette and W.T. Grant have disappeared; certain shopping districts are in decline, e.g. downtowns in Kansas City, Toledo, and Providence; Underground Atlanta boomed and busted and is now being redeveloped; Times Square in New York is going through the same cycle. Even major developers make mistakes; every city has examples like Eden Prairie Plaza in Minneapolis (Exhibit 14.2). At the same time, of course, every urban area is full of visible examples of growth, innovation, and success.

What aspects of the retail landscape should we look for? And how do we interpret them? The previous chapters have discussed some of the changes and their causes, and the corporate procedures in the retail industry. It should be possible to draw some plausible conclusions about many of the events and phenomena that you observe. Vacant stores suggest

## Exhibit 14.2
## EVEN THE MAJORS MAKE MISTAKES!

Despite the experts and location studies, retailers and developers are capable of bad decisions. The Eden Prairie Center in suburban Minneapolis is a classic example of a failure to apply location insights to a corporate decision. Built in 1976 at a cost of $15 million, the center involves two of the country's leading firms: Homart (the second largest shopping center developer) and Sears Roebuck, the largest retailer, as well as Power's (later Donaldson's), now part of Carson, Pirie Scott. The floor area is 750,000 square feet and houses about 100 tenants. As in most regional centers, the national chains are well represented, or were initially.

Since opening, the mall has been plagued by problems – store closures, failing independents, and vacancies – all stemming from low customer traffic. A close look at a map of the area around the center provides some answers. Ten years later the area around the site has still not been fully built-up. The developers misjudged available population forecasts for the metropolitan area as a

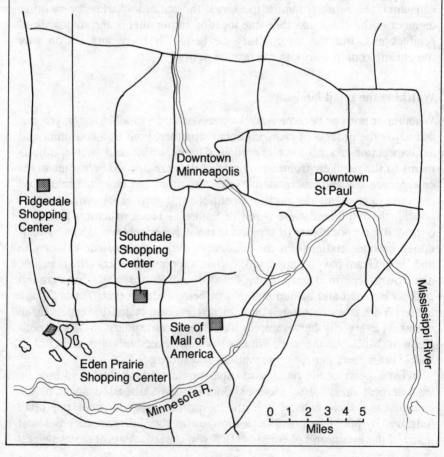

whole, as well as the direction of growth. Its market area is still located on the city side: the mall has to attract customers instead of simply intercepting them. The site itself is surrounded by small lakes that wall it off from nearby residents (like a golf green surrounded by water hazards!), while the access highway system has been long delayed in completion.

The result is a very low level of sales per square foot. With $35 million in 1982 (about $50 per square foot), this center ranked second last among the thirty centers in Minneapolis. Its major competitor, Southdale (only 6 miles away) sold over ten times as much. And here comes the Mall of America.

How many poor locations can major developers and retailers afford? Given the situation disadvantages of this center, renovations or new tenants are unlikely to make much difference. Perhaps the only solution is to wait for more growth.

*Source:* The authors

either that the local market has declined, or that there have been significant changes in the pattern of competition. Increases or decreases in average store size reflect changes in corporate marketing strategy, while the presence of many new merchants in a retail district or shopping mall suggests that the market is changing economically or culturally.

One of the more dramatic sources of change in the landscape is the corporate environment. If you open the business section of the newspaper you read about take-overs, mergers, or bankruptcies in the retail industry. Sure enough, six months or a year later you will observe changes in the store fronts, as some stores go out of business and others take on new roles. You are now in a position to evaluate the marketing and location strategies that were imposed. Which stores changed? And why? What kinds of locations were deemed disposable? How did the merger affect the strategies of other chains in the same retail sector that were not part of the merger?

As we have seen, the retail sector is continually washed by waves of innovation, sometimes minor, sometimes major: new products, store organizations, and outlet locations. Does one chain consistently introduce the new technique first? Does another consistently follow? How does the new procedure affect you as a customer? Are you attracted or repelled? Are some innovations quietly withdrawn after a short period? Are innovations introduced selectively to certain outlets, or do they go to all stores at once? It may depend on whether the chain is a leader or a follower, a dominant or a niche retailer.

Competition is a major preoccupation among retailers. It affects all their decisions about marketing and location strategy. You can watch the competition between two chains like McDonald's and Burger King just as you follow a baseball season. Each action by one chain should generate a response by the other: price wars, new products, a different store format, a major expansion in the downtown location. Do the chains compete head to head? Or do they gradually evolve to specialize in different sectors? Examine their advertising, their special promotions, and the locations of their new stores.

Of course, in the longer term you can track many of the kinds of changes in the retail structure that we have discussed in this book. Are more specialized retailing environments here to stay or just a temporary fad? In what direction is the retail strip near your house heading? Upscale or downscale? What does this tell you about the changes in your neighborhood? To what kind of shopping environments do you find yourself drawn? Where is your money spent? Has convenience become as much a question of time, in the sense of opening hours (or days) as it is of location? Can you predict the conflicts and debates that surround a planning application to build a new shopping plaza? There are plenty of hypotheses to be tested.

In Chapter one we suggested that location analysis was a valid way to learn about the distribution system. Throughout this book we have tried to show that the location perspective expands one's interpretation of larger marketing processes. You have learned how to assess existing retail structure, to explain the changes you observe in the retail system, and to devise marketing strategies. By providing a set of concepts or relationships valid in a variety of situations, the spatial approach helps to integrate the three major elements of the retail system – the consumer, the major actors on the supply side, and the existing retail structure. Table 14.4 draws some parallels between these concepts from spatial analysis and the major themes of marketing studies in general. Each spatial concept has an

**Table 14.4** Parallels between location analysis and marketing

| Location concepts | Associated marketing concepts |
|---|---|
| Accessibility/centrality | Scale economies, business concentration |
| Spatial scale<br>  neighborhood<br>  metropolitan area<br>  nation | Business scale<br>– independent<br>– chain<br>– megachain |
| Distance decay | Market penetration, market share |
| Spatial variation | Segmentation (lifestyle, income, age) |
| Site | Store characteristics |
| Situation | Marketing environment |
| Spatial behavior | Consumer behavior |
| Spatial efficiency, optimal location | Minimum cost distribution systems, network planning |
| Spatial organization of a retail chain | Corporation structures and strategies |

*Source:* The authors

equivalent concept in the broader field of marketing. An understanding of the location problem should permit the reader to grasp the second notion more readily. For instance, the theory of the distance decay of consumer demand within a trade area illuminates the more general concept of market penetration. A spatial market is simply a type of market segment. A familiarity with the varieties of spatial scale leads you easily into the differences between independents, chains, and megachains. Location strategies and the concept of the optimal location for an outlet have clear parallels in the selection of corporate strategies under various conditions.

We can argue that by now you may know more than you think. Location analysis introduces a number of general marketing concepts that may be applied in many different ways. However, we have also tried to demonstrate that our approach has some intrinsic virtues as well. The retail sector is a fascinating activity in its own right. We hope that this book will enable you to understand and enjoy an important part of the landscape, the economy, and the society in which you live.

## Further reading

Bluestone, B., Hanaa, P., Kuhn, S., and Moore, L. (1981) *The Retail Revolution*, Boston: Auburn House.

Bureau of Economic Analysis (1985) *1985 OBERS Regional Projections*, Washington.

Davies, R.L. (1983) 'A computer shopping service for the relatively housebound', *Proceedings of the Applied Geography Conference*, 4: 133–44.

Gordon, W.A. (1984) 'Electronic retailing: trends and implications', in *Development Review and Outlook, 1984–85*, Washington: Urban Land Institute.

Guy, C.M. (1988) 'Information technology and retailing: the implications for analysis and forecasting', in N. Wrigley (ed.) *Store Choice, Store location and Market Analysis*, London: Routledge.

Lumpkin, J.R. (1985) 'Marketplace needs of the elderly: determinant attributes and store choice', *Journal of Retailing* 61, 2: 75–105.

May, E., Ress, W., and Salmon, W.J. (1985) *Future Trends in Retailing: Merchandise Line Trends and Store Trends, 1980–1990*, Cambridge, Massachusetts: Marketing Science Institute.

McDonald, K. (1983) 'The commercial strip: from Main Street to Television Road', *Landscape* 27, 1: 12–19.

Sternlieb, G.W. and Hughes, J.W. (eds) (1988) *America's New Marketing Geography*, New Brunswick, New Jersey: Rutgers University, Center for Urban Policy Research.

Wrigley, N. (1989) 'The lure of the USA: further reflections on the internationalization of British grocery retailing capital', *Environment and Planning, A* 21: 283–8.

# Appendix A

**A glossary of terms used in retail location studies**

Half the difficulty in learning a new subject arises from the vocabulary. It is not simply a matter of learning new words: each academic discipline and industry imposes its own meaning on familiar terms. The list below defines what is meant when a particular word or phrase is used in this book.

*Anchor tenant*: the major store(s) within a planned shopping center that attracts customers to the center. The anchor varies with the scale of the center: regional/department store, community/K mart, neighborhood/supermarket.

*Ancillary mall*: planned center or strip incorporated into apartment or office buildings.

*Business type or activity (retail sector)*: a category of retail establishment characterized by a particular mix of products, e.g. drug store. The Bureau of the Census provides a Standard Industrial Classification (SIC) number.

*Catalytic*: a development sequence in which a major regional shopping center predates residential development and may serve as a community focal point.

*Central Business District (CBD)*: the downtown shopping complex of any discrete urban settlement; the oldest and sometimes largest shopping district, usually, but not necessarily, unplanned.

*Centrality*: the attractiveness of a settlement due to the variety of retail and service facilities it provides. Technically, centrality refers to the excess of retail facilities beyond the settlement's own requirements.

*Central place theory*: a location theory for competing activities that serve spatially dispersed consumers. It was developed to explain the network of small service centers in agriculture regions.

*Consequent*: a development sequence in which planned shopping centers are developed after the residential development (e.g. the 1950s).

*Consumer behavior*: the activities of a household, including purchasing patterns, travel patterns, and preferences for such things as access versus

469

variety, or price versus services, etc.; the more precise and quantitative aspects of lifestyle.

*Consumer satisfaction*: the response of a customer to the distribution system as a whole, and in particular to its accessibility, range of choice, and efficiency.

*Consumer sovereignty*: the notion that retail structure (see below), products, and prices are entirely determined by the preferences of the consumer.

*Convenience goods*: have a very steep spatial demand curve. They are frequently purchased and identical, with a low value/bulk ratio.

*Customer profile*: the income and demographic characteristics of the market for a given store or product.

*Demographics*: the age, sex, and household composition of a market. Some marketing research includes income and locational attributes as well.

*Disposable income*: income available after taxes and contractual commitments (pension plan, insurance, loans, rent, etc.).

*Distribution system*: the chain of information, financial flows, transportation, retail, wholesale, and production facilities that link the point of production to the point of consumption.

*Dominant*: the firm that has the largest share of a market within a retail sector i.e. that has a market share at least half as large again as the next largest firm. Such a firm defines the character of competition within the sector.

*Economies of scale*: factors leading to a decline in the average cost per unit as the quantity sold increases. Typically, economies of scale are larger as fixed costs account for a greater proportion of total costs.

*Efficiency*: from the point of view of the distribution system, a concern for minimizing the total cost per unit of providing a given service.

*Externality*: a cost or benefit exacted on an activity as the result of actions of a second activity over which the first has no control.

*Firm*: a retail chain, franchisor, or developer that makes decisions about retail infrastructure. It differs from the 'mom and pop' retailer in (1) its corporate organization, and (2) its potential for operating a number of different outlets at different locations.

*Fixed costs*: those costs of running a store that do not vary with the amount of goods sold, i.e. the overheads, including rent, utilities, insurance, wages, etc.

*Forecasting*: the selection of a most likely, or appropriate projection of future conditions. The following techniques of forecasting are frequently used.

*Extrapolation*: fits a geometrical curve to past events and projects the curve into the future.

*Ratio*: uses the past relationship between the study area and some larger spatial unit to generate a future value.

*Disaggregate*: treats the study area as the sum of a number of independent growth processes that are forecast separately.

*Indirect*: forecasts future values of some particular characteristic by means of functional relationships with another, known, variable.

*Normative*: the future population of an area is constrained by a policy which may be linked to some optimum or maximum capacity of the environment, or to service inputs.

*Franchising*: an individual entrepreneur operates the business in conjunction with a supplier (the franchisor) and a network of other franchises, with the relationships specified by a contract. In 'product and trade name' franchises the relationship specifies the products (e.g. service stations). In 'business format' franchises the relationship includes operating procedures, quality control, etc. (e.g. fast-food outlets).

*Generative*: refers to those retail outlets that attract customers on their own, e.g. major department stores or large retailers with prominent advertising – Sears or Macy's.

*Good (product)*: a distinct item for sale in a retail or service establishment, e.g. apple, haircut.

*Gross Leasable Area (GLA)*: the area of a shopping plaza that is assigned to stores, i.e. excluding exits, corridors, and open space.

*Gross National Product (GNP)*: the total value of goods and services produced by a national economy in a given year.

*Hierarchy*: although a large region will generate a continuum of unplanned centers of all sizes, individual consumers are typically faced with a subset of centers of discrete sizes. These constitute a hierarchy of centers of various orders, and one can identify typical products that are first available at a particular order in the hierarchy. First-order goods have the smallest threshold and are sold at the lowest level of the hierarchy, i.e. in the smallest centers. High-order goods are sold only in the largest places.

*High-order goods*: are only available in the larger centers of the central place hierarchy; typically shopping goods found in highly specialized shops, as opposed to low-order goods that can be found in every retail cluster.

*Horizontal integration*: occurs when a single firm operates a number of outlets that carry out the same function, but at different locations (as opposed to vertical integration).

*'Hot corner' or 100 per cent intersection*: the central corner within an unplanned retail center, where land values are highest, land use density is greatest, and pedestrian flows are maximal.

*Income-elastic goods (luxury goods)*: those goods for which consumption increases disproportionately rapidly as household income increases, e.g. fur coats.

*Institutional boundaries*: market areas that are defined by governments or corporations in order to restrict spatial competition; for example, post office districts, sales territories, exclusive dealerships.

*Key factors*: those characteristics of site and situation that are thought to be essential in determining the level of sales for an outlet.

*Leasing broker*: the middleman between the shopping center developer and the smaller retail chains. The broker may rent a block of space in a center and sublet it to tenants, or simply match tenants and centers.

*Lifestyle*: the variety of ways in which a household spends its time and money. Typical clusters of activities (hence lifestyles) might include 'suburbia', 'punk', 'swinger', 'intellectual', or various ethnic groups.

*Logistics*: costs to a retail chain of operating an outlet that is spatially separated from the head office – includes administative, warehousing, and shipping costs.

*Luxury goods*: see income elastic goods.

*Major retail center*: a Bureau of the Census definition of a retail cluster, requiring at least twenty-five stores outside the central business district, including a department store with 100,000 square feet. (See also Exhibit 7.1.)

*Margin*: that proportion of a store's sales that is not attributed to the cost of the goods themselves, i.e. the overheads or fixed costs. Note that if goods + margin = sales price, then markup (the per cent increase in value of goods due to the store's actions) = [(margin/goods) × 100] − 100.

*Market*: a set of consumers.

*Market area (trade area)*: the locations served by a particular facility. Penetration (see below) of the trade area will vary with distance. Applebaum distinguishes the primary trade area, which contains 60 per cent of the total trade at the facility, and the secondary trade area, which includes the next 20 per cent.

*Market penetration*: the proportion of households in a specified market that consume a given product.

*Market profile*: breaks down composition of a facility's market area, according to income, demography, and lifestyle.

*Market segments*: the subdivision of a market based on income, demographics, location, lifestyle, or some combination thereof.

*Market share*: proportion of total sales in market obtained by a given facility or chain (see also retail strategy).

*Marketing*: that aspect of business which identifies demand for goods/ services and arranges to supply them by means of an efficient distribution network.

*Marketing geography*: describes the spatial characteristics of marketing activities: the consumers, and the distribution network.

*Merit goods*: are imposed on consumers because some agency considers that they are good for people (or reduce the negative externalities from their non-consumption). Examples include education, recreation, health care, public transportation, opera, books.

*Metropolitan Statistical Area (MSA)*: the Bureau of the Census definition (as of 1984) of an urban area. It includes a central city of 50,000 or more, the surrounding county, and other nearby counties within the laborshed of the central city.

*Multiple purpose trip*: a key concept in central place theory which argues that consumers prefer to visit more than one store per trip, generating positive externalities for neighboring stores

*Nested*: if each lower-order trade area is completely contained within the trade area of the next highest-order center.

*Niche*: a small market, partially isolated from competition by distance or the degree of specialization.

*Oligopoly*: a competitive condition in which several large firms compete on a more or less equal basis, but in the knowledge that an action by any one of them will affect all the rest.

*Point of sale*: monitoring consumer behavior by means of information gathered at the cash register, as opposed to interview or traffic observation.

*Predatory*: when a chain attacks a competitor by setting up an adjacent facility.

*Pre-emptive*: when a chain locates an outlet before the target market is developed.

*Price-density*: value per unit volume of a good.

*Product*: (see good).

*Product line*: a mix of products determined by the producer or supplier, based on supply-side considerations, sometimes distinguished by common packaging, advertising, etc. (e.g. Kenmore appliances).

*Production function*: describes the mix of inputs (wholesale price, labor, rent, utilities, interest, etc.) that combine to make up the selling price of a good.

*Range of a good*: the distance from a store at which (in the absence of competition) demand for the good drops to zero due to transportation costs.

*Retail chain*: a number of stores of the same type (typically five or more) that are owned and operated by the same firm. See also horizontal integration.

*Retail sector*: (see business type) a four-digit code in the standard industrial classification that identifies a retail activity.

*Retail strategy*: the set of policies, including price, product design, outlet location, and advertising that identifies a target market and tries to reach it; frequently reflects the actions of the competition. Examples include market share, segmentation, saturation, etc. In the case of gas stations:

*Market share*: companies attempt to maintain a share of the market within certain limits, high enough to obtain maximum value from advertising geared to larger market units, but not so high as to intensify competition among dealers. Market share implies a widespread exposure to all market segments and a particular concern for location of competitors.

*Saturation*: maximizing access to consumers with many sites (small stations on cheap locations).

*Segmentation*: companies focus on a particular subset of consumers – young, old, rich, or poor – choosing sites to maximize access to this group.

*Cross-merchandising*: companies expand product-mix to attract regular patrons who may need other goods, e.g. milk, cigarettes, newspapers, soft drinks, or provide other services, e.g. mechanics, carwash, etc.

*Discounting*: cutting prices, reducing service, and seeking inexpensive locations.

*Brand loyalty*: emphasizes credit cards; hence an integrated network of facilities available in a variety of daily situations relevant to the credit-card segment, including journey to work and recreational travel.

*Comprehensive development*: emphasizes spatial monopoly. Company identifies an isolated spatial market, or one built into a residential development, caters to it, and plays down brand loyalty.

*Retail structure*: the spatial distribution of retail stores and store types, including the composition of groupings of stores, spacing, and relationship to market.

*Shopping center (planned center)*: a number of retail activities (typically five or more) that are operated separately, but also occupy a single property that is managed by a single firm. As a result, they are typically distinguished from unplanned centers by their design, internal layout, mix of business type and store size, and rental structure.

*Shopping goods*: have very shallow demand curves. They are distinctive (brand name?) products, infrequently purchased, with a high value/bulk ratio. Customers like to compare different stores.

*Simultaneous*: a development sequence in which planned shopping facilities are built at the same time as the residential areas (e.g. the 1960s).

*Site evaluation*: to estimate sales at a facility as a function of various characteristics of the facility, its site, and trade area. Evaluation looks at existing outlets, while selection looks at potential outlets using evaluation models.

*Social system*: the cultural, social, and political environment that shapes our demand for consumer goods, and the ways in which this demand is satisfied; perhaps most clearly evident in the consumption of alcoholic beverages.

*Spatial demand curve*: describes the decline in the likelihood of purchase of a good with distance from the store. This decline is attributable to the costs in time and money of consumer travel, and ultimately to the presence of competitive sources for the product.

*Spatial monopoly*: supplier A has a price advantage over his competitor, B, that is equal to the differential in travel costs to the customer, i.e. $T_B >$ $T_A$. This price advantage can be converted to profit for the retailer, according to the economic principles of monopolistic competition.

*Standard Metropolitan Statistical Area (SMSA)*: (see also metropolitan statistical area) the Bureau of the Census definition of an urban area prior to 1984. Includes a central city of 50,000 or more, the surrounding county, plus adjacent counties within the laborshed of the central city.

*Standard Industrial Classification*: a four-digit code assigned by the Bureau of the Census to each business activity, based on the product or service that it provides. Retail activity codes range from 5210 to 5999.

*Suscipient*: refers to retail activities that serve customers who have been attracted by other land uses, e.g. cigar stores, candy stores, restaurants, adjacent to a theater district.

*Target market identification*: given income, demographic, and lifestyle characteristics of a market, and census information for small areas, the most favorable locations can be identified.

*Thiessen polygons*: a geometric technique that identifies midpoints between competing facilities. Intersections of these midpoint lines may be key sites for future expansion.

*Threshold size*: the minimum market size that will support a retail outlet of a given type. From another point of view, the volume of sales at which the average cost per unit sold declines rapidly. In technical terms: the point at which the demand price becomes equal to, or greater than, the average unit cost.

*Trade area*: see market area.

*Truncation*: if a competitor locates in such a way as to intercept customers before they get to the original store.

*Turnover*: the average number of times the store's inventory is replaced each year, i.e. the ratio of annual sales to current inventory. For food stores perhaps fifteen; fashion stores, five or six.

*Unplanned center*: a cluster of retail stores within the city in which there is a structured internal pattern of locations, achieved by the independent decisions of stores operating within the land market.

*Upscale*: (as opposed to downscale) goods and activities appealing to higher-income households (see income-elastic).

*Urban hierarchy*: in aggregate, this term refers to the wide variation in the size of places (and of services offered) that is observed in every settlement system. Within a small region, or from the point of view of a particular household, this variation is reflected in the form of a small number of centers, each of different size and each offering a different mix of goods, e.g. village, town, city, metropolitan area.

*Vacuum method (needs analysis)*: by forecasting the level of sales in a market and subtracting the sales equivalent of existing retail facilities, a store can anticipate the future sales potential for a new facility.

*Variable costs*: those costs of running a store that are directly related to the quantity of goods sold, e.g. the wholesale cost of the product. See also fixed costs.

*Vertical integration*: occurs when a single firm operates a sequence of activities that provide goods and services for each other. In the distribution system, a major retailer might expand into wholesaling, or even production activities, in order to guarantee a supply of goods of specific quality, or to recoup the advantage of its market power.

# Appendix B

## Sources of data for location analysis

The last decade has witnessed at least three revolutions in the application of data to retail location problems: first, the personal computer and user-friendly packaged programs have made market analysis accessible to everyone; second, the explosion of data sources and data packages has overwhelmed most users; and third, numerous market research agencies have emerged to sell data and/or analysis to anyone in need. As a result, it is impossible to provide a comprehensive list of information services or agencies and, even if it were possible, such a list would be out of date yesterday. This survey is selective, focusing on the source materials rather than the market research products that derive from them.

### Demand (chapters two, nine and eleven)

(1) The fundamental source of information on the magnitude and location of consumer demand is the *Census of Population*, which is taken in April of every tenth year (1970, 1980, 1990, etc.). The results are released at any time from one to three years later. In addition to basic data about the number and location of consumers, the census includes detailed information about household composition, income, race, and employment, plus detailed descriptions of housing consumption.

Because the census reaches into every home in the country, the data can be aggregated into very small spatial units, providing a level of geographic detail unmatched by any other source. The Bureau of the Census releases results for (i) the nation as a whole, (ii) geographic regions (groups of states), (iii) states, (iv) counties (3,000+), (v) counties grouped into Metropolitan Statistical Areas (MSAs) (300+), and (vi) local government units. Within the MSAs, data are further disaggregated into (vii) census tracts (average 4,000 people), (viii) enumeration districts or block groups (average 700 people), and for selected housing and population counts, data on (ix) city blocks. Data are also released for Zip codes and special

477

tabulations are available for special areas defined by the analyst, such as trade areas or planning districts. See Bureau of the Census, *Census of Population, 1990.*

(2) While the spatial detail of the census is unmatched, the long time gaps between census-taking necessitate the use of supplementary information. In order to update the census we can turn to:

(i) Biennial estimates of population and income for all spatial units down to local government units, based on a variety of administrative records from both the federal and state governments – income tax, automobile registrations, vital statistics and school enrolment. See Bureau of the Census, 'Population estimates and projections' *Current Population Reports, Series P-25*, and 'Local population estimates', *Series P-26.*

(ii) Annual estimates of income (from income tax returns) for states, MSAs, counties and Zip codes: See Internal Revenue Service, (annual) *Statistics of Income, 199x: Individual Tax Returns*; Bureau of Economic Analysis (Annual) *Local Area Personal Income.*

(iii) Annual estimates of population for local governments, or sometimes local planning areas, derived from administrative records or planning surveys.

(iv) Annual estimates of employment and payroll (thus income) by sector for counties. By monitoring these data one can measure and project growth and change. Monthly estimates of employment for states and 230 sub-areas are prepared by a separate agency. See Bureau of the Census (annual) *County Business Patterns*; Bureau of Labor Statistics (monthly) *Employment and Earnings.*

(v) Annual estimates (plus forecasts) for MSAs, counties, and Zip codes (or any other spatial unit), prepared by market research firms using all of the above sources. The most accessible examples are: CACI (annual) *The 199x Sourcebook of Demographics and Buying Power for Every Zip Code in the USA* (also includes employment data from *County Business Patterns*); 'Survey of buying power' (annual) *Sales and Marketing Management*(for metropolitan areas), New York: Bill Communications; 'Market guide' (annual) *Editor and Publisher*, (for counties and metropolitan areas), New York. Dun and Bradstreet (annual) *Market Profile Analysis* (for MSAs), New York.

(3) Both the Bureau of the Census and the market research firms generate demographic and economic forecasts from their data, and update them frequently. See Bureau of the Census, *Current Population Reports, Series P-25*; Bureau of Economic Analysis (1985) *1985 OBERS Regional Projections.*

(4) At the level of the nation and the region, many agencies, both public and private, provide short-term economic forecasts (see Predicasts). It is difficult, though, to find long-term projections of the economic environ-

ment. See 'abstracts of forecasts', (quarterly) *Predicasts Forecasts,* Cleveland, Ohio: Predicasts; Conference Board (quarterly) *Statistical Bulletin* (summarizes short-term forecasts of the economy); (quarterly) University of Michigan Survey Research Center, Ann Arbor, *Economic Outlook USA.* National Planning Association (annual) *Regional Economic Projections.*

(5) In order to convert the magnitude of consumer demand into purchasing patterns, we depend on household consumption surveys. The Bureau of Labor Statistics uses home interviews and diaries on a rotating sample of 10,000 households to monitor consumer spending patterns. Results are released every two or three years. See Bureau of Labor Statistics (1986) 'Consumer expenditure survey: diary survey, 1982–83', *Bulletin 2245* or 'consumer expenditure survey: interview survey, 1984–85', *Bulletin 2267* (see Table B.1 for an example). Recent results are summarized in Bureau of the Census (annual) *Statistical Abstract of the United States.*

Mediamark Research, Inc. carries out a similar survey annually. More specialized consumer data are reviewed in *American Demographics* (monthly), American Demographics, Inc., Ithaca, New York. Other consumer information ,including brand and media choice, is provided in Simmons Market Research Bureau, Inc. (biennial) *Study of Media and Markets.*

## *The supply side (chapters three, ten and twelve)*

(1) Every five years since 1929 (irregularly in the early years) very detailed studies of the magnitude and location of retail activity have been undertaken as the *Census of Business* or the *Census of Retail Trade.* For the nation, states, MSAs, counties, local governments, and major retail centers, the census provides the number of stores and firms by Standard Industrial Classification (SIC) category, and the level of sales, employment, and payroll. From this source the Bureau of the Census is able to compile a variety of special tabulations, many of which have been used in this book. For example, there are data on store size, retail chains, competitive structure, various operating costs, and special studies of the activities of women (1977) and racial minorities (1972 and 1977).

(2) These data can be updated by means of monthly surveys, also carried out by the Bureau. First, as noted in the previous section, *County Business Patterns* includes data on the number of retail firms, establishments, employment, and payroll. Second, data on retail sales and inventories are provided for SIC categories or for states and MSAs. See Bureau of the Census (monthly) 'Monthly retail trade, sales and inventories', *Current Business Reports.*

(3) An extraordinary amount of data is available from various private sector sources, although researchers must study the data gathering

**Table B.1** Example of consumer expenditure data. Selected characteristics and weekly expenditures of urban consumer units classified by income before taxes, Diary Survey, 1982–3

| Item | All consumer units | Total reporting | Complete reporting of income | | | | | | |
| --- | --- | --- | --- | --- | --- | --- | --- | --- | --- |
| | | | Less than $5,000 | $5,000 to $9,999 | $10,000 to $14,999 | $15,000 to $19,999 | $20,000 to $29,999 | $30,000 to $39,999 | $40,000 and over |
| Number of consumer units | | | | | | | | | |
| (in thousands) | 73,145 | 56,901 | 7,076 | 9,876 | 8,262 | 6,067 | 11,208 | 6,885 | 7,527 |
| Number of sample diaries | 12,719 | 16,865 | 2,203 | 2,901 | 2,380 | 1,849 | 3,189 | 2,100 | 2,243 |
| Consumer unit characteristics | | | | | | | | | |
| Income before taxes | $21,749 | $21,749 | $2,465 | $7,257 | $12,355 | $17,287 | $24,502 | $34,306 | $57,218 |
| Size of consumer unit | 2.5 | 2.5 | 1.5 | 2.1 | 2.5 | 2.5 | 2.9 | 3.0 | 3.2 |
| Age of reference person | 45.8 | 45.2 | 45.5 | 51.6 | 45.8 | 42.1 | 42.8 | 41.5 | 45.2 |
| Number in consumer unit: | | | | | | | | | |
| Earners | 1.3 | 1.3 | .6 | .7 | 1.1 | 1.3 | 1.6 | 1.9 | 2.1 |
| Vehicles | 1.4 | 1.4 | .5 | .9 | 1.2 | 1.4 | 1.7 | 2.0 | 2.2 |
| Children under 18 | .7 | .7 | .3 | .6 | .7 | .7 | .9 | .9 | .9 |
| Persons 65 and over | .3 | .3 | .3 | .5 | .4 | .2 | .2 | .1 | .1 |
| Percent homeowner | 58 | 57 | 27 | 42 | 49 | 52 | 64 | 75 | 89 |
| Average weekly expenditures | | | | | | | | | |
| Food, total | $55.11 | $56.71 | $25.84 | $35.26 | $46.31 | $53.02 | $65.89 | $75.11 | $97.73 |
| Food at home, total | 35.51 | 36.52 | 16.94 | 26.11 | 32.88 | 35.26 | 42.69 | 46.53 | 55.28 |
| Cereals and bakery products, total | 4.71 | 4.83 | 2.33 | 3.67 | 4.28 | 4.70 | 5.66 | 6.15 | 6.94 |
| Cereals and cereal products | 1.50 | 1.56 | .86 | 1.33 | 1.43 | 1.56 | 1.80 | 1.83 | 2.03 |
| Bakery products | 3.21 | 3.27 | 1.47 | 2.34 | 2.86 | 3.14 | 3.86 | 4.32 | 4.91 |
| Meats, poultry, fish and eggs, total | 11.28 | 11.57 | 5.08 | 8.27 | 10.76 | 10.95 | 13.54 | 14.13 | 18.14 |
| Beef | 4.10 | 4.21 | 1.66 | 2.81 | 3.70 | 4.00 | 5.09 | 5.21 | 6.94 |
| Pork | 2.29 | 2.36 | 1.02 | 1.78 | 2.35 | 2.21 | 2.79 | 2.86 | 3.44 |

| | | | | | | | | | |
|---|---|---|---|---|---|---|---|---|---|
| Other meats | 1.58 | 1.61 | .65 | 1.12 | 1.45 | 1.51 | 1.90 | 2.11 | 2.50 |
| Poultry | 1.50 | 1.55 | .86 | 1.24 | 1.50 | 1.51 | 1.75 | 1.79 | 2.18 |
| Fish and seafood | 1.14 | 1.16 | .48 | .71 | 1.07 | 1.02 | 1.25 | 1.39 | 2.27 |
| Eggs | .66 | .68 | .40 | .61 | .69 | .69 | .76 | .78 | .81 |
| Dairy products, total | 4.79 | 4.88 | 2.34 | 3.46 | 4.32 | 4.74 | 5.75 | 6.21 | 7.33 |
| Fresh milk and cream | 2.42 | 2.46 | 1.34 | 1.96 | 2.31 | 2.41 | 2.90 | 3.01 | 3.19 |
| Other dairy products | 2.37 | 2.42 | 1.00 | 1.50 | 2.01 | 2.33 | 2.86 | 3.20 | 4.14 |
| Fruits and vegetables, total | 5.86 | 5.99 | 3.03 | 4.44 | 5.47 | 5.78 | 6.82 | 7.31 | 9.13 |
| Fresh fruits | 1.80 | 1.81 | .97 | 1.31 | 1.67 | 1.70 | 2.05 | 2.17 | 2.82 |
| Fresh vegetables | 1.74 | 1.79 | .86 | 1.34 | 1.69 | 1.71 | 2.05 | 2.18 | 2.65 |
| Processed fruits | 1.33 | 1.36 | .72 | 1.07 | 1.15 | 1.36 | 1.52 | 1.68 | 2.08 |
| Processed vegetables | 1.00 | 1.03 | .49 | .73 | .95 | 1.01 | 1.20 | 1.28 | 1.58 |
| Other food at home, total | 8.87 | 9.25 | 4.16 | 6.27 | 8.05 | 9.10 | 10.91 | 12.73 | 13.74 |
| Sugar and other sweets | 1.26 | 1.30 | .61 | .93 | 1.18 | 1.27 | 1.57 | 1.64 | 1.90 |
| Fats and oils | .94 | .98 | .47 | .76 | .92 | 1.01 | 1.15 | 1.22 | 1.29 |
| Miscellaneous foods | 3.56 | 3.76 | 1.57 | 2.38 | 3.07 | 3.63 | 4.37 | 5.60 | 5.92 |
| Nonalcoholic beverages | 3.11 | 3.21 | 1.52 | 2.20 | 2.87 | 3.19 | 3.82 | 4.27 | 4.63 |
| Food away from home | 19.60 | 20.18 | 8.89 | 9.15 | 13.43 | 17.76 | 23.21 | 28.58 | 42.45 |
| Alcoholic beverages | 5.46 | 5.73 | 2.23 | 3.26 | 4.28 | 5.01 | 6.04 | 7.53 | 12.33 |
| Tobacco products and smoking supplies | 3.24 | 3.37 | 1.68 | 2.54 | 3.12 | 3.66 | 3.89 | 4.49 | 4.26 |
| Personal care products and services | 4.46 | 4.64 | 2.18 | 2.74 | 3.57 | 3.92 | 5.13 | 6.28 | 8.94 |
| Non-prescription drugs and supplies | 1.85 | 1.94 | .71 | 1.53 | 1.62 | 1.29 | 2.60 | 2.23 | 3.28 |
| Housekeeping supplies | 5.44 | 5.68 | 2.55 | 3.32 | 4.27 | 5.37 | 6.85 | 7.78 | 9.88 |

Source: Bureau of Labor Statistics (1986) 'Consumer expenditure survey: diary survey, 1982–3', Bulletin 2245, Washington: Government Printing Office.

procedures carefully. See, for example, A. Schwartz (1987) 'Dun and Bradstreet's market identifiers and economic geography', *Professional Geographer*, 39, 2: 166–172; Gale Research (1986) *Encyclopedia of Business Information Sources*, 6th edn, Detroit Michigan: Gale Research Co,; National Research Bureau (annual) *Directory of Shopping Centers in the United States and Canada* (see also *Shopping Center World* and The International Council of Shopping Centers).

For retail chains, see Standard and Poor (semi-annual) 'Retail', *Industry Surveys* (a compendium of financial data); National Register Publishing Co. (annual) *Directory of Corporate Affiliations*; Dun's Marketing Services (annual) *Million Dollar Directory* and *Dun's Census of American Business*, based on their own data set, with estimates of stores, sales, employment by SIC, down to the county level (see also their *Reference Book*, which lists firms by city and gives financial strength and credit rating); Cambridge Corporation (annual) *Yearbook on Corporate Mergers, Joint Ventures and Acquisition* and 'Information for industry', (annual) *Mergers and Acquisitions: Almanac and Index*; see also *Chain Store Age* (lists major chains, sales, and number of stores); New York: Lebhar-Friedman. *Fairchild's Financial Manual of Retail Stores*, New York: Fairchild Publications: plus numerous specialized trade journals and yearbooks that summarize and forecast data for a particular retail sector.

Data on franchising is gathered by the International Trade Administration (annual) *Franchising in the Economy*. For specific metropolitan areas, local newspapers often compile maps and descriptions of local business structure. Local planning agencies sometimes evaluate specific retail projects. See Greenwood Press (annual) *Index to Current Urban Documents*.

# Source index

# Subject index